Faith Speaking Understanding

Faith Speaking Understanding

Performing the Drama of Doctrine

Kevin J. Vanhoozer

© 2014 Kevin J. Vanhoozer

First edition
Published by Westminster John Knox Press
Louisville, Kentucky

14 15 16 17 18 19 20 21 22 23—10 9 8 7 6 5 4 3 2 1

All rights reserved. No part of this book may be reproduced or transmitted in any form or by any means, electronic or mechanical, including photocopying, recording, or by any information storage or retrieval system, without permission in writing from the publisher. For information, address Westminster John Knox Press, 100 Witherspoon Street, Louisville, Kentucky 40202-1396. Or contact us online at www.wjkbooks.com.

Unless otherwise indicated, Scripture quotations are from the New Revised Standard Version of the Bible, copyright © 1989 by the Division of Christian Education of the National Council of the Churches of Christ in the U.S.A., and are used by permission. Other versions briefly quoted: ESV, English Standard Version; KJV, King James Version; NASB, New American Standard Bible; NET, New English Translation; NIV, New International Version; RSV, Revised Standard Version.

Book design by Sharon Adams
Cover design by Eric Walljasper

Library of Congress Cataloging-in-Publication Data

Vanhoozer, Kevin J.
 Faith speaking understanding : performing the drama of doctrine / Kevin J. Vanhoozer.—First edition.
   pages cm
 Includes bibliographical references and indexes.
 ISBN 978-0-664-23448-5 (alk. paper)
 1. Theology—Methodology. 2. Theater—Religious aspects—Christianity. 3. Performing arts—Religious aspects—Christianity. 4. Religion and drama. I. Title.
 BR118.V365 2014
 230—dc23
                                                                                                2014004508

∞ The paper used in this publication meets the minimum requirements of the American National Standard for Information Sciences—Permanence of Paper for Printed Library Materials, ANSI Z39.48-1992.

Most Westminster John Knox Press books are available at special quantity discounts when purchased in bulk by corporations, organizations, and special-interest groups. For more information, please e-mail SpecialSales@wjkbooks.com.

To see or to make oneself be seen, to understand and to make oneself be understood, that is the fated circle of humanity; to be actor or spectator, that is the condition of human life.
—Charles Garnier, *Le Théâtre*

The most ancient drama, the drama that rules the world, is the drama of the meeting of God with man.
—Gerardus van der Leeuw, *Sacred and Profane Beauty*

The Acts of the Apostles were to convey that name of Christ Jesus, and to propagate his Gospel over all the world. Beloved, you are Actors upon the same stage too. The uttermost parts of the earth are your scene. Act out the acts of the apostles.
—John Donne, Sermon on Acts 1:8 to the Virginia Company (Nov. 30, 1622)

Contents

Preface	xi
Introduction. "In Accordance with the Scriptures": Local Church as "Living Bible"	1
Playbill: Local Church Makes "Living Bible"	1
Program Notes: What This book Is About	4
Plot: A Brief Synopsis	9

PART 1. BEFORE THE CURTAIN RISES: ON THEOLOGY AND THEATER

1 Doing the Word "on Earth as It Is in Heaven": Introducing the Theater of the Gospel	15
Faith Speaking Understanding: The Challenge	15
The Witness as Doer of the Word: James's Mirror and Jesus' House	18
"Theater" of the Gospel: Definitions and Distinctions	20
Theater as Handmaid to Theology: Metaphor or Model?	25
2 Audience Participation: Loving God, Doing Truth, Being Church	33
"Breaking Down the Dividing Wall": Between Actor and Audience, Pastor and Congregation, Church and World	34
"Walking in the Truth": Participation in Christ	37
"Confessing the Coming of Christ": A Self-Involving Demonstration	41
"Abiding in Doctrine": The Audience as Staging Area	44

viii   Faith Speaking Understanding

PART 2. FAITH SHOWING UNDERSTANDING: HOW DOCTRINE MAKES DISCIPLES AND HOW DISCIPLES DO DOCTRINE

3   The Great Theater of the World: Setting the Twenty-First-Century Stage   51
     Stage: Church, World, and the Contemporary Crisis of Authenticity   53
     Lighting: "A Lamp unto My Feet"   63
     Action: The Essence of Theater   65
     Recapitulation: The Canonical Imperative   71

4   Gospel Theater: The Triune Drama of Redemption   73
     The Play of the Playwright "from Above": A Drama of Trinitarian Proportions   75
     The Players: Human and Other Dramatis Personae   82
     The Play of the Playwright "from Below": A Courtroom Drama of Kingdom and Kinship   89
     Recapitulation: The Orthodox Imperative   110

5   Learning (and Becoming) the Part: "Little Christs"   113
     Roles: Till We Have Faces   114
     Costume: Putting on Christ   120
     Prompts: Word and Spirit as *Aide-Mémoire* and Means of Grace   129
     Recapitulation: The Pauline Imperative   136

6   Forming the Company, Doing Church: Doctrinal Directions for Acting Out Life Together in Christ   139
     Communio Sanctorum: Disciples' Gathering as Command Performance—"Do This"   141
     Scenes of Congregational Life   152
     Rehearsing Communion: The Supper as Summa of the Gospel   160
     Recapitulation: The Catholic-Evangelical Imperative   166

7   Staging the Play in Ten Thousand Places: How the Company of the Gospel Enacts Parables of the Kingdom   169
     Local Church, Local Theater: Where is "in Christ"?   171
     An Interactive Theater of Resident Exiles and Holy Fools   179
     Improvisation: Embodying the Mind of Christ Always, Everywhere, and to Everyone   188
     Recapitulation: The Sapiential Imperative   204

8   (Torn) Curtain: On Earth as He Is in Heaven   207
     Climax: "Sits at the Right Hand of God the Father Almighty"   209

Conflict: Postvictory Theater of the Oppressed	214
Catharsis: Purification of the Heart	220
Recapitulation: The Doxological Imperative	225

Conclusion. Tell and Show: Exhibiting the Gospel in Company with Christ — 229

Exeunt: The Dismissal	232
Encore: The Gloria	234

Appendix. What Has Broadway to Do with Jerusalem? — 239

The Antitheatrical Prejudice: Responding to Historical Objections	239
"The Play's Not the Thing": Responding to Contemporary Objections	243

Selected Bibliography — 253

Index of Scripture References — 261

Index of Subjects — 269

Preface

The Church exists for nothing else but to draw men into Christ, to make them little Christs. If they are not doing that, all the cathedrals, clergy, missions, sermons, even the Bible itself, are simply a waste of time.
—C. S. Lewis, *Mere Christianity*

"Greats," in the context of Oxford University, refers to a four-year program of study in the Greek and Latin classics, which lie at the foundation of the humanities: language, literature, history, and philosophy. C. S. Lewis studied "Greats" during his time at Oxford and spent many happy years reading primary sources. "Greats" still exist, though in 2004 the university revised the curriculum in order to include modern texts outside the ancient canon. What does one learn studying "Greats"? We hear the traditional answer: the humanities teach us how to be fully human. The Oxford Classics Department Web site anticipates the skeptic's objection—a knowledge of the classical world does not lead to any obvious employment—and tries to defeat it: "In our world of rapid social and technological change, it is the capacity to react to new and unforeseen developments with flexibility which employers value most."[1] Studying "Greats" is apparently good training for improvisers, a point to which we shall return in due course.[2]

---

1. Quoted from http://www.classics.ox.ac.uk/admissions/undergraduate/careers.html.
2. See chap. 7 below.

The church too has a "Greats" curriculum that aims to understand not only humanity but divinity as well, a course of study that Calvin sums up as involving "the knowledge of God and of ourselves."[3] In the context of the church, "Greats" involves the education not only of the intellect but also of the heart, as Augustine knew well. Augustine uses the soliloquy, a theatrical device whereby a character shares his thoughts with the audience by speaking them to himself out loud, to wrestle with some basic questions after his conversion: What should be the spiritual and intellectual aspirations of a disciple? What are the marks of genuine discipleship? In the course of his soliloquy, he comes to see that his greatest desire is to know and love "God and the soul," and nothing more.[4] Augustine and Anselm frame the challenge of discipleship, and also the purpose of theology, with their well-known phrase: "faith seeking understanding."

Consider these three "Greats," each one a component in the disciple's curriculum: the Great Commandment ("You shall love the Lord your God with all your heart, and with all your soul, and with all your mind, and with all your strength. . . . You shall love your neighbor as yourself" [Mark 12:30-31]), the Great Commission ("Go therefore and make disciples of all nations" [Matt. 28:19]), and what we might call the Great Conception ("Therefore you are great, O LORD God; for there is no one like you" [2 Sam. 7:22]). The Great Conception alludes to Anselm's famous argument for the existence of God from the concept of Perfect Being: a being "than which nothing greater can be conceived" must necessarily exist, he declared.[5] My variation on Anselm is to relate the greatness of God to the gospel. The gospel (and this is a theme to which we shall frequently return) is not only good but great news: testimony to God's great saving act in Jesus Christ, a *doing* "than which nothing greater can be conceived."

Doing is the operative term, for God's being "than which nothing greater can be conceived" is love, and love is active: a ceaseless self-communication, a sharing of all one is and has.[6] Even God's word is "living and active" (Heb. 4:12). The Great Commandment thus follows from the nature of God, what I am here calling the Great Conception. Note that it is only after Jesus says something about God's nature ("the Lord our God, the Lord is one" [Mark 12:29]) that Jesus then formulates the Great Commandment. The imperative (to love God above all things) follows from the indicative (God *is* above all things, and therefore most to be treasured).

In Mark's Gospel, the scribe who posed the question about the greatest commandment appears to understand and affirm Jesus' answer, acknowledging that God "is one, and besides him there is no other" (12:32) and that the command to love God and neighbor is more important than burnt offerings and sacrifices, the trappings of religion (12:33). Jesus commends the scribe's response, up to

---

3. John Calvin, *Institutes of the Christian Religion* 1.1.
4. Augustine, *Soliloquies* 1.7.
5. Anselm's ontological argument is in *Proslogion* 2 (ca. 1077-78).
6. See my *Remythologizing Theology: Divine Action, Passion, and Authorship* (Cambridge: Cambridge University Press, 2010), esp. chaps. 4 and 9.

a point: "You are not far from the kingdom of God" (12:34). "Not far" is, however, not close enough. It is one thing to know the Great Commandment, another to do it, as we see in Luke's version, in which Jesus replies to his questioner, "You have given the right answer; do this, and you will live" (10:28). The knowledge of God is incomplete without the practice of godliness.

In teaching disciples, as in parenting children, we want at all costs to avoid saying, "Do as I say, not what I do." As we shall see, both children and disciples often learn from example. We know where babies come from, and (more or less) how to raise children; but how do we make disciples, mature children who obey God? Jesus' Great Commission remains as urgent as ever, even if many churches operate with a tragically abbreviated version only, baptizing Christians into the triune name but *failing* to teach them to obey everything that Jesus commanded.[7] Certain translations of the Great Commission inadvertently give us a loophole, allowing us to escape our responsibilities to God's word on a technicality. Strictly speaking, many of us, like the scribe, *observe* and even admire Jesus and his commands, yet as we contemplate him from a safe distance, the way we might observe other curiosities: strange behaviors, cultural oddities, circus acts. This is not the kind of observation that Jesus had in mind. We *observe* his commands by complying with them, not by taking mental notes.

To make disciples is to teach people how to keep the faith. One keeps faith by following Jesus' words rather than merely knowing faith's content. When the apostle Paul says, toward the end of his life, that he has not only "fought the good fight" but has "kept the faith" (2 Tim. 4:7), he means that he has preserved the "healthful words" of the gospel from contamination by the gangrene infection of "profane chatter" (2 Tim. 2:16–17). Such is the responsibility of the church today, those charged with reading, hearing, and keeping the written words of the revelation of Jesus Christ (Rev. 1:1–3). Those who keep the words of and about Jesus will be blessed, and they will be a blessing to others.

Churches today may not hold doctrine in high regard, yet the church, like television, is always educating; the only question is, What is it teaching? In particular, what norms, values, and belief is it conveying through its hidden curriculum, its everyday ways of doing things? Into what scheme of beliefs and practices are churchgoers being socialized? Just whose words are the church following? What one learns in the Christian Greats curriculum are the words of eternal life: life-giving and love-directing words that, when followed, usher in the reign of God.

The present book is about the importance of doctrine for discipleship. In the words of the seventeenth-century English Puritan William Ames: "Theology is the doctrine or teaching [*doctrina*] of living to God."[8] We live to God when we

---

7. Dallas Willard refers to the church's failure to make and teach disciples as the "Great Omission" in *The Great Omission: Rediscovering Jesus' Essential Teachings on Discipleship* (San Francisco: HarperCollins, 2006).

8. William Ames, *The Marrow of Theology* 1.1 (Latin, 1656; ET repr., Grand Rapids: Baker, 1968).

live in accord with the word and will of God, and only when we live to God do we live well. Theology is the art and science of living well to God. Stated more fulsomely: *theology is the serious and joyful attempt to live blessedly with others, before God, in Christ, through the Spirit.* Doctrines are not simply truths to be stored, shelved, and stacked, but indications and directions to be followed, practiced, and enacted. Christian discipleship is a practice of *doing* truth, of learning the way of life that is in Jesus Christ.

This is a book about doing church according to its "Greats" curriculum and the doctrines therein. It is about knowing God by participating in what God has done, is doing, and will do in Christ through the Spirit. It is about schooling our spiritual desire for God by awakening our minds and hearts to what is available to the world in Christ. The "Greats" curriculum of discipleship schools hearts and minds. Desire for God without doctrine is blind; doctrine without desire is empty. The Great Commandment calls us to love God passionately with our hearts, minds, and strength (Mark 12:30). Yet we cannot love God rightly without knowing God, and we cannot know God rightly without understanding what he has done in Jesus Christ. Discipleship depends on Christology, and Christology involves being able to show and tell who Jesus Christ is for us today.

Faith Speaking Understanding sets forth a comprehensive vision of what the church is and what it should be doing; it argues that Christian doctrine is a vital aid to "doing church." I discuss the mission of the church in theatrical terms that emphasize both the locality in which the church performs its faith and the doctrine that directs its performance. Some may question the wisdom of espousing a performance-oriented model. It is tempting for church leaders to want to improve the performance of their churches by looking elsewhere in culture for models of successful enterprise. Success here is measured in terms of observable growth: numbers "saved," money raised, programs offered. And it is tempting for churchgoers to sit back and let the leaders do what needs to be done.

The present work offers a different set of criteria for determining what counts as "success" in performance and discipleship. The theatrical model to be developed in these pages has the merit of putting the dangers associated with a performance mentality front and center: we don't want to go *there* and do *that*. In particular, we don't want to make the mistake of thinking that the clergy are the only ones who "do church," or that growth in discipleship is a matter of what we do (i.e., meritorious works). Doing church is rather a matter of participating in the triune God's prior activity. The church is ultimately a triune production, a theater of the gospel wherein we begin to see how God in Christ is "reconciling the world to himself" (2 Cor. 5:19). Theology is the attempt both to *spell out* and *live out* this knowledge of the reconciling God.

Doctrine is an indispensable help in the church's project of living together in communion and contributing to justice and *shalom* in the wider world. The theatrical model here set forth conceives of doctrine as a vital ingredient for training in humanity and godliness alike (1 Tim 4:7-8). Theology is not merely theoretical, a matter of information and the intellect, but also theatrical, a matter of forming, transforming, and performing "habits of the heart" that lead to action (i.e., works of love).

Some readers may want to know how the present offering relates to my earlier book *The Drama of Doctrine*. That work was intended to contribute to academic discussions about the nature of doctrine and theology. Its audience was primarily professional theologians and graduate students of theology. Only toward the end of the book (part 4, "The Performance") did I began to draw out the practical significance of my proposal, a "directive" theory of doctrine, for individual Christians and the church.

Given its size, density, and ambition (and in particular its bright orange cover), I dubbed *The Drama of Doctrine* "The Great Pumpkin." *Faith Speaking Understanding* is, by contrast, written for everyday Christians, serious students of theology, and pastors. It is a root vegetable for the salt of the earth; not a Great Pumpkin but a Lesser Parsnip. This now is a belated reply to the many requests I have received over the years to make my earlier work more digestible, briefer, and of greater practical benefit (two out of three isn't bad). The present work is no mere abridgment, however. It is an upstart sibling with a swagger of its own, namely, a full-fledged proposal for the role of theology in the church's task of making disciples.

My thinking has continued to develop in the twelve years since I first began thinking about theology in theatrical terms.[9] In the interim, I have taken my show on the road. I am grateful for opportunities to lecture and dialogue with students at Wycliffe College (Toronto), Wheaton College, Trinity Evangelical Divinity School, Covenant College, Covenant Theological Seminary, Southeastern Baptist Theological Seminary, and the Center for Christian Study in Charlottesville, Virginia. It was also a privilege to conduct workshops for faculty at Westmont College, Biola University, Wheaton College, and the various colleges associated with the Erasmus Institute at Amherst, Massachusetts. Thanks are also due those who presented papers interacting with *Drama of Doctrine* to the Evangelical Theology group at the 2006 annual meeting of the American Academy of Religion.

Over the years, I have seen the interdisciplinary power of the theatrical model. In 2007 I found myself speaking on "Theology and Improvisation" at the annual meeting of Musical Improvisers at Northwestern University. Even more surprising was an invitation from Eric Johnson to give a keynote address to the 2008 annual meeting of the Society for Christian Psychology, "Forming the Performers: How Christians Can Use Canon Sense to Bring Us to Our (Theodramatic) Senses." This paper was eventually published in *Edification: The Transdisciplinary Journal of Christian Psychology*, along with responses from eight Christian psychologists.[10]

---

9. The first attempt was "The Voice and the Actor: A Dramatic Proposal about the Ministry and Minstrelsy of Theology," in *Evangelical Futures: A Conversation on Theological Method*, ed. John G. Stackhouse (Grand Rapids: Baker Books, 2000), 61–106.

10. See *Edification: The Transdisciplinary Journal of Christian Psychology* 4 (2010): 5–46.

The past several years have also seen the publication of a number of reviews of *Drama of Doctrine*, some of them critical. This is neither the time nor place to whine about unfair comments or to settle grudges. I shall not often mention my critics by name in the pages that follow, but this does not mean that I have dismissed their concerns. Though their presence is in the wings, offstage, I have learned from them and been encouraged to think harder. For this, I owe my critics thanks, as I do my allies, such as Wesley Vander Lugt, whose doctoral dissertation builds on *The Drama of Doctrine* even while going beyond it, as does the present work.[11]

Faith Speaking Understanding clarifies the biblical basis for orienting theology away from philosophy (at least for a time) and toward theater studies. I shall say more about these reasons below, but for the moment it suffices to say that the present work takes its canonical cue from the book of Acts. Action—God's, the apostles', ours today—is the watchword. I argue that theology best serves the church by seeking and then demonstrating its understanding of what God has said and done in Jesus Christ. This book therefore takes its bearings from the gospel, the good news that the Father has established his reign through the cross, resurrection, and ascension of Christ in the power of the Spirit.

Finally, *Faith Speaking Understanding* never loses sight of the role doctrine plays in the edification of the church, nor of the role the church plays in acting out God's reign on earth as it is in heaven. The thesis of the book is that the world changes most when the church stays the same, that is, faithful to the gospel of Jesus Christ. Accordingly, the local church, its nature and purpose, assumes a prominence in this book that it did not have in *Drama of Doctrine*. The local church is just that: the location or *place* where the rule of God breaks into and thus begins to change the world, through the lives of disciples who have learned to enact God's word in fresh and compelling ways.

I am grateful for the support and feedback I received on dress rehearsals of various chapters from the following individuals: James Gordon, Ike Miller, Steve Pardue, Alex Peirce, Derek Rishmawy, Josh Rodriguez, Bob Ratcliff, my editor at WJK, and not least, my daughters, Mary and Emma. The members of the Deerfield Dinner Discussion group deserve thanks for making chapter 4 the subject of a memorable digestif. I owe a special thanks to the two Fellowships that make up the Center for Pastor Theologians (formerly the Society for the Advancement of Ecclesial Theology) and its two directors, the Rev. Gerald Hiestand and the Rev. Dr. Todd Wilson. The Center's vision is to encourage pastors once again to take up the task of doing theology for the health of the church. It is especially for such aspiring pastor-theologians—pastors who are both doctors of the church and directors of local companies of believers—that I have written the present work, in the hope of addressing the theological anemia in the church and the ecclesial amnesia in the academy. May their tribe increase.

---

11. See the published version, Wesley Vander Lugt, *Living Theodrama: Reimagining Theological Ethics* (Farnham, Surrey, UK: Ashgate, 2014).

I dedicate this book to my wife, Sylvie: for staging quotidian mystery plays that enfold everyday life into the liturgical calendar; for creating a place to nurture family, enjoy friends, and welcome strangers; and for setting the scene for some thirty years of stimulating and delicious dinner-table fellowship. Everyday discipleship as daily devotion: this too is the drama of doctrine, the "Great-ness" in the ordinary.

Introduction:
"In Accordance with the Scriptures"

Local Church as "Living Bible"

> *Christian doctrine is what the church believes, teaches, and confesses as it prays and suffers, serves and obeys, celebrates and awaits the coming of the kingdom of God.*
>
> —Jaroslav Pelikan

PLAYBILL: LOCAL CHURCH MAKES "LIVING BIBLE"

This is a book about learning doctrine for the sake of acting *out* what is *in* Christ: call it the *drama of discipleship*. Nothing in the world is more important than this project: living to God with one another in Christlike ways "in accordance with the Scriptures" (1 Cor. 15:3). This is the way the people of God come to know and express their love for God: by conforming their lives—hearts, souls, minds, and strength (Mark 12:30)—to his will, on earth as it is in heaven. Doctrine gives direction for bearing faithful witness, for *speaking* understanding. Moreover, if action "speaks" louder than words, then faith speaking understanding involves both verbal and nonverbal modes of communication: words and deeds.

Scripture gives authoritative witness to the identity and significance of Jesus Christ. Disciples thus speak understanding when they talk and walk "in accordance with the Scriptures." Living in accordance with the Scriptures—being *biblical*—is thus the disciple's prime directive. To be a follower of Christ is to be a follower of Scripture, in all three senses of "follow": (1) to understand the meaning of what Christ says in Scripture, (2) to respond to his instructions with obedience, and (3) to go after Christ or along "the way" of Christ.

Being biblical is thus a matter not only of theory but also of practice. It is one thing to have a view of biblical authority, quite another to grasp God's word and formulate its truth systematically, and still another not only to state the truth but also to do or *embody* it. Too often, doing theology according to the Scriptures does not include this latter sense. The present proposal works with a robust sense of being biblical that includes all three dimensions: holding a high view of Scripture, using Scripture as a source and norm of Christian doctrine, and embodying Scripture in forms of everyday life. Doing theology "in accordance with the Scriptures" is ultimately a matter of being transformed by the Spirit in order to conform one's heart, mind, and soul to the Bible such that being biblical is indeed a matter of the strength of one's very *being*.

It has been said that church history is essentially the history of biblical interpretation.[1] This is obviously true on one level inasmuch as many important turning points in church history involved conflicting interpretations over particular biblical texts (e.g., the Arian controversy featured disagreement over the meaning of the Son's being "the firstborn of all creation" [Col. 1:15]). It is also true on another level insofar as the story of the church is essentially the story of its attempts to interpret Scripture "bodily," that is, through the shape of its life together. The church is biblical, therefore, when it seeks to embody the words in the power of the Spirit and so become a living commentary. The church is thus not only the "people of the book" but also "the (lived) interpretation of the book."

Followers of Christ seek to be biblical in response to Jesus' prayer: "Thy will be done." God's will is expressed in God's word, and no part of Scripture more resembles a script to be performed than the Law. Yet biblical wisdom too functions like a script to the extent that it asks to be embodied in the life of the people of God. Indeed, there is something intrinsically representational, and thus dramatic, about doing God's will "on earth *as* it is in heaven" (Matt. 6:10). The *as* provides a warrant for thinking about the church's embodied interpretation as a performance that seeks to represent on earth the rule of God as it is in God's own realm. How, then, should the people of God perform "in accordance with the Scriptures"?

In 1985 First Presbyterian Church in Libertyville, Illinois, performed the Scriptures, in public, for the first time. They continued to do so over a span of evenings, once a year for several years. The "Living Bible" became an annual event eagerly anticipated by the whole community. The basic idea was simple: spectators could walk around the church building and see a series of thirteen tableaux, staged for three blocks around the parish hall, representing key moments in the biblical story, including Adam and Eve in the garden of Eden, Noah's ark (with goats, horses, etc.), the nativity, the crucifixion, and the resurrection. The production involved more than 600 actors and 200 volunteers working behind the scenes: there was a director for each scene, set decorators, actors, stagehands,

---

1. Gerhard Ebeling, "Church History Is the History of the Exposition of Scripture," in *The Word of God and Tradition: Historical Studies Interpreting the Divisions of Christianity* (Philadelphia: Fortress Press, 1968), 11–32.

prop makers, painters, costume makers, people to work with sound and light, and so forth.

Performances of the Living Bible ran continuously for two hours on each of the three nights, with shifts of actors taking turns. The actors did not have lines, but they played their parts in silent pantomime to musical accompaniment and prerecorded biblical passages. The centerpiece was the scene depicting the Last Supper, modeled after Leonardo da Vinci's famous painting. Great care was taken to ensure that the hairstyles, tableware, and food corresponded to da Vinci's canvas: "Everything will be true, right down to the round loaves of bread on the table. The painting was meant to capture the moment after Christ told his disciples, 'One among you will betray me.' Our actors will personify as exactly as possible their expressions of disbelief."[2] The thirteen actors in the scene would be moving about and gesticulating and then suddenly freeze, creating a nearly exact replica of the disciples' postures and expressions in da Vinci's painting. It was a very effective moment, often taking the spectators' breath away.[3]

The Living Bible was an effective means of evangelism, of showing the way in which the basic story line of the Bible converges on the event of Jesus Christ. In this sense it was a success. Nevertheless, the present book takes the model of performing the Scriptures in another direction. I am more concerned with the latter half of the Great Commission: with making disciples not in the sense of converting them to Christ but rather in the sense of cultivating in them the mind of Christ, "teaching them to observe" the supreme authority of Christ in every situation (Matt. 28:20 KJV). The church is to be a Living Bible, yes, but not by staging literal repetitions (copies) of biblical scenes. This is one kind of faithfulness, to be sure, that of photographic reduplication. The long-term challenge for disciples, however, is to represent the gospel not by seeking literally to duplicate past scenes but rather by continuing to follow Jesus into the present in ways that are both faithful and (necessarily) creative. It is ultimately the difference between repristination ("dead" theater) and fitting participation (i.e., theater that is vital and vibrant).

Being biblical is a Spirit-enabled way of being that is both generated and governed by God's word. It is a matter of coming to know God through his word and of loving God by doing his word. Theology exists for the sake of God's word, ministering understanding, and this for the purpose of growing disciples. Theology is a response to Paul's injunction: "Let the word of Christ dwell in you richly" (Col. 3:16). The rest of this book attempts to make good on this claim. Part 1 shows why the theatrical model offers important resources for conceiving the challenge of being biblical. Part 2 examines a number of doctrines and shows how they help prepare disciples to play their part in the living Bible, or better, the living body of Jesus Christ.

2. H. Lee Murphy, "Cast of Hundreds Celebrates Bible in Church's Tableaux," reporting an interview with Rev. James Glenn, *Chicago Tribune*, September 18, 1987, http://articles.chicagotribune.com/1987-09-18/entertainment/8703100871_1_scenes-painting-la-grande-jatte.

3. First Presbyterian relaunched the Living Bible program in September 2012.

PROGRAM NOTES: WHAT THIS BOOK IS ABOUT

Faith Speaking Understanding uses a theatrical model to discuss the various ways in which doctrine shapes Christian understanding and forms disciples. Theology serves faith's vocation of speaking and showing understanding, of bringing biblical Christianity to life. The present book seeks to advance this all-important project for the sake of the church's well-being. This is a daunting task that involves several interconnected matters. The present book therefore has nine interrelated themes, each of which serves its principal thesis.

It Is about Being Biblical

The church is "a people of the book" in a dynamic way, bringing it to life by entering into the drama of the Christ that the Scriptures attest "in many and various ways" (Heb. 1:1). Here we may recall what Hans-Georg Gadamer says about interpretation as entering into the "play" of the text, which "always involves something like performing a drama, for the player who takes the play seriously interprets it from within, by belonging to and playing a part in it."[4]

Being biblical means attending to the whole as well as the parts and to the relationship between them. Let us call the kind of scholarly analysis that focuses on particular passages *biblical reasoning in its workday mode*. It is familiar to theologians who view their task as studying the data of Scripture to see what the whole Bible (by which they mean the collation of the parts) has to say about a particular topic. Yet synthesis—keeping the big picture in mind—is just as important and requires imagination: the ability to incorporate the individual parts of Scripture into unifying patterns. Imagination is *biblical reasoning in its Sunday best*, lost in wonder at the creativity of the Creator. Being biblical is a vital means of transformation by the renewing of our minds.

It Is about Theology

Theology is a science in that it pertains to knowing God, but "science" may not be the best label for describing this knowledge or why doctrine matters to disciples. In the secular realm, *science* means the mastery of some domain, summarized in a system of knowledge. To know something scientifically is to be able to control it, use it to our advantage. One does not "master" the project of living blessedly with others before God.

Theology admits of many definitions, but in this context it primarily concerns the process of seeking, finding, and then demonstrating wisdom. We will only be able to rehabilitate doctrine if we are able to view doctrine itself as a helpful bridge that spans the debilitating divide between theory and practice. Theology

---

4. Joel Weinsheimer, "Hermeneutics," in *Contemporary Literary Theory*, ed. G. Douglas Atkins and Laura Morrow (Amherst: University of Massachusetts Press, 1989), 126. See also Hans-Georg Gadamer, *Truth and Method* 2nd rev. ed. (New York: Continuum, 2002), 147–48.

helps disciples to display the *lived* knowledge of the gospel: the mind of Christ embodied and embedded in particular situations. Theology is the art and science of enacting the mind of Christ everywhere, at all times, and to everyone.

It Is about Church Doctrine

We may need to change our picture of doctrine if we are to see it as playing a necessary role in growing disciples.[5] Doctrine refers to the deposit of authorized teaching entrusted to the church' care (1 Tim. 6:20; 2 Tim. 1:14), yet it is more than a body of knowledge. It is instruction whose aim is to form, inform, and transform disciples into doers who can speak, act, and think the way Christ did. Doctrine serves as a finishing school for disciples by helping them to view their lives as Christ did his, as caught up in the great drama of redemption.[6] Doctrine, then, is not simply an inert body of knowledge; rather, it intends an active bodily doing. Church without doctrine to direct it is dazed and confused; yet doctrine without the church to embody it is arid and empty.

It Is about the Gospel of Jesus Christ

The gospel is the good news that Jesus has blazed the way to eternal life with God, making good on God's covenant promise to forgive old sins (Isa. 53:5), give new hearts (Ezek. 36:26; Jer. 31:33), and renew creation (Isa. 65:17; 66:22). The gospel is the joyful proclamation that God has done something to good effect. *God has done something*: the drama of redemption reaches its climax when the Son pours out his life on the cross (Acts 2:23) and when the Father raises him from the dead (2:24) and when the Son again pours out his Spirit (2:33). *To good effect*: those who put their faith in the risen Christ are saved from their sins and have a share, through his Spirit, in his life and sonship (2:38).

It Is about Life

Too many people, even those in the church, dismiss doctrine as dry and dusty, unrelated to the rough and tumble of real life, and perhaps even a little bit unspiritual to the extent that it encourages division in the church, as if logic cannot but assault faith (as if "Blessed are those who believe without thinking!"). Sadly, there is more than a little truth to these caricatures. The fault lies not with doctrine itself, however, but with a misunderstanding of its nature and purpose. A false picture of doctrine as lifeless has held sections of the church captive for too long.

---

5. Matthew Myer Boulton's *Life in God: John Calvin, Practical Formation, and the Future of Protestant Theology* (Grand Rapids: Wm. B. Eerdmans Publishing Co., 2011) makes a similar claim.

6. To be sure, transformation requires more than studying doctrine. Saints are not always good students (and vice versa). At the same time, doctrine is one of the ways in which the Holy Spirit ministers the word of God.

What does the church have to say and do that no other institution can? Nature and society alike abhor a vacuum, and there are many ideologies and agendas waiting to rush in and fill the hearts and minds of the uncommitted. Doctrine orients the church's life by teaching it how to live and what to live for. Indeed, doctrine orients the church to the abundant and eternal life found only in Jesus Christ. For life is more than a matter of biology, more than sheer physical existence: it is a matter of being in fellowship with the triune God. Doctrine forms disciples when it helps the church to act out its new life in Christ. Far from being removed from real life, then, we see that doctrine concerns energies and events that are as real and powerful as anything known in physics or chemistry, energies and events that can turn the world upside down (Acts 17:6).

It Is about the Reign of God

What turned the Thessalonian Jews' world upside down had to do with the apostles' proclamation: "there is another king, Jesus" (Acts 17:7 RSV). The lordship of Christ continues to be disruptive, breaking ideological strangleholds, subverting corrupt loyalties, and exposing idolatry well beyond Thessalonica. The kingdom of God is the breaking in of God's reign to defeat the powers of darkness and disorder. Liberating the oppressed is God's signature mark: Christ's setting the captives free is the highpoint of the dramatic conflict between Satan and the Son of God on a stage that includes both heaven and earth.[7]

It Is about the Church

The church is the place where Christ rules by his word, which dwells in disciples' hearts. The kingdom of God is the domain of Christ's word, that bounded area where Christ's word rules and is joyfully accepted. The church is thus a royal theater: a lived exhibit of the word of truth, grace, and love. In particular, the church is that peculiar place where men and women freely and joyfully do the will of God on earth as it is in heaven.

"I believe in . . . the holy catholic church." This is a bold, often counterintuitive confession of faith, especially in an age where the flaws of various church leaders are all too apparent and where so many people express disappointment in their actual experience of church. Yet bold faith in the reality of church is just as important now as it has always been. The church is the visible presence of the invisible, the tangible experience of the kingdom of God on earth: "Your kingdom come. Your will be done, on earth" (Matt. 6:10). We cannot help but believe in church: it is the firstfruits of the Father's answer to the Lord's own prayer and petition.

---

7. Timothy Gombis describes Jesus' victory over the powers and principalities as having cosmic scope (*The Drama of Ephesians: Participating in the Triumph of God* [Downers Grove, IL: InterVarsity Press, 2010], 24).

Of course, it is not enough merely to believe that the church exists. One must also belong to it, be an active member. What is the nature of this activity? Doctrine aids disciples in discerning what they must say and do in order to be church. In later chapters I will expand upon the claim, as bold as it is relevant, that the people who make up church are the place where the reign of God becomes most visible. The local church is a parable of the kingdom when it acts out the new creation in Christ amid the old here and now. As we shall see, the church is not an empty space (Peter Brook's metaphor for the theater) but a *peopled place* where God exhibits his gospel. What fills the empty space is the body of Jesus Christ.

It Is about Public Theology

Public theology is the church's demonstration of life in Christ—to the glory of God and for the sake of the world. When the people of God display a flourishing life in obedience to Christ in the power of the Spirit, they both glorify God and demonstrate the power and wisdom of the gospel to the world. This penultimate theme encompasses the prior seven claims of "what this book is about."

It is commonplace to think of religion as a quintessentially "private" affair and of Christianity as about one's own personal relationship to Jesus. However, to think that what God has done in Christ is simply to make it possible for individuals to go to heaven is severely to truncate and even distort the gospel. The good news is not only that individual souls can go to heaven but especially that God has established a kingdom of priests, a holy nation (1 Pet. 2:9; cf. Exod. 19:6; Rev. 1:6), and that he has established social peace in reconciling Jews and Gentiles (Eph. 2:14). There is therefore a public aspect to the gospel: on the cross of Christ, God displayed his wrath against sin *and* "disarmed the principalities and powers and made a public example of them, triumphing over them in it" (Col. 2:15 RSV mg.). In the words of the King James Bible, God "made a shew of them openly."

There is therefore a public dimension to the gospel. The relatively new discipline of "public theology" studies ways in which Christian faith should impact public life. The assumption is that the gospel has a significant bearing on all people, not Christians only. Much of what the church says and does takes the form of public witness.

Theology is public in another sense as well. To learn Christian doctrine only from textbooks rather than from participating in the communion of saints is like reading Shakespeare but never encountering a live performance: it may be informative, but it is rarely transformative. Disciples best learn how to *practice* doctrinal truth through *paideia*, an apprentice-based pedagogy that involves following the examples of (i.e., imitating) others who are further along.

Theology is public, finally, inasmuch as it seeks both to demonstrate and participate in the expansion of God's reign in the world. How should it accomplish this vital task? What criteria can we use to determine what demonstrations of the kingdom ought to look like? Can we hope that even successful demonstrations will change the world? These are challenging questions, but the short answer is that doctrine is an essential aid to such demonstrations, to such corporate discipleship.

Can the church's demonstration of the gospel change the world? If so, does this have more to do with changing human hearts or social structures, ideas or institutions? In his work *To Change the World*, James Davison Hunter has argued that what changes the world are not simply great men with great ideas but rather ideas embedded in culture-producing institutions. For better or for ill, the church in North America no longer figures on that list. Not to worry. According to Hunter, the church should be less concerned with seizing social power than with being *faithfully present*: "The vocation of the church is to bear witness to and to be the embodiment of the coming Kingdom of God."[8]

The key term here is *witness*. If the very *existence* of the church, as the "body" of Christ, represents a standing witness to the truth of the gospel, how much more does its *activity* (i.e., its bodily *movement*) do so? It is important to speak the truth, to be sure. Yet to demonstrate the truth of the gospel, the church must both speak and show its understanding. Culture-producing power is "the capacity to define what is real."[9] The church does this by enacting God's word in particular times and places, for it is God's word that defines what is ultimately real.

To witness to God's word is thus not simply to repeat it but also to embrace it as one's framework for seeing and interpreting the reality of God, oneself, others, and the world. All that disciples say and do should therefore bear witness to renewed minds and transformed hearts: "Changing our world depends on changing our hearts: how we *perceive*, *name*, and *act* in the world."[10] The drama of doctrine is never more on display than in disciples' lives as they seek to communicate "the life that is God's life in and for the world,"[11] thus giving evidence of changed minds and hearts.

This is how doctrine directs the church to turn the world upside down: by urging Christians to *do* what they *know*, displaying in the lives of disciples and in local churches the wisdom of Jesus Christ.[12] The church is (or ought to be) a public display of the good news, the supreme good that is found only in union with Jesus Christ. This has been the charge to the church since the beginning: to live out the way, truth, and life of Jesus Christ. The result is a "politics" of the gospel whereby the church engages in public practices for the public good, practices that also characterize the distinctive use of power in the coming reign of

---

8. James Davison Hunter, *To Change the World: The Irony, Tragedy, and Possibility of Christianity in the Late Modern World* (Oxford: Oxford University Press, 2010), 95.

9. Ibid., 178.

10. Mark Labberton, *The Dangerous Act of Loving Your Neighbor: Seeing Others through the Eyes of Jesus* (Downers Grove, IL: InterVarsity Press, 2010), 23.

11. Ibid., 27.

12. For an extended argument to this effect, see C. Kavin Rowe, *World Upside Down: Reading Acts in the Greco-Roman Age* (Oxford: Oxford University Press, 2009), esp. chap. 4.

God—such as gathering together, confessing Jesus, peacemaking, truth-telling, and doing justice.

It Is about Reality

There are plenty of doctrines in the world and plenty of disciples for various causes. What makes Christian doctrine unique, however, is its single-minded and single-hearted focus on knowing God and oneself in Jesus Christ and in directing disciples to demonstrate their understanding of this ultimate reality.

Christian doctrine grows disciples by teaching them to perceive, name, and act in ways that demonstrate the reality of the gospel, speaking and showing *what is* "in Christ." This is also the public, and Pauline, face of the church's mission: "to make the word of God fully known, the mystery hidden for ages and generations but now made manifest to his saints, . . . Christ in you" (Col. 1:25–27). The church is the public revelation of the mystery of salvation. Doctrine exists to aid the church and disciples, not to withdraw from the world into their own enclave but rather to *get real*. Public theology in the sense I am using the term is all about getting real: displaying the real *in Christ*.

PLOT: A BRIEF SYNOPSIS

Faith Speaking Understanding has a two-part structure. Part 1, "Before the Curtain Rises," sets out the contours of the theatrical model for thinking about doctrine and theology as well as my reasons for choosing it.

I begin by expounding the book's title. By speaking understanding, faith begins to *do* the word. Speak-acting is the language of the theater. It also corresponds to the Bible's injunction to be a doer as well as hearer of the word. The obedience of faith and faith's demonstration of understanding involve speech and action alike. I then develop the theatrical analogy further, defining key terms and drawing a number of important conceptual distinctions, especially between Scripture and "script." I also explain my subtitle and distinguish between three different but related senses of "drama of doctrine." Next, I consider whether "theatrical" theology is intended only as a metaphor or as an analogical model for the nature of theology and its subject matter. I consider (and rebut) two objections to the theatrical model, an exercise that makes several important advances beyond my argument in *The Drama of Doctrine* (chap. 1 below).

The next chapter confronts a potentially fatal stumbling block to the theatrical model: perhaps it encourages us to think of the church either as thespians performing for a world from which they are separated or, equally disastrous, as a gathering of passive spectators. In response, I suggest that we view the church as an interactive theater in which there is no "fourth wall" separating actors from audience. As to the problem of encouraging passive spectators, I use 2 John as a template in which to show how doctrine urges disciples to abide not only in truth but also in love, and this means active engagement. The audience itself is thus the staging area for the action and the site of the drama, for the urgent issue—the matter on which the whole play (life itself) turns—is whether disciples take the doctrine of Jesus Christ to heart. The church is the proper domain of doctrine, for it is in the church that the truth of doctrine is learned and demonstrated (chap. 2). This brings part 1, my case for thinking about theology in theatrical terms, to a close.

Part 2 is a constructive proposal for how doctrine functions in the church to make disciples. Every doctrine contributes in one way or another to the church's overall understanding of *what is in Christ* and *what is happening in Christ*. It is the burden of part 2 to draw on doctrine both to understand the church's task—right participation in the drama of the Christ—and to equip disciples to demonstrate that understanding in forms of wise, loving practice.

Part 2 begins where we are, with the church on the twenty-first-century stage, and examines the present crisis of authenticity: Whose words and acts count, and why? What does the church have to offer to the world? In response, I offer the bold claim that the church offers speech and action that accord with the created order (i.e., reality) and thus give true testimony to the meaning of life (chap. 3). Doctrine helps us to view God as God presents himself and the world as God views it. The doctrine of human being and sin helps to clarify the precise nature of the dramatic conflict: the clash of finite and infinite freedoms, human faithlessness and divine faithfulness. Fallen creation is the backdrop for the divine playwright's entrance onto the stage of history in order to execute his dramatic plan of salvation (chap. 4).

To this point the focus has been on how doctrine defines disciples, their nature and purpose. The rest of part 2 deals with how disciples do or perform doctrine. I begin by considering what is perhaps the most obvious objection of all to the theatrical model—that it encourages playacting or hypocrisy—and argue in response that Christian doctrine rather shows us who we truly are in Christ (chap. 5). As I have already argued, Christian faith is not a private affair for individuals but a community-building project. Accordingly, the next two chapters turn their attention to ecclesiology. The role of doctrine in the church is to assist pastors and other church leaders to mount local productions that serve as living parables of the kingdom of God. The church is a place where disciples of Jesus gather to learn his teaching and to practice what they learn, not least by acting out their union with Christ, especially in baptism and the Lord's Supper, two central scenes that rehearse the high point of the drama of redemption (chap. 6). The ministry of word and sacrament not only edifies church members but also prepares them to bear witness to Christ's reign to the wider world, especially by performing spontaneous words of truth and works of love wherever two or three are gathered in Jesus' name (chap. 7).

A brief word about the structure of part 2 is in order. In grammar, we say that a verb is in the *indicative* mood when it expresses simple statements of fact (e.g., "she took of its fruit and ate"; "Jesus wept"). Verbs in the indicative mood *indicate*: they show something; they are symptoms of something. We get the English term from the Latin *indicare* (to point), from which the term *index* finger also derives. In addition to *show* or *state*, the verb *indicate* can also mean *suggest a course of action*, especially in a medical context (e.g., "the presence of symptom *x* indicates treatment *y*").

Each chapter in part 2 sets forth one or more doctrines that indicate some aspect of *what is in Christ*. Following the example of the apostle Paul, each of these indicatives is followed, under the rubric of "recapitulation," by an imperative that makes explicit what is already implicit in the particular aspect of *what is in Christ* under consideration. The imperative is simply a statement of what kind of behavior should follow in order to be indicative of *what is in Christ*. These six imperatives give *direction for the church's self-presentation in everyday life, direction for keeping in step with the truth of the gospel* (Gal. 2:14). They also serve to restate the basic argument in more traditional (i.e., nontheatrical) terms.

Part 2 concludes by considering the ongoing dramatic conflict in light of the drama's climax (victory in Christ) and urges disciples to abide in doctrine in order joyfully to endure until the end (chap. 8). The book concludes with a plea for grateful realism, two exhortations that should govern demonstrations of faith's understanding always, everywhere, and by all, and with a reminder that the process of making disciples involves awakening sleepers to the new creational kingdom inaugurated in Christ. For readers who require further convincing of the merits of a dramatic approach to doctrine, I include an appendix that examines both historical and contemporary objections to drawing theological water from a theatrical well.

PART 1
BEFORE THE CURTAIN RISES
ON THEOLOGY AND THEATER

Chapter 1

Doing the Word "on Earth as It Is in Heaven"

Introducing the Theater of the Gospel

> *Dear children, let us not love with words or tongue but with actions and in truth.*
> —1 John 3:18 NIV

> *The New Testament is not a text to be analyzed so much as a set of scripts for forming a company of performers, a movement that will be Christianity.*
> —Terrence Tilley, *The Disciples' Jesus: Christology as Reconciling Practice*

Anselm famously defined theology in his *Proslogion* (1077–78) as "faith *seeking* understanding." Why, a thousand years later, do I make so bold as to suggest a change? And in what sense is "faith *speaking* understanding" a kind of performance?

FAITH SPEAKING UNDERSTANDING: THE CHALLENGE

Speaking is a form of acting, and action is a kind of speaking ("actions speak louder than words"). Actors give speeches, yet action is the language of the theater. Action, in word and deed, is also the primary means by which the church demonstrates its understanding of the world as the theater of God's glory and of itself as the theater of the gospel.

Disciples do not need to speak Greek to live according to the Scriptures, but they do need to speak *Christian*. However, according to Marcus Borg, a historian of Jesus, this is easier said than done. In his hard-hitting book *Speaking Christian: Why Christian Words Have Lost Their Meaning and Power*, Borg points out a disconnect between the original (i.e., biblical) meaning of many Christian terms and the way Christians use them today.¹ North Americans think they know how to speak Christian, but what they say is actually a gross distortion. Either people do not know Christian words at all, or they have heard them but do not know what they mean, or they think they know what they mean when in fact they mean something completely different.

Borg is not referring to non-Christians only but also to churchgoing Christians unaware of how far the meanings of Christian terms have drifted from their historical biblical roots. The crisis in Christian language (why Johnny can't speak Christian) is also a crisis in the church insofar as language is the stuff of worship, preaching, teaching, and so forth and thus the means by which we "do" church. Accordingly, Borg has written his book as a kind of "Christian primer," a remedial wordbook for people who want to speak authentic Christian—not a lexicon for understanding the Christian "Greats," but at least a graded reader.

How did it happen? How could North American Christians forget basic biblical vocabulary? Borg has two explanations. The first is modernity's "literalization" of language, perhaps under the pressure of science. The second is the captivity of biblical language by a heaven-and-hell framework that (mis)understands the gospel as the message that we can "go to heaven" because Jesus paid the price for our sins. It turns out that "speaking Christian" is a matter not of knowing Greek or memorizing Scripture but rather of using certain biblical ideas as a lens through which to view God, world, and self.

I am as interested as Borg in disciples speaking genuine Christian, because faith attains understanding largely by means of biblical paradigms ("By faith we understand that the worlds were prepared by the word of God" [Heb. 11:3]). I agree with Borg that our understanding must be disciplined by Scripture's way of speaking, and that one key Christian term—*believing*—means considerably more than affirming certain statements to be true.²

"How to understand Christian language is the central conflict in Christianity today."³ If theology trains disciples to speak "proper" (i.e., biblical) Christian, then Borg's claim that "speaking Christian" is in a state of crisis means that theology, too, is in a state of crisis. This is particularly so as concerns theology's presence (unremarkable) and influence (minimal) in the church. The real issue, as Borg rightly observes, concerns what Christianity is about. Is the gospel about the afterlife and what we must believe to get to heaven? Or is it about God's passion for the loving transformation of this present life on earth?⁴ According to Borg, we must choose between two competing visions, the water of contemporary literalism and the wine of biblical symbolism: "What separates them is how the shared

---

1. Marcus J. Borg, *Speaking Christian: Why Christian Words Have Lost Their Meaning and Power—and How They Can Be Restored* (New York: HarperOne, 2011).
2. Borg reports that, before the sixteenth century, the English verb *believe* always had a person rather than a thing as its direct object and was synonymous with *belove* (ibid., 119).
3. Ibid., 231.
4. This simplistic (either-or) distinction may reflect on Borg's own inability to "speak Christian theology."

language is understood."⁵ Indeed! Followers of Jesus should therefore want, above all things, to speak with "a full understanding of every good thing we have in Christ" (cf. Philem. 6). Borg's own speech, no more than a sound bite really, is ultimately too abbreviated to be helpful: "The Christian message reduced to its essentials is: love God (as known in Jesus) and change the world."⁶ Yes—but how?

Speaking Christian is a matter of faith speaking understanding, of theology *articulated*. Each element in this definition is important. *Faith*: what Christians speak is what they have received through faith in the apostolic word of the gospel. As Calvin notes in his *Institutes*, what determines faith as Christian is the word that forms and informs it: "For by his Word, God rendered faith unambiguous forever, a faith that should be superior to all opinion," and to make it permanent, God recorded his oracles on public tablets.⁷ *Speaking*: theology arises when the church realizes "that it must give an account to God for the way in which it speaks."⁸ *Understanding*: everything Christians say gives evidence of their understanding of God's prior word and act, especially as this concerns the history of Jesus and the meaning of the gospel. What is Christianity all about, what did Jesus' death accomplish, and what precisely is the gospel?

"Faith speaking understanding" presupposes knowledge of the grammar of faith: doctrine. Learning the language (and grammar) of faith is both means and end of Christian discipleship. Augustine seemed to think so too, if the opening paragraph of his work *On Christian Doctrine* is any indication: "There are two things on which all interpretation of Scripture depends: the process of discovering what we need to learn, and the process of presenting what we have learnt."⁹ Theology speeds disciples on their way to right seeking and wise speaking: to discovering, with the ultimate aim of presenting, understanding.

What is it to speak, and present, understanding? I agree with George Steiner: to understand something is to be able to translate it.¹⁰ To "speak understanding" is to express the meaning of the gospel in some language; to present understanding is to translate the meaning of the gospel into various forms of language, logic, and life. Christian theology is the task of translating—discovering and presenting—the meaning of the gospel of Jesus Christ for us today. The special vocation of the church is to seek, speak, and show nothing less, and nothing else, than Jesus Christ, and him crucified (1 Cor. 2:2).

---

5. Ibid., 253.
6. Ibid., 238.
7. John Calvin, *Institutes of the Christian Religion* 1.6.2, ed. John T. McNeill, trans. Ford Lewis Battles, LCC (Philadelphia: Westminster Press, 1960). (Hereafter cited as *Inst.*)
8. Karl Barth, *Church Dogmatics*, vol. I/1, trans. Geoffrey Bromiley, 2nd ed. (Edinburgh: T&T Clark, 1975), 3. Under "speaking," Barth includes all that the church says and does in its specific action as a fellowship: "proclamation by preaching and the administration of the sacraments, worship, . . . internal and external mission including works of love amongst the sick, the weak, and those in jeopardy" (I/1:3).
9. Augustine, *On Christian Teaching*, trans. R. H. Green (Oxford: Oxford University Press, 1997), 9.
10. See George Steiner, *After Babel: Aspects of Language and Translation* (London and New York: Oxford University Press, 1975), 47.

THE WITNESS AS DOER OF THE WORD:
JAMES'S MIRROR AND JESUS' HOUSE

It is but a small step from the idea of "presenting" faith's understanding to "performing" it. Or is it? Some readers may rightly worry that to speak of faith and theology in terms of performance is to encourage an activist view (as if Christianity were about works righteousness) or, what is worse, a display of one's supposed skill in righteous living, a sure path to prideful ruin. Those (like me) who speak about "performing" doctrine would do well to keep Jesus' words in mind: "Beware of practicing your piety before others in order to be seen by them; for then you have no reward from your Father in heaven" (Matt. 6:1). Performing with the wrong motivation is an ongoing danger.

There are, however, other motives for performing faith. Indeed, we have only to look to Jesus' own example. Jesus does (i.e., performs) God's will, embodying the reign of God through his willingness to give himself up for the world. There is nothing we can do to add to the finished work and definitive performance of Christ; however, it does not follow that there is nothing for Christians to do. On the contrary, Christ calls his disciples to participate in his work by bearing witness to its achievement and to do so in word and deed. If actions speak louder than words, it is because they lend the weight of behavior (real assent) to belief (nominal assent).

Nominal Christianity falls short of true witness and discipleship. The way witnesses live clarifies the meaning of their words and may even count as an argument for the truth of what they say. The disciples' "performance" of faith must be motivated first and foremost by the love of God. This is the one thing above every other that disciples must perform, as Kierkegaard makes clear in his *Purity of Heart Is to Will One Thing*, one of his "edifying discourses." How, asks Kierkegaard, should the ideal reader respond to his challenge to will one thing only (i.e., the good—God)? "To listen in order to act, this is the highest thing of all."[11] He goes on to compare worship to a theater and himself to a prompter who reminds those on stage of their lines. What the actor says matters because "each word becomes true when embodied in him, true through him."[12] People of faith who would speak understanding cannot therefore be content with speaking only.

For whom do witnesses perform their understanding of the gospel? Clearly, disciples ought to enact their faith out in the open in order to communicate their understanding of God and the gospel to others: "Let your light shine before others, so that they may see your good works and give glory to your Father in heaven" (Matt. 5:16). At the same time, everything that disciples do is potentially a way of worshiping and glorifying God, the audience of one to whom our lived confession of faith is ultimately directed. On this, the apostle Paul and

---

11. Søren Kierkegaard, *Purity of Heart Is to Will One Thing* (New York: HarperOne, 1956), 179.
12. Ibid., 180.

Kierkegaard agree: "We speak, not to please mortals, but to please God who tests our hearts" (1 Thess. 2:4). Kierkegaard compares God to a critical theatergoer "who looks on to see how the lines are spoken."[13] The salient point is that those who receive instruction are not passive listeners but active actors, responsible for *acting out* what they have heard and received. The witness presents faith's understanding by translating it into action.

Witnesses must therefore not only speak but also *do* "Christian." This is the moral of the famous mirror image of the apostle James: "But be doers of the word, and not merely hearers who deceive themselves. For if any are hearers of the word and not doers, they are like those who look at themselves in a mirror; for they look at themselves and, on going away, immediately forget what they were like" (Jas. 1:22–24). By contrast, those who look into the mirror of the word of God—the Two-Testament story of God bringing captives out of bondage—see themselves as they truly are: people who have been brought into the kingdom of light by him who is light. The challenge, then, is to live out, to perform, our Spirit-given freedom: to be not "hearers who forget" but "doers who act" (Jas. 1:25). Doctrine is thus something *dramatic*: something to be not only heard and believed but also demonstrated, done, and *acted out*. The path of becoming Christlike is not passive. Grace is opposed not to effort but to the idea of earning.[14] The key to nurturing disciples is well-directed action.

Jesus himself expects his disciples to perform his doctrine. Toward the end of his teaching on the law in the Sermon on the Mount, Jesus employs the metaphor of house building to make a point similar to James's mirror: "Everyone then who hears these words of mine and acts on them will be like a wise man who built his house on rock" (Matt. 7:24; cf. Ezek. 33:30–33). And again, like James, Jesus contrasts the way of wisdom and true discipleship with an abbreviated hearing that stops short of performance: "And everyone who hears these words of mine and does not act on them will be like a foolish man who built his house on sand" (Matt. 7:26). Dietrich Bonhoeffer rightly calculates the cost of genuine discipleship: "*Only [one] who believes is obedient, and only [one] who is obedient believes.*"[15]

What is ultimately at stake in the idea of performing is the very nature of Christian faith: does belief that fails to issue in behavior count as genuine witness (and understanding) or not? There is something inherently "performatory" about the logic of first-person confessional utterances ("I believe"; "We believe"). Such statements are not merely descriptive, informing others of the contents of one's consciousness, but also *dispositional*, indicating the posture of one's being and behavior toward the content of one's belief. If we believe what we say, we ought to be prepared to stand by it and act appropriately. Believing "is *action-oriented*,

---

13. Ibid., 181.
14. So Dallas Willard, "Live Life to the Full," *Christian Herald*, April 14, 2001, http://www.dwillard.org/articles/artview.asp?artID=5.
15. Dietrich Bonhoeffer, *The Cost of Discipleship*, trans. R. H. Fuller et al. (New York: Touchstone, 1995), 63.

situation-related, and embedded in the *particularities and contingencies* of everyday living."[16] The local church is the community that seeks both to *understand* and *stand by* Christian beliefs. The local church is any place in which the gospel of Jesus Christ gets performed, acted out by disciples who translate it into forms of life, worship, and works of love.

The gospel—the good news of the Father's gracious self-communication in Jesus Christ through the Spirit—is essentially a matter of what God has done for the salvation of the world. At the heart of biblical Christianity is a series of divine acts that together constitute the drama of redemption. The present book sets forth a vision of the church as the theater of the gospel (a community gathered to act out its faith) and theology as a species of what we could call *theodramatics*: the attempt to discover and present—to seek, speak, and show—the church's understanding of what God has done, is doing, and will do in Jesus Christ. Theodramatics is faith's attempt to speak understanding by discovering, and then participating in, what the triune God—Father, Son, and Spirit—is doing in and through Christ for the salvation of the world.

A disciple is one who seeks to speak, act, and live in ways that *bear witness to the truth, goodness, and beauty of Jesus Christ*. If the disciple is a truth-bearer that presents faith's understanding, then the theologian is best viewed as a minister of understanding; for getting understanding is prerequisite to presenting it. What is *understanding*? It is not simply head knowledge; it is more than theoretical. Church towers are not made of ivory. To understand one's faith is to know how to get on with it: how to practice it and what to *do* with it. Hence the purpose of this book is to give direction to disciples for understanding the drama of redemption. Therefrom arises my thesis: the recovery of doctrine is essential to the task of discipleship, demonstrating understanding of God's word by doing it. Doctrine is less theoretical than it is theatrical, a matter of *doing*—speaking and showing—what we have heard and understood.

"THEATER" OF THE GOSPEL: DEFINITIONS AND DISTINCTIONS

At this point readers may want to know why I feel the need to make a difficult subject, Christian doctrine, even harder by pairing it with something as esoteric, distant, and inappropriate as drama. Fair question. I have four principal reasons. First and most fundamental: the subject matter of the Bible, God's redemptive words and deeds in the history of Israel that culminates in Jesus Christ, is inherently *theodramatic*, a matter of what God (*theos*) has said and done (*draō*) in history. At the heart of Christianity is not merely an *idea* of God but rather God's self-communicating *words* and *acts*. The gospel is not a

---

16. Anthony C. Thiselton, *The Hermeneutics of Doctrine* (Grand Rapids: Wm. B. Eerdmans Publishing Co., 2007), 21.

universal truth but an announcement of God's saving work in Christ. Second, the language of the theater, and theater studies in general, provides additional images and concepts by which to bridge the theory/practice dichotomy mentioned above. The theatrical model encourages us to relate the lived *form* of our discipleship to the *content* of our doctrines. Third, following from the preceding: the aim of Christian theology is not merely to add to our stockpile of theoretical knowledge but to cultivate disciples who can display the mind of Christ in every situation. Knowledge is static, but wisdom—lived knowledge—is dynamic and hence dramatic. Finally, the notion that the Christian life is a drama in which I have a role to play, with other believers, gives renewed urgency to everyday discipleship. In an age of apathy, the drama of doctrine reminds us that we are here to participate in God's mission to a wanting world. The opportunity to make a difference in the world by performing the drama of doctrine ought to be enough to get even jaded churchgoers out of bed on Monday morning.

Doctrine is instruction about God and direction for playing one's role in the same drama of salvation that lies at the heart of the Scriptures. Doing theology according to the Scriptures means displaying our understanding of what God is doing in the world and of our place in it. It's all about doing the will of King Jesus amid the kingdoms of this world. If *dramatics* is the study or practice of acting in plays, then *theodramatics* is the study or practice of acting in God's royal theater.

I have no interest in making theater studies the queen of the sciences. On the contrary, my appeal to the language of drama and the theater, like my appeal to philosophical concepts, is strictly ministerial. This means that whatever authority or usefulness the theatrical paradigm may have derives from its ability to minister—communicate, teach, apply—the truth and power of Scripture and its theological subject matter, nothing else. I would never go so far as to say that it is *necessary* to employ the theatrical mode, though I do believe that sometimes it may be *expedient* to do so. The theory-practice dichotomy that still bedevils many a theological curriculum serves neither seminary nor church. There is a debilitating dichotomy between what Christians believe (doctrine) and how they live their lives (discipleship). It is not always apparent, for example, what practical bearing doctrines such as the Trinity or even the atonement have on the rough and tumble of daily life. Thus what better antidote than to present doctrine as *theatrical direction for understanding discipleship*—instruction in wise living, teaching how believers are able not only to know but also to love God, do the truth, and be the church?

To repeat: it is not the primary aim of the present work to offer an apology for doing theatrical theology. The main burden of the book concerns the role of doctrine in the life of the church. It is not about using the theatrical model magisterially, as if it had some kind of authority of its own, but rather of using it ministerially, as something that serves the edifying end of making disciples. Personally, I have found the model to be a powerful resource for envisioning how to move from Scripture to theology, how to participate fittingly in the drama of redemption. Thinking of theology in theatrical terms helps me better understand William Ames's aforementioned definition of theology as the project of *living to God*. So, while each chapter wears theatrical garb, the substance of the proposal does not depend on the validity of the theatrical model. Still, a few words of clarification would not be amiss (one way to minister understanding is to avoid misunderstanding). What follows is an attempt to draw a few conceptual distinctions that will help head off at the pass a number of possible confusions (we consider objections to the theatrical model in the appendix).

It is rare to find analytic philosophers mucking about in theatrical metaphors or theater directors overly concerned with logical inference and conceptual precision. Yet there is something to be said for combining the analytic rigor of the one with the imaginative breadth of the other. How, then, ought an analytically inclined theologian distinguish drama from theater, written plays from performance, or for that matter, scripts from Scripture?

Here is a provisional definition: a "drama" delivers a unified sequence of action that a "script" preserves or prescribes in writing, which human enactors bodily represent and enact by a "performance" in a "theater" (*theatron* = a place for seeing).[17] Although the etymology of drama (*drao* = to act, do, take action) suggests a meaning close to "performance" (i.e., doing), it is more common to associate drama with a type of literature designed for stage representation and performance with the "live" enactment of the written drama. Drama is thus the text of a play; theater is its actual production in some place (not necessarily an indoor three-walled space with an audience); a performance-interpretation is that which brings the text, a mere skeleton, to onstage flesh-and-blood life. Theater is therefore the verbalization and visualization—the lived *exhibit*—of drama.

There is thus an organic connection between drama and theater similar to that of musical score and performance. Though not all theorists would agree, I think it unnecessarily reductionist to identify drama with the play script. It can be a verb as well: to "dramatize" is to bring to embodied life a script, scenario, or idea as a theatrical performance. Unlike narrative texts that represent a sequence of action in the third person ("he said, she did"), the words that comprise drama are spoken in the first and second person. While dramas can accommodate third-person narration and first-person monologue, they are essentially dialogical in form (i.e., one person presenting oneself to others).

Theater is not a static thing but a happening, a happening that involves more than physical events. The medium of theater is not physical but personal: human action and interaction. Theater happens whenever one or more persons present

---

17. See also Richard Schechner, "Drama, Script, Theater, and Performance," in *Essays on Performance Theory, 1970–1976* (New York: Drama Book Specialists, 1977), 36–61.

themselves to others in space and time.[18] *At the heart of both drama and theater, then, is communicative action in word and deed.*[19]

What happens in theaters is often a matter of life and death. Consider, for example, theaters of war or surgical theaters. Interestingly, the apostle Paul compares his apostolic ministry to a theatrical spectacle: "For I think that God has exhibited us apostles as last of all, as though sentenced to death, because we have become a spectacle [*theatron*] to the world, to angels and to mortals" (1 Cor. 4:9). God puts the apostles on display, and the apostles participate in the play by administering Christ in their speaking, acting, and suffering. Not only that: Paul urges his readers "be imitators of me" (1 Cor. 4:16), thus bequeathing his vocation of being a theater of the gospel to the church today.

There is more. While the church is the theater of the gospel, creation is, in Calvin's words, the theater of God's glory. As creatures in God's world, humans are spectators of God's works.[20] We have a front-row seat in what Calvin calls "this magnificent theater of heaven and earth," yet even so we fail to know God.[21] In order to see the spectacle of God's works in creation, we need the Scriptures, which bring focus as the "spectacles of faith."[22] Calvin has in mind the metaphor of eyeglasses. It is only with the aid of Scripture that we can "read" the book of nature correctly. Yet Scripture recounts a whole series of supernatural spectacles, God's mighty acts, by which God reveals *who* he is (e.g., the only true God) by *what* he does (e.g., making and keeping his promises). God thus exhibits not only the apostles but also himself in the great theater of the world.

In summary: drama is a shaped sequence of action, especially dialogical action, with a beginning, middle, and end. Performance is the realization or actualization of drama. Theater is the space-time performance by which persons present themselves—their being—to others: "Activity is the basic medium of theater. It is the only channel through which presentational ideas can be projected."[23] Speaking is the preeminent human communicative activity. The theater is thus the space-time of dialogical action.

At this point it is tempting to identify Scripture with the dramatic script.[24] This is partially true but not wholly correct. A script contains plot development, dialogue (i.e., the words that the characters are to say), and stage direction (i.e., indications of what the characters should do). It is true that dramatic scripts exist to be performed, just as texts exist to be read and interpreted. Yet one

---

18. I owe this definition, and my analysis of the relationship of drama to theater in general, to Bernard Beckerman, *Dynamics of Drama: Theory and Method of Analysis* (New York: Alfred A. Knopf, 1970), 10.
19. Silence and suffering also have their place in drama.
20. Calvin, *Inst.* 1.6.2.
21. Ibid., 2.6.1.
22. Ibid., 1.6.1.
23. Beckerman, *Dynamics of Drama*, 13.
24. I may have succumbed to this temptation in *The Drama of Doctrine: A Canonical-Linguistic Approach to Christian Theology* (Louisville, KY: Westminster John Knox Press, 2005). Accordingly, in chap. 3 of the present work, I associate Scripture less with a script than with the lights that illumine the stage and allow us to see what is going on.

should not too hastily identify Scripture with a play script.[25] It is true that Jesus' words must be not only heard but also obeyed; yet not all of Scripture is law. To be sure, some parts of Scripture call for direct repetition (e.g., the Lord's Prayer). Other portions of Scripture prescribe principles of behavior (e.g., the Ten Commandments), suggest templates for behavior (e.g., Jesus' cross), or inform us of what has already happened and is never again to be repeated (e.g., the flood). Still others *ought not* to be repeated (e.g., Israel's conquest of Canaan; Judas's betrayal of Jesus). How then does Holy Scripture stand in relation to the drama of redemption and the church as the theater of the gospel?

Scripture alone is the normative specification of what God has done in Israel and in Jesus Christ to redeem sinners and renew creation. The prophets and apostles who authored it are less scribes who script lines for the church than transcribers who have produced an authoritative record of God's work, an inspired transcript: "*It is the transcript of the love of God in the loving and gracious quest for wandering man. . . . Scripture is the transcript of Jesus Christ.*"[26] In an important sense, the Bible is *not* a script in the sense of a detailed blueprint for action (or the future); this was the moral of our remarks concerning the live performance of biblical scenes known as the "Living Bible." In a looser sense, however, Scripture remains the church's script, a divinely commissioned and authorized written witness to the ongoing drama of redemption, for which doctrine gives direction to disciples for understanding and participation. Scripture not only transcribes but also prescribes, authorizing spiritual medicine (e.g., the fear of the Lord; faith) that, if taken as directed, leads to beneficial and healthy results: wisdom, *salus* (welfare).

Scripture itself is part of the dramatic action. This is most obvious in New Testament passages where the interpretation of the Old Testament is at issue (and where is it not?). In such cases, the drama is the activity of biblical interpretation: What are the apostolic authors *doing* with the Law and the Prophets? How are they reading the Psalms and the Wisdom literature in light of the person and work of Jesus Christ? What generates the drama is the word of the Lord coming to people (e.g., prophets; kings). The history of Israel, for example, often depended on how its kings responded to the word of the Lord. The same is true of the history of the church. In short: the Bible not only reports the word of God but is itself a form of the divine address. There is theodrama wherever there is divine address awaiting human response. What the church ultimately has to perform is not a holy script but rather the theodrama that Scripture describes, transcribes, and prescribes. This is the sense in which the believing community is to be biblical, the sense in which the church best constitutes a living Bible.

---

25. Thanks to Wes Vander Lugt for help with this insight.
26. Bernard Ramm, *Special Revelation and the Word of God: An Essay on the Contemporary Problem of Revelation* (Grand Rapids: Wm. B. Eerdmans Publishing Co., 1961), 186.

THEATER AS HANDMAID TO THEOLOGY: METAPHOR OR MODEL?

Paul uses a racing metaphor to describe the Christian life (1 Cor. 9:24), but he is no more suggesting that disciples go to the track than I am urging them to sign up for acting classes. What, then, is the purpose of the theatrical language? It is all about vision-casting: helping disciples to see how doctrines do not merely state the truth but also encourage one to live and lean into it, to *do* the truth (John 3:21; 1 John 1:6).

Theatrical theology concerns faith speaking and showing understanding. It is all about the church's attempt to explain, and then act out, the meaning and significance of the theodrama of which Scripture is the authorized account: script, transcript, prescript. Theatrical theology serves the project of *gospel exhibition*: the living out of Christian faith in the theater of the world. Like all comparisons, however, this one too can be pushed too far. Before going further, then, it will be helpful to examine the appropriateness of the theatrical model, both in respect to doctrine and that which doctrine is about: redemption. In what sense are theology and the gospel itself dramatic?

"Drama" of Doctrine

The principal drama of which Scripture serves as transcript, script, and prescript concerns the mighty acts in word and deed of the triune God: theodrama. What, then, does it mean to perform the drama *of doctrine*? To answer this we must first define *doctrine*.

Doctrine (Lat. *doctrina*; Gk. *didaskalia*) means "teaching, instruction." It is what the church believes (on the basis of the Bible) and teaches, both explicitly in its creeds and confessions and implicitly in its way of life. It is no coincidence that Paul's Pastoral epistles (1–2 Timothy, Titus) are replete with references to doctrine, for doctrine at its best exercises a pastoral function: correcting error, deepening understanding, fostering wisdom, funding endurance, encouraging godliness. Doctrine is necessary, in part, because there is false teaching and evildoing. So doctrine combats false teaching, the "doctrines of demons" (1 Tim. 4:1 RSV). It does so by preserving teaching that accords with the apostolic preaching of the gospel and with biblical revelation more generally. In the Pastoral Epistles, the "sure word" of the gospel is the touchstone for "sound doctrine" (Titus 1:9 RSV).

What is the nature of "sound doctrine," a phrase Paul uses five times (1 Tim. 1:10; 2 Tim. 1:13; 4:3; Titus 1:9; 2:1)? That doctrine is "sound" (Gk. *hygiainō*, lit., "hygienic") suggests that its teaching is more than technically true. On several occasions Paul introduces his teaching with a variation on the following formula: "the saying is sure [i.e., trustworthy] and worthy of full acceptance" (1 Tim. 1:15; 3:1; 4:9; 2 Tim. 2:11; Titus 3:8). These trustworthy sayings are more than propositional statements to be gathered into a system of truths, more than a collection of authoritative statements by Chairman Paul. They are rather statements of *understanding* that indicate a grasp of the meaning and significance of what God has done in Christ. Accordingly, they are statements that call for personal (and practical) appropriation, not mere theoretical acknowledgment. They are statements that call for their hearers to exercise trust and to respond not only with one's mind but also with one's whole being: heart, soul, and strength. Doctrine explicitly tells us *what is* and *how things are*; it also implicitly asks us to trust that *this is how things are* to the point of staking one's life on it.

Doctrine is a special kind of teaching that instructs the head, orients the heart, and guides the hand. It tells us what we should believe (*credenda*), what we may hope (*speranda*), and what we should do (*agenda*). As such, it provides direction for faith, hope, and love alike. Sound doctrine is biblically grounded direction that both corresponds to the gospel and also engenders godliness, combining the privilege of knowing God with the responsibility of living righteously out of love for God. As such, "godliness" is a sign of authentic Christian faith. It is the lived knowledge of God, the truth of the gospel bearing the fruit of godliness. Sound doctrine is teaching that is good for us, direction that makes for sound living and human flourishing.

How does doctrine perform such marvelous feats? By providing summary statements of the story line of the Bible and insights into its key players and events. Doctrine thus provides us with a dramatic framework for viewing God and his relationship to the world in a new, true light. If the Scriptures are the Christian's spectacles of faith, doctrine is the disciple's spectacles of understanding. Doctrine helps us understand both what God is doing in the world in and through Christ and what we are to do in response. Specific doctrines, like Christology and Pneumatology, help us understand the principal *dramatis personae* (as does the doctrine of the Trinity); other doctrines, like the doctrine of original sin or the doctrine of the atonement, help us to understand the action (what kind of story are we part of?). Eschatology teaches about the ending of the story and thus of how to live toward it.

Christian doctrine thus provides a very particular kind of teaching: *direction*, both dramatic and theatrical. More pointedly: doctrine gives us direction for articulating and appropriating our understanding of biblical Christianity. Doctrines give us, first, direction for understanding the theodrama, the great drama of redemption that begins with Israel's exodus and reaches its climax with Jesus' *exodos* from Jerusalem (i.e., his "departure" or death on a cross [Luke 9:31]). Various doctrines also yield particular vantage points from which to understand the meaning of the whole theodrama. What we are to believe, hope, and do is related to a prior question: Of what story (drama) do I find myself a part? Sound doctrine ultimately orients disciples to the true story of the world. Put differently, sound doctrine ministers reality, a created and redeemed order to which wisdom willingly conforms, for there is no other order.

In sum: we come to understand the drama of redemption that lies at the heart of Scripture and our role in it through doctrinal direction. Doctrine first gives disciples direction for *understanding* the drama, the identity of God, the chief protagonist, and the meaning of what God has done (call this theoretical understanding). Then, in a second move, doctrine gives disciples directions for *demonstrating* their understanding by speaking and acting in ways that display their grasp of the action and their willingness to participate in it (call this theatrical understanding).

Now that we have explained *doctrine*, we are in a better position to see what I mean by the *drama* of doctrine. It will help to keep in mind the following three senses:

1. The drama *behind* the doctrine. This refers to what God has already said and done in the histories of Israel and Jesus Christ. The Bible is the transcript of the divine-human interaction that forms the heart of the drama, and that allows us to see the Old and New Testaments as progressive stages in a single unified plot. In this case the "drama" refers to the sequence of historical actions recorded by Scripture (a covenantal history) that has already been accomplished and of which Scripture is a part (as covenant document).

2. The drama *of* doctrine. This refers to the church's attempt to understand the drama behind the doctrine, especially the meaning and significance of what God was doing in Jesus Christ. There is drama in the development of doctrine not least because, as we have seen, false teaching is an ever-present danger and because from the beginning darkness has struggled to overcome light (Gen. 1:2; Isa. 60:2; John 1:5). Scripture here functions as source and norm, providing both the basic narrative on which theology reflects and seminal statements of its meaning and significance.

3. The drama *in front of* the doctrine. This refers to the present scene in which the church finds itself and to the very real demand on disciples to participate fittingly in the ongoing triune action, thus demonstrating their understanding of senses 1 and 2 (above). Here Scripture functions as prompt and prescript, encouraging the people of God to display the meaning and truth of the gospel by living in wise ways that exhibit the mind of Christ in bodily (i.e., corporate) form.

Doctrine is dramatic, then, because it concerns the church's efforts to perform it, to speak and show its understanding of what God is doing in Christ to renew creation. Disciples are not onlookers who keep a safe distance but witnesses who stake their lives on the good news that the triune God is actively at work in all situations to rescue and redeem. What the church needs now are not passive spectators but active participants, actors who can follow doctrinal directions.

"Drama" of Redemption

Many writers refer to the "drama" of redemption. Is it only a figure of speech? As mentioned previously, the essence of drama is persons presenting themselves to one another, largely through language, but also through deeds. This is precisely what God does in making himself known to Adam, Abraham, Moses, and others. Divine address and human response comprise the two-beat rhythm of the history that forms the backbone of biblical narrative. The medium of theater, like theology, is interpersonal interaction. And if having a plot that unifies this interpersonal interaction is a necessary and sufficient condition of drama, then the history that Scripture recounts is indeed dramatic.

Erving Goffman uses the theater as a framework for conducting sociological research. The way persons present themselves to others in everyday life is similar to the way an actor renders a character to an audience. Goffman's particular interest involves the ways individuals try to control the impressions that others form of them. They do so through their self-presentations (i.e., performances), "all the activity of a given participant on a given occasion which serves to influence in any way any of the other participants."[27] As we shall see in later chapters, this theatrical framework opens up new possibilities for thinking about hypocrisy. The salient point, however, is that the theater is, for Goffman, a conceptual scheme that allows him further to explore the human condition.[28]

The apostle Paul was adept at using metaphors to communicate the saving significance of Jesus' death, employing imagery drawn from the battlefield (victory), temple (sacrifice), commerce (redemption of slaves), and lawcourt (justification). We have also observed his appeal to imagery drawn from the theater ("We have become a spectacle [*theatron*]" [1 Cor. 4:9]) as well as Calvin's description of creation as the "theater" of God's glory (see above). The question is whether theater is one of the "metaphors we live by" and, if so, whether it has the potential and staying power to become a comprehensive model.[29] Models are extended metaphors that view one reality (e.g., God) in terms of another (e.g., theater director).

Theater serves as an appropriate model for the relationship of Christian doctrine to discipleship because (1) theology's subject matter is intrinsically dramatic, a series of actions united by a plot (i.e., the theatrical model is conducive to understanding and ordering Scripture); (2) the drama of God's self-communication structures theological understanding (i.e., the theatrical model is conducive to systematizing belief and ordering doctrine); and (3) the drama of redemption orients and prompts human action (i.e., the theatrical model is conducive to illumining life and ordering love). Human existence with others before God is theatrical and indeed a model that Christians can live by, thus generating promising possibilities for both thought and action. For the theatrical model is both explanatory and exploratory: it helps us grasp what God has done, and it helps us navigate our way forward. Understanding God as Rock, for example, is helpful as far as it goes, but it goes only so far toward

27. Erving Goffman, *The Presentation of Self in Everyday Life* (New York: Doubleday, 1959), 15.
28. Victor Turner makes a similar proposal for anthropology, defining human beings as *homo performans* and using the theatrical model to make sense of cultural rituals. See his *Drama, Fields, and Metaphors: Symbolic Action in Human Society* (Ithaca, NY: Cornell University Press, 1975); idem, *The Anthropology of Performance* (New York: PAJ Publications, 1987).
29. See George Lakoff and Mark Johnson, *Metaphors We Live By*, 2nd ed. (Chicago: University of Chicago Press, 2003).

explaining and exploring the ways of God. In contrast, the theatrical model encourages us to think of the triune God as simultaneously playwright, actor, and director of the drama of human history. As we shall see, this is a more fecund and generative model for thinking about both God and the Christian life than "rock" and "walk" respectively.

To conceive of the gospel as dramatic and theology as theatrical is to embrace a meaningful, imaginative vision for thinking about reality and about discipleship. And just in time, too. For the prevailing naturalistic world picture by which many people live today leaves little scope for meaningful human action or meaning. According to some neo-Darwinian evolutionary models, human action is best explained (or is it explained away?) by reference to the unifying story of genetic engineering. History is less the story of self-presentation than self-propagation. Nature is the theater not of God's glory but of the violent struggle of DNA to survive and thrive from one generation to the next. If this is the ultimate framework by which to understand our existence, then we of all species are "most to be pitied" (1 Cor. 15:19).

I agree with Dorothy Sayers: "The Christian faith is the most exciting drama that ever staggered the imagination of man — and the dogma is the drama."[30] At the heart of the drama, the crucial point on which the whole plot pivots, is the question "What think ye of Christ?" (Matt. 22:42 KJV). In claiming that the dogma *is* the drama, Sayers has in mind the story line of Jesus summarized in the Apostles' Creed: "conceived . . . born . . . suffered . . . was crucified, died, buried . . . rose again . . . ascended . . . will come again." It is hard to believe, Sayers playfully suggests, "that anything so interesting, so exciting, and so dramatic can be the orthodox Creed of the Church."[31] The drama of doctrine, summarized by creedal Christianity, is a model not only for viewing but also for participating in reality. It is precisely this invitation to orient oneself in the world as an actor in the divine drama of redemption that makes theatrical theology superior to narrative theology. Disciples are not mere storytellers but *story-dwellers*.

That disciples are story-dwellers is another way of claiming the superiority of theatrical over narrative theology. Before going any further, however, we must consider two potential objections to the very enterprise of theatrical theology.

Objection 1. "Dramas are representational, but 'theodrama' does not represent anything." Speaking well of God is the theologian's first, and most important, task. To go wrong in one's doctrine of God is to go wrong everywhere, for theology concerns the relationship of just this God to just this world. That is why the present objection, which concerns not misrepresentation but the impossibility of representation, kept me up half the night (Michael Pakaluk, you owe me three hours' sleep). Here is the problem in a nutshell: drama is about the representation or imitation of something "more real" (i.e., the real story) than the actors and actions themselves. Children can play at representing

---

30. Dorothy L. Sayers, *Creed or Chaos?* (New York: Harcourt, Brace & Co., 1949), 3.
31. Ibid., 20.

their parents, just as the Greeks played at representing the actions (antics!) of their gods on stage. Pakaluk asks: "But if God is the actor, whom is He going to represent? Who or what is the greater Reality which his actions might imitate and strive to be like?"[32] Surely the Creator God is not merely *pretending* to be a heavenly Father! Pakaluk is happy enough to speak of God as acting, but not of God as an actor. He asks, What in the world is the biblical theodrama representing?

Answer: Nothing in the world, but rather something in eternity. *God's mighty acts in history "represent" the perfections of God's eternal nature and the outworking of God's eternal decree.* Revelation (i.e., God's self-presentation in historical word and deed) is essentially representational. The historical missions of Son (e.g., incarnation) and Spirit represent eternal processions (e.g., begetting). What God does in time represents the way God is in eternity. God is on earth as he is in heaven!

The technical term for God's self-presentation, his presence and activity in history, is "economy" (*oikonomia*). The economic Trinity (i.e., the way God is "for us" in time) represents in history the light, life, and love that characterize the "essential" or "immanent" Trinity (i.e., the way God is "in himself" in eternity).[33] Recall the opening verses of Hebrews: in the past God spoke to our fathers by the prophets, but in these last days he has presented himself to us by his Son, who is "the exact imprint of God's very being" (Heb. 1:3). What God does in time as Father, Son, and Spirit represents what and who God eternally is. God the triune actor is acting in history (the economic Trinity), representing God the triune Author (the immanent Trinity).[34]

In sum: the dramatic story of which the church is called to be a part represents the outworking of a divine decree or plot conceived "before the foundation of the world" (John 17:24; Eph. 1:4; 1 Pet. 1:20). The people of God too participate in the historical representation or unfolding of God's eternal plan. Doctrine guides disciples not to playact but to get real. While the finite may not be able to *contain* the infinite (*finitum non capax infiniti*), it may be able dramatically to *represent* it.[35] Indeed, human beings are created in the image of God and charged with the task of glorifying him. The Son glorifies the Father by dramatically finishing the work he was given to do (John 17:1–4). Disciples imitate the Son, who is the definitive image of God and dramatic representation of God's being (Heb. 1:3) when they too glorify God in their bodies by performing works of grateful obedience (1 Cor. 6:20).

---

32. Michael Pakaluk, "The Play's Not the Thing," *Edification: The Transdisciplinary Journal of Christian Psychology* 4 (2010): 29.

33. I shall return to this theme in chap. 4 below.

34. See Fred Sanders, *The Image of the Immanent Trinity: Rahner's Rule and the Theological Interpretation of Scripture* (New York and Frankfurt: Peter Lang, 2005); and my *Remythologizing Theology: Divine Action, Passion, and Authorship* (Cambridge: Cambridge University Press, 2010), 70–72 and chap. 5.

35. The context of Calvin's *finitum* formula was the debate with Lutherans over the ubiquity of Christ's flesh in the Lord's Supper.

Objection 2. "The theatrical model is merely window dressing, does no real work, and ultimately only gets in the way of the task of systematic theology." Where the first objector accuses the theatrical model of getting in the way of Scripture, this second objection charges it with hindering the handmaiden's proper work. According to its critics, the theatrical model plays, at best, a merely cosmetic rather than substantive role, putting rouge on the queen's cheeks, perhaps a curl in her hair—all in all, a trifling service with which theologians can easily dispense.

On the contrary: The theatrical model provides us with a fresh way of integrating knowing, doing, and being. It charts a middle way between theology as an inductive science that arranges biblical "facts" into a system of theoretical knowledge on the one hand and a moralistic science that arranges biblical commands into a practical system of right and wrong. The apostle Paul was neither academic theologian nor ethicist; instead, he was a pastor *and* theologian who speaks about the "is" and the "ought" in Christ at one and the same time: "Paul's ethical vision is shaped by the death, resurrection, and ascension of Jesus, and the sending of the Spirit."[36] Paul's goal is to instruct his readers by inducting them into the story of Jesus Christ. Paul urges us to conform our thoughts and lives to the contours of the theodrama, in particular to the death and resurrection reality that we find at its climax. The theatrical model is doing real work to the extent that it facilitates and extends Paul's integrative and edifying vision. The theatrical model is doing real systematic work when it helps to unify Scripture and vivify disciples.

Is it truly "systematic"? We need to define our terms. A "system" of theology must ultimately give "an orderly account" concerning the things of which Scripture informs us (Luke 1:3–4). Theology need not rely on some philosophical method in order to be systematic; there are other ways to pursue coherence and consistency. The idea that the world is the theater of God's action and that a single dramatic plot links the two Testaments is one way of arranging the various elements in the Bible into a meaningful whole. Furthermore, *theodramatic* coherence and consistency accord with the subject matter of theology itself. A theodramatic systematics includes a concern for *logical* coherence and consistency but cannot be reduced to it, for its primary concern, the pastoral, is aimed at helping disciples better understand the theodramatic plot: how God's plan conceived before the foundation of the world is now being worked out through the Word made flesh.[37] And, as I have been arguing, to understand this drama requires one not only to look at it from a critical distance but also to participate in it, to begin to live out its truth, to live *into* its truth. *Theatrical theology is essentially a matter of wisdom (i.e., lived theodramatic knowledge).*

---

36. Timothy Gombis, *Paul: A Guide for the Perplexed* (London: T& T Clark International, 2010), 62.

37. See the discussion in Gale Heide, *Timeless Truths in the Hands of History: A Short History of System in Theology* (Eugene, OR: Pickwick Publications, 2012), esp. 6.

Theology is systematic when it shows how the various doctrines relate to one another and how God relates to everything else.[38] The dramatic model is one such systematic attempt to show just that and to do it in such a way as to cultivate theoretical and practical understanding. In ministering understanding, the theatrical model avoids the modernist extreme of valuing thought over action as well as the narrativist tendency to make action more important than thought.[39] The only truly effective response to this dichotomy is to show how the theatrical model actually ministers understanding (i.e., reflective practice), how it actually helps disciples grasp the orders of creation and redemption "in Christ," and how the church fits in.

It is perhaps fitting that its critics decry the theatrical model for its relative "weakness." Theater studies are, no doubt, "weak" and "foolish" in comparison to more prestigious academic disciplines like physics and philosophy. Could this be another chapter in the history of God's using weak and foolish things to demonstrate the peculiar wisdom of the cross?

What counts at the end of the debate, of course, is not the theatrical model itself but rather the understanding of reality, "being in Christ," that it ministers and administers. The substance of my argument—that doctrine fosters understanding, helping disciples to speak and show their faith in meaningful forms—does not depend upon the theatrical analogy. Nor should one think that the dramatic model focuses only on *doing* the good or merely encourages disciples to be activists. While it is true that the gospel demands a response (the obedience of faith), the drama of doctrine involves more (but not less) than working for the social implications of the gospel. It requires professing its truth, doing right, and acquiring right desires. The theatrical model, rightly handled, encourages disciples to participate in or enact the truth, goodness, and beauty of Jesus Christ.

---

38. See A. N. Williams, *The Architecture of Theology: Structure, System, and Ratio* (Oxford: Oxford University Press, 2011).

39. For more on the contrast between modern and narrative theology, see Gale Heide, *System and Story: Narrative Critique and Construction in Theology* (Eugene, OR: Pickwick Publications, 2009).

Chapter 2

Audience Participation
Loving God, Doing Truth, Being Church

> *What is important is not that God is a spectator and participant in our life today, but that we are attentive listeners and participants in God's action in the sacred story, the story of Christ on earth.*
> —Dietrich Bonhoeffer, *Life Together*

If the world is the theater of God's glory, and world history is the theater of God's gospel, where is the audience, and what is its role? This is an important question, one that could potentially develop into a decisive objection to the theatrical model to the extent that it makes disciples into passive spectators rather than active participants in the drama of redemption. To recall William Ames's definition, theology is "the doctrine or teaching of living to God." It follows that the aim of doctrine is to shape both belief *and* behavior.

To act out truth—to correspond to *what is*—is ultimately to participate in the way and life of Jesus Christ, the one who is truth incarnate: the embodied word, wisdom, and love of God. Accordingly, after briefly reflecting on the nature of the actor-audience relationship in the theater of the gospel, we turn to 2 John as a framework from which to consider the close connection between love and truth in the life of followers of Christ. It is precisely this tie that renders doctrine a matter of drama, and that requires the audience to be more than passive observers. Second John treats the importance for followers of Christ in local churches to *do* as well as *speak* the truth in love (cf. Eph. 4:15–16).

"BREAKING DOWN THE DIVIDING WALL": BETWEEN ACTOR AND AUDIENCE, PASTOR AND CONGREGATION, CHURCH AND WORLD

For he is our peace, who has made us both one, and has broken down the dividing wall of hostility.

—Ephesians 2:14 RSV

From one angle, God is the only audience that counts, the all-knowing, all-seeing audience of One. Kierkegaard depicts God as "the critical theatergoer, who looks on to see how the lines are spoken."[1] Indeed, only God *can* be audience to everything that happens in the world, for no one else is in a position to observe what Kierkegaard calls the "Drama of Dramas": "to God, world history is the royal stage where he, not accidentally but essentially, is the only spectator, because he is the only one who *can* be that."[2] My interest in this section, however, is with human audiences.

The so-called "fourth wall" is the imaginary barrier that stands in front of a traditional three-walled theatrical stage and separates the actors from the audience. It is the invisible window into the world-of-the-play through which the spectators watch the action unfold. The French philosopher and critic Denis Diderot came up with the notion in his study of eighteenth-century French theater. The net effect of the concept was to heighten the boundary between the world depicted by the actors and the world of the audience and to limit the participation of the audience in order to maintain the illusion of a self-enclosed onstage reality. Diderot wanted actors to act as if the audience were not even there; this, he thought, was the best way to maintain their respective autonomy.[3]

Diderot was also editor of the famous *Encyclopédie* whose goal was to assemble all the scattered knowledge that humans had garnered about the sciences, arts, and crafts and to present it systematically. His aim was "to change the way people think," and his notion of the "fourth wall" certainly changed the way people thought about the theater. Prior to Diderot (I'm thinking primarily of the medieval "Mystery Plays," but also of Shakespeare), there was usually some kind of physical interaction between actors and audience. In one sense, the "fourth wall" perfectly suits the Age of the Enlightenment and the privilege it accorded to critical distance, abstraction, and neutral observation

---

1. Kierkegaard, *Purity of Heart*, 161.
2. Søren Kierkegaard, *Concluding Unscientific Postscript to Philosophical Fragments* (Princeton, NJ: Princeton University Press, 1992), 158.
3. See Denis Diderot, *De la poésie dramatique* (1758), in *Œuvres complètes, édition critique et annotée*, ed. J. Fabre, H. Dieckmann, J. Proust, and J. Varloot (DPV), 33 vols. (Paris: Hermann, 1975–2004), 10:373. See also Michael Fried, *Absorption and Theatricality: Painting and Beholder in the Age of Diderot* (Berkeley: University of California Press, 1980).

(i.e., "theory"). However, even in the church there is often a tendency to erect a "fourth wall" between what leaders do at the front of the church and what happens in the congregation. The fourth wall here functions not as a theatrical convention but rather as an obstacle to genuine worship insofar as it cordons off the congregation from the doxological action. To think of the area at the front of the church as a stage and the congregation as the audience goes directly against my intentions in employing a theatrical model.

A "fourth wall" can appear not only within the church but also between the church and the world. The "church before the watching world" has too often been a sorry spectacle, a demonstration not of the wisdom of Christ but of human folly. *Some* distinction, even separation, must of course remain if the church is to be salt and light, a holy nation, and a kingdom of priests. We dare not simply erase the difference or distance between actors and audience, as in some form of experimental theater. At the same time, it is important, in the words of the apostle Paul, to "break down the dividing wall," not of hostility (cf. Eph. 2:14) but of *passivity* (within the church) and *incomprehensibility* (between church and world).

One way to break down the dividing wall of passivity between church leaders and congregations is to adopt the theatrical model for thinking about doctrine and discipleship. And, if we think of the church-world relationship in terms of *interactive* rather than traditional theater, then the theatrical model suggests a way to break down the dividing wall of incomprehensibility between church and world as well.[4] Instead of espousing some theory of interactive theater, however, we would do well to take our bearings from the New Testament itself.

As any student of the New Testament knows, each book had a historical occasion, a distinct purpose or set of purposes, and was written for a particular audience.[5] Knowing something about the intended audience, which is a part of what it means to determine the original context, is often helpful in discerning the author's meaning. This is one way in which the audience "participates" in the action.

The other and more important way in which the audience participates in the apostolic discourse is to make the appropriate response, not of applause but of belief and the obedience of faith: "These [signs that Jesus did] are written that you may come to believe that Jesus is the Messiah, the Son of God, and that through believing you may have life in his name" (John 20:31). This is what all the authors of the New Testament summon and solicit their readers to do: to enter into the name, the story, and the very identity of Jesus Christ, to the extent that they, the reading audience, take up *their* crosses, thereby following the example of the apostles. In sum: the New Testament documents were

---

4. In this section I am indebted to Wesley Vander Lugt's post "Church beyond the Fourth Wall," August 10, 2010, http://www.transpositions.co.uk/2010/10/church-beyond-the-fourth-wall/.

5. The first scholarly work to suggest that each Gospel had a different audience was Burton H. Streeter's *The Four Gospels: A Study of Origins* . . . (London: Macmillan & Co., 1924).

written in order to involve—nay, *conscript*—the audience in the dramatic action of redemption. This is interactive theater at its finest.

To whom, exactly, was the New Testament written? Who is the audience? Richard Bauckham argues that the Gospels were most likely written for general circulation: "Their implied readership is not specific but indefinite: any and every Christian community in the late-first-century Roman Empire."[6] Whether the original audience was particular or general, the church, in receiving the Bible as Scripture, acknowledges that it is the primary addressee of God's word written.[7] As Jesus exhorted his followers to "take up their cross daily" (Luke 9:23), so the New Testament authors expected their audience to participate in what God the Father was doing in the Son through the Spirit (cf. 1 Cor. 15:31).

There is no alibi for biblical interpretation. Those who read or hear God's Word may not excuse themselves from responding on the grounds that they are only the "audience." God's word comes to individuals and awaits a response. To speak of the priesthood or even "playerhood" of all believers is not to say that each individual is his own pope but rather that each person has a role to play in biblical interpretation. The apostle Paul expresses this point beautifully in comparing the church at Corinth (i.e., the community of Christ-followers gathered there) to a letter addressed to a general audience, the whole world: "You yourselves are our letter of recommendation, written on your hearts, to be known and read by all men" (2 Cor. 3:2 RSV). The church therefore has an "epistolary" mission to the world.

To think of the church as an acting company that performs the drama at the heart of the Gospels and apostolic letters is to view the church-world relationship in terms of interactive theater, and this in two senses. First, the church is interactive theater because the whole people of God, and not only the official ministers and church leaders, participate in the production, which includes not only what happens during worship but afterward as well. Second, the church is interactive theater because it seeks to engage the world even as it remains distinct from it. It is less a matter of "the church *before* the watching world" than "the church *in* [though not *of*] the watching world.[8]

In the same way that the audience of original readers was to respond to the apostolic writings by participating in the action, so the church as a whole continues to respond, "performing" in order to invite into the action the watching world, the audience beyond the fourth wall. Of course, the world is *already* involved in the action, inadvertently participating, for good or for ill, in the drama of redemption, even if only by way of ignoring or rejecting it. In interactive theater, there is no strict separation between the actors and audience.

---

6. Richard Bauckham, "For Whom Were Gospels Written?," in *The Gospels for All Christians: Rethinking the Gospel Audiences*, ed. R. Bauckham (Grand Rapids: Wm. B. Eerdmans Publishing Co., 1998), 1–2.

7. See Edward W. Klink III, ed., *The Audience of the Gospels: Further Conversation about the Origin and Function of the Gospels in Early Christianity* (London: T&T Clark International, 2010), esp. the chapters by Klink himself and Craig Blomberg.

8. In chap. 7 below we shall return to the church as interactive theater.

Everyone is part of the theatrical experience; every person and everything is either consciously or inadvertently playing a part in the drama of redemption. The "audience"—those who read the Bible, those who hear it preached—is invariably being drawn into the same drama in which the biblical authors have been caught up. The audience, I have suggested, is the staging area for the main conflict: turning hearts that are set against God back to God.

In the final analysis, it is Christian doctrine that breaks down the "dividing walls" of passivity and incomprehensibility. It breaks down the wall of passivity because the word of God demands a response: faith is something to be done, acted out. It breaks down the wall of incomprehensibility to the extent that the world begins to understand what God and the gospel mean by watching and interacting with the church. For, when the church responds to the word of God as it ought, the church demonstrates the love of God and the mind of Christ, in word and in deed. Just as the church comes to understand the love of God by attending to the story of Jesus and getting caught up in the gospel story, so the church in turn renders that story intelligible when it lives out the truth of the gospel.[9]

"WALKING IN THE TRUTH": PARTICIPATION IN CHRIST

I was overjoyed to find some of your children walking in the truth, just as we have been commanded by the Father.

—2 John 4

There is a long and venerable theological tradition according to which creatures "participate" in their Creator simply by existing. If God is the source of all being, so the reasoning goes, then anything that exists will reflect something of God the way a piece of workmanship reflects something of its creator. The "something" in question is nothing so specific as color, size, weight, physical composition, or any other quality that can be perceived by the senses. On the contrary, the creature participates not in the properties of this or that kind of being but in the properties of being itself, what medieval thinkers called "transcendentals": properties that exceed all particular classes of things but can nevertheless be affirmed of any and all beings, so long as they exist.

The three most important transcendentals are the "Platonic triad": truth, goodness, and beauty.[10] The basic idea is that being presents itself under a certain aspect. Something is true because it unveils itself, presents itself as knowable;

---

9. In part 2 we shall return to the notion that the church-world relationship is best described in terms of interactive theater.
10. Aristotle introduced the concept in *Metaphysics* 10, his study of what we can know of reality in general. Medieval thinkers tended to identify five transcendental categories: being, unity, goodness, truth, and beauty. Thomas Aquinas focused on unity, truth, and goodness (see Jan A.

good, because it gives itself, presents itself as desirable; beautiful, because it bedazzles, presents itself as delightful. Truth, goodness, and beauty are aspects of any being whatsoever. A rose by any other name would be just as true, good, and beautiful because, as an existent, it participates, however partially, in the perfections of its Creator (i.e., the divine attributes).

In our present disenchanted age, where the world no longer seems "charged with the grandeur of God" (in the words of Gerard Manley Hopkins), the idea that we participate in the deep mysteries of reality is proving attractive to many theologians, Roman Catholic, Protestant, and evangelical alike. Again, the key idea is that every entity, and thus every human being, participates in the "transcendental" qualities of being simply by virtue of its existence. Some characterize this participation as sacramental, even going so far as to speak of "sacramental ontology": "the conviction that historical realities of the created order served as divinely ordained, sacramental means leading to eternal divine mysteries."[11] There is much to admire in such attempts to probe beneath the surface reality of things by inquiring into their transcendental grounding. The question is whether this is the kind of audience participation in the gospel that the New Testament describes and requires.

Let us begin with *being*. In the first place, the New Testament declares that being is not a generic or impersonal substance or power in which we participate but something personal. Jesus Christ is "the exact imprint of God's very being" (Heb. 1:3). And while no one has ever seen God, the Word that was with God and was God in the beginning (John 1:1) is also the Son who has "explained" or "exegeted [*exēgēsato*] God" (John 1:18, Gk.).[12] Perfect being, the being than which nothing greater can be conceived, therefore has a face.

To know truth, goodness, and beauty, one has to do more than think about the concept of perfect being. Instead, one must begin with the claim that the Son exegetes the Father. To do so is to see the history of Jesus on earth (i.e., God's being in time) as corresponding to the being of God as it is in heaven (i.e., God's being in eternity). God *is* in himself as he *is* in the history of Jesus Christ. Stated differently: God *is* as he *does* in Jesus Christ. We discover what God is like not by examining the concept of perfect being, as philosophers might do, but rather by attending to the life of Jesus Christ. Doctrines acquire their content from an analysis of what God has done. Who God is and what God is like is on full display in the life of Jesus of Nazareth.

Aertsen, *Medieval Philosophy and the Transcendentals: The Case of Thomas Aquinas* [Leiden: E. J. Brill, 1996]).

11. Hans Boersma, *Nouvelle Théologie and Sacramental Ontology: A Return to Mystery* (Oxford: Oxford University Press, 2009), 289. See also idem, *Heavenly Participation: The Weaving of a Sacramental Tapestry* (Grand Rapids: Wm. B. Eerdmans Publishing Co., 2011).

12. For a defense of this translation, see Robert H. Gundry, "How the Word in John's Prologue Pervades the Rest of the Fourth Gospel," esp. Addendum II, "In Defense of 'Exegesis' in John 1:18," in *The Old Is Better: New Testament Essays in Support of Traditional Interpretations* (Tübingen: Mohr Siebeck, 2005), 361–62.

The divine perfections of God's nature are enacted in the history of Jesus Christ, as they are in everything that God says and does. Yet we only get a firm hold on the meaning of these attributes when we attend to the concrete action that culminates in Christ's cross and resurrection. What, for example, is God's love? "We know love by this, that he laid down his life for us" (1 John 3:16). "In this is love, . . . that he sent his Son to be the atoning sacrifice for our sins" (1 John 4:10; cf. Rom. 5:8); "Greater love has no one than this, that someone lay down his life for his friends" (John 15:13 ESV). In Jesus Christ, God lays down his life not only for his friends but also for his enemies.

God is love: an eternal self-giving and communicative activity oriented to communion ("that they may be one, even as we are one" [John 17:11 RSV]). What should we now say about the transcendentals? Just this: truth, goodness, and beauty are ultimately qualifications of love (God's self-giving being) and the works of love (God's self-giving acts). Furthermore, because God's being is *active*, it may be better to think of the transcendentals as *theatricals*: perfections of a divine *doing* (i.e., loving) than which nothing greater can be conceived.

The payoff for thinking of the transcendentals as theatricals comes when we return to the question of audience participation. Fully to participate in truth, goodness, and beauty requires creatures to do more than merely exist. For the ultimate criterion of truth, goodness, and beauty is not generic "being" but rather the particular being—the person, words, works, and history of Jesus Christ.[13] The truth, goodness, and beauty of God are the truth, goodness, and beauty of dramatic action: the life, death, and resurrection of Jesus Christ. It is *that*, God's communicative activity in Jesus Christ, in which the Holy Spirit enables the audience (i.e., disciples) rightly to participate.

The brief but profound Second Letter of John to a local church ("the elect lady" [2 John 1]) is a model exercise in theatrical theology inasmuch as it was written to encourage its audience to participate in (i.e., to take part in or act out) the love and truth of God revealed in Jesus Christ: the divine "theatricals." The main point I wish to glean from 2 John, however, is that sound doctrine not only explains what God is doing in Jesus Christ but also shows us how to participate in it, for our good and God's glory. Truth makes us free (John 8:32), not in some abstract sense of the term, but specifically to share in God's *love*.

In a scant 245 words, what one commentator calls a "postcard epistle,"[14] 2 John exhorts its readers to act out the truth and love of Jesus Christ and to preserve the message of Jesus Christ from false teachers. To walk in the truth (2 John 4) is to follow or "walk around" in self-giving love to one another (v. 6), for the truth is that God is love and has commanded us to "love one another" (v. 5).

"Walking in the truth" (v. 4) reminds us that the truth is something to be done as well as believed. The truth of Jesus Christ is not simply information

---

13. See Aidan Nichols, *A Key to Balthasar: Hans Urs von Balthasar on Beauty, Goodness, and Truth* (Grand Rapids: Baker Academic, 2011).
14. Daniel L. Akin, *1, 2, 3 John*, New American Commentary (Nashville: Broadman & Holman, 2001), 217.

about him, but God's own self-communication. Jesus is the truth because he is God's self-communicative activity. To follow or walk in truth is to follow or walk in love. Second John is not spouting sentimental nonsense. The author has not confounded epistemology (truth) with ethics (love) but rather sketched their proper relation, as a brief excursus into 1 Peter will help make clear.

Peter too speaks of the importance of the saints' "obedience the truth" in the context of the love that Christians are to show to one another (1 Pet. 1:22). This truth is not a general concept but the gospel: the proclamation of God's being in loving, self-communicative activity in the person and work of Jesus Christ. This is why Peter can later remind believers to "obey the gospel of God" (1 Pet. 4:17; cf. 2 Thess. 1:8). What sense does it make to speak of "obeying" the gospel or, for that matter, *doing* truth (John 3:21; 1 John 1:6)?

What on the surface may look like a category mistake is simplicity itself once we begin thinking in terms of theatricals. For included in the demand to "behold" what God has done in Christ is the requirement to conform our lives to this truth. The gospel of what God has done in Jesus Christ is also the gospel of God's being-with-us and for-us. The truth of the gospel—*what is* "in Christ"—is the criterion for truth, goodness, and beauty alike. Put differently: the truth of the gospel is directed not only to our heads but also to our hearts and hands. To "obey" or conform to the truth of the gospel is a whole-person affair.

Ecce homo. "Behold the man!" (John 19:5 KJV). Truth was standing before Pilate, but he failed to take the time necessary to discern it: "'What is truth?' And when [Pilate] had said this, he went out" (John 18:38). Truth for Pilate was something to mention in a throwaway line; Pilate did not walk in the truth but away from the truth. By way of contrast, disciples obey the truth and the gospel when they *take hold* of what they *behold* and let the drama of the Christ serve as the metanarrative or control story of their own lives. Implicit in the phrase "Behold the man!" is the demand to conform our thinking, doing, and desiring to *what is* in Christ. *What is* in Christ is, among other things, "God . . . reconciling the world to himself" (2 Cor. 5:19). The imperative (i.e., to love God above all earthly things) follows from the indicative (i.e., the demonstration in the cross of Christ that God, as love, is above all things). God is the being than which nothing greater can be conceived because his *doing* is such that nothing greater can be conceived. This is why we should be thinking in terms of theatricals, not transcendentals. The goal of discipleship is not being per se but rather *being-in-Christ*. Creatures cannot participate in God's reconciling activity the way that disciples ought to participate merely by existing.[15] On the contrary, participating in the gospel requires the Spirit-enabled obedience of faith.

---

15. Of course, there is a sense in which even those who are neither disciples nor believers participate in reconciliation by virtue of common grace to the extent that they perform acts of civic good or use their natural gifts (such as music) in inadvertent witness to God's light, life, and love. See Richard Mouw, *He Shines in All That's Fair: Culture and Common Grace* (Grand Rapids: Wm. B. Eerdmans Publishing Co., 2002).

We are now in a better position to see why 2 John joins truth and love at the hip. Fully to know *what is* in Christ is to have experienced God in loving action: "We love him because he first loved us" (1 John 4:19, mg.). We can go further: the net effect of following the truth of the gospel of God is to grow in godliness (i.e., Christlikeness). We know God's love in Christ truly only when we participate in it and share it with others. To "walk in the truth" is ultimately to participate in the love of God by acting out our being-in-Christ. This is the purpose of doctrine: to teach disciples the surpassing worth of being-in-Christ (cf. Phil. 3:8). And this is what it means to be *church*.

"CONFESSING THE COMING OF CHRIST": A SELF-INVOLVING DEMONSTRATION

> *Many deceivers have gone out into the world, those who do not confess that Jesus Christ has come in the flesh.*
> —2 John 7

To follow, walk in, or do the truth involves not only knowing the truth of the gospel but also *acknowledging* it to be so. Specifically, disciples must acknowledge "that Jesus Christ has come" (2 John 7). *Confessing* is one of the primary ways the audience participates in the ongoing action.

To "confess" [*homologeō*] the coming of Christ is to do more than say words or repeat certain lines. Nor is it simply a matter of asserting the content of one's belief. To confess is rather to acknowledge, which is a self-involving speech act.[16] In self-involving speech acts, speakers do not simply refer to a state of affairs, but they take up a particular posture toward it. The speakers are prepared to *stand by* their words (i.e., to take a stand), to borrow a phrase from Wendell Berry.[17]

Like other self-involving speech acts, *confessing* commits speakers to adopting a certain attitude in relation to the subject matter. When I confess with saints the world over "I believe in God the Father Almighty, Maker of heaven and earth," I am doing more than stating a fact. I am declaring my ultimate commitments, my deepest identity. Confessional statements "bring together both the content (what is confessed) and the force or stance with which it is

---

16. See the fine study by Richard Briggs, *Words in Action: Speech Act Theory and Biblical Interpretation* (Edinburgh & New York: T&T Clark, 2001), esp. chaps. 5–6. Briggs draws on the seminal work by Donald D. Evans, *The Logic of Self-Involvement: A Philosophical Study of Everyday Language with Special Reference to the Christian Use of Language about God as Creator* (London: SCM Press, 1963).

17. Wendell Berry, "Standing by Words," in *Standing by Words: Essays* (Berkeley, CA: Counterpoint, 1983), 24–63.

confessed."[18] Confessional statements combine truth claims (what John Searle calls "assertives") with the implicit promise of faithful action ("commissives").[19]

The particular truth that concerns discipleship is the acknowledgement that "Jesus Christ has come in the flesh" (2 John 7). Confessing the coming of Christ in the flesh is a self-involving speech act that counts both as an assertion (i.e., a statement about *what is* the case) and commitment to a future course of action (i.e., living in the light of *what is*). Second John is all about this dual character or confession, which is why we have a stress on truth *and* love. To confess the coming of Christ in the flesh is to declare that one is involved in the drama of redemption not as a spectator but as an active follower of Jesus.

The coming of Christ in the flesh lies at the very heart of the theodrama, which the Bible everywhere attests. In due course we shall have more to say about the contents of the theodrama. For present purposes it suffices to say that confessing the coming (present tense) of Christ is to recall what was, to state what is, and to anticipate what "is to come" (Rev. 1:4). For Jesus is the one who was promised to come (Gen. 3:15), the one who has come in the flesh (John 1:14), and the one who will come again (Acts 1:11). To confess Christ as "the coming one" is thus to acknowledge the centrality of the incarnation, the permanent significance of the God-man: "the same yesterday and today and forever" (Heb. 13:8).

"Many deceivers have gone out into the world, those who do not confess that Jesus Christ has come in the flesh" (2 John 7). Second John would not exist if it were not for the presence and activity of false teachers. Perhaps in the phrase "gone out into the world" we can even hear an echo of Jesus' Great Commission as recorded in the longer ending of Mark: "Go into all the world and proclaim the good news to the whole creation" (16:15). False teachers are on a mission too. Second John calls them "deceivers" and "antichrists." This is inflammatory language, but we can better see what is at stake when we realize that anti-confessions too are self-involving. Those who refuse to acknowledge the coming of Christ, those who *deny* him, are also declaring their ultimate commitments and deepest identities. To behold this man is no spectator sport. In the end, there are no passive spectators: "Whoever is not with me is against me" (Matt. 12:30).

Many readers may think that the language of "deceiver" and "antichrist" is excessive. Is this perhaps an instance of taking doctrine *too* seriously? No, it is not, for both the identity of God and the gospel are at stake in the confession of the coming of Christ. Those who deny that Christ has come in the flesh deny *what is* in Christ. They deny, first, the reality of the Mediator who bridges the abyss between holy God and sinful humans; and second, the abolition of the dividing wall of hostility between Jew and Greek. Not to acknowledge that Christ has

---

18. Briggs, *Words in Action*, 192–93.
19. For a classification of speech acts, see John R. Searle, "A Taxonomy of Illocutionary Acts," in *Expression and Meaning: Studies in the Theory of Speech Acts* (Cambridge: Cambridge University Press, 1979), 58–75.

come in the flesh (Phil. 2:6-7) is to fail to recognize the self-communicating nature of God (i.e., that God has extended himself in order to come to us). The failure to acknowledge Christ's coming in the flesh is nothing less than a denial of the reality of God's love, which is to say, a denial of the reality of God, since "God is love" (1 John 4:8).[20] To lose the truth of the incarnation, then, is to lose the meaning of the theodrama, the truth about the love of God and, ultimately, one's grip on reality.

There are, in fact, two ways to deny the love of God. The theoretical way is to fail to acknowledge that Christ has come in the flesh. Yet it is possible to affirm the idea theoretically while denying it in practice. One denies it in practice by failing to live in its light, to walk around in its truth. This is a performative contradiction of the gospel. Hence John exhorts his readers, "Watch yourselves" (2 John 8 ESV). To watch oneself acting—to watch not only that my deeds correspond to my words but also that my life is attuned to the reality of *what is* in Christ—is to be actor and audience at once. The point, again, is that the audience of 2 John participates in the love and truth of God's being-for-us (and our being-for-one-another) only when it makes good on its confession that Christ has indeed come in the flesh.

Confession need not always be verbal. The Gospels record a remarkable example of a self-involving acknowledgement of Christ's coming in the flesh by the woman who anoints Jesus with oil, an act that speaks volumes both about Jesus' identity and her own (Matt. 26:6–13; Mark 14:3–9; John 12:1–8; cf. Luke 7:36–50). Two features about this strange act are particularly noteworthy. First, it comes at a key point in the drama and is arguably the catalyst for Judas's betrayal, since he objected to the waste (the oil cost the equivalent of a full year's wages): "Why was this perfume not sold for three hundred denarii and the money given to the poor?" (John 12:5). The second striking feature is the very different way Jesus responds: "Why do you trouble the woman? For she has done a beautiful [*kalon*] thing to me" (Matt. 26:10 RSV).

Calvin calls the woman's act "an extraordinary performance,"[21] and so it was. We recognize it as a fitting act of devotion that indirectly communicated who Jesus was. Jesus himself viewed it as particularly appropriate, interpreting it as an advance preparation of his body for burial, thus ensuring that the anointing would be regarded as an act laden with dramatic irony. In this light, we can say that Judas's criticism of the woman already betrays him as one of the *antichrists* against which 2 John warns us.[22] The woman's act was entirely fitting, and her timing was impeccable. Yet in refusing to acknowledge the rightness of the woman's act, Judas fails to acknowledge who Jesus is.

---

20. See also the discussion in 1 John 4:1–5:12.
21. John Calvin, *Commentary on a Harmony of the Evangelists* (Edinburgh: Calvin Translation Society, 1866), 3:188.
22. The rest of the disciples are mere passive spectators. They are neither condemned nor praised. Rather, in Calvin's words, "Christ gently reproves the disciples . . . for not entertaining sufficiently honorable views of his future reign" (ibid., 191).

"She has done a beautiful thing." Jesus says that what she has done will be told "in remembrance of her" wherever and whenever the gospel is preached (Matt. 26:13; Mark 14:9). Calvin says that people from every nation "will applaud this action."[23] How extraordinary! Surely this is a minor scene performed by a bit player. What could possibly evoke a global standing ovation? Just this: the woman's act rightly acknowledges the coming of Jesus Christ. This is why it is true, good, and beautiful, a fitting participation in the reality of God's love made flesh. The woman symbolically and lovingly acts out the gospel truth, and consequently she serves as a paradigm for how believing audiences everywhere should respond to the coming of the Christ.

"ABIDING IN DOCTRINE": THE AUDIENCE AS STAGING AREA

Any one who goes ahead and does not abide in the doctrine of Christ does not have God.

—2 John 9 RSV

True disciples do not merely profess but also abide in Christ (John 15:4). To abide in Christ is to abide in his word (8:31) and to have his word, Spirit, and truth abiding in us (2 John 2). Disciples abide in Jesus' word by keeping his commands, and to obey his word is to abide in his love (John 15:9). These interconnecting Johannine themes are well known, though nonetheless profound. Less familiar, however, is the idea of abiding in the *doctrine* or teaching [*didachē*] of Christ (2 John 9).[24] What might it mean to "abide" in doctrine—Christology, for instance?

The clue is to see doctrinal instruction (teaching) as a self- and *other*-involving speech act. Like confessing, teaching doctrine involves much more than asserting facts. Whereas confessing combines assertives (statements) and commissives, teaching combines assertives and *directives*. Imparting and receiving information is only part of what transpires in teaching and learning. The good teacher, of Christian doctrine or anything else, knows that one must not only *state facts* but also *show how*.[25] One successfully *shows how* only when others are able to follow directions to "go and do likewise" (Luke 10:37). Recall Ludwig Wittgenstein's

---

23. Ibid.
24. Interpreters debate whether the author is referring to the teaching about Christ (objective genitive) or to Christ's own teaching (subjective genitive). The context suggests the former inasmuch as John is writing his epistle to combat false teaching (bad Christology). It is something of a moot point, however, because Jesus' own teaching concerned the significance of his own person and work. Either way, then, John wants his reader to abide in sound Christology.
25. See the discussion in Gabriel Moran, *Showing How: The Act of Teaching* (Valley Forge, PA: Trinity Press International, 1997).

comment that a learner attains understanding at the point of being able to say, "Now I know how to go on."[26] Call it *performance pedagogy*, training in how to go on: "Teaching is showing someone how to live and how to die."[27] Doctrine teaches disciples not only how to *speak* but also how to *do* the truth, the truth in question being *what is* "in Christ."

There is, of course, important information that teachers of doctrine need to communicate (e.g., "He is risen!"). Yet what sets Christian disciples apart is not simply the content of their belief but rather how they relate to it. Doctrine does more than state facts: it offers interpretive frameworks. Disciples interpret their knowledge and experience in the light of the drama of the Christ. How, for example, does one learn to "count it all joy . . . when you meet various trials" (Jas. 1:2 RSV)? Doctrine teaches us how to do this by directing us to view all things as part of God's providential plan (Eph. 1:9–10) and purpose (Rom. 8:28).[28] Disciples therefore learn how to interpret everyday experience eschatologically (i.e., in light of the climax and conclusion of the theodrama, the fulfillment of God's reign on earth).

Jesus' own teaching is a case in point. While at times he taught directly, with straightforward propositions (e.g., "The Lord is one" [Mark 12:29]), his preferred form of teaching was indirect. He taught his core subject (i.e., the coming of the kingdom of God) in parables (metaphors extended into narratives) and, like some of the Old Testament prophets before him, performed parabolic actions (Jer. 19; Ezek. 4; John 2:13–22). Jesus taught in parables because he was trying to do more than add this or that fact to our repertoire of factual knowledge. Jesus' curriculum was more ambitious: his aim was to change his disciples' worldview, beliefs, values, and practices alike, reframing how we think about ourselves and even how we experience God, the world, and ourselves. To abide in the doctrine of Christ means, at least in part, keeping this eschatological framework uppermost in one's mind. To abide in the doctrine of Christ is to remember that the reign of God has come into the world, unexpectedly, in Jesus' person and work, and to let this headline news color and shape one's everyday experience.

The "kingdom of God" is God's powerful presence and communicative activity in our world. To abide in the doctrine of Christ means remembering that one is a citizen of this kingdom, and that means participating, through the Spirit, in the expansion of God's reign. God's kingdom is not empirically observable (Luke 17:20) nor is it confined to particular space-time locations as are worldly entities. Jesus nevertheless reprimands the Pharisees for not seeing it: "The kingdom of God is among [*entos*] you" (Luke 17:21). By way of contrast, disciples abide in doctrine when they discern *what is* in Christ and demonstrate the reality of the kingdom by living it out.

26. Ludwig Wittgenstein, *Philosophical Investigations* (New York: Macmillan, 1953), §151.
27. Moran, *Showing How*, 41.
28. I am borrowing from, and modifying, Briggs's discussion of teaching as a New Testament speech act. See his *Words in Action*, esp. 271–73.

Where is the kingdom of God? The primary locus of God's reign is in hearts of believers (cf. Prov. 4:23), and it is they who give it visibility. It follows that the audience, those to whom God's word and acts are addressed, is the primary stage of the action as well. For whether or not one abides in the truth depends not merely on the theoretical positions one holds but on the orientation of one's heart. To abide in doctrine involves one's head, heart, and hand alike.

Audience participation is part and parcel of the theater of the gospel. Indeed, to invite others into the action—the triune communicative action oriented to communion and reconciliation—is the very purpose of the play (cf. Col. 1:20). Theology is theatrical, not only because it is a response to what God has done, but also because teaching and learning demand a lived demonstration of our understanding. As God has communicated to us, so we must communicate our understanding of that communication to others, not least by abiding in doctrine.

The church, then, is the domain of doctrine. The company of faith is the place where the love of God and the truth of doctrine are demonstrated (i.e., acted out), both in the way believers interact with one another and with those outside the church. The church is both school of discipleship and stage for interactive theater. For in the final analysis, men and women are the site where the most important action of the drama, the coming of God's kingdom, takes place. The audience itself is ultimately the theater of God's glory, the place that best exhibits the kingdom of God: God's reign in human hearts and minds. Doctrine helps shape what was formerly an amorphous group into the people of God: a place wherein to see God's presence and activity. The church has become the theater of the gospel, and in this theater, there are no passive spectators, only engaged participants, acting out *what is* in Christ. Dietrich Bonhoeffer perfectly expresses the idea: "Of ultimate importance, then, is not that I become good, or that the condition of the world be improved by my efforts, but that the reality of God show itself everywhere to be the ultimate reality."[29]

Our backstage tour of theatrical theological prolegomena is now complete. The curtain is about to rise. Yet in a sense it already has, for the method I have set forth is already informed by Christian doctrine. Like an extended overture, we have already heard snatches of melodies to come. That is because the subject *matter* of theology should determine the methodological *manner* in which we approach it. If we let the matter govern the method, we will break down not only the "fourth wall" that separates the audience from the action but also the "first wall" that too often separates the backstage scaffolding (i.e., theological method) from the action onstage (i.e., the communication of the Christ).

Theater happens whenever one person observes another. Walking across the stage—"the empty space," to cite the British theater director Peter Brook—is not as simple as it sounds, even when one is not attempting to walk in truth (3 John 4).[30] What many people fear more than anything else is public speaking.

---

29. Dietrich Bonhoeffer, *Ethics*, vol. 6 of *Dietrich Bonhoeffer Works* (Minneapolis: Augsburg-Fortress, 2005), 48.

30. Peter Brook, *The Empty Space* (New York: Atheneum, 1968).

Yet disciples must be prepared to give answers to anyone who asks them a reason for the hope that is within them (1 Pet. 3:15). Love (of truth) may cast out this fear of going onstage, though we still need to decide what to say and do when we get there. Are we ready to go on? In fact, we are always already onstage, and for many centuries, the church has been center stage. How then should we, as disciples, walk across the stage? What exactly does it mean, or look like, to "walk in the truth"? It is the task of doctrine to direct disciples to fill empty spaces and empty moments with redemptive speech and action. At its best, theology helps form us into people who can walk across the stage of world history like Christ. It is to that task that we now turn.

PART 2
FAITH SHOWING UNDERSTANDING
HOW DOCTRINE MAKES DISCIPLES AND HOW DISCIPLES DO DOCTRINE

Chapter 3

The Great Theater of the World

Setting the Twenty-First-Century Stage

> *On a shattered and deserted stage, without a script or prompter, the actor is free to improvise his part.*
> —Maurice Natanson, "Jean Paul Sartre's Philosophy of Freedom"

Why is there something rather than nothing? Theologians have a short answer to this perennial philosophical conundrum. There is something rather than nothing because God spoke the world into existence and himself into the world: "Let there be light . . . life . . . love."

To be or not to be is *not* the question for disciples of Jesus Christ. We are here not by our own choice but on account of a prior divine summons: God "calls into existence the things that do not exist" (Rom. 4:17). Consequently, we find ourselves always/already in the world—*thrown* into existence, to use Martin Heidegger's term.[1] The theologically correct way of putting it is to say not that we have been thrown but rather *cast* into the world, *called* into existence for a purpose: "to be holy and blameless, . . . his children through Jesus Christ" (Eph. 1:4–5).

This was and is God's will in heaven that is being worked out on earth. God chose a people "before the foundation of the world," before the stage was set. That we have been called into being for a purpose is perhaps the fundamental

---

1. *Being and Time*, trans. John Macquarrie and Edward Robinson (Oxford: Basil Blackwell, 1980), 321.

human truth: we have been called into being to be potential covenant partners with God and respond to his call in ways that glorify him.

The great Spanish playwright Pedro Calderón de la Barca rightly grasped this insight at the heart of the doctrines of creation and election in his 1635 play, *The Great Theater of the World*. In Calderon's play, God is the director and the Word is his stage manager, costuming every person who comes into the world with the necessary props to play the role they have been given. The Prompter encourages each player to "Do good, for God is God."

That was then. Some four centuries later many people are not so sure. The waters of modern and postmodern chaos again threaten the orders of creation (Gen 1:2). Some are as likely to ask "*Is* God God?" or to announce "God is dead" as to confess "God is God." Others who continue to confess it no longer know what "God" means. Still others say good riddance. According to Sam Harris, the problem with religious beliefs is that they eventually lead us to kill one another: "As long as it is acceptable for a person to believe that he knows how God wants everyone on earth to live, we will continue to murder one another on account of our myths."[2]

"Do good, for God is God." To speak of the "death" of God is to say that the traditional idea of God as the Creator of all things has become, for some, a practical impossibility. In our scientific age, a materialist picture of the world now holds many captive. Add to that the postmodern suspicion that all truth claims are in fact disguised bids for power and you get a potent mix of skepticism and cynicism, a cocktail guaranteed to make one's blood run *old* before its time. It is difficult in the extreme for faith to speak understanding into plausibility structures that have no room for God. Without God, how can we do what is good? Without God, what becomes of meaningful, authentic human existence?

We are onstage, in the here and now of the twenty-first century. Yet the "here" has become something of an empty space, a point devoid of meaning, and the "now," likewise, has become a detached moment bereft of any sense of an ending (hence the epigraph on Sartre above). If public speaking is indeed what people most fear, how much more challenging is it now to be on stage. Why am I here? What should I do and say? How ought I to walk through an empty space? Unaided reason is unable to answer our questions, nor does science have any answers. Many therefore simply imitate what they see other people doing, *strutting* across the stage like so many American Idols. Others *slink* across the stage, hoping that no one will notice.

The crisis of our post-Christian present stems from our having to walk across the stage, even when we do not quite know how to do so. There is no alibi for acting. The church is on the world stage, with many others, and we have been called into being for a particular purpose: to "live for the praise of his glory" (Eph. 1:12). Why is there something rather than nothing to say and do? There

---

2. Sam Harris, *The End of Faith: Religion, Terror, and the Future of Reason* (New York: W. W. Norton & Co., 2005), 134.

is something to say and do because there is a created order in which God has chosen to put us for a purpose. There is therefore an understanding to speak, a way to walk, a wisdom to enact.

"Do good, for God is God." Everything that needs to be said is implicit in this tightly bound sentence. "God is God" tells us what ultimately "is"; "do good" tells us what ought to follow from this "is." The indicative *indicates* the imperative. To say *what is* suggests a course of fitting action, which is why doctrine and discipleship are joined at the hip. And this brings us to the contemporary crisis in the church: when doctrine dwindles, disciples can only limp. It is difficult to walk with a dislocated hip.

STAGE: CHURCH, WORLD, AND THE CONTEMPORARY CRISIS OF AUTHENTICITY

The first thing to do when the curtain rises is to take in the stage and setting. Where are we? What scene are we playing? How should disciples be walking across the stage? What should they be saying and doing? These questions have become particularly acute in the present church, in a time and place where Christian doctrine is in eclipse. We begin with a series of book reports that help us take the measure of the church's twenty-first-century context.

Doctrine in the Church: Four Reports on the State of the Knowledge of God

All four books agree: these days, doctrine does not receive much positive publicity. In fact, what press it gets is almost uniformly negative: it's unspiritual, it's irrelevant, it's divisive, it's boring. What can one say to these accusations except "guilty as charged"? Here is what I want to say: while doctrine *can* be dry, dull, and debilitating to life and love, it *need* not be so.

Doctrine is inevitable. We've all been *indoctrinated*: everyone has absorbed some system of beliefs and values. Just as our gestures and our accents give us away as people who have been raised in the Midwest or the South or elsewhere, so much of what we believe gives evidence of how, when, and where we have been brought up. Someone has said that all television is education; the only question is, What is it teaching? The same could be said of culture in general. Indoctrination is always happening: in homes, schools, the workplace, sometimes even in church. The only question is whether it is truly Christian.

A number of recent works have observed a tectonic shift in the role doctrine plays in Christian faith and life for the younger generation. In *The Transformation of American Religion: How We Actually Live Our Faith*, Alan Wolfe, a sociologist, argues that American religion in our time is utterly different from what it was a generation ago. "In every aspect of religious life, American faith has met American culture—and American culture has triumphed. . . . The faithful in the United States are remarkably like everyone else."³ Why should this be? By way of reply, Wolfe points to "the strange disappearance of doctrine": "Talk of hell, damnation, and even sin has been replaced by a nonjudgmental language of understanding and empathy. Gone are the arguments over doctrine and theology; if most believers cannot for the life of them recall what makes Luther different from Calvin, there is no need for [disagreement and schism]."⁴ What matters to most people now is *spirituality*—the feeling of intimacy with God—not doctrine. Notably, Wolfe found that doctrine is an endangered species in conservative and liberal Protestant churches alike: "Evangelical churches lack doctrine because they want to attract new members. Mainline churches lack doctrine because they want to hold on to those declining numbers of members they have."⁵ Wolfe also surmises that the decreasing importance of doctrine in providing guidance for moral and religious views may be a generational phenomenon, at least for Roman Catholics, but probably for others as well: "The younger the Catholic, the more likely he or she holds the view that individuals are the appropriate decision makers."⁶

Youth is the operative term in Christian Smith's *Soul Searching: The Religious and Spiritual Lives of American Teenagers*. Smith too is a sociologist who spent four years trying to understand thirteen-to-seventeen-year-olds—no small feat. He discovered that the majority of American teenagers are still religious, believers active in their churches. However, they are "*incredibly inarticulate* about their faith, their religious beliefs and practices, and its meaning or place in their lives."⁷ This does not mean that they do not hold to certain doctrines. On the contrary, Smith says they have an implicit theology: "Moralistic Therapeutic Deism," or MTD for short (an apt acronym for a socially transmitted disease).

Adherents to MTD are often affiliated with traditional faith communities, unaware that they are practicing something very different from their historic faith communities. It has also infected people who no longer go to church, so much so that it may be "the new mainstream American religious faith for our culturally post-Christian, individualistic, mass-consumer capitalist society."⁸ If those who hold this faith could articulate it as a creed, it might go something like this:

> I believe in a creator God who orders and watches over life on earth. I believe that God wants people to be good: to act nice to one another [the

---

3. Alan Wolfe, *The Transformation of American Religion: How We Actually Live Our Faith* (New York: Free Press, 2003), 3.
4. Ibid.
5. Ibid., 87. A related issue concerns the future of denominations in a postdoctrinal age. See, e.g., David S. Dockery, ed., *Southern Baptists, Evangelicals, and the Future of Denominationalism* (Nashville: B&H Academic, 2011).
6. Ibid., 88.
7. Christian Smith, *Soul Searching: The Religious and Spiritual Lives of American Teenagers* (New York: Oxford University Press, 2005), 131.
8. Kenda Creasy Dean, *After Christian: What the Faith of Our Teenagers Is Telling the American Church* (New York: Oxford University Press, 2010), 205.

"moralistic" tenet]. I believe that the central goal of life is to be happy and feel good about oneself [the "therapeutic" tenet]. I believe that God is not involved in my life except when I need God to solve a problem. I believe that good people go to heaven. Virtual worlds without end, Amen.

This, too, is doctrine, but alas: it expresses an unbiblical, non-Trinitarian faith. The God of Moral-Therapeutic Deism neither dies on a cross nor transforms people through his Spirit. And its doctrine, not the holiness but the *niceness* of God, is only skin deep, a superficial lotion that fails to cut reality at its joint and marrow. Make no mistake: the theology of MTD is formative insofar as it encourages a particular pattern of individual and community life. No sacrificial self-giving here: the God of MTD is not bracing Love but bland amiability. MTD is a theological design for living *boringly* forever.

This brings me to a third book, David Wells's *The Courage to Be Protestant: Truth-Lovers, Marketers, and Emergents in the Postmodern World*, a broad indictment of contemporary North American evangelicalism. We can sum up his overall thesis in one sentence: the twenty-first-century evangelical church is on the verge of selling its Protestant birthright, *sola scriptura*, for a mess of pottage, *sola cultura*. Put differently: the evangelical church finds itself in danger of being indoctrinated by culture rather than Scripture. There is too much concern with what works and sells than with gospel truth. It is tempting, and better for one's self-esteem, to be "like other nations" (1 Sam. 8:20) than to be a resident alien, a marginalized weakling, or a fool. In these postmodern days, says Wells, doctrines are decidedly of low social status: "When all is said and done today, many evangelicals are indifferent to doctrine—certainly they are when they 'do church.'"[9] The problem, certainly, is how we are to "do church" without a good grasp of the doctrine of the church. We need to know something about the nature and mission of the church, why God invented it.

The last book in my brief stage-setting survey is Harvey Cox's *The Future of Faith*. Like Wolfe and Smith, Cox too observes a sea change taking place in what it means to be "religious." Religion globally is on the upswing. The big surprise of our secular age is that religion has not gone quietly into that good night. As to fundamentalism, however, Cox thinks it is dying from overconfidence in the correctness of its doctrine. We are entering a third stage of church history. According to Cox, the first stage, the apostolic Age of Faith, was concerned with following the way of Jesus, especially his moral teaching. However, during the second stage, the Age of Belief, between the fourth century and the twentieth, the church became preoccupied with Christology instead of following Jesus Christ himself.

Cox is heavily invested in the old liberal distinction between the "pure" personal faith in Jesus that allegedly characterized the early church and the preoccupation with doctrine that the church contracted from its exposure to

---

9. David F. Wells, *The Courage to Be Protestant* (Grand Rapids: Wm. B. Eerdmans Publishing Co., 2008), 3.

Greek philosophy: "Emphasis on belief began to grow when these primitive instruction kits [viz., baptismal formulas] thickened into catechisms, replacing faith *in* Jesus with tenets *about* him."[10]

Whereas Wells laments the loss of doctrine, Cox sees it as a return to something like the Age of Faith. He believes that we are entering into what he calls a third period, marked by resistance to authoritative institutions and creeds and a concern for vibrant spirituality rather than sound doctrine: the Age of the Spirit. He likes Aldous Huxley's variation on the Lord's Prayer: "Give us this day our daily faith, but deliver us from *beliefs*."[11] Cox even claims that creeds "were always something theologians invented, often to stake out spheres of authority. The vast body of lay Christians knew little about them and cared less."[12] No doubt Cox approves of Prince Charles recasting the sovereign role vis-à-vis the Church of England from "Defender of *the* Faith" to "Defender of *Faith*."

In one sense I am sympathetic to Cox's cause. As I have been arguing throughout, disciples must not only believe but also *act out* their beliefs. I am all for "living the message." Here we need to ask Cox worrisome but relevant questions: What *is* the message? *Can* faith bereft of specific beliefs speak understanding? If so, understanding *of what?* My concern is that the only thing Cox has to say to young people seeking spirituality is "Do good."[13] But why should we do good? And what is the good if it is not somehow rooted in the nature and work of God? Cox's Age of the Spirit needs a normative Word. For while belief without faith is empty, faith without belief is blind.

A Doctrinal Offering: Getting the Message Across in an Experience Economy

What does the church have to offer the world that no other institution can? Is it belief or faith? A set of doctrines or a style of spirituality? The very way of posing the question is discouraging, for it reminds us that the church is onstage with others, many of whom are clamoring for the attention and loyalty of the audience. Even more alarming are congregations that suffer attention deficit disorder whenever someone even mentions doctrine.

To be sure, what the church has to offer that no other institution can offer is the gospel of Jesus Christ, an invitation to life with God and fellowship in his family. This involves more, but not less, than teaching about Jesus Christ. Proclaiming the truth is important, a sine qua non, yet the church's vocation goes further. The mission of the church is to offer a taste of truth: a personal experience of the gospel, a relationship with Jesus Christ.

---

10. Harvey Cox, *The Future of Faith* (New York: HarperCollins, 2009), 5.
11. Ibid., 213, emphasis added.
12. Ibid., 221.
13. Perhaps Cox is not worried about this. He does point out that Asian religions are hard pressed to set forth lists of their "beliefs" (ibid.).

To speak in terms of church "offerings" is to risk speaking as if the church were in competition with other service providers, and in a sense, it is. There are any number of truths, "gospels," and salvations presently available in the cultural and intellectual marketplace, as there are in the business market. And this brings me to Joseph Pine and James Gilmore's fascinating book *The Experience Economy: Work Is Theatre and Every Business a Stage*.[14] The book helps us understand why doctrine is in decline even if its stated subject is the world of business rather than the church.

Companies exist to sell things. In the old days, companies traded commodities: *raw material* was the "offering." With the industrial revolution, companies began to manufacture goods: the *product* was the offering. In the postindustrial age, companies provide services: the *operation* (e.g., haircutting, housecleaning) is the offering. Companies that want to gain a competitive edge must distinguish their goods and services from those of their competitors. The way to do that, Pine and Gilmore contend, is to offer an *experience*. When one buys a Caramel Macchiato from Starbucks, one is buying not merely raw materials (i.e., coffee beans) or a product (the drink) or even a service but rather an experience (and thus a memory): "He pays to spend time enjoying a series of memorable events that a company stages—as in a theatrical play—to engage him in a personal way."[15] We have moved through various economies: from Agrarian to Industrial, then Service, and finally to an *Experience* Economy.

The twenty-first-century stage is filled with companies of actors, each with some kind of experience to offer. Pine and Gilmore trace the beginnings of the Experience Economy to Walt Disney. Disneyland not only sells products and delivers services but, more important, creates memorable experiences, involving guests in familiar stories: "Companies stage an experience whenever they *engage* customers, connecting with them in a personal, memorable way."[16]

The rise of the Experience Economy is significant for the church on several levels. First, it reminds us that our deepest desires are not for temporal goods (things) but meaningful personal experiences and interpersonal relationships. Augustine had it right: "Our hearts are restless until they find their rest in thee."[17] Second, it reminds us that the church is not the only institution offering meaningful personal experiences or interpersonal relationships (think Match.com). Of course, the church has often had to proclaim the gospel in pluralistic situations. There was plenty of competition for the fledgling church in ancient Rome. Third, the very idea of subscribing to the latest in marketing strategies will no doubt prove tempting to some churches, the "seeker-sensitive" in particular. We must resist the temptation. The distinct experiential end in question in the church, communion with God and others, neither justifies nor

---

14. B. Joseph Pine II and James H. Gilmore, *The Experience Economy: Work Is Theatre and Every Business a Stage* (Boston: Harvard Business School Press, 1999; updated ed., 2011).
15. Ibid., 2.
16. Ibid., 3.
17. *Confessions*, 1.1.

fits many marketing means. The increase of the kingdom of God owes more to the work of the Spirit than to Madison Avenue.

If I here invoke *The Experience Economy*, it is not to be on the cutting edge of marketing but rather of discipleship. The church may well be a theater that stages experiences in order to engage guests; there is nevertheless something distinctive about the company of saints and the kinds of experiences they stage. The challenge is to specify this difference, just as we need to distinguish true acting from playacting (i.e., hypocrisy) in speaking of the church as the "theater" of the gospel. The biggest difference, of course, is that the church is a theater for experiencing the risen Christ, something that is not susceptible to commodification, for the initiative always lies with Christ.

Nevertheless, there are significant areas of overlap between the worlds of business, theater, and church, many of which are quite instructive. Pine and Gilmore draw a number of helpful distinctions. For example, guests are "entertained" when they remain passive spectators but "engaged" when they become active participants. Clearly, my theatrical model urges the church to offer experiences that engage rather than merely entertain. This applies to the teaching of doctrine as well: the armchair disciple is a contradiction in terms.

Pine and Gilmore appeal to theater as a model for understanding economic offerings. In the Experience Economy, businesses need to realize that they must offer more than goods and services to stay competitive: "Any work observed directly by a customer must be recognized as an act of theatre."[18] The offering is the performance itself, insofar as it generates a memorable experience. It is but a short step from the idea of a memorable experience to one that leaves a permanent mark: "The experiences we have affect who we are, what we can accomplish, and where we are going, and we will increasingly ask companies to stage experiences that change us."[19]

What is everywhere on offer on the twenty-first-century stage are promises of *life-transforming experiences*.[20] Indeed, personal transformations represent a distinct economic offering, an experience that is not merely memorable but also *effectual*. Transformation changes the *being* of the buyer. It follows that *the customer is the product*.[21] The ultimate economic offering is the opportunity to become the *new you*.

This brings us back to the present challenge for the church: How can it distinguish its offerings, including the promise of a transformed (i.e., spiritual) life, from all the other offerings currently in the personal transformation market? Pine and Gilmore conclude their book with some constructive suggestions, the most intriguing of which concerns the role of worldview in business offerings: "In the years ahead, we think that companies and their customers

---

18. Pine and Gilmore, *Experience Economy*, 106.
19. Ibid., 163.
20. Pine and Gilmore cite higher education as one "business" that stages educational experiences and promises to transform their client/guests (ibid., 168).
21. This is also the title of chap. 9 in ibid.

will increasingly acknowledge rival worldviews—ideologies, if you will—as the legitimate domain of business and as differentiators of competing offerings."[22] To restate their idea in terms of the present work: in the years ahead, companies will be staging differing *doctrinal* experiences. Pine and Gilmore themselves acknowledge the role of something resembling religious belief: "We believe buyers will purchase transformations according to the set of eternal principles the seller seeks to embrace—what together they believe will last."[23] The authors actually conclude their book with an explicit Christian confession. While the ultimate transformative experience would doubtless be *perfection*, they believe that we can be perfected (i.e., saved; sanctified) only by God's grace, and this is not for sale. Still, it is salutary, even for Christians, to realize that "every business is a stage for glorifying something."[24]

The Crisis of Doctrine and Discipleship: Which Identity? Whose Authenticity?

The argument in the present book is that the church is a theater of the gospel in which disciples stage previews of the coming kingdom of God. What the church has to offer the world that no other institution can is indeed "economic" in the traditional theological sense of the term (*oikonomia* [Eph. 1:10; 3:9]): the historical outworking of God's plan of salvation. Complicating the church's mission, however, is the fact that there are so many other "companies" staging different "economic" offerings. We are all too aware of the mixed monetary motives of those who stage economic or ideological offerings. Those who manage not to become cynical nevertheless find themselves with a plethora of offerings from which to choose. The sheer preponderance of the various gospels on offer—promises to transform your life in this way or that—results in *doctrine* fatigue, the refusal to believe that any one person or institution has exclusive rights to Truth.

Dorothy Sayers was right. It appears that we have to choose between creed and chaos. The contemporary stage is indeed chaotic and cacophonous, and for this reason it resembles an ancient stage: "In those days there was no king in Israel; all the people did what was right in their own eyes" (Judg. 17:6; 21:25). It also resembles the future time foretold by Jesus: "For many will come in my name, saying, 'I am the Messiah!' and they will lead many astray" (Matt. 24:5). But how can we recognize the true Christ, the right creed? These currents on the twenty-first-century stage add up to a major crisis for the church, particular in the West, a crisis not only over authority but also over *authenticity*: being true to one's true self.

Gilmore and Pine have written a sequel to *The Experience Economy* that addresses the following paradox: the more we realize that experiences are staged,

---

22. Ibid., 206.
23. Ibid.
24. Ibid.

the more we require the assurance of the real. If an offering is perceived as less than real, it will be branded as inauthentic, counterfeit, fake. Accordingly, they titled their book *Authenticity: What Consumers Really Want*. Any company that wants its offerings to be competitive in today's marketplace of product and ideas must stage *authentic* experiences. In their words: "Your business offerings must get real."[25] The new business imperative is to manage, not people but *perceptions*.[26]

Gilmore and Pine rightly identify the key question: "*Can businesses help individuals find authenticity in a world where people no longer esteem our most basic social institutions?*"[27] They spend most of their book offering suggestions as to how companies can render their offerings authentic, though they are under no illusions as to how difficult this is: "The very act of *saying* something is authentic immediately leads consumers to *doubt* said authenticity."[28] One wonders whether authenticity, like love, can ever be a commodity, especially when the companies offering it have mixed motives that include not only the consumer's satisfaction but also the company's bottom line and profit margin.

What is authenticity? The English term derives from the Greek *authentikos*, meaning "primary" or "original" (i.e., "authorial"). Something is authentic if it is what it purports to be, and this often implies a historical connection to its alleged source (e.g., an authentic Shakespeare sonnet, Rembrandt painting, or Henry Aaron home-run ball). In connection with the experience economy, the most important aspects of authenticity are (1) being real ("Authenticity is reality without sham")[29] and (2) being true to or becoming more oneself.

Gilmore and Pine cite the examples of Eden Alternative and ServiceMaster as companies that score high on the scale of authenticity. The former's aim is to transform the nursing-home experience from being lonely, boring, and meaningless into an "authentic" community of elders. Eden is not simply a home but a "habitat" in which residents can interact with plants, animals, and children. There are opportunities to give as well as receive care (the antidote to loneliness and meaninglessness). There are not only routines but also spontaneous events in which unscripted interactions take place (the antidote to boredom). Obviously, Eden Alternative is not *the* Eden; no human institution is perfect, or even paradisal. Nevertheless, the church must take note: it is hard to refute "doctrine" that generates meaningful community life.

---

25. B. Joseph Pine II and James H. Gilmore, *Authenticity: What Consumers Really Want* (Boston: Harvard Business School, 2007), 3.

26. Lest the reader misunderstand, let me repeat that it is not my purpose to suggest that the church is like other business and that all it need do is employ the latest marketing techniques. On the contrary, I am suggesting that it is precisely these techniques that have precipitated the crisis over authority and authenticity. I also think that these works provide important insights into the nature of the present cultural moment.

27. Ibid., 28, emphasis original.

28. Ibid., 43.

29. Thomas DuBay, *Authenticity: A Biblical Theology of Discernment* (San Francisco: Ignatius Press, 1997), 26.

ServiceMaster is authentic because it has a purpose beyond profit that is true to who they are. C. William Pollard, the company's former CEO, calls its purpose—to honor God, to help people develop, to pursue excellence, to grow profitable—the "soul" of the firm.[30] The company comes across as authentic because what they do is true to who they are, and what they say they are to others is indeed who they are. Not all companies are what they represent themselves to be, however. Phoniness abounds.

Twenty-first-century individuals may be less confident than their predecessors that they can discern what is really real—after all, so much reality is media manufactured and socially constructed—yet these same individuals are more confident when it comes to the importance of being true to oneself, to one's personality, spirit, and dreams. If a company can persuade consumers that it will help them to follow or realize their dreams, it will likely turn a profit. The problem, as Gilmore and Pine rightly note, is that "the sole determinate of the authenticity of any economic offering is the individual perceiving the offering."[31] That is because (or so the thinking goes) no one knows me better than I do myself. This alleged self-knowledge is also doctrine, however. As such, it can be true or false.

Charles Taylor, a philosopher, views this belief in the importance of being true to oneself as the hallmark of "The Age of Authenticity," which is one way of thinking about the present secular age.[32] The Age of Authenticity has its roots in the expressive individualism of the Romantic period, in particular the idea "that each one of us has his/her own way of realizing our humanity, and that it is important to find and live out one's own, as against surrendering to conformity with a model imposed on us from outside, by society, or the previous generation, or religious or political authority."[33] Unfortunately for doctrine, it is associated with *all* of the above. As we saw in Cox, *spirituality* is in; *belief* is out.

Not so fast. The Age of Authenticity relies on certain doctrines, too, as Alan Ehrenhalt observes in *The Lost City: The Forgotten Virtues of Community in America*, a study of life in Chicago in the 1950s and afterward: "Most of us in America believe a few simple propositions that seem so clear and self-evident they scarcely need to be said. Choice is a good thing in life, and the more of it we have, the happier we are. Authority is inherently suspect; nobody should have the right to tell others what to think or how to behave."[34] At first blush there would seem to be no place for doctrine inasmuch as it is a form of *authoritative* teaching. Upon closer inspection, however, we see that this statement appeals

---

30. C. William Pollard, *The Soul of the Firm* (New York: Harper Collins; Grand Rapids: Zondervan, 1996).
31. Pine and Gilmore, *Authenticity*, 92.
32. Charles Taylor, *A Secular Age* (Cambridge, MA: Belknap Press of Harvard University Press, 2007), chap. 13.
33. Ibid., 475.
34. Alan Ehrenhalt, *The Lost City: The Forgotten Virtues of Community in America* (New York: BasicBooks, 1995), 2.

to authority too. Indeed, it is a secular creed, complete with tacit appeal to the authority of the majority.

Taylor worries that the appeal to authenticity has the ironic effect of making authentic community more difficult as individuals head off to find themselves. We need to state the obvious questions: *Are* individuals the ultimate authorities as to what is best for them? Is authentic existence something we can decide for ourselves?

There is only one human nature. Martin Heidegger got this right at least. Once we are "thrown" into the world, it is up to us to decide what to do with our existence. To be human is to be finite yet free. How I shall be, how I walk across the stage of life, is my decision. To fail to decide, to let others (the "they") decide for me, is to renege on my freedom and fall into inauthentic existence. To the extent that I conform to social conventions, I am not my *own* self but a "they-self."[35] By way of contrast, authenticity for Heidegger, an existentialist philosopher, means resolutely facing one's "ownmost" possibility: the inevitable prospect of one's own mortality. To be human is to have limited time and to know it. That is why he describes human existence as being-toward-death. Authenticity for Heidegger means constantly preparing to play one's own death scene. My counterclaim, to be worked out during the course of the present book, is that the only way to achieve authenticity is to come to a true view of one's true nature, namely, theological anthropology: the Christian doctrine that human beings are created in God's image. "What does it mean to be human?" may be a multiple-choice question, but it does not admit of a multiple-choice answer.

To sum up: we are living in a time when Christian doctrine is in decline, just when the world and the church need it most. For myriad companies are offering myriad gospels, all of which more or less promise to transform individuals into their true selves. However, all these offers presuppose doctrine: ideas about what is good for us. What the church has to offer is not simply one more idea of the good, but rather an announcement that the good has actually been realized, and is being realized, and will be realized even more in Christ. The church knows—not because it is clever but because it has been told— where we come from, what we are, why we are here, and what our purpose is: "Beloved, we are God's children now; it does not yet appear what we shall be, but we know that when he appears we shall be like him" (1 John 3:2 RSV). There is nothing more authentic than being transformed into the image of Jesus Christ, the prototype of true humanity. What the church has to offer to the world is not only the message but also a practical demonstration of salvation: the transformed identity of those who not only bear the image of Christ but also stand in right relationship to him; the promise of reconciled communities; the reality of being-toward-resurrection.

---

35. Martin Heidegger, *Being and Time*, trans. John Macquarrie and Edward Robinson (Oxford: Basil Blackwell, 1980), 167.

LIGHTING: "A LAMP UNTO MY FEET"

The world stage on which we live and move and have our being is vast and complex. Who can comprehend it? In order to understand our contemporary context and the shape twenty-first-century discipleship should take, we need to make sure that we are seeing things correctly. We need a framework with which to interpret and integrate our experience, to find our way, and to discern authentic from inauthentic ways of being.

In part 1, I wondered whether Scripture is the disciples' holy script. We concluded that a supplementary image may be that of a transcript: a divinely authorized record of God's word and acts in the histories of Israel, Jesus Christ, and the early church. Let me suggest now that, precisely as divine transcript, with the Spirit's speaking in and through human authors, the Bible is also what provides stage lighting. "Your word is a lamp to my feet and a light to my path" (Ps. 119:105; cf. 2 Pet. 1:19). The spectacles of faith, Calvin's celebrated image for thinking about Scripture in terms of corrective lenses, are also *footlights*: the means by which we see the stage clearly and make our way across it.

"'Let there be light'; and there was light" (Gen. 1:3). What illumines the stage is God's word, the word that spoke forth the created order in the beginning, the incarnate word whose activity eventually restores and perfects that original order, and the word written that attests to the Word through and for whom all things were made (Col. 1:16). From the very beginning, it was God's word that, to use Plato's phrase, "carved nature at its joints."[36] The most basic division in the created order, between light and darkness, day and night, proceeds from God's luminous word. There is wisdom in letting God's word light one's way because it is God's word that formed the created order and then formulated the laws that order rightful human action, distinguishing moral day (i.e., right) from night (i.e., wrong).

God's word is a lamp to disciples' feet because *God* is light, and his word illumines the way of all flesh. The psalmist has in mind God's verbal instruction recorded in the Ten Commandments and the book of Deuteronomy, because Psalm 119 celebrates the gift of *torah*.[37] The law is a pedagogue, a guide to holy living. To follow any other rule for life is soon to become entangled in frightful mazes. To associate God's word with light is to contrast it with the dark counsels of a fallen world. In Calvin's words: "Unless the word of God enlighten men's path, the whole of their life is enveloped in darkness and obscurity, so that they cannot do anything else than miserably wander from the right way."[38]

---

36. Plato, *Phaedrus* 265d–266a.
37. Geoffrey W. Grogan, *Psalms* (Grand Rapids: Wm. B. Eerdmans Publishing Co., 2008), 263.
38. John Calvin, *Commentary on the Book of Psalms* (Grand Rapids: Wm. B. Eerdmans Publishing Co., 1949), on Ps. 119:105.

God's word is light because, in many and various ways, God's speech illuminates reality.[39] It reveals the truth, makes things known, and enables us to see how things are. It is against this backdrop that we must read the Fourth Gospel's testimony to Jesus as the light. The incarnation of God's Word represents an unprecedented historical manifestation of light: "The true light, which enlightens everyone, was coming into the world" (John 1:9). "God is light" (1 John 1:5), and what comes from God is also light. It is through the light of the Son that the Father, who is light itself, is known. Similarly, it is through the light afforded by Scripture that we are able to see Jesus as the Christ, "the light of the world" (John 8:12; 9:5). Scripture is a lighthouse, not the ultimate source of the light, but the "house" through which the Spirit makes shine upon our hearts the light of Jesus Christ, the knowledge of the God who is light.

"The unfolding of your words gives light; it imparts understanding to the simple" (Ps. 119:130). The Bible is not an expression of the prophets' and apostles' religious experience but a transcript of the drama of redemption in whose light everything else comes into proper focus. This is how Scripture constitutes the spectacles of faith: it provides the corrective lenses and the mediated light by which to "read" our world and interpret our experience rightly. This is why John Robinson was able to say, in his 1620 farewell speech to the pilgrims who would land at Plymouth, "I am verily persuaded the Lord hath more truth and light yet to break forth from His holy word." Robinson is not saying that he expects new revelatory content to break forth; rather, he is expressing his confidence that the Spirit will continue to use Scripture to communicate Jesus Christ and so illuminate further stages of church history.

Disciples are children of light (John 12:36; cf. Eph. 5:8; 1 Thess. 5:5) who are to walk in the light (1 John 1:7), namely, "the light of the knowledge of the glory of God in the face of Jesus Christ" (2 Cor. 4:6). The key point is that Scripture participates in the light of Jesus Christ, as Peter makes clear in his reflection on the event of Jesus' transfiguration: "So we have the prophetic message more fully confirmed. You will do well to be attentive to this as to a lamp shining in a dark place" (2 Pet. 1:19). It was the prophetic word that alone interpreted the significance of the apostles' witnessing Jesus' transfiguration. Had it not been for the law and the prophets (represented by the two figures who appeared with Jesus on the mountain [Matt. 17:1–7]), Peter would not have known that he had just witnessed the fulfillment of the prophetic word (i.e., the enthronement of the promised Messiah).

Faith speaking understanding is a matter of *talking* in the light, that is, in ways that follow the way the biblical authors use key terms and the longer

---

39. Strictly speaking, divine illumination is the Spirit's act in the economy of triune communication. Scripture does not automatically or magically shed light, but only as the Spirit uses it to overcome hard-heartedness and dark-mindedness. See John B. Webster, "Illumination," *Journal of Reformed Theology* 5 (2011): 325–40.

canonical grooves.⁴⁰ We only see the world stage rightly when we view it in the light of the biblical transcripts, that is, through Spirit-enabled faith in the word of God. Scripture provides light because it illumines the theological depth dimension of both stage and action.⁴¹ Furthermore, we learn how disciples are to speak and act by reading accounts of what they said and did in concrete situations. Looking at the stage with the light of Scripture reminds us that every situation is an opportunity to walk in the light, to act in ways that demonstrate our understanding of the play (the subject of the next chapter).

Jesus is the *apaugasma* (brightness, effulgence, radiance) and the "exact imprint of God's very being" (Heb. 1:3). It is in Jesus' characteristic activity that the light shines (i.e., makes God known). Simply by being what it is, light does something. So it is with Jesus. What he says and does reveals who he is, and hence who the Father is. Surely it is significant that Jesus' claim to be the light of the world (John 9:5) is dramatized by the scene in which he cures and counsels the man born blind (John 9).⁴² Scripture likewise is light because it enlightens, enabling us to see and understand what is happening on the stage of world history, at least as concerns the struggle of light against darkness and the church's role in it. In sum: the Bible—the Spirit speaking in and through Scripture—lights up the stage by opening our eyes to the drama unfolding upon it, and to our own vocation as church to become "the light of the world" (Matt. 5:14).

ACTION: THE ESSENCE OF THEATER

The stage is the environment of a theatrical presentation, the space and time in which one person engages another. The doctrine of creation reminds us that the world is indeed an environment for interaction between persons, a space and time in which something can be done. To speak of doing God's will on earth as it is in heaven reminds us of the Creator-creature distinction while recognizing the dynamic relation between them. The doctrine of creation also reminds us that the world is a stage for presentations of God's glory.

In the next chapter we shall examine the particular contours and themes of the theodrama, the great play of creation. The focus here is on the stage

---

40. In *The Drama of Doctrine*, part 3, I outline six ways in which theologians are to speak and act canonically (i.e., be biblical, walk in the light). These ways constitute the backbone of the canonical-linguistic approach, the heart of which is the suggestion that the norm of Christian theology is a function of the way language is used in the biblical canon rather than ecclesial culture. The relationship between Scripture and church theology is asymmetrical: the wisdom embodied in the canon must govern the church's speech, thinking, and action today rather than vice versa.

41. This is not to suggest that light from Scripture removes all dark corners from the universe. There are certain depths (e.g., evil) that we will never understand and certain heights (e.g., divine perfections) that will ever elude our grasp, for God "dwells in unapproachable light" (1 Tim. 6:16).

42. C. H. Dodd notes that light has a discriminating function as well. The coming of light into the world clearly demarcates the children of light from the children of darkness, who refuse to love it (*The Interpretation of the Fourth Gospel* [Cambridge: Cambridge University Press, 1953], 210).

as the setting for action in space and time. After all, action is the language of the theater—but what kind of action? Not every happening is necessarily theatrical, for the simple reason that not every movement is the act of an actor or agent. There is a difference between reflex bodily movements like breathing and blinking and intentional bodily movements like holding one's breath or winking. Winking is a kind of saying, just as saying is a kind of doing. Humans can do things with words and say things with their bodies. And this is what makes for theater: embodied speech. Insofar as it sets the necessary temporal and spatial conditions for embodied personal agents, creation is the great theater of *communicative* action.

Act and Being as Communicative

While the focus of theater is spoken action and actions that speak, there is a sense in which everything in creation communicates its nature. The movement of Venus through the night sky is a predictable event, but it is not theatrical—unless one views it as the result of God's creative speech act that set its course ("The heavens are telling the glory of God" [Ps. 19:1]). Strictly speaking, Venus is not an agent or actor, but an object of an actor's (or in this case, a Creator's) action. However, because God is the Actor whose agency is behind all things, there is a sense in which even natural events are instances of indirect divine discourse.

The concept of drama reminds us that we should not draw too fine a distinction between speaking and acting. As we have seen, God even sets the stage by speaking ("Let there be light"). What God creates reveals something about God. God's very act of creating is thus an unveiling, a parting of the curtain that partitions God's space-time as it were in heaven (the realm of the eternal) from the space and time of the created world (the temporal). Creation thus both reveals something and sets the stage for further revelation, the (dramatic) representation of God's being "on earth as it is in heaven."

Should not theology be concerned with the essential truths of God's being rather than suggesting, as I am about to do here, that the essence of theater (and theology) is action? In chapter 1, I defended the present approach from the charge that it reduces theology to a kind of moral activism by relating doing to believing. Believing, I said there, is not merely propositional but also dispositional, a matter not only of processing intellectual content but also of acting it out. We now add to that account by relating doing to *being*.

Consider, once again, the phenomenon of light. Light *enlightens*. Its very being is an activity (i.e., electromagnetic radiation at a speed of 186,281 miles per second). God is light, and God's being too is a matter of his activity. In more traditional theological terms: God's essence is his existence. The concept "essence" is a sure sign that we are in the vicinity of ontology and metaphysics, and so we are, at least momentarily. Ontology has to do with categorizing the sort of reality beings have; metaphysics provides general categories with which to understand the whole system of created reality.[43]

When we look at the world stage in the light of Scripture, we see that God has both ordered creation (by separating the heavens above from the earth below, water from land) and filled it with various kinds of things (e.g., the sun, vegetation, fish, birds, land animals). Upon closer inspection, however, what we have on stage are not a collection of static disparate things but "a dynamic network of dispositional forces and habits."[44] Put differently: things have natures, but a thing's nature is its essential tendency to act in a certain way, according to the "law" of its being. Creatures are made "after their kind," with an abiding character that disposes them to present themselves according to their respective natures, in certain ways rather than others. Everything that exists communicates what it is (essence) simply by being what it is (i.e., acting in character).

To think of reality in this way is to approach a *dramatic* metaphysic in which the universe is a theater for reality, a staging area where everything that is, from magnesium to manatees, can be what it is and strut its "stuff." *Everything that is seeks to communicate itself insofar as it is possible, given its particular nature.* What populate reality are not static substances but active agents, personal and impersonal entities alike that act in character and communicate their nature through their characteristic activity. What we have on the world stage, then, are various kinds of beings presenting themselves to one another by acting out their existence and essence (i.e., *that* they are and *what* they are). To be is to *act out*, to communicate one's own particular existence. The universe is a network of entities that are constantly giving and receiving, acting on others and being acted on in return.

God has essential dispositions (nature) too, though he is no creature. God, who is Being itself, also has a self-communicating nature: "God is love" (1 John 4:8). Love is essentially communicative because its characteristic activity is sharing (i.e., *communicare* = making common) and self-giving for the sake of the other. It is God's nature always and everywhere to be in communicative activity.[45] God reveals his nature to Moses by revealing his name: "I AM WHO I AM" (Exod. 3:14). From this slim starting point, Thomas Aquinas derives what has been called the "metaphysics of the Exodus," namely, the idea that God is "Being itself." Aquinas's most basic metaphysical principle, according to some

---

43. Ancient philosophers considered metaphysics, the "science of presence" that studies what it means to *be*, to be "first philosophy," the most fundamental aspect.
44. This is Sang Hyun Lee's phrase to describe Jonathan Edwards's conception of reality (*The Philosophical Theology of Jonathan Edwards* [1988], expanded ed. [Princeton: Princeton University Press, 2000], 4).
45. For a fuller argument, see my *Remythologizing Theology*, esp. chap. 4. In making this claim I am standing on the shoulders of theological giants, esp. Thomas Aquinas and Jonathan Edwards. On Thomas, see W. Norris Clarke, *Explorations in Metaphysics: Being—God—Person* (Notre Dame, IN: University of Notre Dame Press, 1994). On Edwards, see William M. Schweitzer, *God Is a Communicative Being: Divine Communicativeness and Harmony in the Theology of Jonathan Edwards* (London: T&T Clark, 2012).

Thomists, amounts to just this: *"Action is the self-revelation of being."*[46] This principle accords well with what we see in Scripture too. Creation is the stage for a covenantal drama, for clearly the human creature is the crown and center (some would say "microcosm") of creation. Unlike other creatures that cannot help but act according to their natures, however, Adam and Eve were created with the fearsome ability to deny their true natures and deny their Creator. God created men and women with dispositions most like his own, including, in a limited (i.e., finite) measure, freedom. Though created for fellowship with God, the human creature has the mysterious ability to turn away.

The material principle underlying the drama of creation is the subject of the following chapter. At present we are concerned with the formal principle: *communicative action*. Communicative action is the heart of both the theater and metaphysics. It is the reason why there is something rather than nothing. Creation is the divinely designed space for the action of embodied creatures that interact with one another, and with God, in time. More particularly, it is the stage for the history of God's covenantal dealings with his human creatures. Make no mistake: for God to be who he is, God does not need the world. He has perfect life in and of himself: his light, life, and love circulate eternally in and between the Father, Son, and Spirit. Still, in his freedom God has decided not to keep his light, life, and love to himself but to share it with what is not-God: creation, and the human creature in particular.

God sets the stage by speaking the created order into being. Even more amazing: the God whose word spoke forth the universe verbally addresses particular human creatures. The stage-setting takes up a scant two chapters of the Bible. The vast majority of Scripture focuses on God's communicative initiatives to human beings (e.g., Adam, Abraham, Moses, Israel) and the way in which human beings respond (or fail to respond). Often these take the form of "the word of the LORD" coming to a particular individual. In the New Testament, however, the word of the Lord comes in the humanity of Jesus Christ, "the Word . . . made flesh" (John 1:14 KJV).

Creation as Stage for Divine-Human Communicative Interaction

We are now in a better position to see the appropriateness of the theatrical model. What both Scripture and Christianity highlight is the communicative action between the triune Creator God and human creatures: the dialogue between infinite and finite freedom. Even before we examine *what* actors say to one another, we can confidently say that communicative action, in word and deed, constitutes the primary form of dramatic action. Yes, it is important to know the stage upon which we play our existence. Yet what really counts is a grasp of the plot: what has been said and done? How should I now respond? With this query we return to where this chapter began: the contemporary crisis

---

46. Clarke, *Explorations in Metaphysics*, 45.

of authenticity in an age where apparently God no longer oversees the action in what has therefore become the not-so-great theater of the world.

Why is there something to say and do rather than nothing? Here is Jonathan Edwards's reply: "The great and universal end of God's creating the world was to communicate himself. God is a communicative being."[47] God has given human creatures the dignity of communicative causality, the godlike ability to *do* things by *saying*. More important, God has given human beings the privilege of responding to and participating in his own self-communication. As we shall see, this is indeed our most fundamental vocation: rightly to answer the call that called us into being. The drama of world history spotlights both the divine communicative initiative and the human response.

What kind of response, what kind of communicative action, is *authentically* human? One that fulfills the human vocation of corresponding to God's prior communicative initiatives. The proper response to a divine command, for example, is obedience; to a divine promise, trust; to a divine assertion, belief. Here the prophetic and apostolic word must be our guide, the chief criterion for discerning authentic human performances on the world stage. Just as authentic musical performance depends on recovering testimony of how early instruments were originally played, so disciples must rely on the apostolic testimony of those who first walked the Way. Even if they are not physically present to question, we can still discern what they would probably say about many, though not all, contemporary situations.

Authentic Being-in-Act

Is there "authenticity" in theatrical performance? If by authentic one means a historically accurate reproduction of an original performance, then the answer is probably "no." There are other ways of being true to the original than duplication (recall the "Living Bible"). Besides, the original audience, first-century Palestinian Jews, Samaritans, Romans, and others throughout the empire, is no longer here. Nevertheless, there are very good reasons to think that we can recover the Author's original intention for the play and very bad reasons for thinking that we could do better by filling the play with our own intentions, purposes, and points. In the words of one historian of the theater: "We ought to aim to mount them [revivals] in ways that might have made sense to their authors and original performers, not as mere pretexts for the display of our own theatrical virtuosity."[48]

For Heidegger, human beings achieve authentic existence when they resolutely face the inevitability of their own death and let that resolution color

---

47. Jonathan Edwards, *The "Miscellanies": Entry Nos. A–Z, AA–ZZ, 1–500*, A-500; in *The Works of Jonathan Edwards*, vol. 13, ed. Thomas A. Schafer (New Haven: Yale University Press, 1994), 410.

48. Jonas Barish, "Is There 'Authenticity' in Theatrical Performance?," *Modern Language Review* 89, no. 4 (1994): 831.

every other scene they play. Perhaps this is the best answer a philosopher can give to the question "Why is there something to do rather than nothing?" Theology, however, goes further. Indeed, one purpose of doctrine is to give disciples directions for achieving authentic existence: for being real, for becoming true to themselves (i.e., true to the design-plan of their Creator), and for following a way of life that rightly responds to the divine vocation that defines them. What doctrine gives disciples is testimony to *what is in Christ*, which includes everything one needs to know about true deity and true (i.e., authentic) humanity.

Disciples walk across the stage authentically when they speak understanding of Jesus Christ and follow his way. Jesus Christ is the paradigm for authentic human existence because he is the Logos made flesh, the Creator made creature. In his historical performance we therefore see how the original design plan was to have been fulfilled. We will examine the design plan, and Jesus' performance, in the next chapter. For the moment it suffices to call attention to the persona and work of Jesus as the criterion for discerning authentic existence. We learn from God's self-communication in Jesus that humans exist for fellowship with God and "the praise of his glory" (Eph. 1:12).

Jesus Christ is the preeminent "faithful and true witness," the one whose words and deeds communicate God's very being more than anyone else, because this same witness is also "the origin of God's creation" (Rev. 3:14), the original template, structure, and source through whom all things have their being (Col. 1:16). To his designated followers, Jesus commands, "You will be my witnesses" (Acts 1:8). As such, the apostles participate in Jesus' testimony about himself, handing on (*paradosis* - 1 Cor. 11:2; 2 Thess. 2:15) the communication of the Christ: "what we have heard, what we have seen with our eyes, what we have looked at and touched with our hands, concerning the word of life" (1 John 1:1). As the apostles extend the dominical communicative action, so disciples today, secondhand witnesses, extend the apostolic testimony.

The stage is thus set . . . for martyrdom. To be a martyr is first and foremost to be a witness, one who indicates, in life or death, *what is in Christ*. Martyrdom is indeed the authentic vocation of followers of Jesus and, indeed, of all human creatures and followers of Jesus: to bear witness to the great things God has done in all creation and preeminently in the history of Jesus Christ. Unlike Heidegger, who believed that authenticity was a matter of always being prepared for one's death scene, Christians must always be prepared to bear witness in the courtroom drama of world history, where the most important judgment to be made is whether Jesus is Lord.

And so it has been since the beginning. Soon after the apostles exited the stage, early Christians were summoned to court. In AD 180, a group that has come to be known as the Scillitan martyrs stood trial for sedition or, more exactly, for refusing to swear by "the genius of the emperor." A trial transcript records one Saturnis, a proconsul, urging the Christians, "Cease to be of this persuasion," to which Vertia responds, "I am a Christian," and Secunda, "What I am, that I wish to be." These early martyrs conceive their very being ("what I am") in terms of their identity in Christ: "Christian martyrdom is merely the working out, in particular circumstance, of the identity in which individual Christians participate."[49]

This is only one of many incidents mentioned in the "Acts of the Martyrs," official court records of early Christian martyrs. There were many acts to follow, and no doubt many yet to come. For being a Christian means giving one's life over to the task of bearing witness to the word that has given us life. Genuine discipleship and authentic Christian identity always involve martyrdom—bearing witness—in life and, if necessary, in death. In the final analysis, the world stage is a theater for Christian martyrdom where disciples demonstrate their understanding and authenticity by their Spirit-enabled ability to play scenes of being-toward-resurrection.

RECAPITULATION: THE CANONICAL IMPERATIVE

"Recapitulation," in the context of rhetoric, refers to an argument's final summation, the end of the speech where a speaker drives home his final points. Irenaeus applies the term to Jesus' life and work, not simply to say that Jesus repeats the history of Adam and Israel, doing right what they did wrong, but also that Jesus is the Father's "summary statement": "Christ is the Logos of the Father, the logic or purpose in and through which the whole divine economy is conceived and implemented."[50] Or, in terms of the present work: Christ is God in self-communicative action, a précis of the play of the world.

Here in similar fashion, I want to recapitulate the argument of the present chapter by calling attention to some aspect of *what is in Christ*. Doctrine waxes not only lyrical but also metaphysical when it sets forth *what is in Christ*. This is why doctrine matters: it is indicative of reality. Indeed, in ministering understanding of *what is in Christ*, theology ministers reality.

We began this chapter by reviewing the present situation of doctrine in the church. The crisis of doctrine today is in large part due to the perception that the traditional Christian doctrines are a step removed from the particulars of daily life. At the same time, doctrine is inevitable, and even the attempt to recapture the vitality of early Christian spirituality (i.e., "faith") ultimately involves beliefs about what is or is not the case. So does any attempt at personal transformation. Doctrine of some kind or another is inevitable.

I then claimed, following Calvin, that we can only interpret our experience correctly when we view it through the narrative lens of Scripture. I also argued that Scripture itself, as prophetic and apostolic testimony to Jesus Christ, participates in the Son's own communicative action (light from light). Implicit

---

49. Michael Jensen, *Martyrdom and Identity: The Self on Trial* (London: T&T Clark, 2010), 3.
50. R. R. Reno and John O'Keefe, *Sanctified Vision: An Introduction to Early Christian Interpretation of the Bible* (Baltimore: Johns Hopkins University Press, 2005), 39.

in this understanding of Scripture is the corresponding imperative: walk as children of light.

Nothing is more difficult, we said at the outset, than having to walk across an empty stage, especially when it is dark. The canonical imperative—to view God, the world stage, and oneself in the light of Scripture—is the normative specification of the disciple's walk. In short: Scripture provides the rule for walking across the stage of life. The canon provides normative guidance for both walking and talking the faith. It is not only a rule of faith, but also the rule for faith's understanding that obtains not only in the ancient Near East, but also in today's North America, Europe, the global South, and throughout the world.

The canonical imperative is simply another way of speaking about biblical authority. It is a way of recapitulating what the Reformers called *sola scriptura*. Scripture is to be the disciples' supreme authority *because* it sheds light on the One who is the light of the world and on all other beings in the world. Scripture is the *formal principle* that governs "faith speaking understanding." The canon helps us see that the world, far from being an empty space, is a formed place, a fitting stage for communicative action. The canon further aids us in understanding that the existence of human beings was not a random occurrence but part of God's eternal plan. Finally, the canon explains why there is something rather than nothing for humans to do: We have been called into being to bear witness to the goodness of God. Accordingly, the canon is also our rule of authenticity. It is the one word that defines us at the root of our being because it is the authorized word of the Author of all things.

The canonical imperative is not "do good, for God is God" but rather, "Do God's word, for God is God [i.e., the Creator]." The biblical canon is a rule not only of thumb but also of hand, head, and heart—a rule for the whole body and everything we do with it. The canon helps us know what to do in order to glorify God in everything. Last, the canon is the norm for Christian witness. Insofar as bearing witness means being a martyr, then we could well view the canon as a rule for martyrdom. These are the authoritative texts that direct Christians how to bear witness in word and act, life and death, to the realities indicated by the gospel of Jesus Christ.

This chapter has treated the *formal* aspects of Christian discipleship: the form of spatial-temporal life on stage, the formal principle of authority, the formal principle of the theater (i.e., communicative action). The forms are in place: the stage is set, the lights are lit. We turn now to consider the material principle of the great theater of the world: the covenantal history whereby the Father shows himself to be a loving Lord, the Spirit, the giver of Life, and the Son, the Light of the world, *King for us.*

Chapter 4

Gospel Theater

The Triune Drama of Redemption

> *Jesus said to them, "Very truly, I tell you, the Son can do nothing on his own, but only what he sees the Father doing; for whatever the Father does, the Son does likewise. The Father loves the Son and shows him all that he himself is doing; and he will show him greater works than these, so that you will be astonished."*
>
> — John 5:19–20

The doctrine of the Trinity is the beginning and end, the source and substance, of the Christian message of salvation. Stated provocatively: the doctrine of the Trinity is longhand for the gospel: the announcement that God has gone out of his way—out of himself, in the sense that he has poured himself out in self-giving love, in bone and blood—for us and our salvation.[1] Insofar as believers are united to Jesus Christ, they enjoy all the rights and privileges that pertain to the Son's sonship, and that means basking in the eternal love (communion), light (knowledge), and life (joy) of God the Father, Son, and Spirit.

The purpose of the present chapter is to spell out this claim in greater detail so that disciples will have a better idea of the nature of salvation, the raison d'être of Christian faith and the essence of Christianity. This requires going beyond the merely formal categories like communicative action that we examined in the last chapter to say what God has actually done. What is the substance, the material

---

1. Conversely, the gospel is "shorthand" for the doctrine of the Trinity, its temporal realization in the economy of redemption. For a more extended treatment of this idea in connection with an interpretation of John 5:19–20, see my "At Play in the Theodrama of the Lord: The Triune God of the Gospel," in *Theatrical Theology: Explorations in Performing the Faith*, ed. Trevor Hart and Wesley Vander Lugt (Eugene, OR: Cascade, 2014).

principle, of the drama of redemption? What kind of drama is it in which disciples play a part? It is impossible to answer these questions without invoking the doctrine of the Trinity. The principal claim set forth in this chapter is that the main action of the play of salvation, establishing covenantal communion, corresponds to God's eternal triune being. To anticipate: *God's mighty work in the history of redemption enacts the perfections of God's inner life.*

The play progressively resolves a dramatic mystery, the mystery of the gospel (Eph. 1:9–10; 3:9; 6:19): the answer to the paradox of how a righteous God could save the unrighteous while still remaining righteous is inexplicable apart from a consideration of the triune God. Indeed, this is how the doctrine of the Trinity emerged in the first place. The church fathers realized that the life and death and resurrection of Jesus could not have saving significance unless the incarnate Son was of the same substance (*homoousios*) with the Father. Take away the deity of Jesus, and the drama turns into a tragedy with a long scene of an innocent man being tortured.

What is the route from the heavenly bliss of the eternal God to the suffering of Jesus' death on the cross? Does it have anything to do with the way of the Christ that his disciples are to follow? There is an intimate connection between heaven and earth: God is God in both realms. And, as we shall see, there is even a certain dramatic dimension in God's perfect life, to the extent that the latter consists in *communicative action oriented to communion*. If "love makes the world go round," it is only because love "goes round," circulates, between the divine persons eternally. It is precisely into this circulation of love, light, and life that disciples enter when, through the Spirit, they act out *what is in Christ*.

We turn, then, to consider the manner in which the drama of redemption, *what has happened and now is in Christ*, is a Trinitarian affair. The previous chapter identified communicative action as the *formal principle* of the drama of redemption; now this chapter sets forth *covenant* and *kingdom* as the drama's chief material principles, the concrete form and telos of redemptive history.

We begin by thinking about the drama of redemption from the perspective of the divine playwright ("from above"). Because history was conceived in eternity, we begin "from above." We only know this retroactively because of what we have seen with our eyes, heard with our ears, and touched with our hands. Yet because the playwright conceived the play in eternity, it is appropriate to begin there, insofar as we can reconstruct it, as it were, from what we know by looking into the rearview mirror of redemptive history. The history of redemption represents, in time, the "drama" of God's own eternal Trinitarian being, the triune reality of God in himself, before the world stage even existed. Creation here appears as the theater of God's righteousness (i.e., covenant faithfulness). We then examine the other actors in the drama, particularly as they figure as communicative agents implicated in the covenant history of the coming kingdom.

The final section examines the drama of redemption from the perspective of those who have experienced its historical unfolding ("from below"). Here too we see that what gets played out in time is nothing less than the way God is in eternity. This is a crucial point, for it explains why doctrine gives disciples directions for "doing" heaven on earth: the whole drama of redemption turns on the ending entering into time. As we shall see, the purpose of the play is to ensure *communion* between players and Playwright. The main action of the play concerns the way in which the covenant Mediator—Jesus Christ, the Playwright become player—achieves this God-man communion. *What is in Christ* is nothing less than adoption into the triune life: a fellowship in the Son, through the Spirit, with the Father.

THE PLAY OF THE PLAYWRIGHT "FROM ABOVE": A DRAMA OF TRINITARIAN PROPORTIONS

Some readers, upon considering these things, may go away sorrowful, questioning whether anyone can know God as God is in himself. Such an attempt surely represents the worst kind of speculative theology: pointless, fruitless, and feckless. The concern is legitimate but in this case unwarranted, for I propose to begin not with an abstract concept of God as perfect being but with the particular way God demonstrates his perfection through his redemptive work. From God's self-presentation in history (*ad extra*), we extrapolate to God's perfection in himself (*in se*). In sum: we can only think about God's perfect triune life in eternity in the light—the afterglow, as it were—of the gospel, the revelation of God and his goodwill toward us displayed in and through the incarnation of Jesus Christ.

"And the Word Was God": The Eternal Communication of the Son

"In the beginning was the Word, and the Word was with God, and the Word was God" (John 1:1). If the Word was in the beginning, what was it saying, and to whom? To the old chestnut "What was God doing before creation?," is the correct answer *uttering a soliloquy*, "To be perfect being, or not to be"? As the history of Jesus eventually makes clear, the Word with God in the beginning also speaks *to* God. It is most significant in this regard that one of the most characteristic things the Son does while on earth is communicate with the Father (e.g., John 12:27–28). The way the Father and Son interact in time (i.e., the economy) corresponds to the relationship of Father and Son in eternity.

Is there "drama" in the Trinity? Yes, but only in the sense that there is communicative activity. Scripture depicts the life of the Father, Son, and Spirit as *perfect doing*: a "drama" than which nothing greater can be conceived, a ceaseless activity of free and loving communication ("making common") that makes for triune communion. The good news of the gospel is that human creatures too can share in this eternal fellowship. God's communicative activity resulting in communion, God's sharing his perfections, is the substance of salvation. The good news is triune: the Father shares his light, life, and love in the Son through the Spirit. But we are getting ahead of ourselves.

We gain a precious peek into God's inner life by attending to the communicative interaction of Father and Son in history, particularly where it is on conspicuous display in the Fourth Gospel. There are three main topics of conversation: mutual glorification, the giving of life, the sharing of love. Significantly, the dialogues "come at crucial moments in the narrative of the unfolding drama of the Trinity, and they mark the nodal points of the inner relations of the Trinity, worked out in time and space."[2] For example, we hear the Father addressing the Son as the Spirit descends upon Jesus at his baptism: "You are my Son, the beloved; with you I am well pleased" (Mark 1:11; cf. Luke 3:22; Matt. 3:17), or again at the theologically pregnant moment of Jesus' transfiguration (Matt. 17:1–5; Mark 9:2–8; Luke 9:28–36).

The voice of the Father is a comparatively rare occurrence in the New Testament. More often we overhear the Son addressing the Father. Before raising Lazarus from the dead, Jesus says, "Father, I thank you for having heard me" (John 11:41). When he realizes that the hour has come he prays, "Father, glorify your name" (12:28), only to be answered by a voice from heaven: "I have glorified it, and I will glorify it again." The Spirit, too, plays a communicative role. Jesus says, "He [the Spirit] will glorify me, because he will take what is mine and declare it to you" (John 16:14). As with everything God does, then, communicative action too is triune: a unified action with three aspects. The three persons are distinct communicative agents that nevertheless share the perfection of communicative agency in common.

Glorification is the communication of God's glory, the publication of God's excellence. It is also the main topic of Jesus' longest prayer, the high-priestly prayer of John 17, spoken on the eve of the drama's climax. What is striking is how Father and Son glorify, make known the glory of, one another: "Father, the hour has come; glorify your Son so that the Son may glorify you" (John 17:1). Tellingly, however, Jesus indicates that his historical glorification (being "lifted up" on the cross [John 3:14; 8:28; 12:32–33]) only makes known something he enjoyed in eternity: "So now, Father, glorify me in your own presence with the glory that I had in your presence before the world existed" (John 17:5). In the words of the seventeenth-century Scottish minister Robert Leighton: "It is most true of the Blessed Trinity, *Satis amplum alter alteri theatrum sumus* [each of us is to the other a theater large enough]."[3]

There is divine revelation because the way God is in the economy or history of salvation corresponds to the way God is in himself. The Father, Son, and Spirit are simply continuing, in time, the communicative activity that characterizes their eternal perfect life. The Word made flesh makes known the communicative activity that was with God and was God in the beginning. "God" is therefore the name for this common communicative (e.g., glorifying) being of the three

---

2. Oliver Davies, *A Theology of Compassion* (London: SCM Press, 2001), 199–200.
3. Robert Leighton, *The Whole Works of Archbishop Leighton*, vol. 1, *A Practical Commentary upon the First Epistle of Peter* (London: Ogle, Duncan & Co., 1820), 154, on 1 Pet. 1:23.

persons.[4] The Father-Son communications that we discover at key moments of Jesus' history are simply the communicative face of the perichoresis (mutual indwelling) that characterizes God's eternal triune being. This inner-Trinitarian conversation is perfect: there is complete union, and thus communion, between the communicants, in glorious contrast to the incomplete and broken nature of most human communicative ventures, verbal or otherwise.

Pactum Salutis: A More Excellent (and Dialogical) Decree?

The Son is not simply the Word that God speaks into human history but the Word that was with God from the beginning. The perfect life of God is an eternal fellowship of Father, Son, and Spirit: a mutual admiration society, a communion. God is light: the communicative activity (glorifying) by which Father, Son, and Spirit respectively publish their divine perfections. God is love: the communicative activity by which God as it were extends himself to share his life, everything he is and has, with others. God is life: the power of communicative action (i.e., the power to be and hence the power of self-presentation).

To say that God communicates his life, light, and love *by* his light, life, and love is to say that the Father communicates himself in the Son through the Spirit. For example, the Father eternally communicates his life to the Son (John 5:26). The Son is thus "the Author of life" (Acts 3:15) as the Spirit is "giver of life" (John 6:63). The Father does not "create" but "begets" the Son and "breathes" the Spirit. The technical term for such begetting and breathing is "processions": the Son and the Spirit eternally proceed from the Father, even while being fully God themselves. The life of God consists in these processions or relations. The point is that God, in himself, is fully alive: a triune communication of life.

The eternal life held out to those who put their faith in Jesus Christ (John 3:16) is just that: God's eternal life. The good news of the gospel is that God determined from eternity not to keep his own company only. It is this decision, this free self-determination on God's part to be with us and for us, that constitutes the ultimate basis and substance of the gospel. It is the drama *behind* the drama that gets played out in the history of salvation and, as such, it is worth investigating further. Insofar as all Christian doctrine has to do with God, it is absolutely vital that we acquire right knowledge of the one with whom we are dealing. We therefore need to clarify the fullness of God, the plenitude of his perfect life, in order to speak of how God acts (in time) as the one he is (in eternity).

In the beginning was the Word: not an indeterminate om, an empty divine mantra, but on the contrary a fulsome divine decree with gospel content, the "Yes" of Christ uttered "before the foundation of the world" (Eph. 1:4), God's eternal plan of salvation for the purpose of his glory. The divine decree is a far

---

4. In making this suggestion, I am but following in the footsteps of Jonathan Edwards. See Schweitzer, *God Is a Communicative Being*, esp. chap. 1.

cry from its frequent caricature as fatalistic determinism. This latter doctrine undermines discipleship altogether: Why bother *doing* anything if the results are fixed in advance? That way lie resignation and wretchedness. Better to view the decree as God's determination to extend his family: "He destined us for adoption as his children through Jesus Christ" (Eph. 1:5). Above all, the notion of a divine decree ensures that redemption was not a divine afterthought. Indeed, Jesus declares that he came from heaven "not to do my own will, but the will of him who sent me" (John 6:38).

There are good biblical reasons to expand the idea of an eternal divine decree in a more dialogical direction. This, at least, was the conclusion of post-Reformation Reformed theologians who discerned, through a careful reading of Scripture, a *pactum salutis* (i.e., the intra-Trinitarian "pact of salvation") between the Father and the Son. Consider, for example, Paul's reference to "the plan of the mystery hidden for ages in God, . . . in accordance with the eternal purpose that he has carried out in Christ Jesus our Lord" (Eph. 3:9, 11). To be sure, Scripture does not wear the notion of a *pactum salutis* on its sleeve, but like the doctrine of the Trinity, it appears to be a necessary implication of what is said explicitly.[5] Minimally, it says that both the Father and the Son freely formed a partnership, agreeing on a plan from before the foundation of the world that would be executed on the stage of space-time history: "You were ransomed . . . with the precious blood of Christ. . . . He was destined before the foundation of the world, but was revealed at the end of the ages for your sake" (1 Pet. 1:18–21). The *historia salutis* is thus the dramatic representation in space and time of the eternal *pactum salutis*. This is all to say that the eternal divine decree is dialogical, the work of more than one communicative agent.

What disciples need to know is that the gospel of salvation has an eternal foundation in the counsel of God. The triune God both keeps his own counsel and takes counsel within himself. The "pact" is a *covenant* of redemption, a solemn and binding agreement between Father and Son as to the particular form that God's saving righteousness will take in history.[6] The Son freely commits to taking on the role and obligations of human creatures (servant, son), including the consequences of their failure to fulfill these obligations ("No one takes it [my life] from me, but I lay it down of my own accord. I have power to lay it down, and I have power to take it up again. I have received this command from my Father" [John 10:18]). The Father freely commits to redeem the people the Son represents, to sustain the Son in his work, and to glorify him at its completion. It is not a contract but a coauthored *script*, an emplotted sequence of actions whereby Father and Son honor one another as they, together with the

---

5. See Richard A. Muller, "Toward the *Pactum Salutis*: Locating the Origins of a Concept," *Mid-America Journal of Theology* 18 (2007): 11–65.

6. Herman Bavinck describes the *pactum salutis* "as a covenant between the *three* persons in the divine being itself" (*Reformed Dogmatics*, vol. 3 [Grand Rapids: Baker Academic, 2006], 213, emphasis added).

Holy Spirit, move history toward a glorious conclusion: "that God may be all in all" (1 Cor. 15:28).

As mentioned earlier, there is solid exegetical ground for the idea of an "eternal covenant" of redemption (Heb. 13:20).[7] Bavinck's survey is particularly helpful, calling attention to the Son's status as God's servant who has been assigned a specific task (Isa. 53:10; John 6:38–40; 10:18; 12:49; 17:4), for which he receives a reward for the obedience accomplished (Isa. 53:10–12; John 17:24; Eph. 1:20–22; Phil. 2:9–11).[8] Further, Jesus is aware that the Father has conferred (Gk. *diatithemai* = to make a covenant) on him a kingdom (Luke 22:28–30), and Hebrews 7:20–22 refers to the oath-swearing (a covenantal sign) of Psalm 110:4, which testifies to God's having made the Son "a priest forever according to the order of Melchizedek."

It appears that the Son is reckoned a covenant mediator (e.g., priest, king) even before his incarnation. Indeed, the Son consents to being sent *before* the economy proper gets underway, *before* he takes on "the form of a slave" (Phil. 2:7). The incarnation is itself a part (the first part) of the outworking of the covenant of redemption (Phil. 2:6–7). Similarly, far from being an event that "overtook" Jesus or caught him by surprise, the cross is rather the climax of the covenant of redemption, the point at which the Son both completes his task and is "lifted up" (Phil. 2:7–8; John 3:14; 8:28; 12:32–33). In short: the Son determined to play the part of the crucified one before the foundation of the earth: "Vicarious satisfaction has its foundation in the counsel of the Triune God, in the life of supreme, perfect and eternal love, in the unshakable covenant of redemption. Based on the ordinances of that covenant, Christ takes the place of his own and exchanges their sin for his righteousness, their death for his life."[9]

The concept of the *pactum salutis* thus stands for the Trinitarian grounding *ad intra* (i.e., the covenant of redemption) of the Trinitarian work *ad extra* of salvation (i.e., the history of redemption). The drama of redemption is the historical outworking of God's promise to himself to be who he is (the Father, Son, and Spirit *for us*). This thought brings us to soteriological ground zero, the verge of salvation history. God's eternal triune being is not merely conversational but *covenantal*: "The pact of salvation made known to us the relationships and life of the three persons in the Divine Being as a covenantal life. . . . Here, within the Divine Being, the covenant flourishes to the full."[10] It is in this sense

---

7. Both Bavinck and John Webster, while proponents of the idea of a covenant of redemption, are aware of the risk of speculation when one tries to peer into eternity. Bavinck is dismissive of the 17th-century Reformed tendency to appeal to Zech. 6:13 as the locus classicus of the doctrine (*Reformed Dogmatics*, 2 [2004]: 213). Webster admits that the objections to the doctrine are substantial but insists that they are not decisive ("'It Was the Will of the Lord to Bruise Him': Soteriology and the Doctrine of God," in *God of Salvation: Soteriology in Theological Perspective*, ed. Ivor J. Davidson and Murray A. Rae [Farnham, UK: Ashgate, 2011], 29).

8. Bavinck, *Reformed Dogmatics*, 2:214.

9. Ibid., 406.

10. Ibid., 214.

that the *pactum salutis* expands the notion of the divine decree in a dialogical direction. Whereas the decree stresses the oneness of God (i.e., one will), the covenant of redemption highlights the three divine persons and the role in the plan of salvation apportioned to each.

What at first glance appears speculative—the notion of a covenant of redemption concluded in eternity—upon closer inspection becomes perhaps the best way to understand the love of God. Though some theologians complain that the covenant of redemption resembles a legal contract, it is more accurately viewed as a mutual commitment forged out of triune love for the lost (i.e., sinners) and for the creation in bondage to corruption (Rom. 8:20–22).[11] Furthermore, the covenant of redemption helps us better see the divine decree and the will of God in terms not of sheer cause but rather sovereign loving purpose, namely, God's self-determination to share his life with those who are not God while still retaining his perfections, including righteousness. What appears to be an intractable problem on the plane of history, how to reconcile divine sovereignty and human freedom, is resolved in eternity by the Son's free self-determination to accept the Father's sovereign will. In other words, in the covenant of redemption "the greatest freedom and the most perfect agreement coincide."[12] The covenant of redemption is a kind of script to which the Son is a willing conscript, and this primordial harmony of divine sovereignty and freedom continues on the plane of history when the Son, in his obedient humanity, freely says at the drama's climax, "Not my will but yours be done" (Luke 22:42).

The gospel is the execution and exhibition in time and space of what was freely decided in eternity. This is why the doctrine of the Trinity is good news. It is good news, first, because it informs us that God is not an impersonal causal force but is an interpersonal loving communion. What was God doing before he created the heavens and the earth? We are now in a position to hazard an answer: not "concocting hell for those who pry into mysteries," but rather *covenanting* our salvation. Second, the Trinity is good news because it informs us that God has chosen not to be God without us, for the Son determined from eternity to be *with us* in his humanity and *for us* in his death. Far from being speculative, then, the doctrine of the *pactum salutis* is a source of strength for disciples everywhere. Indeed, J. I. Packer claims that neither the gospel nor the Trinity nor Jesus Christ is properly understood until viewed in terms of the covenant: "In highlighting the thought that covenantal communion is the inner life of God, covenant theology makes the truth of the Trinity more meaningful than it can otherwise be."[13]

---

11. For a critical perspective, see Myk Habets, "The Doctrine of Election in Evangelical Calvinism: T. F. Torrance as a Case Study," *Irish Theological Quarterly* 73 (2008): 334–54.

12. Bavinck, *Reformed Dogmatics*, 2:215.

13. J. I. Packer, "Introduction" to Herman Witsius, *The Economy of the Covenants between God and Man: Comprehending a Complete Body of Divinity*, 2 vols. (repr., Escondido, CA: The den Dulk Christian Foundation, 1990), 1:9.

A Missional Drama of Trinitarian Processions and Proportions

There is one more doctrinal perspective from which to get a handle on the playwright's play "from above," that is, a view into the immanent life of God himself that is the ultimate ground of the drama of redemption, and it too contributes to a thick description of God's life (i.e., God's communicative activity). The technical term is "processions," but we can think of them as God's self-communication *ad intra* (in contrast to the "missions," which are self-communications *ad extra*). Again, it will be crucial to attend to Scripture as one ventures to say something about God's immanent life. To recall our key assumption: if Jesus is indeed the revelation of the Father, then the way God is in Christ corresponds to the way God is in himself.

How, then, is God in himself? To say that God "is" is to say that God exists, that he is living, which is to say that God is communicative in and of himself. God's being is communicative in the sense that it is a ceaseless sharing or making common of his light, life, and love. The perfect life of God consists in various personal relations: the Father's *begetting* the Son, the Son's *being begotten*, and the Spirit's *proceeding* from the Father and the Son. These relations of origin—paternity, filiation, spiration—*are* God's perfect life.[14] Think of them as forms of self-communication: the Father begets the Son by sharing his own being, by uttering a Word that is a mirror image or repetition of himself.[15] Each of these processions represents a way that God relates to himself, a form of his self-communication that is also a mode of God's unique perfection. As such, they form what Jonathan Edwards calls "the economy of the persons of the Trinity."[16]

The whole drama of redemption that results in *what is in Christ* has its root in God's perfect life in himself. That was the conclusion to our brief study of the *pactum salutis* above, and it is our claim here as well. Viewed "from above," from the perspective of the divine playwright, the drama of redemption is made up of a series of sendings or missions (from Lat. *missio* = sending) that originate with the Father. These divine missions, the "sendings" of the Son and Spirit that comprise the history of salvation, are but the historical realizations of the eternal processions. Consider: the "missions" are the Father's sending the Son, the Son's obedient going out, and the Spirit's being breathed out at Pentecost to sanctify, adopt, and perfect those who through faith are united to the Son. The missions correspond exactly to the eternal processions (i.e., begetting, being begotten, being spirated): "These missions repeat *ad extra* the relations *ad intra*."[17] The missions of the Son and Spirit are the acting out, in time, of what has been going

---

14. See John Webster, "God's Perfect Life," in *God's Life in Trinity*, ed. Miroslav Volf and Michael Welker (Minneapolis: Fortress Press, 2006), 143–52.

15. In all essential respects, the Son is the same as the Father: "very God from very God." The sole difference is that the Father begets and the Son is begotten.

16. Jonathan Edwards, *Discourse on the Trinity*, in *Writings on the Trinity, Grace, and Faith* (New Haven: Yale University Press, 2003), 135.

17. Webster, "Soteriology and the Doctrine of God," 26.

on in God's triune life eternally. They are *dramatico-historical representations* (for lack of a better term) of the eternal processions. To state it axiomatically: the economic Trinity *dramatically represents* the immanent Trinity.

Mission lies at the very heart of Christian thinking about God (and, we shall see, our thinking about the church). The triune God of the gospel is a missionary God who repeatedly goes out of himself, sending himself forth twice—first as the Son, then as the Spirit—for the sake of communicating and establishing fellowship with others. Viewed "from above," the drama of redemption is essentially missional: "Christ's mission is to use his life to reveal the Father. He is a word, expressing the Writer's thought, an Actor putting the Playwright's idea into action, and thus an idea which shows us the whole mind of the Writer."[18] The missions repeat in time and dramatically re-present the eternal processions.

The doctrine of the Trinity, in identifying the leading actors, is at the same time a précis of the whole drama. The divine dramatis personae, the processions that become missions, *are* the drama. God communicates himself, through himself, to what is not himself. What becomes played out, in time, is the perfection of God's eternal life: "What we encounter with concentrated historical force in Son and Spirit is the reality in time of a divine movement of sending which is itself the repetition of God's self."[19] The drama is trustworthy because it shows us God as God really is. What gets played (poured!) out on the stage of world history is nothing less than the heart of God: not Nietzsche's will to power but the triune God's will to communion.

That God who is fully and perfectly love in himself decided to extend that love still further is a mystery that exceeds our comprehension: "what wondrous love is this," that God freely communicates himself—his love, knowledge, and life—through himself. More wondrous still is the fact that Jesus wants to send his disciples to extend this circle of love even further. Make no mistake: disciples have been given the privilege and responsibility of participating in the triune mission and thus the drama of redemption. Hence comes our vocation, as disciples and as human beings, to participate rightly in a drama conceived in eternity and, when the time was right, played out in history.[20]

THE PLAYERS: HUMAN AND OTHER DRAMATIS PERSONAE

"God does not play the world drama all on his own; he makes room for man to join in the acting."[21] As we move from the eternal drama played out between the three divine persons to the historical drama that unfolds below, it is appropriate

---

18. Francesca Murphy, *The Comedy of Revelation* (Edinburgh: T&T Clark, 2000), 338.
19. Webster, "Soteriology and the Doctrine of God," 27.
20. Chapter 5 treats the nature of the individual's participation; chaps. 6–7 deal with the church's participation.
21. Hans Urs von Balthasar, *Theo-drama*, vol. 2, *The Dramatis Personae: Man in God* (San Francisco: Ignatius Press, 1990), 91.

to consider other players who figure prominently. In particular, we want to say something about what it is to be a person, for the interactive theater of the gospel is all about persons communicating and relating to one another. In the previous chapter I suggested that self-communicative action functions as a metaphysical principle, that everything on the stage of the world communicates its nature, either voluntarily or involuntarily. To speak of the dramatis personae of the theater of the gospel is to focus on one kind of creature in particular, however: *persons*. We have begun from above, with an exploration of divine personhood, in order to avoid projecting ideas of human personhood onto God.[22] For, as Karl Barth notes, "It is not God who is a person by extension, but we."[23]

This is not the place for a full-fledged theological anthropology. Here we deal only with what disciples need to know about their humanity in order to achieve self-understanding, which is to say, knowledge of themselves as actors in a divine drama. Later chapters will examine the doctrine of sanctification with respect to how human actors can play their parts well, participating rightly in the evangelical action.

Adam and His Children

Human life is dramatic: our very first line, usually uttered on a delivery room stage, is an inarticulate existential cry that, being translated, means, "I'm alive, help!" As we age, we continue to cry out: in helplessness, frustration, anger, and despair as well as in greeting, triumph, love, and delight. Disciples cry out too: "Lord, have mercy!" "He is risen!" "Come, Holy Spirit!" "Alleluia!" We cry out to others in the hope that we will be heard: "The cry is seen as a form of primary utterance in scripture and in life, a sign of intensity and importance, in itself a dramatic event that calls for wise discernment and response."[24]

Cry and response: the phenomenon gets us close to what defines us as persons created in the image of God. As we have seen, God's own triune life is one of communicative activity (e.g., glorification), even dialogue (e.g., the *pactum salutis*). Theologians have difficulty identifying a single trait that constitutes the *imago Dei*. It is dangerous to isolate one property, like rationality, as the sole definition of the image. Some theologians therefore work from another angle, arguing that we should be looking not for a particular property but at the relational nature of God. There are many kinds of relations, however: logical, causal, temporal, spatial, and so forth. Much harm has been done in thinking of other people as objects to be used instrumentally (e.g., in terms of "I-it"

---

22. This was the basic premise behind my *Remythologizing Theology*. The alternative is something like a Feuerbachian projection whereby human traits are predicated of God. In viewing God as personal, we are not speaking in anthropomorphic terms, for human personhood is itself derivative: theomorphic.

23. Karl Barth, *Church Dogmatics*, II/1, trans. Geoffrey Bromiley, (Edinburgh: T&T Clark, 1957), 272.

24. David F. Ford, *The Future of Christian Theology* (Oxford: Wiley-Blackwell, 2011), 55.

relations). Accordingly, the purpose of this brief section is to characterize the kind of activities and "I-Thou" relations characteristic of and distinct to persons.

Human beings are God's physical representatives on earth: living icons, statues of flesh standing in for the king, emissaries able to engage in the varieties of communicative action that characterize interpersonal covenantal relations. The concept of communicative agency is well suited both to preserve and to integrate the traditional emphasis on the image of God as rationality with the newer emphasis on relatedness. From the very beginning, Scripture records persons as presenting themselves to and engaging with one another by means of communicative action. The very first thing God does with the human creatures he created is address them with a command: "You may freely eat of every tree of the garden; but of the tree of the knowledge of good and evil you shall not eat" (Gen. 2:16–17). And later in the story, "The Lord God called to the man, and said to him, 'Where are you?'" (3:9).

God's addresses to various individuals (e.g., Abraham, Moses, David, the prophets) represent key developments in the biblical drama. Indeed, one of the typical forms of divine intervention is *interjection*: "Abraham!" (Gen. 22:1); "Jacob! Jacob!" (Gen. 46:2 NIV); "Moses! Moses!" (Exod. 3:4 NIV); "Samuel!" (1 Sam. 3:6); "Saul, Saul, why are you persecuting me?" (Acts 9:4); "Ananias!" (Acts 9:10 NIV). Let us draw a preliminary conclusion: to be a person is to be an answerable agent. A person is one who can respond to a call: "Here I am" (Gen. 22:1; Gen. 46:2; Exod. 3:4; 1 Sam. 3:6; Ps. 40:7; Isa. 6:8; Acts 9:10).

Paul Ricoeur's hermeneutic philosophy, his attempt to state the meaning of the "I am," relies on the notion of self-attestation.[25] According to Ricoeur, we come to understand ourselves as we attest our capacity to say and do things, not least in response to the words and deeds of others. These interactions with other persons come to take on the shape of a story. Persons are also able to recognize themselves as characters in a unified narrative that recounts the things one has done or suffered (i.e., the story of one's life). Narrative attestation means that I identify myself as the one who does things (i.e., take initiatives) and as the one to whom things are done: "We become the people we are as our identities are shaped through the patterns of communication and response in which we are engaged."[26] Being a person is less a matter of stating "I think, therefore I am" (Descartes) than of the way we habitually say (or fail to say) "Here I am." To be a person is to be answerable, and this implies being a communicative agent.

The theatrical model is well suited to this focus on the person as communicative agent. We need to go further, however, because communicative capacity is a merely formal notion. Yes, to be a person is to be answerable to God, but what has God said? To what kind of divine communicative initiative are human persons to respond? The answer should now be obvious. Just as the three persons in the Godhead covenanted together, so God *covenants* with his

---

25. See Paul Ricoeur, *Oneself as Another* (Chicago: University of Chicago Press, 1992).
26. Alistair I. McFayden, *The Call to Personhood: A Christian Theory of the Individual in Social Relationships* (Cambridge: Cambridge University Press, 1990), 7.

human interlocutors. The aforementioned divine interjections are for the most part aspects of covenantal discourse. Much, if not all, of what God says pertains in one sense or another to this or that covenant: its institution, administration, and culmination. In particular, the eternal election of a people in Christ gets dramatically played out in history as God elects a series of individuals and then a "nation" (Israel) to be his "treasured possession," through which "all the families of the earth shall be blessed" (Gen. 12:2–3; Exod. 19:5–6).

In sum: persons are *answerable agents in covenantal relation with others*.[27] This is true of divine and human persons alike. Theological anthropology views human persons as players in a divinely produced drama, as speakers and actors able to make communicative initiatives and covenantal responses.[28] Human persons are summoned by many others—parents by children, husbands by wives, friends by friends, judges by victims, and so forth—and achieve their particular characters in their patterns of response. God too summons human actors, often by name, to take part in the action. Everything thus depends on whether and how the creature responds to the call of its Creator. The call is covenantal: "Come, let us be together." Because they are in God's image, human persons cannot be autonomous individuals. For *sharing* with others is implicit in the very concept of communicative agency. Human persons are communicative subjects in covenantal relation *designed for communion*, with God and with one another. Everything in the drama thus depends on how the human creature responds to the words of others and, in particular, how Spirit-empowered believers respond to God's covenantal word. Will the human creature play its designated part, keeping words as covenant keepers, or breaking words as covenant breakers?

Jesus Christ and His Ministering Angels

Whether humans would keep covenant was a rhetorical question. We know that human persons have violated their true natures by turning a deaf ear and disobedient heart to the divine address. Human persons have contradicted their natures by refusing to let God's word "sound through" them (*per + sonare* = to sound through): everyone refused except for one, our Savior, Jesus Christ. Jesus Christ is both God's fulfilled promise and humanity's right response. As the God-man covenant mediator, Jesus Christ fulfills both sides of the covenantal relation through his distinct communicative activity.

In the first place, Jesus is God's own word, "the image of God" (2 Cor. 4:4), very God of very God, God the Son incarnate. As such, he is the fulfillment of the protevangelium, the promise God made to Adam and Eve that Eve's

---

27. There is a sense in which all communication is covenantal inasmuch as entering into conversation with someone implies that we agree to abide by what I have elsewhere termed the "covenant of discourse" (see my "From Speech Acts to Scripture Acts: The Covenant of Discourse and the Discourse of the Covenant," in *After Pentecost: Philosophy and Theology of Language and Biblical interpretation*, ed. Craig Bartholomew [Grand Rapids: Zondervan, 2001], 1–49).

28. See further my "Human Being, Individual and Social," in *The Cambridge Companion to Christian Doctrine*, ed. Colin Gunton (Cambridge: Cambridge University Press, 1997), 158–88.

seed will crush the serpent's head (Gen. 3:15). Jesus is what makes good God's promise to Abraham to establish an everlasting covenant to be God to Abraham and his descendants (Gen. 17:6–8). He is realization of God's word to David to establish from his line a kingdom that would have no end (2 Sam. 7:12–14). Jesus is the vindication of God's self-naming as the one who is "abounding in steadfast love and faithfulness" (Exod. 34:6; cf. John 1:14). The drama of the Christ shows the lengths to which God freely goes to bind himself to his word. If "our word is our bond," how much more is that the case with the Word that is God: Jesus is the promise-keeping of God made flesh, made good, made gospel.

Jesus is also the fully human word of obedient response and hence the exemplar of true humanity. In assuming humanity, the eternal Son had a genuine human experience, lived an authentic human history: "For we have not a high priest who is unable to sympathize with our weaknesses, but we have one who in every respect has been tested as we are, yet without sin" (Heb. 4:15). Jesus' communicative action was consistently truthful: "No deceit was found in his mouth" (1 Pet. 2:22). Because Jesus, unlike Adam and everyone else, kept covenant with God, he is the "image of the man of heaven" (1 Cor. 15:49). Better: the life that Jesus acts out on earth is the exact representation of the drama that subsists in God's own eternal being. As we shall see, Jesus is the exemplary person whose faithful communicative actions maintain right covenantal relations, thus proving to be the crucial factor in the drama of redemption.

To this point, we have argued that persons are answerable agents who make communicative initiatives and respond to the initiatives of others. In addition to God and human persons, there is another class of players, "a little higher" than the humans (cf. Heb. 2:7, 9). Angels from time to time appear as actors in crucial scenes of the drama of redemption. The absence of narratives about angels is noteworthy. Angels are supporting actors, marginal figures but nevertheless truly *supporting* inasmuch as their role often seems to consist of reinforcing the divine communicative action. Karl Barth's comment is apt: "They do not exist and act independently or autonomously. They have no history or aims or achievements of their own."[29]

According to the Scriptures, the raison d'être of angels is to minister and magnify God's own communicative action. Their primary role is that of herald, announcing what God is doing, may do, or will do. Thus an angel informs Abraham and Sarah of the birth of Isaac, prefiguring the annunciation to Mary of the birth of Jesus, an event later confirmed by a whole choir of angels (Luke 2:10–11). Angels were also the first communicative agents on the scene of Jesus' resurrection (Matt. 28:5–7; Luke 24:4–7) and later his ascension (Acts 1:10–11). In general, they seem to speed the church's ministry of the word (Acts 5:19; 8:26; 10:22; 16:9). It is also an angel who heralds the vision of the drama's end

---

29. Barth, *Church Dogmatics*, III/3, trans. Geoffrey Bromiley (Edinburgh: T&T Clark, 1961), 480.

(Rev. 1:1). Barth rightly notes that angels are "the heavenly entourage of the God who acts from heaven to earth."[30]

Satan and His Minions

There is one more group of players to consider. What exactly should we say about Satan and his messengers (i.e., the demons)? Are they persons too? At least one demon in addition to Satan has a name ("Legion" [Mark 5:9; Luke 8:30]), and Satan has an important speaking part in the drama. Indeed, Satan is largely responsible for the conflict that propels the drama forward. As a first approximation, we might say that Satan and his minions are communicative agents oriented to covenantal discord and division. However, even this is to pay the devil too great a compliment.

If Satan and his minions are to be viewed as persons, then it is only because they possess a peculiarly improper or corrupt kind of communicative agency. The very first words that Satan uttered in the garden sowed distrust: "Did God say?" (Gen. 3:1; cf. Rev. 12:9). Then, like toddlers who resist parental authority, Satan said *no*: "You will not die" (3:4). Satan's third speech act conjured up an alternative reality: "You will be like God, knowing good and evil" (3:5). In each case, Satan craftily questions God's word, the same word that had just ordered creation and created Adam and Eve. Satan's verbal ploys are nothing short of an assault on the Creator and created order alike.

True words represent reality. Satan's words deny and distort reality. This is why Jesus can say of Satan that he "does not stand in the truth, because there is no truth in him. When he lies, he speaks according to his own nature, for he is a liar and the father of lies" (John 8:44). It is precisely for this reason that Satan's communicative agency is not only ethically wrong but also ontologically improper. Lies bring to mind things that fail to correspond to anything real. A lie is a misbegotten, short-circuited speech act whose utterance (what one claims to be true) contradicts what one conceives (what one knows to be false). The lie is oriented not to *what is* but to *what is not*. To "exchange the truth for a lie" (Rom. 1:25) is thus to orient oneself to nothing of lasting substance.

Satan is indeed a player in the drama, yet his performance is uniformly negative. Satan's "agency" is defective; all he can do is deceive and dissemble. Paul warns the Corinthians that "Satan disguises himself as an angel of light" (2 Cor. 11:14). These disguises are rhetorical ploys, for what insinuates itself into the drama of redemption is *disinformation*. In the parable of the Sower, for example, Jesus depicts Satan as disrupting the economy of communication: "When they [i.e., people newly exposed to the gospel] hear, Satan immediately comes and takes away the word that is sown in them" (Mark 4:15).

The one concrete message that Satan communicated was itself a corruption of the truth: the devil "put it into the heart of Judas . . . to betray him [Jesus]"

---

30. Ibid., 451.

(John 13:2). This speech act too was only parasitic: instead of handing Jesus *on,* as in apostolic tradition, Judas in Luke 22:28 hands him *over,* as in betrayal (the Greek term, *paradidomi,* is the same). That Satan continues to bring about infelicitous speech acts even after Jesus' resurrection is evident in Peter's pointed question to Ananias: "Why has Satan filled your heart to lie to the Holy Spirit and to keep back part of the proceeds of the land?" (Acts 5:3). Lies, lies, and more lies (John 8:44).

Satan's communicative agency is defective yet effective. On the one hand, he is unable to state the truth, to produce a felicitous speech act, or to bring about understanding. On the other hand, he is able to dissuade people from the true, the good, and the beautiful. His communicative acts do not bring about understanding, but they do produce results. This is, as I have indicated, a strange, improper form of personhood. Indeed, we might say that Satan disguises himself as a communicative agent but is actually only a manipulator. For, strictly speaking, liars do not communicate ("make common"), for they hold back with the left half of their forked tongue what they offer with their right. What the liar "makes common" is but smoke and mirrors, mere pretense. The discourse of the liar is the static that distorts genuine communicative action, the noise that interferes with true understanding.[31]

Satan therefore has no *positive* communicative agency. He has no causal power to compel obedience, only a cunning power that presents opportunities for corruption. Satan can do nothing with words but gesture vainly. How then shall we interpret Paul's ascribing "power" to Satan (2 Thess. 2:9a)? Upon closer inspection we see that it is no true power at all, only the power of nothingness, the power of illusion, "signs, lying wonders, and every kind of wicked deception" (2 Thess. 2:9b–10). Yet Paul also warns Timothy about some who will depart from the faith "by paying attention to deceitful spirits and teachings of demons" (1 Tim. 4:1).

It is Satan's counterfeit communicative agency that accounts for the original and ongoing conflict in the drama. Satan's words tempted Adam and Eve to disobey God. After the fall, distrust of God's word and disobedience to God's word became second nature to the human creature. The people of Israel failed to respond rightly to God's word, as did its kings. Both people and kings failed again even when confronted by the Word incarnate. But Jesus Christ did not fail. He too was tempted in the wilderness for forty temporal units (days, not years) but responded rightly, using the word of God to ward off the wiles of the devil (Luke 4:4, 8, 12).

Satan's communicative agency is pathological, a conjuring trick with words. Nevertheless, though it lacks positive being, it remains a paradoxical factor in the drama, hence disciples must remain vigilant: "But I am afraid that as the

---

31. When Paul speaks about "principalities and powers," he is often thinking about the destructive and enslaving effect of idolatry, which is another kind of lie inasmuch as it solicits devotion to what is-not. See the discussion in Timothy Gombis, *The Drama of Ephesians: Participating in the Triumph of God* (Downers Grove, IL: InterVarsity Press, 2010), 44–48.

serpent deceived Eve by its cunning, your thoughts will be led astray from a sincere and pure devotion to Jesus Christ" (2 Cor. 11:3). Gregory of Nyssa believed that Satan was defeated by his own medicine: Jesus' apparent weakness in Gethsemane deceived Satan into thinking that he could defeat Jesus and keep his prisoner in Sheol. On this view, Satan's "fall" in a garden (Gethsemane, not Eden) was only poetic justice, not to mention dramatic irony: "The emphasis on Christ's deception of the devil in the garden of Gethsemane, which seems to detract from the centrality of the crucifixion, is in fact a typological requirement intended to mirror and thus reverse the *devil's* deception of Eve in the garden of Eden."[32]

THE PLAY OF THE PLAYWRIGHT "FROM BELOW": A COURTROOM DRAMA OF KINGDOM AND KINSHIP

The essence of Christianity is neither metaphysical nor moral but dramatic: in history the triune God executes the plan conceived in eternity, speaking and acting in order to redeem humanity and restore creation. The gospel displays an act than which none greater can be conceived or dramatized.

To this point we have examined the triune drama of redemption from the perspective of the eternal triune decree (i.e., "from above") and introduced the major dramatis personae who will play out the drama in history. Now we turn to examine the play from a human and historical point of view (i.e., "from below"), where the focus is on the execution of the plan of salvation in history: this is speaking of the *economic* Trinity rather than the immanent Trinity. What is of the utmost importance to keep in mind, however, is the continuing fundamental importance of the Trinity, only now it is the *missions* of Son and Spirit (and thus the history of Jesus Christ) rather than their eternal *processions* that take center stage. We must also keep in mind that we are dealing with one drama that has two aspects, not with two different dramas: it is precisely the eternal God, complete in himself, who enters into our history to offer us eternal life.

How, then, are the two perspectives on the drama of redemption (from above, from below) related? This is a subtle question that pertains to the relationship of the immanent to the economic Trinity (i.e., God *in se* and God *ad extra*) and of eternity to time. It is wrong to speak of *two* dramas, as if the one (economic) were not the outworking of the other (immanent). It is also incorrect to think that the dramas are numerically identical, for this would collapse eternity into what happens in time, and fuse God's being (without remainder) into his historical becoming. Eternity is the sphere of God's life (i.e., the sharing of God's knowledge, love, and joy between Father, Son, and Spirit). By way of contrast,

---

32. Nicholas Constas, "The Last Temptation of Satan: Divine Deception in Greek Patristic Interpretations of the Passion Narratives," *Harvard Theological Review* 97 (2004): 155.

time is the sphere of God's communicative action in relation to creation: time is the "space," as it were, for finite existence.[33] Both time and eternity, then, are forms of communicative action. The triune eternal communicative action (i.e., the *pactum salutis*) thus corresponds to the triune historical communicative action (i.e., the *historia salutis*). Some might call this correspondence relation "analogy," in which case we could speak of the *analogia dramatis*: the play "from below" is analogous to the play "from above."

C. S. Lewis approaches the question from a different though complementary direction, in terms of causes rather than communications: "Did Ophelia die because Shakespeare for poetic reasons wanted her to die at that moment—or because the branch broke? I think one would have to say, 'For both reasons.' Every event in the play happens as a result of other events in the play, but also every event happens because the poet wants it to happen. All events in the play are Shakespearian events; similarly all events in the real world are providential events."[34] On this view, the drama of redemption is the playwright realizing his "poetic" intention through the providential ordering of historical events.

The purpose of this section is to examine this providential ordering as it has been played out in the crucible of history. Clearly, the mission of the Son was the salvation of the world, and somehow Jesus' death and resurrection were crucial to accomplishing this mission. But why? What is happening in the history of Israel and in Jesus' history? How ought we to understand the playwright's play "from below"? To answer these questions, we had best turn to the testimony of the prophets and apostles.

"Then beginning with Moses and all the prophets, he interpreted to them the things about himself in all the scriptures" (Luke 24:27). One thing is already clear: the play presents *what is in Christ*. I have used this phrase on several occasions, but to this point I have said only that it is indicative of reality. We can now be more precise. The content of *what is in Christ* is nothing less than true deity and true humanity. What we come to know when we see *what is in Christ* is the full measure of the love of God and the full stature of his human image. We come to learn about the reality of God's nature and human nature and about the reality of the relationship between the two. *What is in Christ* is nothing less than the prime theological truth, the most important indicative of all.

Entrances, Exits, and Returns: Between Earth and Heaven, History and Eschatology

At its most basic level, the theodrama is a matter of the historical entrances and exoduses of God. The action of the drama of redemption is largely made up of comings and goings (and returns). The first premise of Christian theology is

---

33. Even nonorganic entities like radioactive isotopes require time to be what they are (i.e., "communicate" their natures) and to decay. Uranium-238, e.g., has a "half-life" of about 4.5 billion years.

34. C. S. Lewis, *Miracles* (New York: HarperCollins, 1996), 221.

that God *can* enter into the world because he *has* done so in Jesus Christ. Yet in Scripture it is clear from the start that the God who created the heavens and the earth is free to come and go as he pleases. This is what it means to be Lord of space and time. The Bible regularly depicts God as entering into communicative contact, even conversation, with a number of human individuals (e.g., Adam, Noah, Abraham), prophets, priests, kings, as well as the whole people of Israel. On occasion there are visual cues to God's presence and activity (e.g., the pillar of fire that led Israel), but most often what enters the human stage is the word of the Lord (e.g., "the word of the LORD came to . . ."). All the more reason to attend to the appearance of Jesus on the scene, the word of the Lord become *flesh* (John 1:14).

"He came down from heaven" (John 3:13 KJV). There are other things that Scripture depicts as entering the world stage from heaven. In addition to God's "voice from heaven" (Dan. 4:31; Matt. 3:17), we read of manna come down from heaven in blessing (Exod. 16:4) as well as fire from heaven come down in judgment (2 Kgs. 1:12). The manna and the fire are placeholders for the Son's entry from heaven: Jesus is "the bread of life" (John 6:31–35) as well as the one upon whom the terrible cup of God's wrath is poured out on the cross (Rom. 1:18; Isa. 51:22; Matt. 26:39).

Where is heaven? Is it literally "up" there? The psalmist declares, "The LORD looks down from heaven on humankind, to see if there are any who are wise" (Ps. 14:2). The medieval morality plays took this image literally, installing God in heaven on a platform above the stage, which represented earth. It is true that Scripture often uses the term "heaven" to refer to the physical sky and the entities (e.g., sun, stars) found there (Gen. 1:20, 17), but the Son entered the earthly stage by descending bodily, not from the sky but "from David according to the flesh" (Rom. 1:3). "Heaven" is also the term for God's abode, the immaterial "place" where God and his angels dwell. We cannot locate heaven on a map, however, nor can we speak confidently about its metaphysics.

Heaven and eternity stand to God's presence and activity as space and time do for our only human presence and activity. In each case, the former provides the "place" for communicative activity—divine and human existence respectively. It would be a grave mistake, however, to think that God's existence is *on the same level* as human existence. On the contrary, the Creator is utterly distinct from the created order, for the triune God has life in himself, whereas everything creaturely depends on God's breath to sustain its existence.

Where is heaven? Though there is an absolute distinction between Creator and creation, there is also a relation between them: the Creator is able to enter into creation, thanks to the missions of Son and Spirit. If heaven is the place where God dwells, and if God can make his dwelling on earth, then we should not think of heaven and earth as entirely distinct. We should not think of heaven as an entirely remote place that has nothing to do with life on earth. Rather, heaven names the place where God's will is joyfully done. It is the future ("the age to come") for which we hope. Perhaps, in this sense, the right question to ask is "*When* is heaven?"[35]

The entrances of the Son and Spirit from heaven may be less "from above" than "from the end." In both the Old and New Testaments, the people of God set their hope on the great act of restoration that God promised to do in the future. Heaven is another way of thinking about "the age to come," when the evils of the present age would be no more. When Jesus "came down from heaven," he brought a bit of heaven with him. The bulk of Jesus' teaching in the Gospel of Matthew concerns the kingdom of heaven. The kingdom is not only "at hand" but also "upon" those who witness Jesus' kingdom-indicating miracles (Matt. 12:28; Luke 11:20 RSV). When John the Baptist's disciples ask Jesus if he is indeed "the one who is to come" (Luke 7:19), the Messiah on whom Israel has set its hope, Jesus answers not with words but deeds: he cured many of disease, cast out demons, gave sight to the blind, and raised the dead (Luke 7:21–22). Through these works, Jesus was beginning to bring heaven to earth, the end of time (eschatology) into the middle (history).[36]

The entrance of the Son in the incarnation is the climactic, but not exclusive, entrance of God onto the stage of world history. There are also some dramatic exits, or exoduses. The great saving event of the Old Testament was an exodus out of Egypt. The great saving event in the New Testament is the "departure" (Gk. *exodus*) Jesus makes in Jerusalem, a euphemism for his death on a cross (Luke 9:31).[37] There is therefore a "gospel" in Exodus and an "exodus" in the Gospels. In each case, the mighty saving act of God takes the form of an "exit." The first exodus, God's miraculous delivery of Israel from its oppression in Egypt, was an event of high drama, a long-awaited fulfillment of God's earlier promise to Abraham. Yahweh promises deliverance (Exod. 3:7–8) and delivers on his promise (Deut. 20:1). The exodus is not simply a great escape but the event in which God creates a people for himself: a "treasured possession" (Exod. 19:5) and "holy nation" (19:6). The exodus is not only a saving event but also a saving relationship. The exodus thus becomes the single act that, more than any other, serves to identify the God of Israel: "I am the LORD your God, who brought you out of the land of Egypt, out of the house of slavery" (Exod. 20:2).

Israel's exodus from Egypt turns out to be only a preview of an even greater saving event: the cross. This "new exodus," like the original, is God's mighty saving act. Indeed, Jesus' dramatic exit is arguably the high point of the drama, or would have been, except that he *returns*. The gospel is the message that the crucified one *is risen* (Luke 24:34). The one who has departed has returned,

---

35. See N. T. Wright, *Surprised by Hope: Rethinking Heaven, the Resurrection, and the Mission of the Church* (New York: HarperCollins, 2008).

36. Wolfhart Pannenberg exceeds others in describing Jesus' resurrection as an actual anticipation of the end of history. See his *Basic Questions in Theology*, vol. 1 (Philadelphia: Fortress Press, 1970), chap. 2.

37. See Michael Parsons, *The Departure of Jesus in Luke–Acts*, JSNTSup 21 (Sheffield: Sheffield Academic Press, 1987).

making an exit and entrance that stand somehow as crucial pivot points in the plan of salvation (more on this in the following section).

Jesus' resurrection from the dead is not yet the end of the play, only the beginning of the end. There are more exits and entrances to come. For example, after forty days with his disciples, Jesus leaves them again: "While he was blessing them, he withdrew from them and was carried up into heaven" (Luke 24:51). Jesus had explained to his disciples why it was to their advantage that he "go away": if he did not go away, "the Advocate" (i.e., the Holy Spirit) would not come (John 16:7). The ascension-exit of Jesus thus makes possible the entry, the *mission*, of the Holy Spirit, recorded in Acts 2 in the story of Pentecost. Notice that it is Jesus' cross, resurrection, and ascension that enable him to return to heaven, there to pour out the Spirit: "If I go, I will send him to you" (John 16:7).[38] What appear to us, from below, as entrances and exoduses are, viewed from above, the result of heavenly sendings (i.e., missions).

That the risen Jesus ascended into heaven means that he is now in heaven in bodily form. This does not mean that we can pinpoint Jesus' location in our universe. Rather, as we have seen, heaven is the place of God's abode. Heaven and earth are not two regions on the same space-time continuum but two different dimensions that, because God is sovereign Creator, overlap and intersect. It is precisely because Jesus is raised and ascended into heaven that he is really *present* everywhere on earth, though his presence is not discernible by the capacities of the present age. God's presence and activity is of a different, eschatological order, partaking of a different kind of space-time, yet it is able to make a difference in our spatio-temporal order: a telltale sign that it is real. As we shall see, heaven becomes real on earth to the extent that God's word and Spirit begin to rule in human hearts.

The drama of redemption ends not with an exit but with a final reentry. After Jesus' ascension, Luke reports that two men in white robes inform the disciples, "This Jesus, who was taken up from you into heaven, will come in the same way as you saw him go into heaven" (Acts 1:11). With the apostles, Christians now await "the blessed hope and the manifestation of the glory of our great God and Savior, Jesus Christ" (Titus 2:13). The drama of redemption will draw to a spectacular close when the risen and ascended Jesus comes again, this time *with* heaven. In the words of the Nicene Creed: "He will come again, . . . and his kingdom will have no end." Eschatology too is part of the gospel. The good news includes the idea that Christ will come again, bringing heaven to earth in a way that realizes God's original good purpose for creation.

For present purposes, the significant point is that the drama or economy of redemption is an ordered sequence of comings and goings, entrances and exits from the world stage. The theodrama is the story of God's triune being freely extending itself in order to communicate God's light, life, and love to

---

38. For a theological reflection on the significance of the ascension, see Douglas Farrow, *Ascension Theology* (London and New York: T&T Clark, 2011).

creatures, so that they in turn could give themselves to God and one another. The drama turns on God's triune mission to the world, his two-handed outreach to a creation that had spurned him. The drama is about how the human players, notably Israel, respond to the mission, and in particular to the words (and Word) sent from God. Now we turn to examine the way these various comings and goings can be viewed as a unified action. Yes, there are important entrances and exits, but what kind of drama is it?

Exploring the Divine Comedy

What Kind of Play?

The goal of the present section is to characterize God's triune mission to the world in terms of the biblical story line. How do the biblical authors think about God's plan of salvation as they experience it from below? Is the conflict resolved and, if so, how? What kind of play, in general terms, describes the various comings and goings?

The best-known form of serious drama is tragedy. Both ancient and modern tragedies wrestle with the fundamental questions of human existence, in particular that of suffering, both deserved and undeserved. In ancient tragedy, the tragic hero is no match for hostile gods or impassive Fate, yet nevertheless displays courage in the face of impossible odds. This stance comes close to Heidegger's notion of authentic existence as the resolute facing of being-toward-death. In tragedy, the universe either conspires against us (ancient) or is indifferent to our plight (modern). The climax is the tragic event or catastrophe that befalls the central figure, prompting the audience to react in fear and pity.

The story of God's missionary outreach to the world is not a tragedy. True, the central figure does suffer unjustly (even Pilate thinks Jesus is innocent), but the play ultimately does not end with blood on the stage. In spite of the cross, the drama of the Christ is no tragedy. It is no tragedy because Jesus' life is not taken from him but freely laid down (John 10:17–18). Moreover, Jesus' death loses its sting when the Father vindicates him by raising him from the dead, the first step in putting all injustice to rights (1 Cor. 15:55).

Comedies too can be serious dramas that examine the human condition. Whereas tragedies often deal with the nobility or royalty (e.g., *King Lear*), comedy treats commoners, or makes the noble appear more common. One of the characteristic aspects of comedy is the tendency to bring the proud down a notch, though in a kinder, gentler fashion than tragedy. Comedy often turns social conventions on their heads; indeed, such comic inversion is often the focus of the play. The divine comedy of Christ's exchanging the form of God for the form of a slave (Phil. 2:5–8) represents the greatest inversion of all. The difference between comedy and tragedy is, in the final analysis, a matter of endings: tragedy begins well but ends badly; comedy begins with a complication but ends well—in this case, with every knee in heaven and on earth bending at, and every tongue confessing, the name of Jesus Christ as Lord (Phil. 2:10–11).

If I belabor the point, it is because disciples should know what kind of drama they are playing. Yes, bad things happen to good people, but in the end, all things will be well because subject to God, so that "God will be all in all" (1 Cor. 15:28). What lies at the heart of the drama, the cross, is not a catastrophe but what J. R. R. Tolkien terms a *eucatastrophe*: a cataclysmic event with a *beneficial* effect (we shall return to that *eu-* in due course).[39] The news is good (*euangelion*, gospel) because a good than which nothing greater can be dramatized has been done: "In Christ God was reconciling the world to himself" (2 Cor. 5:19). Moreover, the way God reconciles the world to himself is comical because it completely subverts expectations, as well as the prevailing social orders. Disciples who participate in the subversive divine comedy may well find themselves accused of "turning the world upside down" (Acts 17:6). Finally, like many other comedies, this one too ends with a wedding: the marriage of the Lamb (Rev. 19:7, 9).

How Many Acts? Plotting the Drama

It is not surprising that a number of biblical theologians have adopted the rubric "drama of redemption." Though the Bible itself does not use the category "drama," the key ingredients are there, as we have seen. *Drama* does a particularly good job at focusing on the story line of salvation history, so much so that a number of scholars have suggested that the biblical drama may be divided up into various "acts."

The biblical roots for recounting the various acts in the drama of redemption may go back to ancient Israel, to doxology rather than dogmatics: "I will tell of all your wonderful deeds" (Ps. 9:1). In particular, Israel was to remember not only the divine commands and covenants but also what the Lord did: to Pharaoh and all Egypt (Deut. 7:18), to Israel during the forty years of wilderness wanderings (8:2), to Israel as punishment for covenant disobedience. The clearest example of a recital of God's mighty acts in the Old Testament is Joshua 24:1–18 (cf. Pss.78; 106; Ezek. 20).

Several speeches in the book of Acts bring the narrative up to date, notably Peter's Pentecost sermon (2:14–36) and Stephen's martyr speech (7:2–53), by relating God's mighty acts in the history of Israel to the history of Jesus.[40] Some of Paul's Epistles appear to contain elements of creedal traditions that sum up the most important new developments in the drama. For example, Paul mentions four stages in the Christ event: "Christ died for our sins, . . . was buried, . . . was raised on the third day, . . . appeared to Cephas, then to the twelve" (1 Cor. 15:3–5). Other such Pauline passages include Christ's incarnation (Phil. 2:6–7) and role in creation (Col. 1:15–16). Just how many "acts" are there in the theodrama?

---

39. J. R. R. Tolkien, "On Faith Stories," in *Essays Presented to Charles Williams*, ed. C. S. Lewis (Grand Rapids: Wm. B. Eerdmans Publishing Co., 1966), 81.
40. Simon J. Kistemaker counts 26 speeches, including 8 by Peter, Stephen's long speech, 9 by Paul, and several others ("The Speeches in Acts," *Criswell Theological Review* 5, no. 1 [1990]: 31–41).

Biblical theology comes into its own at this point, tracing the progress of redemptive history in the Bible's own terms. Even so, not all biblical theologians agree as to how the material should be divided. Still, *drama* provides a helpful framework for dealing with the unity and diversity of Scripture. There is one playwright, one underlying drama, one beginning and ending, but many actors, scenes, events, and themes. Correctly identifying the number of acts in the theodrama furthers the cause of faith speaking understanding, and this on two levels. First, it helps us better to understand the unity and diversity of Scripture (i.e., one play with many acts); second, it helps disciples to understand better where they are in the story. This second point will prove critical in later chapters.

Two, maybe three, desiderata ought to govern the way we conceive the drama's plot. The most important thing is to do justice to the story line of Scripture. To omit something essential to the story is to risk compromising the logic of the gospel. We can call this first criterion "canonical comprehensiveness." Conversely, for the sake of explanatory power, it is important to focus on essential developments only. The goal here is to find the simplest yet also most powerful outline, the story line that can account for the integrity of the whole plot in the least amount of moves. We can call this second criterion "theodramatic loveliness," lovely because it provides the most understanding in the briefest compass.[41]

The minimum number of acts in the Christian theodrama would appear to be three (creation-fall-redemption), though there is some debate as to whether the third act does sufficient justice to the already/*not-yet* nature of redemption.[42] Some point out that at present we enjoy only the firstfruit of redemption, because the consummation is yet to come: "*The continuities and discontinuities of an inaugurated eschatology are not possible to communicate with a three-act script of the canon's theo-drama.*"[43]

N. T. Wright's suggestion of a five-act play has proved even more influential, spawning several variations: (1) Creation, (2) Fall, (3) Israel, (4) Jesus, (5) Church.[44] On Wright's reading, the church knows about the first four acts, and at least the first scene of act 5, but is otherwise in the position of needing to work out the rest of the fifth act for themselves. Sam Wells follows Wright's lead, but not without criticizing him at points. For example, Wells thinks it a mistake to make the church rather than the eschaton the end of the story. He also thinks that Jesus should be in the middle of the story, not least because he

---

41. For "loveliness" as a criterion of understanding, see Peter Lipton, *Inference to the Best Explanation*, 2nd ed. (London: Routledge, 2004), esp. chap. 9. David H. Wenkel makes a similar appeal to comprehensiveness and simplicity in "The Most Simple and Comprehensive Script for the Theo-drama of Scripture: Three Acts or Four?," *Scottish Bulletin of Evangelical Theology* 30 (2012): 78–90.

42. Alternately, some might suggest an even simpler, two-act scheme, following Paul in Rom. 5: Adam (act 1) and Christ (act 2).

43. Wenkel, "The Most Simple and Comprehensive Script," 85.

44. N. T. Wright, "How Can the Bible Be Authoritative?," *Vox evangelica* 21 (1991): 7–32, esp. 18–19; cf. the similar treatment in his *The New Testament and the People of God*, vol. 1 of *Christian Origins and the Question of God* (Minneapolis: Fortress Press, 1992), 140–43.

is the mediator ("middle-man"). He also objects to treating the fall as a separate act, for this implies that the fall is an act of God.[45]

Wells's amended version therefore looks like this: (1) Creation, (2) Israel, (3) Jesus, (4) Church, (5) Eschaton. As to Creation, "the drama of this act is that there was too much love in the Trinity for God to keep it to himself."[46] The fall is a moment in act 1, a "human misconstrual of God's created gift of freedom."[47] The third act, Jesus, is when the Playwright enters the play and creates the church, thus confounding Israel's notion that it was in a three-act play (creation, Israel, Messiah). The church is in act 4, charged with being the body of Christ in a world where other dramas jostle and sometimes prevail. That there is a fifth act means that Christians, while called to be faithful, do not need to usher in the kingdom with their own resources alone.

Finally, Craig Bartholomew and Michael Goheen propose a six-act story line in *The Drama of Scripture: Finding Our Place in the Biblical Story*. Again, their concern is to do justice to both the unity and diversity of Scripture, for without a unified story line, both Scripture and its followers are "in danger of being absorbed into whatever *other* story is shaping our culture."[48] They want Scripture to be the control story of Christian lives, the go-to text to answer the basic meaning-of-life questions: Who am I? Why am I here? What's happening? Where (in the story) am I? What time is it? We can only answer such questions, they rightly point out, if we know of what story we find ourselves a part.[49] What sets off their proposal is their focus on God's mission (related to the kingdom) and their addition of a sixth act: the *new* creation. Hence (1) Creation: God establishes his kingdom, (2) Fall: rebellion in the kingdom, (3) Redemption initiated: the King chooses Israel, (4) Redemption accomplished: the King comes, (5) Mission of the church: spreading the news of the King, (6) Redemption completed: the return of the King.[50]

Each of the above schemas makes helpful points, yet none adequately analyzes just what is to be counted as an act. In the context of theater, an act is a major division of a play that signals a change of time and/or place and is susceptible of being further divided into various scenes. In the context of theology, however, it is better to think of each act as a vital ingredient in the historical outworking (i.e., economy) of the divine decree. As such, each act is "according to the definite plan and foreknowledge of God" (Acts 2:23). What we need is a way of marking the historical progression of a single unified action. As we shall see, the biblical themes of "covenant" and "kingdom" go a long way toward answering this need.

---

45. Samuel Wells, *Improvisation: The Drama of Christian Ethics* (Grand Rapids: Brazos Press, 2004), 52–53.
46. Ibid., 53.
47. Ibid.
48. Craig G. Bartholomew and Michael W. Goheen, *The Drama of Scripture: Finding Our Place in the Biblical Story* (Grand Rapids: Baker Academic, 2004), 12.
49. Bartholomew and Goheen follow both N. T. Wright and Lesslie Newbigin in thinking that story is a cognitive instrument, an indispensable means for articulating a worldview and thus for gaining understanding. See Wright, *The New Testament and the People of God*, chaps. 2–3; Newbigin, *The Gospel in a Pluralistic Society* (Grand Rapids: Wm. B. Eerdmans Publishing Co., 1989), 15.
50. The authors helpfully devote a chapter to each act.

A biblical-theological account of Scripture's unity and diversity works best with a five-act scheme. Unlike Wright, or Bartholomew and Goheen, I have chosen not to view Adam's fall as an act in its own right. The Christian story is a theodrama that, by definition, focuses on the acts of God. Indeed, each of the five acts set forth below is put in motion with a mighty speech act of God:

Act 1. Creation, the setting for everything that follows (Gen. 1–11)

Act 2. Election of Abraham/Israel (Gen. 12–Mal.)

Act 3. Sending of the Son/Jesus (the Gospels)

Act 4. Sending of the Spirit/Church (Acts–Jude)

Act 5. Return of the King/day of the Lord/consummation/new creation (Rev.)

There are, of course, connections between what happens in earlier and later acts. Events in act 1 reverberate throughout the play. The fall of Adam is particularly noteworthy in this regard inasmuch as it explains the presence of *conflict in all five acts*. In each case, the conflict arises because the human players fail rightly to respond to God's word. Adam and Eve disobey God's command. This rupture of God's good created order elicits immediate judgment on God's part. Adam and Eve suffer exile from the garden, and this forced departure is arguably the catalyst that sets the whole drama in motion. Yet another of God's speech acts, the promise that Eve's offspring will defeat the offspring of the serpent (Gen. 3:15), equally provides the dynamic that propels the drama forward. The question that act 1 leaves in suspense is simply this: Will God's special creature, his representative on earth, ever return to God and fulfill the vocation for which men and women were called into existence in the first place, to stand in for God on earth?

This question, and the dramatic conflict, carries over into act 2. Israel and its kings similarly fail to keep God's law, and they too suffer exile. God brings his people back to Jerusalem, but this time they fail to recognize or respect God's Word incarnate. The question for the church in act 4 is whether we too will fail to recognize and respect God's word written, hence the warnings about false teaching (2 Cor. 11:13; 2 Pet. 2:1; 1 John 4:1) and falling away (Mark 13:22; Heb. 3:12). Finally, the book of Revelation's mention of the false prophet and the beast suggest that there will be satanic conflict until the end. Disciples do well to remember the nature of the conflict: will we side with those who respond to God's word rightly or with those who question, distort, and deny it?

What Is It About? Three Interpretations

We turn now from diversity to unity, from the number of acts the play has to what it is fundamentally about. Broadly speaking, the great play of the world is about God's renewing a broken creation. From the perspective of the human actors, it is about keeping and losing and then being given faith. It is a drama in which both divine and human players show themselves to be either faithful or faithless. It is a story about how God keeps his word even when his human images cannot. More specifically, the play has something to do with creation, kingdom, and covenant. Each of these three leading themes or frameworks has its own biblical theologians willing to champion its centrality. I will briefly review some representative approaches and then present my own integrative proposal.[51]

1. *The drama of new creation.* We begin with Greg Beale's *A New Testament Biblical Theology* because, as he announces with his subtitle, *The Unfolding of the Old Testament in the New*, the key to the whole play is contained in its opening scenes.[52] There is another advantage to starting with Beale: he explicitly addresses the question of the Bible's story line. According to Beale, Genesis 1–3 introduces key themes and patterns that the rest of the Old and New Testaments develop and from which they never depart. His focus is on the unity of the organic process of revelation and redemption.

Beale subscribes to what appears to be a three-act version of the play: creation, judgment, new creation. He sees Eden as a cosmic temple, a fit dwelling place for God, especially when we appreciate how kings in the ancient Near East would build temples to commemorate their victories and celebrate their reigns. The rest of the play concerns what God has to do when Adam and Eve are no longer fit to remain in God's presence. God seeks to reestablish a dwelling place in Israel's tabernacle and temple, but these ultimately are only shadows of something greater to come: the paradisal city-temple (Rev. 21:2), which is also equated with a "new heaven and a new earth" (21:1): "My thesis is that the Old Testament tabernacle and temples were symbolically designed to point to the cosmic eschatological reality that God's tabernacling presence, formerly limited to the holy of holies, was to be extended through the whole earth."[53]

For Beale, "movement towards an eschatological goal" is a major theme in the Old Testament story line and then again in the New.[54] All the action in the play is pushing forward toward the end, when God establishes the new creation through Jesus' death and resurrection and coming of the Spirit. Everything that happens in, to, and through Jesus Christ is eschatological inasmuch as it inaugurates the new creational reign of God. Jesus, too, is the temple of God,

---

51. The following survey is illustrative, not comprehensive. Richard Hays thinks the New Testament authors stress the same underlying story by attending to three focal images: creation, cross, and community (*The Moral Vision of the New Testament: A Contemporary Introduction to New Testament Ethics* [San Francisco: HarperSanFrancisco, 1996], chap. 10). For another theme (i.e., mission) that integrates the biblical story line, see Christopher J. H. Wright's *The Mission of God: Unlocking the Bible's Grand Narrative* (Downers Grove, IL: InterVarsity Press, 2006).

52. Gregory K. Beale, *A New Testament Biblical Theology* (Grand Rapids: Baker Academic, 2011).

53. G. K. Beale, *The Temple and the Church's Mission: A Biblical Theology of the Dwelling Place of God* (Downers Grove, IL: InterVarsity Press, 2004), 25.

54. Beale, *A New Testament Biblical Theology*, 15.

but through his work his people once again themselves become a temple fit for God's indwelling presence.

2. *The drama of the kingdom.* A number of authors view the play as telling the story of the progress of the kingdom of God, how God becomes king (but not without a fight).[55] Despite the relative infrequency of the phrase "kingdom of God" from the Old Testament, it is clear that, from the beginning, God is the ruler over all creation, and hence over all creatures and human kingdoms (Pss. 93:1; 96:4–10). This is why God can give dominion over the rest of creation to the human pair created in his image (Gen. 1:26–28). However, Adam and Eve failed to rule rightly in God's stead, as also failed the kings of Israel after them. Consequently, the world is now under the dominion of the powers of darkness. Interestingly, the motif of divine kingship achieves dramatic prominence primarily because the world resists and rejects God's authoritative rule.

The promise of a Davidic king, whose throne would endure forever, nevertheless fueled Israel's hope, as did the apocalyptic imagery of the coming Son of Man (Dan. 7:13–14). As John Bright says, "It is the kingdom of God toward which all history moves."[56] The Gospels present Jesus as this Son of Man, who has brought God's kingdom in his own person. On this view the gospel is the good news that the Father Almighty, Maker of heaven and earth, has fulfilled his promise to David (2 Sam. 7:8–16) and established his reign in Jesus Christ through the Holy Spirit.[57] Wright claims that the New Testament authors "all think that Jesus is already in charge of the world.... That is what they understood by 'God's kingdom.'"[58] However, this kingdom is both present and future, awaiting definitive consummation, and it is this eschatological tension that drives the drama forward to its climactic confrontation and conclusion, where God's reign will be recognized as extending over all (1 Cor. 15:24; Rev. 1:5–7).

3. *The drama of covenant.* Yet a third way of construing the divine play is to plot its covenantal progression. Bartholomew and Goheen, likening the canon to a cathedral, suggest that "kingdom" and "covenant" each present a strong claim to be the main door through which to enter in. They then go on to ask whether kingdom and covenant are two different doors or the same door. Their answer: "covenant and kingdom are like two sides of the same coin, evoking the same reality in slightly different ways."[59] They associate the kingdom with

---

55. See George Ladd, *A Theology of the New Testament*, rev. ed. (Grand Rapids: Wm. B. Eerdmans Publishing Co., 1993); Graeme Goldsworthy, *According to Plan: The Unfolding Revelation of God in the Bible* (Downers Grove, IL: InterVarsity Press, 2002); Stephen G. Dempster, *Dominion and Dynasty: A Biblical Theology of the Old Testament* (Downers Grove, IL: InterVarsity Press, 2003); N. T. Wright, *How God Became King: The Forgotten Story of the Gospels* (New York: HarperOne, 2012).

56. John Bright, *The Kingdom of God: The Biblical Concept and Its Meaning for the Church* (Nashville: Abingdon Press, 1957), 92.

57. See Graeme Goldsworthy, *Gospel and Kingdom: A Christian Interpretation of the Old Testament* (Exeter: Paternoster Press, 1981).

58. Wright, *How God Became King*, 16.

59. Bartholomew and Goheen, *The Drama of Scripture*, 24.

the reign of God over the whole of creation and covenant with the special relationship that God institutes with Israel. However, kings often established covenants, and the covenant that God made with Israel eventually encompasses the whole of creation, so in the end it is difference in emphasis only. Others disagree, seeing the covenant rather than the kingdom as the best way to view the God-world relationship, from creation to consummation.[60] After all, God makes covenants with Noah, Abraham, Moses, and David, and the prophets look forward to the "new covenant" (Jer. 31:31–33) that the New Testament announces as mediated by Jesus Christ (Luke 22:20; 1 Cor. 11:25; Heb. 9:15).

What is a covenant? This has been the subject of no little scholarly dispute over the past decades.[61] There have been many proposed definitions, based in large part on perceived parallels with ancient Near Eastern practices, but even in the Bible itself the notion is quite flexible: "It is used to refer to international treaties (Josh. 9:6; 1 Kgs. 15:19), clan alliances (Gen. 14:13), personal agreements (Gen. 31:44), national agreements (Jer. 34:8, 10), and loyalty agreements (1 Sam. 20:14–17), including marriage (Mal. 2:14)."[62] Gordon Hugenberger expresses the core idea: "A covenant, in its normal sense, is an elected, as opposed to natural, relationship of obligation under oath."[63] Even more succinctly: "a *bĕrît* [Hebrew for "covenant"] is a relationship involving an oath-bound commitment."[64] The key to distinguishing the different kinds of covenants we see in Scripture depends on who takes the oath (i.e., who undertakes the covenantal obligations). Obligations can be unilaterally assumed, unilaterally assigned to another, or they can be bilateral (i.e., mutual).

Scott Hahn's *Kinship by Covenant* argues that Scripture presents a unified covenantal drama. Though the covenants vary in form and content, they ultimately serve as a means by which to integrate aliens into a familial structure. While some covenants emphasize either the ethical, juridical, or cultic aspects, covenants in general are essentially means for extending familial relationships: "The familial nature of covenants is their unifying factor."[65] In sum: the various

---

60. See, e.g., Walther Eichrodt, *Theology of the Old Testament*, 2 vols. (London: SCM Press, 1961–67); W. J. Dumbrell, *Covenant and Creation: A Theology of the Old Testament Covenants* (Exeter: Paternoster Press, 1984). For a caution on overextending the concept of covenant beyond what exegesis warrants, as so-called covenant theology is wont to do, see Paul R. Williamson, *Sealed with an Oath: Covenant in God's Unfolding Purpose* (Downers Grove, IL: InterVarsity Press, 2007), 30–31.

61. See the surveys in Williamson, *Sealed with an Oath*, 19–29; Scott Hahn, *Kinship through Covenant: A Canonical Approach to the Fulfillment of God's Saving Promises* (New Haven: Yale University Press, 2009), 1–31; Peter J. Gentry and Stephen J. Wellum, *Kingdom through Covenant: A Biblical-Theological Understanding of the Covenants* (Wheaton, IL: Crossway, 2012), 129–45.

62. Gentry and Wellum, *Kingdom through Covenant*, 130–31.

63. George Hugenberger, *Marriage as a Covenant: A Study of Biblical Law and Ethics Governing Marriage Developed from the Perspective of Malachi* (Leiden Netherlands: E. J. Brill, 1994), 11.

64. Gentry and Wellum, *Kingdom through Covenant*, 132.

65. Hahn, *Kinship through Covenant*, 333. The extended family was "the central framework for the legal, religious, and political activities of ancient Semitic society" (3). Hahn is especially concerned to rebut the notion that the covenant is a contract, since "contract" conveys only the legal aspect and excludes familial, cultic, and other dimensions (8).

covenants in the biblical story fit into a pattern: "a drama of the development of the covenant relationship between father and son, that is, between God and his people."[66] The *cantus firmus* (melodic theme) of the theodrama is God's single-minded purpose to extend his family: "*covenant establishes kinship.*"[67] Where are we? In a story about the Father-son bond between God and his people, his extended family of adopted sons and daughters (Israel, the church): "God's relationship with Israel is thus guided by a filial pedagogy culminating in Christ."[68]

Peter Gentry and Stephen Wellum also believe that the covenants constitute the framework of the biblical story, though they emphasize not "kinship" *by* covenant (Hahn) but rather "kingdom" *through* covenant. They criticize Beale for exaggerating the importance of creation[69] and Goldsworthy, among others, for exaggerating the importance of kingdom.[70] Their proposal has the merit of seeking to integrate the themes of creation and kingdom, but without collapsing them into one another, as Bartholomew and Goheen seem willing to do. They also seek to do justice to the theme of creation inasmuch as covenant concerns the relationship between the Creator and his creation. Their thesis: covenant is essential to the "plot" of Scripture, and only by appreciating the progression of the various covenants (the "backbone of the biblical narrative"), and their relationship to the new covenant inaugurated in the person and work of Jesus Christ, can one discern correctly the "whole purpose of God" (Acts 20:27).

It is not necessary to decide which theme should have priority over the others. While *covenant* provides a way to divide the story into several acts, *kingdom* keeps the story unified. God, the king of the universe, created humankind to be vice-regents, ruling creation on his behalf. However, Adam and Eve, together with their progeny, reject God's rule. The rest of the drama concerns God's attempts to restore his rule and right relations with his created image-bearers *through* a succession of covenants. For example, Solomon's temple is a place, like Eden, where fellowship with God can once again be enjoyed, though it is only a temporary and provisional solution. Ultimately it will take a new covenant, a new temple, a new king, as well as a new and utterly unexpected kind of victory: the cross.

A Covenantal Courtroom Drama: The Trial of the Great King

Before moving on, it might be helpful to retrace our journey. We are seeking to understand the nature of the playwright's play "from below," from the perspective of its unfolding in human history. We have suggested that (1) the

---

66. Ibid., 338.
67. Ibid., 28.
68. Ibid., 334; cf. Paul Kalluveettil's observation: "Thus a covenant implies an adoption into the household, an extension of kinship" (*Declaration and Covenant* [Rome: Biblical Institute Press, 1982], 205).
69. Gentry and Wellum, *Kingdom through Covenant*, 13.
70. Ibid., 96.

play has five acts; (2) the unifying principle has something to do with the kingdom of God; (3) the diversity has something to do with the succession of covenants; (4) the telos of the play is the new creation; and (5) at the center of the play stand the cross, resurrection, ascension, and return of Jesus Christ, the great King (Ps. 89:3–4; Luke 1:32–33). I now submit that all these themes are elements in an ongoing courtroom drama in which both covenant servants and covenant Lord appear alternately to be on trial.

This is not the place to work out the detailed picture; we have time only for broad-brush strokes. The big picture depicts God's communicative action in covenantal settings oriented to Creator-creature communion. It features the triune God relating to his creation as sovereign King, exercising and expanding his rule by means of his covenantal words, which bind him to his people and regulate his people's behavior.[71] At every point, the question is whether and to what extent human persons are living in right relatedness (i.e., righteousness), with God and others (i.e., neighbors). The alarming answer: not so much. The kingdom of God, God's people living under God's blessed rule in God's place, proves to be devastatingly and mortally elusive.

The ultimate covenant blessing is communion: "I will take you as my people, and I will be your God" (Exod. 6:7; Jer. 11:4; Ezek. 36:28); "I will be your father, and you shall be my sons and daughters" (2 Cor. 6:18). The sobering truth, however, is that human creatures rebelled against God's rule, casting the whole of creation into disorder and falling well short of right relatedness. Yet, as in every relationship, each side takes turns blaming the other. Divorce is even threatened. In short: the divine comedy threatens to degenerate into an unseemly courtroom drama marked by mutual accusations. One suspects that Satan, the "accuser" (Zech. 3:1; Rev. 12:10), is well pleased at the turn of events. Yet not all is as it seems. The Great King, who is also Judge, is about to work the greatest plot twist ever told. . . .

"Courtroom drama" gets at the heart of God's covenant history with his people. Who is on trial? Not only the rebellious children of Israel, but also their Lord: Will he be as good as his covenant word? In essence, the courtroom drama is both a trial of the great King and covenant Lord—of God's truth, goodness, and beauty—yet also of the covenant people, their faith, wisdom, and love. This is the play in which disciples too participate, as we shall see in due course.

Covenant Lawsuit

"I call heaven and earth to witness against you" (Deut. 4:26; 30:19; 31:28). Unlike the unconditional promise God made with Abraham (Gen. 12:2–3), the Sinai covenant imposed certain obligations on Israel (see Deut. 4:1–40), the most important being covenant loyalty to Yahweh: "You shall have no other gods before me" (Exod. 20:3). This requirement, to remain in a "monogamous"

---

71. For a fuller development of these ideas, see Scott R. Swain, *Trinity, Revelation, and Reading: A Theological Introduction to the Bible and Its Interpretation* (London: T&T Clark, 2011), 17–33.

relationship with Yahweh, is only fitting in a relationship of exclusive love. As we saw above, the covenant is like a marriage: the blessing is communion, but the condition is faithfulness. Alas, Israel "went a whoring after other gods" (Judg. 2:17 KJV), committing spiritual adultery and leading Jeremiah to wonder whether Israel had landed in a divorce court (Jer. 3:8). Of all the words that disciples could hear, surely the worst is "I never knew you; go away from me" (Matt. 7:23).

Everything in the play depends on how human creatures respond to God's word. Right response to God's word entails right relatedness to God (and vice versa). God establishes his covenants unilaterally: it is entirely by grace that the Maker of heaven and earth chooses to enter into a privileged relationship with Israel. The covenants typically include both privileges (e.g., promises on God's part of blessings for obedience) and responsibilities (e.g., obligations to obedience on Israel's part). The history of Israel is largely the story of Israel's covenant faithfulness and unfaithfulness (primarily the latter).

Two other features of God's covenant with Israel bear mention. First, covenant faithlessness would not go unpunished. There were consequences to the shape of Israel's response to God's word. Second, there were provisions to preserve the covenant in writing (e.g., the "book of the covenant" [Exod. 24:7; Deut. 29:21]), a documentary witness to the solemn agreement. There are other witnesses as well, and it is these that give the biblical play the feel of a courtroom drama.

"I call heaven and earth to witness against you" (Deut. 4:26; 30:19; 31:28). On several occasions, God sends his prophets to announce a lawsuit against his people for breach of covenant: "Here the word of the LORD, O people of Israel; for the LORD has an indictment [*rîb*] against the inhabitants of the land. There is no faithfulness or loyalty, and no knowledge of God in the land" (Hos. 4:1). A number of biblical scholars have examined this covenant lawsuit motif.[72] The trial typically includes the prosecutor's accusation before heaven and earth, summoned as witnesses: "Hear, O heavens, and listen, O earth; for the LORD has spoken: I reared children and brought them up, but they have rebelled against me" (Isa. 1:2).[73] The trial proceeds when the Judge (who is also the plaintiff) declares his right to press charges, reads the charges, notes the inability of making the situation right through foreign gods or empty rites, and then pronounces judgment.

---

72. See the excellent survey by Richard M. Davidson, "The Divine Covenant Lawsuit Motif in Canonical Perspective," *Journal of the Adventist Theological Society* 21 (2010): 45–84. Davidson counts 44 references to God's *rîb* in the Old Testament. Most are "positive" in the sense that they lead to someone's vindication, not condemnation, though the longer passages that contain the whole covenant lawsuit structure tend to be negative.

73. Other passages that invoke heaven and earth as witnesses include Deut. 4:26; 32:1, 6, 10, 15; Mic. 6:1–8; Jer. 2:4–13; and Ps. 50. See Herbert B. Huffman, "The Covenant Lawsuit in the Prophets," *Journal of Biblical Literature* 78 (1959): 285–95; and Julien Harvey, *Le plaidoyer prophétique contra Israël après la rupture de l'alliance: Étude d'une formule littéraire de l'Ancien Testament* (Bruges-Paris: Desclée de Brouwer, 1967).

As the book of Job shows, humans can bring a case against God (Job 23:1-7; cf. 40:1-9). For present purposes, however, I shall focus primarily on Yahweh's case against Israel (see Deut. 32; Hos. 4-5; Mic. 6:1-8). The context for these covenant lawsuits is "the emergency situation in which the prophet sees it as his task to force the people to return to the covenant relationship with Yahweh by forcing them to come to an awareness of what this relationship demands of them."[74]

The great theater of the world turns out to be a courtroom in which defendants and prosecutors plead their respective cases and witnesses give testimony: "Get up! Defend yourself before the mountains! Present your case before the hills! . . . For the LORD has a case [*rîb*] against his people; he has a dispute [*rîb*] with Israel!" (Mic. 6:1-2 NET). Israel is charged with a number of counts, all variations of what we could call *aggravated covenant assault*. For example, Amos charges Israel with oppressing the poor, committing sexual immorality, and profane worship (Amos 2:6-8). God calls a variety of witnesses that attest the justice of his cause, his righteousness as over against Israel's unrighteousness. In Deuteronomy, Moses calls heaven and earth as witnesses. In Amos 3:9-10, God calls "Assyria and . . . Egypt" (RSV, LXX) as witnesses of Israel's oppression of the poor (Egypt being a particularly ironic choice, given Israel's earlier oppression there). God is both plaintiff and judge. Israel is tried not by jury but by divine fury, which is what the righteousness of God resembles when it confronts unrighteousness. Covenant lawsuit, far from being a marginal theme, "constitutes a motif that suffuses the entire warp and woof of the Bible from Genesis to Revelation."[75]

There is another kind of covenant trial worth mentioning in this context, the informal hearing (or rather *watching*) whereby one party is put to various kinds of tests in order to determine their character and heart. The paradigm case here is God's testing Abraham's faith by asking him to sacrifice his son Isaac (Gen. 22:1-2). God puts individuals and nations to the test, not to incite them to disobedience but rather to confirm them in either their covenant faithfulness or unfaithfulness, as the case may be (Jas. 1:13). While not a formal covenant lawsuit, such informal testing nevertheless represents a kind of covenant trial and, as such, belongs in the broad canonical sweep of the courtroom theodrama. It is against this backdrop of covenant lawsuit and trial that we best view the New Testament testimony to Jesus Christ.

The Trial of the Second Adam: Mosaic Prophet, Melchizidekian Priest, and Davidic King

"Who do you say that I am?" (Matt. 16:15; Mark 8:29; Luke 9:20). Jesus' question to his first disciples remains the question for disciples in every

---

74. Kirsten Nielsen, *Yahweh as Prosecutor and Judge* (Sheffield: JSOT Press, 1978), 61.
75. Davidson, "The Divine Covenant Lawsuit Motif," 70. Davidson attempts to make good on this claim in the rest of his essay, noting that the covenant lawsuit structure forms a virtual mirror image of Israel's covenant-making pattern, as elaborated by Meredith Kline's *Treaty of the Great King: The Covenant Structure of Deuteronomy* (Grand Rapids: Wm. B. Eerdmans Publishing Co., 1963), with the exception that the *witnesses* are placed at the beginning of the lawsuit rather than at the end of the covenant document.

generation, and thus the question for us today. It is related to the central issue of the Old Testament: the identity of Yahweh.[76] In particular, the question is whether Yahweh is the one true God, the God who will remain true to his word. However, God turns the tables and brings a case against Israel and the nations: the nations fail to recognize God, and Israel fails in its servant role to be a light to the nations. What begins as a trial of God becomes a trial of those who sought to try him. The trial motif is especially prominent in the contest between Elijah and the prophets of Baal (1 Kgs. 18), where what is at stake is the identity of Yahweh as an agent of covenant blessings (i.e., rain). The identity of Yahweh is again at stake in Isaiah 40–55, where the issue is whether Yahweh is the ultimate agent behind King Cyrus's victories: "Yahweh and his witnesses are placed on one side and the gods of the nations and their supporters on the other."[77]

"Who do you say that I am?" Jesus answers this question throughout the Fourth Gospel by means of his words and deeds. Jesus not only tells the truth (8:45) but also says that he has come into the world to bear witness to the truth (18:37) and, what is more, even claims himself to be the truth (14:6). In particular, Jesus claims to have a special relationship with the Father, which some listeners interpret as a blasphemous claim to be equal with God (5:18). Jesus claims to be the only one who has seen the Father (6:46) and the only one through whom the Father can be seen (14:7). Jesus claims that the Father is "in" him as he is "in" the Father (14:10) and that whoever hates him hates the Father also (15:23). In some sense, Jesus claims to be part of the very identity of the Father.

Two charges against Jesus result in his arrest and trial. The Jewish leaders brought him to Pilate, the Roman governor, saying rather vaguely that he is an "evildoer" (John 18:30 RSV). Pilate cross-examines Jesus, concluding, "I find no crime in him" (19:6 RSV), to which the Jewish leaders retort: "We have a law, and by that law he ought to die, because he has made himself the Son of God" (19:7 RSV). Pilate, clearly reluctant to involve himself in the intramural matters of Jewish theology, again tries to release him (19:12) only to hear an even more chilling charge brought against Jesus: he has sought to make himself not only like God but also like *Caesar* (19:12). The Jewish leaders then seal their covenant fate, forgetting the great King of Israel and instead professing, "We have no king but Caesar" (19:15 RSV). Jesus is found guilty in both the religious trial of the Jewish Sanhedrin and the political trial of Rome.

The trial and death of Jesus are the focal point of all four Gospels. The cross, after all, was a death sentence pronounced by the court. The Fourth Gospel features Jesus' trial before the former high priest Annas (18:12–23), before the

---

76. Walter Brueggemann organizes his whole Old Testament theology around this question: "I have focused on the metaphor and imagery of the courtroom trial in order to regard the theological substance of the Old Testament as a series of claims asserted for Yahweh, God of Israel" (*Theology of the Old Testament: Testimony, Dispute, Advocacy* [Minneapolis: Fortress, 1997], xvi).

77. Allison A. Trites, *The New Testament Concept of Witness* (Cambridge: Cambridge University Press, 1977), 44.

current high priest Caiaphas and the Sanhedrin (18:24–27), and finally before Pilate (18:28–19:16). Yet, as several commentators have noted, *the whole of John's Gospel is structured as a courtroom drama*. For example, Andreas Köstenberger speaks of "the cosmic trial motif" that serves as the backdrop to the historical action in John's Gospel. This trial does not pit Yahweh against the nations but God (light) against the world (darkness).[78] Indeed, Jesus is on trial *throughout* the Fourth Gospel, as amply attested by the frequent mention of notions such as *witness*, *testimony*, and *judgment*.

The Fourth Gospel is a courtroom drama where what is on trial is nothing less than *God's truth claim*. In the Old Testament, "truth" (*'ĕmet*) carries connotations of reliability and, in particular, covenant faithfulness. What is being tried is covenant faithfulness: the righteousness of God. Andrew Lincoln argues that throughout his Gospel John self-consciously employs the Old Testament lawsuit motif, especially the lawsuits in Isaiah 40–55, perhaps because his readers were similarly undergoing various kinds of trial for their own evangelical truth claims.[79] He is especially struck by the frequency with which notions like testimony and judgment appear in the Fourth Gospel, well before Jesus' official trial. For example, the noun *witness* or *testimony* (*martyria*) appears fourteen times and the verb thirty-three times. In the courtroom drama that is the Fourth Gospel, *everything* seems to be giving testimony, either voluntarily (e.g., the man born blind [9:17, 24–26]) or inadvertently (e.g., Caiaphas [18:14]).

The star witness, of course, is Jesus himself. It is his testimony to his heavenly Father (John 3:31–35), as well as his claim that the Father has borne witness to him (5:37), that become the occasions for the violent reprisal against him. In John's Gospel, not only what Jesus says but also everything he does, especially his miracles, are signs (*sēmeia*) that speak to his true identity. Yet multiple additional witnesses have walk-on parts: John the Baptist (1:6, 7, 15, 27, 29, 32–34; 5:33), the Samaritan woman (4:19, 29), Moses (5:45–46), the man born blind (John 9), to name but a few. Again, what is on trial is Jesus' truth claim, or rather, his claim to be God's truth: the revelation (true knowledge) and righteousness (true covenant faithfulness) of God.

Although the Fourth Gospel may be the only one structured as a courtroom drama, the Synoptics are certainly aware of the "trial" aspect of Jesus' mission. Each includes the narrative of Jesus' temptation by Satan, whose forty-day wilderness testing (Matt. 4:1–2) corresponds to Israel's forty-year wilderness wanderings. This, too, is a trial, a test that helps the reader to discern who Jesus truly is.[80] Luke's Gospel traces Jesus' genealogy back not to Abraham, as Matthew does, but to Adam (Luke 3:38), and then in the next verse introduces

---

78. Andreas J. Köstenberger, *A Theology of John's Gospel and Letters* (Grand Rapids: Zondervan, 2009), 436–56.
79. Andrew T. Lincoln, *Truth on Trial: The Lawsuit Motif in the Fourth Gospel* (Peabody, MA: Hendrickson Publishers, 2000).
80. According to Michael Jensen, "a trial (*probatio*) is an external and public event; a temptation (*tentatio*) is more internal and personal" (*Martyrdom and Identity*, 166).

the temptation narrative. This sequence is no accident: rather, the Gospels intentionally identify Jesus with both Adam and Israel and their respective trials. Whereas the first Adam succumbs to the temptation to hearken to Satan rather than God, Jesus rebuffs Satan with God's word (Luke 4:4, 10, 12). Paul also contrasts the obedience of the second Adam with the disobedience of the first (Rom. 5:12–21).

Taken together, the Gospels and the rest of the New Testament represent a cumulative testimony as to Jesus' identity: he is the second Adam; a true prophet, greater than Moses (Deut. 18:15–16; 34:10–11; cf. Acts 3:22; Heb. 3:3); a true priest, according to the order of Melchizedek (Ps. 110:4; Heb. 5:10; 6:20); a true king, greater than David (Matt. 12:42, 21:9; Eph. 1:20–21). He is God's vindicated (i.e., resurrected) truth claim: he is the truth about God, the truth about humanity, and the truth about the relationship between God and humanity. He is God's covenant faithfulness, both its promise and judgment.

"Who do you say that I am?" I say that you are the righteousness of God.[81]

Disciples in the Dock: Martyrdom and Covenant Identity

Back to the Fourth Gospel. Lincoln is right to observe, "The Fourth Gospel is not simply about a trial; it is itself a testimony in the trial."[82] The Gospel is so structured that the reader is drawn into the courtroom drama, placed on the jury, or perhaps the witness stand, and thus obliged to take a stand for or against John's testimony. There can be little doubt that the author uses his rhetorical skills to bring about a crisis in the reader, a crisis that can be relieved only by making a judgment [*krisis*] about Jesus: "These [things] are written that you may believe that Jesus is the Christ, the Son of God, and that believing you have life in his name" (John 20:31 RSV). The Gospel closes with another reminder that the reader has been privy to courtroom testimony, for the author identifies himself as an eyewitness: "This is the disciple who is testifying to these things and has written them, and we know that his testimony is true" (John 21:24).[83]

In play here are at least two levels of dramatic irony. First, it is ironic that though Jesus is the one who appears to be on trial, in fact it is those sitting in judgment who are themselves being judged. It is the working out of what was said in the prologue: "He was in the world, . . . yet the world did not know him" (John 1:10). It is also ironic that readers in the know about this first level of irony are caught up themselves on a second level: it is not enough to see the shortcomings of the Jewish and Roman leaders if one does not come to a right judgment oneself. The sober truth is that the person now on trial in the Fourth Gospel is not Jesus, not even Pilate, but contemporary readers. And we are on trial not only when we happen to be reading the Fourth Gospel, but at every

---

81. We shall say more about this topic in the next chapter.
82. Lincoln, *Truth on Trial*, 170.
83. See also my "The Hermeneutics of I-Witness Testimony: John 21:20–24 and the 'Death' of the 'Author,'" in *Understanding Poets and Prophets*, ed. A. Graeme Auld (Sheffield: Sheffield Academic Press, 1993), 366–87.

moment of every day: "Every human meeting is judgment, is crisis, is a situation in which we are called either to receive Christ or to be Christ's messenger to the person whom we are meeting."[84]

It follows that all human beings, like the heavens and earth, are called upon to be witnesses to the trial of truth at the heart of the gospel. Jesus is the preeminent witness-martyr, the one who, unlike Adam and Israel, successfully passes the test of covenant faithfulness, even though it cost him his life. Jesus is the righteousness of God because he demonstrates right relatedness to God through his true testimony. In similar fashion, the risen Christ calls his followers to give true testimony to his identity: "You are witnesses [*martyres*] of these things" (Luke 24:48; cf. Isa. 43:10). Theology speaks understanding when it can say what form fidelity to the vocation of truthful witness ought to take today.

Christian doctrine prepares disciple-witnesses to give true testimony in the courtroom drama of daily life. The way we live each day bears eloquent testimony to what we truly believe (and believe in). Doctrine helps disciples to bear true witness, to put others in the position of coming to know (believe and understand) the gospel of Jesus Christ. Bearing witness is often costly; the cost of discipleship is martyrdom, whether in life or in death. Our role in the courtroom drama of the covenant, to bear witness, is itself a trial. Kierkegaard speaks of "suffering for the doctrine."[85] This suffering is necessary, which is why bearing testimony is a trial, because of what we have to say: the kingdom of God is cruciform in nature. This is not a popular message to those accustomed to worldly power.[86]

What is finally on trial in the covenantal courtroom drama of the Christ is the truth about the nature of God's reign and the identity of the king. In their everyday speech and action, disciples bear witness as to which king and whose kingdom they ultimately serve. In this light, Jesus' words to his disciples are especially apt: "You are those who have stood by me *in my trials*; as my Father *covenanted* [*diatithemai*] *a kingdom* to me, so do I *covenant a kingdom* to you" (Luke 22:28–29, my trans.). A crown awaits the faithful witness.

The book of Revelation identifies Jesus Christ as the paramount "faithful witness, . . . and the ruler of kings on earth" (1:5 RSV). Yet the king accedes to his throne only through his death on a cross. The great King, the Lion of Judah, is also the slain Lamb (5:5–6). And so it shall be with Jesus' disciples: they must first give faithful witness before ruling with their Lord, and bearing faithful witness implies bearing a cross. In the New Testament, a *martyr* is first and foremost a witness, a player in the great courtroom drama of the world. Testimony begins in the context of a judicial trial but quickly becomes an existential trial when the

---

84. Anthony Bloom, *Beginning to Pray* (New York: Paulist Press, 1970), 75.

85. Søren Kierkegaard, *For Self-Examination: Judge for Yourself*, Kierkegaard's Writings vol. 21, ed. and tr. Howard V. Hong and Edna H. Hong (Princeton, NJ: Princeton University Press, 1991), 201.

86. For a further examination of the overlapping ideas of witness and martyr, see my "The Trials of Truth: Mission, Martyrdom, and the Epistemology of the Cross," in *First Theology: God, Scripture, and Hermeneutics* (Downers Grove, IL: InterVarsity Press, 2002), 337–73.

witnesses suffer for their testimony. This is what happened to Stephen, the first known Christian martyr. Paul later recalls how "the blood of [Christ's] witness Stephen was shed" (Acts 22:20).

Martyrdom is an important theme in the book of Revelation, which speaks to both the issue of the covenant lawsuit and also the nature of true discipleship. The blood of the martyrs cries out from under the altar after the opening of the fifth seal, "Sovereign Lord, holy and true, how long will it be before you judge and avenge our blood?" (6:10). The rest of the book is a response to this question. The covenant courtroom briefly becomes a cosmic battleground before order is reestablished in the heavenly court and a final judgment pronounced before the Great White Throne: "Books were opened, . . . and the dead were judged by what was written in the books, by what they had done" (20:12 RSV). At this point, when the books are closed, the curtain comes down on the old heaven and earth. Meanwhile, the true disciple "keeps the words of the prophecy of this book" (22:7; cf. 1:3) by preparing for the trials, and the blessed hope, that await. Doctrine is a precious help for disciples seeking to fulfill their covenantal vocation as faithful witnesses and martyrs.

RECAPITULATION: THE ORTHODOX IMPERATIVE

"Ontogeny recapitulates phylogeny." This pithy formula states Ernst Haeckel's hypothesis that as an organism develops from embryo to adult (ontogeny), it goes through stages that resemble the whole evolutionary process of its ancestors (phylogeny).[87] I only introduce this celebrated (though now thoroughly discredited) aphorism in order to set forth another, to which I am strongly committed: "Economy recapitulates ontology" (with the doctrine of the Trinity in mind, of course).

This chapter illustrates that "economy recapitulates ontology" by observing the way in which the dramatic play "from below" (i.e., the missions of Son and Spirit from the Father that comprise the economic Trinity) recapitulates the play as seen "from above" (i.e., the processions of the immanent or ontological Trinity). In particular, we have focused on the way in which the Father and Son bring about communion in the kingdom through covenantal communicative action (and passion). The plan of salvation, life in and through the Son (i.e., *what is in Christ*), was conceived in eternity and executed in history. The gospel is Trinitarian through and through.[88] Economy recapitulates ontology.

---

87. Ernst Haeckel, *The Riddle of the Universe at the Close of the Nineteenth Century* (New York and London: Harper & Brothers Publishers, 1900), 81.

88. See also Fred Sanders's statement, "The gospel is Trinitarian, and the Trinity is the gospel" (*The Deep Things of God: How the Trinity Changes Everything* [Wheaton, IL: Crossway, 2010], 10). Sanders also sees a connection between the economic and the ontological, through he rephrases the principle as "first the reality, then the explanation" (35).

The *orthodox imperative* is shorthand for the necessity of affirming the ancient Trinitarian and christological doctrines associated with the Councils of Nicaea (325), Constantinople I (381), and Chalcedon (451). Whence comes this necessity? Is not the doctrine of the Trinity a highly abstruse, even arcane, piece of Greek theologizing? Is not the notion of the hypostatic union an outdated remnant of Greek metaphysics? No, they are not. On the contrary: the doctrine of the Trinity is absolutely central for the project of faith speaking understanding for, in a real sense, the drama *is* the triune dramatis personae: Father, Son, and Spirit. That was the whole point of observing the connection between the eternal processions within the Godhead and the historical missions of the Son and Spirit. We can only understand what is happening in the history of Jesus Christ if we understand who Jesus is and how, as Son of God, his person and work is related to God the Father. Indeed, the whole play is about how the triune Playwright comes down from heaven, unites himself with his human creatures, and then reunites earth with heaven. As to Chalcedon, the logic of the gospel and the coherence of the theodrama depend on the Son being fully God and man: hence the importance of the doctrine of the incarnation as well.

The Trinity is the ground, grammar, and guarantee of the gospel. As such, it is central for the project of faith speaking understanding: "Trinitarianism is the encompassing framework within which all Christian thought takes place and within which Christian confession finds its grounding presuppositions. It is the deep grammar of all the central Christian affirmations."[89] The Trinity guarantees the gospel by explaining how those who lack righteousness can nevertheless enjoy right relatedness to the God of all righteousness. The drama of the Christ is the story of how the Father extends his family, opening up space in the eternal triune life for human creatures that enter into the Son's sonship through the Spirit.

The gospel is good news only if one relates to it rightly. The demons believe *that* Jesus is the Christ, but they do not believe *in* (or *into*, Gk. *eis*) him (Luke 4:41; cf. Jas. 2:19). *Knowing about* is one thing; *personal commitment* or *trust* in a person is quite another. Right knowledge ("orthodoxy") is ultimately hollow if it is not accompanied by right love. Disciples must not only speak the truth in love (Eph. 4:15) but also love the truth (2 Thess. 2:10) they speak. Faith speaking understanding must be heartfelt. With this thought, we move from the logic of the gospel to the logic of the martyr.

The faithful witness must not just parrot the good news of *what is in Christ* but also *participate* in it. What does this mean? It means, first, that disciples must play their part in the courtroom drama of the covenant, bearing true witness to the things that happened to Jesus in Jerusalem (Luke 24:18), passing along the apostolic testimony concerning Jesus Christ, what the first Christians heard, saw with their eyes, looked upon, and touched with their hands (1 John 1:1). It

---

89. Sanders, *The Deep Things of God*, 46. Sanders helpfully adds: "Whereas the Trinity in salvation history just is the gospel, the Trinity in itself is the background of the gospel" (93).

means, second, that disciples bear witness to the gospel by joining in the triune play of reconciliation whereby God is making all things new through Christ in the Spirit (2 Cor. 5:17–19). It means, third, identifying Jesus Christ as the great King, attesting his status as true prophet, priest, and king. In this way disciples continue, by way of participatory attestation, Christ's own mission: the prophetic activity of forthtelling God's word and will, in particular the contours of the new covenant; the priestly activity of praying in Jesus' name and celebrating his sacrifice; even the kingly activity of working in cruciform ways for justice, peace, and righteousness. It means, finally, participating in the death and resurrection of Jesus, as individuals and as churches, thereby realizing our new existence "in Christ" and, in the process, becoming harbingers and flagships of the reality of the gospel. To witness to *what is in Christ* is to participate in the coming of his kingdom. It is to these important meanings of participating in Christ that we now turn.

Chapter 5

Learning (and Becoming) the Part

"Little Christs"

> *Every Christian is to become a little Christ. The whole purpose of becoming a Christian is simply nothing else.*
>
> —C. S. Lewis, *Mere Christianity*

Understanding what God is doing in Christ is already a significant achievement. As we saw in the previous chapter, the doctrines of the Trinity and the incarnation go a long way toward ministering understanding. Those who correctly identify the divine dramatis personae already have a sense of the missional nature, and hence the plot, of the divine playwright's play. There is someone rather than nothing because God saw fit to share his triune life with creatures made in his own image. Still, this awe-inspiring vision of the meaning and purpose of cosmic history does not tell me how *I* am to take part in the action. What should I be doing during my fleeting moments on the stage of the great theater of the world?

The first Gentiles who may have asked themselves this question had the advantage of apostolic tuition under Saul and Barnabas: "For an entire year they met with the church and taught a great many people, and it was in Antioch that the disciples were first called 'Christians'" (Acts 11:26). At first glance, the two ideas do not seem even remotely connected: the apostles taught new believers; someone called these believers "Christians" for the first time. Further reflection suggests, however, that the two ideas may be deeply connected. It is worth teasing out this train of thought. The Gentiles would not have known "Christ" was Hebrew for "anointed one" rather than the name of a person. To name Jesus' followers "Christians" is therefore to name them "Christ's people," the followers of a particular person rather than, say, a political movement. "Christians" are therefore partisans of Christ, people who advocate the cause of Christ, people who even play the part of Christ, acting like Christ.[1]

And this perhaps explains why Saul and Barnabas needed to spend a year in Antioch to teach doctrine. Doctrine that is merely informative is nothing but a noisy gong or a clanging cymbal whose percussive force does not extend to shaping character. One does not become a "Christ person," however, simply by learning one or two new facts, even if those facts concern what happened to Jesus in Jerusalem. Something more is needed if doctrine is to have a transformative impact on Christian character and help disciples to imitate Christ. In any case, it is profoundly appropriate that we first encounter the term "Christian" in the context of a Gentile community taking a crash course in apostolic teaching (i.e., theology). For we too, like the early Gentile Christians, learn theology in order to learn our parts as "little Christs."

The peculiar vocation of the Christian is to be Christlike. Doctrine helps us fulfill our vocations as disciples to the extent that it not only identifies the Christ but also assists us in growing into his image, "to the measure of the full stature of Christ" (Eph. 4:13). How does doctrine, mere teaching, perform so great a feat? In and of itself, it cannot. Doctrines are not how-to manuals whose paint-by-number instructions one simply follows in the flesh. They are rather indications of reality, expositions and explorations of *what is in Christ*, that the Holy Spirit uses to sanctify our imaginations and renew our minds: means of grace that enable us to see ourselves, in the mirror of Scripture, as we truly are and as we are becoming. In the words of C. S. Lewis: "The Church exists for nothing else but to draw men into Christ, to make them little Christs. If they are not doing that, all the cathedrals, clergy, missions, sermons, even the Bible itself, are simply a waste of time. God became Man for no other purpose. It is even doubtful, you know, whether the whole universe was created for any other purpose."[2] We can add *doctrine* to Lewis's list of things that waste time if it is not forming disciples into little Christs.

ROLES: TILL WE HAVE FACES

At this point a critical and attentive reader might justifiably leap up and cry "Aha! Just as I thought. Your theatrical mumbo jumbo simply encourages Christians to *playact* their faith, to indulge in childish fancies and pretend games about heaven." It is a serious objection and raises serious questions: Who do we say we

---

1. The early Christians themselves apparently preferred the self-designation "the Way" (Acts 9:2; 19:9; 24:14; 24:22). The term "Christian" is found only in Acts 11:26; 26:28; and 1 Pet. 4:16. Jesus identifies himself with "the way, and the truth, and the life" (John 14:6), so the discrepancy implies no contradiction, only a different emphasis.

2. C. S. Lewis, *Mere Christianity* (New York: Touchstone, 1996), 171.

really are? How do we present ourselves to others? And do our self-conceptions and self-presentations correspond to reality? Such questions become even more complicated when we realize that they are the staple of identity politics: the struggle over an individual's or a community's right to identify or name oneself or itself, to give oneself a public face. The *face* is the site of contemporary ideological warfare, a conflict of interpretations over what it means to be human and over who gets to say who I am.

Does one's face reveal who one is, or does it mask who we are? Is identity a matter of nature (fateful necessity) or nurture (free choice)? Is there a human nature (i.e., a universally shared human identity)? Or is it social roles, the parts we play, all the way down? Am I born with my identity, or can I make it up as I go along? These questions pertain not only to identity but also to authenticity: How can I be true to myself before I know who "I" am? To a certain extent the theater is a fitting emblem of an age inclined to think that personal identity is a matter of individual and social construction. What goes on my face is *makeup*, the rouge of rhetorical construction.

There are, then, two related problems: first, that the theatrical model privileges artificiality and arbitrariness (i.e., the idea that we can play any role we choose); second, that the theatrical model encourages playacting. Neither of these outcomes is conducive to discipleship. Christian theologians must therefore face these suspicions squarely, and we shall. But before we do, I want to thank my imagined critic for the question, for it opens up a whole field of questions concerning how disciples answer Christ's call and become the part they play.

Arbitrary Roles or Answerable Selves?

The origin of the Latin term *persona* was the theater, in which context it means "mask." Today it refers to the different roles a person plays (e.g., son, student, husband, colleague, friend, father, etc.). One's "persona" refers to the way one presents oneself to others, the way one appears in the world. The question is whether a theatrical model encourages people to think that an individual is *nothing but the roles one plays*, nothing but the masks one wears. Is there a stable identity, a person rather than a *persona*, behind the many roles one plays?

The exalted sovereign self of modernity—Descartes's "I think therefore I am"—has been brought low by postmodern thinkers for whom fragmentation (the *shattered* self) is the better watchword. Contemporary psychology, with its assumption that persons are not unified wholes but consist rather of multiple subpersonalities (i.e., roles), lends scientific credence to the postmodern claim that identity is either socially determined or socially constructed. As one psychologist puts it, "People are not what they used to be."[3] Why not? Because

---

3. Léon Turner, *Theology, Psychology, and the Plural Self* (Farnham, Surrey, UK: Ashgate, 2008), 9. Turner apparently wanted to title his book "For We Are Many": The Unclean Spirit's Explanation of Why He Was Called 'Legion' (Mark 5:9)."

the self is not as stable and singular as it is used to be: "There is now a broad consensus amongst psychologists of all kinds, from psychoanalysts to cognitive psychologists, that the self must be understood at some level as a multiplicity."[4] The person, we could say, has dissolved into a plurality of personae. That we can choose which self we wish to be is the "gospel" not only of the human but the natural sciences as well, to the extent that the latter suggest that we can, through biotechnology, choose to be "better than well."

To be sure, the apostle Paul happily acknowledges that he plays many roles: to the Jews he becomes a Jew, to the weak he becomes weak, and so on. Indeed, "I have become all things to all people" (1 Cor. 9:22). Paul role-plays in order to minister to many kinds of people, but is he making the postmoderns' or psychologists' point about having a plurality of selves? On the contrary, he is saying, "It is still *I*, Paul the apostle, playing these various roles." And the self that is the true Paul, underneath these various roles, is not the Cartesian *cogito* but the Christian *vocatio*: the self that God has called into existence from what did not exist (Rom. 4:17), the self that is called by, and in turn calls on, Jesus Christ.

What accounts for the coherence of the individual self, the assurance of being oneself acting and suffering, is precisely the notion of a communicative agent in covenantal relations in a dramatic context. Paul's personal narrative was anything but continuous: he made a complete turnaround from persecuting to preaching Christ. What continuity of the self one has is ultimately a matter of theodramatic coherence: *how* we relate to the word of our covenanting Creator God reveals *who* we are.

The doctrines of creation and election speak understanding into our perplexed present-day situation that so easily confuses roles with selves, personae with persons. Together, these doctrines remind us that who I am is fundamentally a matter of God's choice before it is mine. We have been called into being and have received the ultimate casting call. Our vocation follows from our prior evocation; for while we were yet in the womb, God appointed us to the role of persons who bear his image and have been set apart for his purpose. God alone knows the person under the mask (Gal. 4:9). As we have seen, to be a person is to be an answerable agent, one who is able and thus responsible to respond to the call of God and of others. Hence our identity is not an arbitrarily chosen role, but a matter of how we respond to our theological vocation to image God so as to glorify and enjoy him forever.

Is there an integral self beneath the many roles people play? There is, but it is not the vaunted knowing subject of modernity. It is rather the self known and called by God (Gal. 4:9; 1 Cor. 13:12). God knows who we are beneath our several social masks. This is not to deny the significance of a number of commonly employed identifiers, including gender, ethnicity, and class. It is to

---

4. Léon Turner, "Behind the Mask," *Edification: The Transdisciplinary Journal of Christian Psychology* 4 (2010): 38.

say, however, that these external indicators are secondary rather than primary (1 Cor. 12:13; Gal. 3:28; Col. 3:11). Personal identity is first and foremost a matter of our answerable agency, of the shape of our characteristic response to the word and call of God.

Hypocrisy or Authenticity?

To be or merely to *pretend* to be: that is the question for the actor as well as the disciple. We saw earlier that disciples are to be authentic as opposed to false and faithless witnesses. One way to bear false witness is to pretend to be something that one is not. And this is the heart of the second objection, that the theatrical model encourages actors merely to go through the external motions rather than to experience the inner emotions and convictions from which action springs. It is one thing to *mimic* faith, quite another to achieve a true mimesis (from Gk. *mimēsis*, imitation) of the great cloud of witnesses that make up the biblical roll call of faith (Heb. 11:1-38).

The great merit of the theatrical model is not that it encourages such playacting but rather that it *exposes* it. It exposes it by drawing a distinction between "good" and "bad" actors. The distinction, roughly, is between merely *playing* a role and *becoming* the role one plays. The danger is real, and both the theater and theology have a name for it. In the theater, they call it *mechanical acting*; the New Testament names it *hypocrisy*.

Jesus singles out hypocrites for special criticism: "Woe to you, scribes and Pharisees, hypocrites! For you are like whitewashed tombs, which on the outside look beautiful, but inside they are full of the bones of the dead and all kinds of filth. So you also on the outside look righteous to others, but inside you are full of hypocrisy and lawlessness" (Matt. 23:27-28). It is possible that Jesus' use of the term reflects something of the presence of Hellenistic theaters in first-century Palestine, in which case the emphasis would be on the *deceptive* nature of the performance.[5] What Jesus goes on to say about the Pharisees leaves us in no doubt as to his meaning: on the outside the hypocrites pretend to be what they are not on the inside. There is a contradiction between their outward appearance and the inner reality of their hearts. Jesus thus criticizes hypocrites not for being bad actors but for being godless. It is the moral and spiritual corruption of their hearts that evacuates their actions of authenticity.

Almost all of Jesus' denunciations of hypocrisy have to do with the lack of coinciding fit between outward appearance and inner reality. Hypocrites treat prayer as a kind of public performance because they care about being seen (Matt. 6:5). The hypocrites we always have with us, as we see from Jesus' citation of the Old Testament: "'Isaiah prophesied rightly about you hypocrites, as it is written, "This people honors me with their lips, but their hearts are far from me"'" (Mark 7:6). There is a disastrous disconnect in the way the hypocrites respond to God's

---

5. See R. A. Batey, "Jesus and the Theatre," *New Testament Studies* 30 (1984): 563-74.

word, appearing to obey it but in reality greeting it with a heartfelt denial. It is the hypocrite who hears the word but fails to do it. And by calling attention to the importance of hearing and doing, the theatrical model does not exacerbate hypocrisy but exposes it.

Those who are aware of the danger of hypocrisy are better prepared to pursue the goal of integration, the process of conforming one's external appearance to one's inner reality. By contrast, hypocrisy describes the fateful fracturing of inner and outer self, the inability to achieve identity, the "oneness" or coherence of an integral self. Hypocrisy is wrong not only because it deceives others but also because it injures oneself.

As to the objection that the theatrical model encourages hypocrisy, the Russian director and acting teacher Constantin Stanislavski shared the same concern to avoid hypocrisy. His "system" for teaching actors how to learn their roles rejects overacting, clichés, mannerisms, and other types of what he calls *mechanical acting*. The mechanical actor reproduces outward expressions without actually experiencing what they express. In mechanical acting there is a conspicuous gap between the inner and outer man; it is the theatrical equivalent of hypocrisy. In Stanislavski's words: "Never allow yourself externally to portray anything that you have not inwardly experienced."[6] He also warned his students against the use of a mirror: "It teaches an actor to watch the outside rather than the inside of his soul."[7] In particular, Stanislavski encouraged his actors not to *mimic* but actually to experience, through memory, the emotions of the characters they portray.

The great actor is able authentically to render not only a character's emotions but also the motives. No part of Stanislavski's system is better known than his insistence that actors learn not only their lines but also everything about the characters they play. The key to becoming the part one plays is not makeup or costuming but the *inner* preparation. Actors must wrestle with the question of what they would do *if* they really were a certain character (the "magic if"): "If you speak any lines, or do anything, mechanically, without fully realizing who you are, where you came from, why, what you want, where you are going, and what you will do when you get there, you will be acting without imagination."[8] The actor's imagination is especially important. One has to imagine how a certain kind of person would act in a particular way given a certain set of circumstances, and then one has to believe it: "*Everything must be real in the imaginary life of the actor.*"[9] We can only achieve truth on stage when we have faith in our part, when we sincerely believe in what we are doing and know who we are.

Finally, Stanislavski believed that the actor is given not only the "task" of learning the assigned part but also the "higher task" of entering into the horizon of meaning that encompasses the role. *Everything* an actor does on stage should

---

6. Constantin Stanislavski, *An Actor Prepares* (New York: Routledge, 1964), 31.
7. Ibid., 21.
8. Ibid., 77.
9. Ibid., 171, emphasis original.

be related to the main idea of the play, which he called its "superobjective": "The main theme must be firmly fixed in an actor's mind throughout the performance."[10] Disciples in the drama of redemption take note: *the ultimate goal of the actor is not simply to play a role but to project the main idea of the play.* From when we get out of bed in the morning to the time we retire at night, the disciple would do well to keep in mind the Christian superobjective (i.e., the big theodramatic picture): "Whatever you do, in word or deed, do everything in the name of the Lord Jesus, giving thanks to God the Father through him" (Col. 3:17).

Doctrine helps disciples act with authenticity, to learn their new roles to the point where they become not mechanical but *organic* actors. The apostle Paul exhorts his readers "Let love be genuine [*anypokritos*]" (Rom. 12:9), using the alpha privative (*an-*) to express the opposite of "hypocritical" (*hypokritos*, pretending). Similarly, the authentic (the genuine, natural, or organic) is the opposite of mechanical or artificial. We may deceive others, but there is no fooling God, hence "the first act of prayer is to choose such words of prayer as are completely true to what you are."[11]

Jesus is not the only one to call someone a hypocrite. The apostle Paul does it to Peter's face in a particularly instructive episode. It is clear, from Peter's vision and subsequent amazement at the Gentiles' receiving the Holy Spirit (Acts 10), Peter understood that God did not distinguish between Jews and Gentiles, so long as they had faith in Christ. He therefore felt free to eat (and thereby fellowship) with Gentiles in Antioch without requiring them to undergo circumcision. However, when representatives from the Jewish church at Jerusalem arrived on the scene ("certain people came from James"), Peter "drew back and kept himself separate for fear of the circumcision faction" (Gal. 2:12), and the other Jewish Christians "joined him in this hypocrisy, so that even Barnabas was led astray by their hypocrisy" (2:13).[12]

Here something more than table manners or even hypocrisy is at stake. Paul says that he "opposed him [Cephas] to his face, because he stood self-condemned" (2:11). What lies behind this strong language is the fact that, once again, Peter has denied Christ. To be precise: he has denied by his actions *what is in Christ*, namely, the gracious inclusion of uncircumcised Gentiles in the new covenant. *Peter's actions deny the gospel.* Paul therefore charges Peter, Barnabas, and the rest of the Jewish Christians in Antioch with acting out false doctrine, with behaving in a way that does not correspond to the truth: "They were not acting consistently [*orthopodeō*] with the truth of the gospel" (Gal. 2:14). This saying is noteworthy: first, because right opinion (orthodoxy) requires right walking (orthopedics, orthopraxy) in order to be rightly related to the truth of

---

10. Ibid., 295.
11. Bloom, *Beginning to Pray*, 49.
12. I am here following the translation by Robert Gundry in his *Commentary on the New Testament: Verse-by-Verse Explanations with a Literal Translation* (Peabody, MA: Hendrickson Publishers, 2010), 737.

the gospel; second, because our "walk" may not correspond fully to the truth but be moving toward it. The first point underlines the importance of avoiding the inner/outer inconsistency that is the essence of hypocrisy. The second point poses the question to which we now turn: is it hypocritical to present oneself as "already" at a point if one is "not yet" entirely there?

COSTUME: PUTTING ON CHRIST

Among the truths that we discover in examining *what is in Christ* is the truth about who we are: what it means to be human. The good news of the gospel is that everything has been made new in Christ, including human persons (2 Cor. 5:17). Christian doctrine rips away our socially constructed masks and reveals us as we truly are by showing us *what is in Christ*. We need, however, to return to the initial objection, that the theatrical model encourages hypocrisy, especially in light of Paul's injunction to "put on the Lord Jesus Christ" (Rom. 13:14). This sounds as though Christ is some kind of clothing. Paul tells the Colossians that they have "clothed" themselves with "the new self" (Col. 3:10), complete with "accessories" such as "compassion, kindness, humility, meekness, and patience " (3:12–13). Love completes the outfit: "Above all, clothe yourselves with love" (3:14).

"Putting on" is an ambiguous notion. To *put on* a costume may be a way of *putting one over* on someone. A "put-on" can mean a deception. Does doctrine exacerbate the risk of hypocrisy when it encourages saints to "put on" Christ? C. S. Lewis poses the question in his inimitable way. In a chapter from *Mere Christianity* titled "Let's Pretend," Lewis asks us to consider what we are doing when we utter the first two words of the Lord's Prayer: "Our Father." Saying those words means that we are putting ourselves in the place of a child of God: "To put it bluntly, you are *dressing up as Christ*."[13] Lewis observes that dressing up as Christ is "a piece of outrageous cheek. But the odd thing is that He has ordered us to do it."[14] Why? Because often, says Lewis, "the only way to get a quality in reality is to start behaving as if you had it already."[15] There is "good" as well as "bad" pretending, he suggests. I want to say something similar about the way disciples play their parts, the performance of the saints, and the special kind of pretending that we may associate with Christian doctrine.

The Christian's Outfit

In order to play their roles correctly, there are a number of things that disciples have to put off before putting on others. Paul gives his readers whole lists of things that should be in the disciples' wardrobe and things that should not be

---

13. C. S. Lewis, *Mere Christianity*, 163, emphasis original.
14. Ibid.
15. Ibid.

worn. The "things" in questions are actually behaviors, actions that, if they become habitual, are formative of character, for better or for worse. Things to "put off" include "anger, wrath, malice, slander" (Col. 3:8)—things we do with words and deeds. It is not simply particular acts that Paul wants us to put off, however, but rather the whole "old self [*palaion anthrōpon*] with its practices" (Col. 3:9; cf. Eph. 4:22). Paul elsewhere (Rom. 5:12–6:8) says that this "old self" was crucified with Christ, and in context he seems to be referring to what we were "in Adam" (i.e., in an earlier stage of the theodrama, in this age rather than in the age to come). Disciples must discard their "Adam" costume.

Conversely, there are several new garments to put on: "the armor of light" (Rom 13:12); "the likeness of God" (Eph. 4:24); "the whole armor of God" (6:11); "the breastplate of righteousness" (6:14); "the breastplate of faith and love, and for a helmet the hope of salvation" (1 Thess. 5:8); even "immortality" (1 Cor. 15:53–54) and a "heavenly dwelling" (2 Cor. 5:2). Paul again summarizes the wardrobe by encouraging disciples to put on "the new self" (Col. 3:10) or, stated even more succinctly, "Christ" (Rom 13:14; Gal 3:27).

What does it mean to "put on" Christ? No one gains superpower simply by putting on a Superman costume, so what gives disciples the right to think that they can become little Christs or that they can clothe themselves with Christ's righteousness? Isn't pretending to be righteous when one is not the very essence of hypocrisy? The answer to this question is not as straightforward as one might think, particularly if C. S. Lewis is right about "good" pretending. It is to this possibility that we now turn.

Putting On: The Fundamental Issue

The fundamental issue is whether acting a part (e.g., putting on Christ, kindness, humility, etc.) is always hypocritical, or whether there is a sense in which it can be viewed as authentic. Can disciples *become* rather than merely playact the part they have been given to play? This issue is related to a more general concern about the moralism that seems to hover around, or haunt, the very notion of *performing*. What the two concerns have in common is a worry about viewing the Christian life in terms of performance or *acting out*. Is it possible truly to *become* virtuous by *acting* virtuously?

Jennifer Herdt agrees with Lewis that often the only way to acquire a virtue is to start behaving as if one had it already. So far, so theodramatic—and even Aristotelian: "According to Aristotle, we acquire virtues largely by habituation, that is, by acting as if we already possess them."[16] In Herdt's view, Luther and other Protestant theologians were suspicious of such attempts to acquire virtue, however, because they worried that these attempts would encourage pride and self-love, not to mention reliance on one's own works rather than God's grace.

---

16. Jennifer Herdt, *Putting on Virtue: The Legacy of the Splendid Vices* (Chicago: University of Chicago Press, 2008), 23.

What appear to be virtues are, on this account, mere *semblances* of virtue. For Luther, nothing we *do*, no "external" practice or activity, can ever produce Christian righteousness. We do not become little Christs by mimicking Christ's behavior. Mimicry, seeking to put on Christ after the flesh, is "mere" imitation, an external, superficial, fruitless, and deceptive enterprise.

This Protestant anxiety has Augustinian roots. To suggest that disciples can, by dint of their own effort, do the right thing—make themselves righteous—is to succumb to a kind of Pelagian can-do, self-help mentality, where "ought" (i.e., "be ye holy") implies "can." This Augustinian anxiety in turn has Pauline roots. Paul insists that righteousness comes through faith in Christ, not through the "works of the law" (i.e., moralism) for the simple reason that sinners are unable to keep the law (Rom. 3:19–28; Gal. 2:16; 3:10).[17] An even more telling example comes from the book of Hebrews: "For since the law has but a shadow of the good things to come instead of the true form of these realities, it can never, by the same sacrifices which are continually offered year after year, make perfect those who draw near. . . . And every priest stands daily at his service, offering repeatedly the same sacrifices, which can never take away sins" (10:1, 11 RSV). This is not to say that offering sacrifices is a futile exercise (they have typological significance, pointing to the definitive sacrifice of Jesus Christ), only that performing sacrifices does not make a person righteous.

Herdt traces a different Augustinian path to a more positive conclusion, one that recognizes a legitimate place for moral striving (i.e., acting virtuously): "There is no other way to become what we are called to be except by acting a part."[18] The hero of Herdt's alternative account is Erasmus. Erasmus is open to the possibility that even those who do not explicitly confess Christ may be walking "in his steps" to the extent that they are imitating other moral exemplars whose beauty they do recognize. It is as if those who act according to their *better natures* begin to be assimilated to Christ by *grace*: "Erasmus offers what could be considered a performance conception of virtue: we develop the virtues only by enacting them, and so transform being through doing."[19] Erasmus adds two important caveats (to which we shall return): first, we must remember that we have not yet arrived at complete Christlikeness but are on the way; second, we are not acting independently, but rather are participating in divine agency.

Herdt worries that Protestants like Luther are unable to give a meaningful account of moral agency and psychology if persons can act virtuously only after God creates new wills and hearts. Grace works *through* nature to improve it, not

---

17. This is not the place to enter into extended discussion of "old" and "new" perspectives on Paul or of the nature of Judaism. For my own view on what Paul means by justification, see my "Wrighting the Wrongs of the Reformation? The State of the Union with Christ in St. Paul and Protestant Soteriology," in *Jesus, Paul, and the People of God: A Theological Dialogue with N. T. Wright*, ed. Richard Hays and Nicholas Perrin (Downers Grove, IL: InterVarsity Press, 2011), 235–58.
18. Herdt, *Putting on Virtue*, 168.
19. Ibid., 128.

on nature to transform it, she thinks.[20] The difference is not insignificant: with Erasmus, Herdt wants to say that those who strive to act virtuously are playing Christ (i.e., imitating Christ) even if they do not explicitly know Christ (or have faith in Christ). She devotes a chapter to examining a theatrical conception of virtue that she finds in the plays of Jacob Bidermann (1578–1639), the great Jesuit playwright. For seventeenth-century Jesuits, the theater was nothing less than a means of character and even spiritual formation. For example, Bidermann's *Philemon Martyr* tells the story "of a pagan actor who is *converted* to Christianity in the course of *acting the part* of a Christian."[21] Conversion is not only the sincerest form of flattery but also the limit case for the idea that we become the part we play. The issue concerns the nature of "the power exercised over them by attractive exemplars."[22]

Can we by *imitating* become like God? Can we by acting (*mimēsis*) not only pretend to be but actually become virtuous, or must we simply wait for God's transforming grace to make us new creatures? Finally, to what extent does this either-or (i.e., humans acting virtuously vs. God acting graciously) wrongly force us to view human and divine agency as in competition with one another? On Herdt's account, persons acquire virtue by mimetic (imitative) action, by playing a part. We can be inspired to "go and do likewise" by exemplars whose acts and lives we find attractive (Luke 10:37). For example, we want to be like the woman who did a "beautiful thing," anointing Jesus' feet with oil (Mark 14:6 RSV). More important, we want to be like Christ and those who follow him. While Herdt rightly calls our attention to the role of acting virtuously in order to become virtuous, we need to strengthen her account by insisting that what disciples ultimately must act out is not fiction (what if) but reality (what is), namely, their being in Christ.

Mimesis: Acting Out

Imitation (*mimēsis*) is an important biblical principle. Saints are to imitate both good (3 John 11) and God (Eph. 5:1). If this direction were all that disciples had to go on, they would have difficulty determining what to do: it is hard to imitate abstractions. Fortunately, most biblical references to imitation are more specific. Paul repeatedly encourages his readers to imitate his own conduct and concrete example: "be imitators [*mimētai*] of me" (1 Cor. 4:16). If that still sounds too abstract, Paul is happy to give specifics. He encourages the church at Thessalonica, for example, to imitate his willingness to work night and day in order not to be a burden while he was with them (2 Thess. 3:7-9).

---

20. This is similar to Thomas Aquinas's conception of cooperative grace whereby God uses our acts of love, mercy, and goodness to transform us into loving, merciful, and good persons (*Summa theologiae* I-II Q. 111 art. 2).
21. Herdt, *Putting on Virtue*, 128, emphasis added.
22. Ibid., 344.

What makes Paul the paradigm of discipleship is his absolute focus on, and passion for, imitating Christ: "Be imitators of me, as I am of Christ" (1 Cor. 11:1). Interestingly, the letter's first call to become Paul's imitators (4:16) occurs just after his confession of weakness and litany of tribulations, culminating with his description of apostles as the "refuse" (NIV) or "rubbish of the world" (4:13). This is only fitting, for what Paul seeks to imitate is the cruciform way of Jesus Christ: to act out Christ is to imitate the weakness of the cross. Though he does not use the term *mimēsis* in Philippians 2, the idea of imitation is clearly there when Paul encourages the Philippians to imitate Christ's attitude or mind. Because Jesus humbled himself unto death, so should we (Phil. 2:5–8). Indeed, perhaps the most distinctive virtue that disciples are to put on is Christian— which is to say, *Christ's*—humility: selflessness, the quality of regarding oneself as having less importance than others (Phil. 2:3).

Disciples imitate their masters. Masters are role models because their actions provide a template that guides the actions of their followers. In Jesus' case, he even gave his disciples the very words they were to say to God in order to pray like him: "Pray then in this way: Our Father in heaven . . ." (Matt. 6:9). Yet questions remain: Imitation may be the sincerest form of flattery, but is it a means of sanctification? Does repeating Jesus' words constitute true prayer? Does acting humbly like Paul make someone humble?

The Austrian philosopher Ludwig Wittgenstein had fiercely loyal disciples at Cambridge University, where he taught in the 1930s and 1940s. Gilbert Ryle, another philosopher, remarked after one visit to Cambridge that "veneration for Wittgenstein was so incontinent that my mentions of any other philosopher were greeted with jeers."[23] His student-disciples wore tweed jackets and white open-necked shirts identical to Wittgenstein's. They even tried to imitate his mannerisms, expressions, catchwords, and tone of voice, going so far as to put their hands over their foreheads and cry "Ja!" when they approved of something said—never mind that they did not otherwise speak German: "How religiously the inner circle of the disciples followed the master has a comical air to it: sleeping in narrow beds, wearing sneakers, carrying vegetables in string bags to let them breathe, and putting celery in water when serving it for dinner."[24]

If it walks, talks, and mocks like a Wittgenstein, is it truly Wittgensteinian? Some of his disciples apparently out-Wittgensteined Wittgenstein, "for the master himself was not as ascetic as is often presented."[25] One wonders whether these forms of external imitations get beyond mimicry to true mimesis. Sadly, imitating mannerisms do not make a person. The conclusion should be obvious: his disciples were striving to be like Wittgenstein "according to the flesh" (Rom. 8:5, 13).

---

23. Cited in David Edmonds and John Eidinow, *Wittgenstein's Poker: The Story of a Ten-Minute Argument between Two Great Philosophers* (New York: HarperCollins, 2001), 31.
24. Ibid., 34.
25. Ibid.

Something similar takes place in Charles Sheldon's best-selling 1897 *In His Steps*, a fictional account of what happens to a congregation when its pastor challenges them systematically to imitate Jesus. The story begins with the Rev. Maxwell preaching on 1 Peter 2:21: "For to this you have been called, because Christ also suffered for you, leaving you an example, so that you should follow in his steps." At the conclusion of the service, a homeless man stands up and asks, "What does it mean to follow his steps? What does it mean to imitate him?" After speaking, he collapses and then dies some days later. The following week, Rev. Maxwell asks for volunteers who will pledge not to do anything for an entire year without first asking, "What would Jesus do?" Those who take the pledge must act exactly as Jesus would, no matter what the consequence. The bulk of Sheldon's book traces the stories of the various church members who try to act out what they think Jesus would do. Interestingly, most remain at their secular posts: the newspaper editor does not quit his job, for example, though he does decide not to devote a three-column story to a prizefight, carry advertisements for whiskey, or print a Sunday edition!

Contrast Sheldon's *In His Steps* with Thomas à Kempis's fifteenth-century devotional masterpiece *The Imitation of Christ*, a critique of those who try to reproduce the "externals" of Jesus' life (e.g., poverty) rather than focusing on the "internal" spiritual source from which the former flow. It is one thing to follow stage directions ("stand here, do this"), quite another to follow directions for what Thomas calls the "interior life" ("Let not your hearts be troubled" [John 14:1 RSV]; "Rejoice always" [1 Thess. 5:16]).

Paul's "I die every day!" (1 Cor. 15:31) presents what is perhaps the most extreme challenge for the imitator-disciple and actor. Here too, Paul is simply imitating Christ: "If any want to become my followers, let them deny themselves and take up their cross daily and follow me" (Luke 9:23). Is dying daily, the cruciform pattern of Jesus' life, a matter of external action or internal passivity? Can we learn to die daily by going through some series of external motions? Is this what it means to "act out" the Christian life? On the contrary: taking up one's cross involves not simply doing certain things but also having the right desires and motivations. Ultimately we must lose ourselves in order to find ourselves; we must crucify the thought that we can imitate Christ through our own resources. The way forward is to see that the genuine imitation of Christ is always a matter of acting *from the inside out*.[26] Union with Christ is the Christian watchword: what disciples act *out* is their being *in* Christ.

Christos: What/Who/How Disciples Act Out

To be, or not to be, *in Christ*: that *is* the question, but not something that disciples can answer for themselves. Disciples can only act out Christ if Christ

---

26. See also Larry Bouchard, *Theater and Integrity: Emptying Selves in Drama, Ethics, and Religion* (Evanston, IL: Northwestern University Press, 2011).

is first in them. Paul speaks of the Father delivering sinners from the dominion of darkness, characterized by deep-set opposition to God, and transferring them to the kingdom of his beloved Son (Col. 1:13). This delivering is theodramatic: only God can break the power of sin in a person's life, reorient one's heart and mind, and put one in the orbit of the Son's resurrection life. The "transfer" of sinners from one kingdom to another is less geographic than temporal, a transition from the old to new, from this age to the age to come. This transfer is not quite time travel, but it does involve the end of history inbreaking into the middle, the new creation inbreaking into the midst of the old.

Doctrine not only informs us of what God was and is doing in Christ (i.e., the drama); it is also a precious indication that aids disciples to discern what *they* are doing in Christ (i.e., being clothed with a new costume/status) and what Christ is doing in them (i.e., communicating new life). In particular, a number of doctrines associated with soteriology expand on the truth that what is in Christ is *us*—disciples, members of his body, the church. Indeed, one way to summarize the good news of the gospel is by describing the twin aspects of this new state of affairs: *we in Christ* and *Christ in us*.

Acting out Christ turns out to be a function of our participation in Christ's history (the "already" of his death and resurrection) and future (the "not-yet" of his final victory and exaltation). Call it eschatological participation, a this-age taking part in the reality of the age to come. Eschatological participation in Christ's new life is possible only through faith in the word, in the gospel of Jesus Christ, and the power of the Holy Spirit. In sum: disciples can only act out Christ because the Father has first incorporated them into the Son through the Holy Spirit. The drama of discipleship is the progressive realization that one's own existence owes everything to the drama of the Christ: "I have been crucified with Christ; and it is no longer I who live, but it is Christ who lives in me" (Gal. 2:19–20).

It is vitally important that disciples not confuse the *is* of *what is in Christ* with *as if*. Paul is not playing make-believe when he says, "It is Christ who lives in me." He does not say, "It is *as if* Christ lives in me." This gets us no further than a pious fiction. This is *bad* pretending. At the same time, in making clear *what is in Christ*, doctrine does have recourse to the imagination. This is so because the *is* is *eschatological*. Disciples really do enjoy union with Christ *already*, thanks to the indwelling Holy Spirit, even though they have *not yet* attained to the full measure of Christlikeness. Doctrine that sets forth *what is in Christ* requires a robust eschatological imagining, a faith-based seeing that perceives what is *not yet* complete, our salvation, as *already* finished, because of our union with Christ.

Here is the crucial point: what Lewis calls "good pretending" is not a fiction but an eschatological reality. Though it is not visible to the naked eye, the eye of faith sees that those who put their faith in the gospel of Jesus Christ truly (i.e., eschatologically) participate in Christ. God transfers saints from the old age to the new so that they now participate in the nature and history of Christ instead of the history of Adam. To be *in Christ* is to participate in a new,

Spirit-empowered resurrection mode of existence, to live and move and have our being in a new sphere, "transplanted into a new soil and a new climate, and both soil and climate are Christ."[27]

To be in Christ is to be restored to what humans were created to be: persons who actively image God by representing his cause and embodying his rule at all times and places. Christ fulfills humanity's destiny by perfectly obeying God's will, thereby fulfilling the covenant role first assigned to Adam. To be in Christ is to recover one's true humanity and deepest identity, as covenant servants—prophets, priests, and vice-regents—of the covenant Lord. To be "in Christ" is therefore to be not an arbitrary but an authentic and answerable self, a disciple who responds to God's call like Samuel ("Here I am!" [1 Sam. 3:4]) and Mary ("Let it be with me according to your word" [Luke 1:38]). To be in Christ is to have both a new orientation and a new power: the Holy Spirit, the giver of life (2 Cor. 3:6). What disciples ultimately act out on the stage of world history is their eternal election in Christ.[28]

Earlier we picked on Peter as an example of one whose actions denied the gospel. It is only appropriate, then, that we now take our bearings from Peter's own words to the early church about what it means to act out our union with Christ by which we become "participants of the divine nature" (2 Pet. 1:4). Calvin helpfully explains that the word *nature* (in 2 Pet. 1:4) refers not to God's essence but quality (i.e., godliness): the chief end of humanity is conformity to the image of God in Jesus Christ.[29] Peter, this disciple-errant, has clearly learned his lesson. He now understands that humans do not have resources in and of themselves to follow, much less to become like Christ. Rather, it is Jesus' own power that gives us "everything needed for life and godliness" (1:3). Virtue is not something that we can acquire simply by redoubling our merely human efforts, even though it is something that Peter expects disciples to act out (1:5–7).

Peter explains the key to acting out Christ: it is the knowledge of "his precious and very great promises" (1:4), meaning the covenantal knowledge that, in Christ, God has fulfilled his promise to bring about "new heavens and a new earth" (3:13) and to give sinners new natures (hearts). Peter knows that for those in Christ, a new life in a new world has dawned, which is why he goes on to say that through this promise we "may escape from the corruption that is in the world" (1:4). This is similar to Paul's idea that anyone in Christ "puts on imperishability" (1 Cor. 15:54; cf. Phil. 3:21).[30] Creatures participate in the

---

27. James S. Stewart, *A Man in Christ: The Vital Elements of St. Paul's Religion* (Grand Rapids: Baker, 1975), 157.

28. Marcus Peter Johnson, *One with Christ: An Evangelical Theology of Salvation* (Wheaton, IL: Crossway, 2013), 33–39.

29. See John Calvin, *Commentary on the Second Epistle of Peter*, on 1:4; in *Commentaries on the Epistle of Paul to the Hebrews and the First and Second Epistles of St. Peter* (Grand Rapids: Wm. B. Eerdmans Publishing Co., 1963).

30. James M. Starr devotes an extended discussion of 2 Pet. 1:4 in relation to Paul's theology of union with Christ in his *Sharers in Divine Nature: 2 Peter 1:4 in Its Hellenistic Context* (Stockholm: Almqvist & Wiksell, 2000), 167–216.

divine nature inasmuch as the Spirit unites them to Christ, enabling them "to share *by grace* in the sonship that Christ has by nature."[31]

The Holy Spirit is the one who, through faith, unites us to Christ. Christ lives in us by the Spirit; the Spirit is the "dresser" who clothes disciple-actors with Christ's righteousness. Disciples do not need to repeat the once-for-all sacrifice of Jesus, but they do bear witness to its definitiveness by the way they now live, namely, as citizens of heaven who have been transferred from the domain of death into the kingdom of God. How then ought disciples act out Christ? According to Peter, by participating in the drama of the Christ through faith, supplementing faith with the seven other virtues he mentions: moral excellence, knowledge, self-control, steadfastness, godliness, brotherly affection, and love (2 Pet. 1:5–7)—qualities all defined ultimately by what is in Christ.

The disciple who does not act out Christ in these ways is "nearsighted and blind, and is forgetful of the cleansing of past sins" (1:9). Stated differently: those who do not act out Christ have forgotten their standing *in* Christ. They suffer from a deficit of eschatological imagination, unable to accept the first article of faith: "If anyone is in Christ, there is a new creation" (2 Cor. 5:17).

Doctrine is quintessentially evangelical when it explicates the good news of the gospel, what Calvin calls the "double grace" that follows from our union with Christ.[32] The doctrines of justification and sanctification both speak of what is in Christ, declare *that* it is, and in so doing, inform disciples of their new and authentic identities. First, justification: "we in Christ" (Rom. 6:3–4; 1 John 2:28). Those who are by faith in Christ are incorporated into his story of obedient sonship. They are forgiven sinners and adopted children who enjoy a new standing (a right relation, a relation of rightness) in the family of God. What is in Christ is perfect filial obedience, and those who are united to him enjoy all the rights and privileges that accompany sonship. In Luther's words: "The *Logos* puts on our form and pattern, our image and likeness, so that it may clothe us with its image, its pattern, and its likeness."[33]

Second, sanctification: "Christ in us" (Gal. 2:20; 1 John 3:24). It is not enough to have the status of Christ's righteous sonship; disciples also want to become children who live lives pleasing to God by becoming more like Christ. If justification is the indicative of one's union with Christ, sanctification is the imperative. The ongoing challenge of the Christian life is to act out the truth of our union with Christ. To be sure, our efforts to live holy lives do not justify us. We put on Christ by faith, yet it requires effort to act out what faith has received, namely, our union with Christ. To put on Christ means not only that we bear his name ("Christopher" = *Christophóroi* Gk. lit. "Christ bearing") but also that we bear his image (1 Cor. 15:49), the abuse he endured (Heb. 13:13),

---

31. Douglas Harink, *1 and 2 Peter*, BTCB (Grand Rapids: Brazos Press, 2009), 144.

32. See esp. J. Todd Billings, *Union with Christ: Reframing Theology and Ministry for the Church* (Grand Rapids: Baker Academic, 2011).

33. Martin Luther, *Werke: Kritische Gesamtausgabe*, Weimarer Ausgabe [= WA] (Weimar: Böhlaus, 1964), 1:28, 25–32.

and even his death in our bodies (2 Cor. 4:10). However, even this work is ultimately rooted in God's gracious doing in Christ through the Spirit: "Work out your own salvation with fear and trembling, for it is God who is at work in you, enabling you both to will and to work" (Phil. 2:12-13).

In learning to act out their new life in Christ, disciples begin to enact their true humanity, for humans are made in the image of God, of which Christ alone is perfect exemplar (2 Cor. 4:4; Col. 1:15). As Son of Man, Christ is the second Adam, the definitive covenant servant, the paradigm prophet, priest, and king. God has cast human beings in the play of the world to be not mask-wearing persona but holy icons, persons who with "unveiled faces" (2 Cor. 3:18) increasingly reflect God's character in all they do and so: "You shall be holy, for I am holy" (1 Pet. 1:16). All those who have put on Christ are equipped to play the part. To act out our being in Christ is to put into practice the new life and the new covenant we have in him (2 Pet. 1:8-10).

It only remains to stress that acting out what is in Christ has nothing to do with playacting or pretending. On the contrary, to act out our new identity in Christ—to put on Christ, the costume of Christ's righteousness—is gradually to realize, one day at a time, the truth of our "eternal weight of glory." To put on Christ, it takes eschatological imagination, the ability to see as "already" started what is "not yet" complete. Society is all too ready to dress us in the conventional costumes of the day, but these roles betray our true selves, for the disciple's life "is hidden with Christ in God" (Col. 3:3). It follows that by acting out Christ, disciples are not pretending but rather getting real: for reality is first and foremost *what is in Christ*.

PROMPTS: WORD AND SPIRIT AS *AIDE-MÉMOIRE* AND MEANS OF GRACE

Imitating Christ is no burden for genuine disciples who act out only what, or rather who, is in them. The disciple's mandate is simply "Become who you already are [in Christ] (cf. Col. 3:1-4)." Here we may recall what was said earlier about James's mirror and the importance of being not merely hearers but also doers of the word. To attend to God's word, "the perfect law, the law of liberty" (1:25) is indeed like looking into a mirror; for we see ourselves there in light of the gospel, the word that frees us from the task of becoming righteous through our own resources ("works"). And yet James expects us to do "works," not in order to become worthy of union with Christ but as a fruit of that union: "I by my works will show you my faith" (2:18).

The real work of discipleship, growing into our parts as "little Christs," therefore remains, not as a condition but as a consequence of our salvation. We have been elected, cast in the role of Jesus' disciples, not because we were holy but in order "to be holy" (Eph. 1:4). If disciples are to become Christlike, they must do more than learn their lines; they must also develop their characters.

And in order to avoid hypocrisy, disciples must do more than go through the external motions of saints; they must also be sanctified. Sanctification too is ultimately God's work, yet God works not simply "on" but "with" his saints. When it comes to Christlikeness, character development is a matter of spiritual formation. It is ultimately the Holy Spirit who conforms disciples to Christ through the ministry of the word of the gospel.

The significance of word and Spirit for Christian character development is clear from the very first mention of disciples in Paul's earliest epistle. Paul writes approvingly of the Thessalonians' example of faith, hope, and love, prompted by the gospel that came in word and in the power of the Holy Spirit (1 Thess. 1:2–5a). Paul's own example contributed as well: "You know what kind of persons we proved to be among you for your sake" (1:5b). The Thessalonian disciples became, in turn, "imitators [*mimētai*] of us and of the Lord," because, in spite of persecution, they "received the word with joy inspired by the Holy Spirit" (1:6). Christian character is indeed developed through hardship, for the way of Jesus Christ is joyful endurance. It is precisely the Thessalonians' joyful welcome of the word through faith that renders them Christlike, so much so that Paul says they in turn have become "role models" to all the believers in neighboring regions, indeed, "in every place" (1:7–8).

With the example of the Thessalonians before us, now we turn to examine how word and Spirit serve as helps and catalysts, holy prompts, to disciples who seek not only to learn their lines but also to develop their characters In order to become the role they play. Word and Spirit are means of grace, prompts God uses to help disciples put on the character of Christ.[34]

Sermon: An External Ministry of the Word

> *The devil cares nothing about the written Word, but where one speaks and preaches it, there he takes to flight.*
> —Martin Luther, cited by Meusner, *Luther the Preacher*

Luther's grand claim for the power that accompanies preaching rings somewhat hollow in a culture where words, spoken or written, are increasingly viewed with suspicion or deemed powerless to effect genuine change, especially after an election year. There are more media than ever but fewer and fewer forums where people sit passively to listen to one person talking for more than a few minutes. And whoever does have the impertinence to speak continuously for twenty minutes or so had better not preface or conclude the discourse with a

---

34. Cf. the Heidelberg Catechism, Question 65: "Since then we are made partakers of Christ and all his benefits by faith only, whence doth this faith proceed? Answer: From the Holy Ghost, who works faith in our hearts by the preaching of the gospel, and confirms it by the use of the sacraments." In the next chapter I will examine two more words that serve as means of grace for Christian character formation: the visible word (i.e., sacraments) of baptism and the Lord's Supper.

"Thus saith the Lord." The response to such a scandalous claim would likely be not "Thanks be to God" but "Well, that's your opinion."[35]

In the next chapter we shall have more to say about the role of doctrine and teaching in the church. Our immediate concern is with preaching as a means of grace that reminds disciples who they are, from where they have come, and why they are here. As a means of grace, preaching plays a vital role in the economy of Christian character development. In speaking of "character development," I mean to highlight not the formation of moral values but rather the sense of who one is and what role one is playing. Before we set out to acquire this or that virtue, we must know who we are playing, a challenging prospect in an age where many see roles as arbitrary social constructions and personal identities as graven images. In an age where many use surgical techniques to approximate their ideal image, it is easy to think of identity as a commodity that can be bought (or stolen). A good deal of advertising draws consumers into dramas whose happy ending depends only on making the right purchase ("I shop, therefore I am"). Identity has also become the focus of politics, where individuals group together on the basis of their differences from others. Which differences define us? Which differences ought to define us? Wretched indeterminate ethnic-gendered person that I am! Who can bespeak the meaning and purpose of this body, this site of political warfare?

True identity is not a function of ethnicity or any other kind of denominational label, including church denominations, but rather of one's relationship to Jesus Christ: "Whoever is not with me is against me" (Matt. 12:30; Luke 11:23). The good news is that we do not need to act like Christ in order to be right with God: Christ has acted on our behalf and now invites us to act on his behalf. The best means of true character development is therefore theodramatic self-understanding: understanding oneself as caught up in God's play of making all things new in and through Christ. Preaching is perhaps the supreme instance of "faith speaking understanding." Indeed, the preacher's raison d'être is to minister the word, that is, to minister greater understanding of the faith to people of faith and to move them toward the obedience of faith.

What sets Christian preaching apart from every other form of discourse is not only its authoritative source (Scripture) and unique content (gospel), but also its function as the primary means by which God's word cultivates Christ in the believer. Preaching is a means of grace because it presents, and makes present, Christ and what is in Christ. In so doing, it reminds listeners who they are and prepares them for their role in the ongoing drama of the Christ. It accomplishes these ends not primarily by informing congregations about systems of theology but rather by forming disciples, and it forms disciples by transforming the interpretive frameworks by which they lead their lives. Gospel preaching takes subevangelical thought captive, exposing the emptiness of other narratives that

---

35. See Lance B. Paper, *The Scandal of Having Something to Say: Ricoeur and the Possibility of Postliberal Preaching* (Waco: Baylor University Press, 2013).

seek to colonize our imaginations. Gospel preaching speaks forth the true story of the world: that all things "are from him and through him and to him" (Rom. 11:36). To preach Christ is to exhort disciples not to live in the world as if some other story were true. For the disciple, there is no other drama (Gal. 1:6–7): there is only the call to follow Christ.

Preachers minister understanding from faith to faith by helping disciples both to view their lives as caught up in the drama of redemption and then to determine what they can say and do in order rightly to participate in that drama. Put differently: preachers help their listeners act out who they are in Christ. "The unfolding of your words gives light; it imparts understanding to the simple" (Ps. 119:130). Preaching "unfolds" (explicates) what has been "enfolded" (implied) in Scripture: the world "of" the text. Disciples attain understanding when they come to see who and where they are in the drama of redemption. We understand a situation when we grasp what we are to do in it, and we demonstrate our understanding by doing it. Philosophers seek understanding too. For example, Martin Heidegger wrote about authentic being-in-the-world, but he got no further than being-toward-death. Preachers of the gospel bring good news: they speak forth authentic being-in-Christ, a being-toward resurrection.

Preaching presents Christ. It does so by setting forth Christ's presence in three related ways: in Scripture, saint, and sermon.

1. *Christ's presence in Scripture.* Preachers are simply following Jesus' own example when they find Christ in Scripture. From his first sermon in Nazareth (Luke 4:16–22) to his postresurrection "walk through the Bible" on the way to Emmaus (24:13–27), Jesus opened the Scriptures and explained how they referred to him (24:27). Obviously Christ is present in the New Testament. To preach Christ from the Old Testament, however, "means that we preach, not synagogue sermons, but sermons that take account of the full drama of redemption, and its realization in Christ."[36] It is not, therefore, a matter of appealing to Jesus as a moral example, for in an important respect his work was unique. Jesus is the central character in the drama of redemption for he is both covenant Lord and Servant, the God-man Mediator (Rom. 1:1–6).[37] His story contributes to our self-understanding because we now see ourselves as the beneficiaries of his utterly unique and marvelous work.

2. *Christ's presence in saints.* To say "we in Christ" and "Christ in us" is to say that we participate in Christ's story and he in ours. It is not a matter of transubstantiation or "transubjectification": we are not absorbed into Christ's being; we remain ourselves. Nevertheless, as Calvin insisted, there is a real, spiritual union: a *communion*. Saints participate in a spiritual yet real way in Christ's story and history, his identity and status, his theodramatic death and resurrection. To be in Christ is to be already in one sense what we are not yet in another: "Our relation with [Christ] is real and not fictive, although we have the

---

36. Edmund Clowney, *Preaching Christ in All of Scripture* (Wheaton, IL: Crossway, 2003), 11.
37. See ibid., 11–20.

reality of these eschatological states of affairs in faith and in hope."[38] Christ is present as the disciple's past, present, and future. Preaching reminds disciples of their being-in-Christ and urges them to act Christ out.

3. *Christ's presence in sermon.* In viewing preaching as itself a form of the word of God, Karl Barth was simply echoing the Reformers. Calvin says that those who proclaim the Word faithfully "must therefore be listened to, as if God himself descends from heaven."[39] In Bonhoeffer's words, "Christ is . . . present . . . as the Word of the Church, i.e., as the spoken word of preaching."[40] When the word of God is rightly expounded, it is as if Christ himself were speaking. Indeed, Augustine identifies Christ as the "Inner Teacher" who imparts understanding. Luther's account of what happens in the event of preaching is less didactic than dramatic: "Preaching continues the battle begun by the saving event and is itself the saving event."[41] This is only fitting: the sermon is the theodrama's western front, as it were, the cutting edge of the word's forward progress as it conquers new territory, one heart at a time.

The purpose of the sermon is not merely to describe the theodrama, what is taking in place in Christ, but in addition to *inscribe* it on listening hearts. Preaching is doubly theodramatic: it not only proclaims the advance of God's kingdom through the cross of Christ but also is itself an ingredient in that same advance: "In preaching, an ordinary human being . . . stands over against the people of God in the name of God and proclaims the word of God."[42] This is the way the kingdom of God and the church have always advanced: through the ministry of the word.

Preaching is the prime ministry of the biblical word. Through the sermon, the preacher sets forth in speech what is in Christ. What does it have to do with us? Instead of asking how the text "applies" to us in our day and age, as if the important thing is to discover how the text relates to our world, it is better to think in terms of inserting oneself into the world of the biblical text, which is the true story of our world. Aristotle famously defines truth as saying of what is *that* it is.[43] Preachers do that and more: sermons urge us to speak, think, and act in ways that correspond to what is in Christ. Preachers thereby minister not only the word but also understanding, a grasp of what a situation requires of us, because gospel sermons ultimately minister reality. They orient us to God, the world, and ourselves by reminding us of what God, in Christ through the Spirit, is doing in the world with and for us.

---

38. Hans Burger, *Being in Christ: A Biblical and Systematic Investigation in a Reformed Perspective* (Eugene, OR: Wipf & Stock, 2009), 552.

39. John Calvin, *Ioannis Calvini opera quae supersunt omni*, 24156; cited in Herman J. Selderhuis, ed., *The Calvin Handbook* (Grand Rapids: Wm. B. Eerdmans Publishing Co., 2009), 178.

40. Dietrich Bonhoeffer, *Christology* (London: Collins, 1966), 52.

41. Martin Luther, *Luther's Works*, vol. 51, *Sermons 1*, ed. John W. Doberstein (Philadelphia: Fortress Press, 1959), xx.

42. John Leith, *Introduction to the Reformed Tradition: A Way of Being the Christian Community* (Atlanta: John Knox Press, 1977), 228.

43. Aristotle, *Metaphysics* 1011b25.

Preaching is a means of grace because it opens our eyes (or rather, our imaginations, the "eyes of your heart" [Eph. 1:18]) to the presence and activity of the risen Christ. The ministry of the word, preaching and teaching alike, trains our minds, hearts, and imaginations so that we develop good canonical habits of viewing everyday life in theodramatic perspective (*sub specie theodramatis*). Insofar as sermons insert us into the drama of redemption and hence help us to understand our parts, accept our identities, and grow into our assigned roles—to that extent they become ministerial aids in transforming us into the image of the one whose words define reality. Preaching is a prompt to put on Christ. Sermons say what is in Christ with a view to conforming the congregation's hearts, wills, and minds to this reality.

There are, of course, other ministries of the Word, such as teaching or pastoral counseling.[44] Our term "catechesis" (Gk. *katēchēsis* = instruction) derives from a Greek verb (*ēcheō*) that means "echo," and this is a fitting image for the purpose of preaching too. The purpose of the ministry of the word is to reproduce it in people's lives. Preaching is a prompt: a timely reminder that both informs and incites to action, the action being the inner realization of Christ's rule. Preaching helps us to find ourselves in Christ in order to act Christ out.

Spirit: The Inner Ministry of the Word

Words are impotent unless and until hearers take them in and give them a home. The word must be taken to heart: "incardiated."[45] Only the Holy Spirit can give us ears to hear and hearts to receive God's word. If the words of Scripture and its proclamation are the means of grace, then the Spirit is their prime minister: "No one can say 'Jesus is Lord' except by the Holy Spirit" (1 Cor. 12:3). Scripture and sermon become saving words only when the Spirit impresses them upon our minds and hearts so as to secure heartfelt assent. The Spirit writes both law and gospel on human hearts (Jer. 31:33; 2 Cor. 3:6). Calvin says that it is only when the Spirit seals Scripture (and we could add: seals preaching) on one's heart that we can say that the word *exhibits Christ*.[46]

The Spirit is the one who unites us to Christ and seals the union with words of promise and comfort, even while stimulating us with other words of exhortation and hope. The point is that word and Spirit belong together, and only together do they efficaciously exhibit and confirm *what is in Christ*. The process by which the Spirit impresses the word upon our hearts, leading us to grasp who we are in light of the gospel, is character development in the most radical sense of the

---

44. On Christian counseling, see my "Forming the Performers: How Christians Can Use Canon Sense to Bring Us to Our (Theodramatic) Senses," *Edification: Journal of the Society for Christian Psychology* vol. 4, no. 1 (2010): 5–16.

45. Cf. Bernard Ramm: "The Holy Spirit is the *internal* minister of the Word who speaks the compelling and persuasive Word to the human heart" (*The Witness of the Spirit: An Essay on the Contemporary Relevance of the Internal Witness of the Holy Spirit* [Grand Rapids: Wm. B. Eerdmans Publishing Co., 1960], 17).

46. Calvin, *Inst.* 1.9.3.

term. Such Spirit-enabled character development is nothing less than spiritual formation, which in turn is an aspect of sanctification.

Character development, learning to become the role we play, is another way to speak of spiritual formation, that process by which the Holy Spirit forms the life of Christ in us. Spiritual formation begins when I recognize my history as intimately connected to that of Jesus: "I am called (by the Father), I am crucified (with the Son), I am conformed (to the image of the Son by the Spirit)." Spiritual formation is therefore grounded in the reality of our union with Christ: "I am what in Christ through the Spirit I become" (cf. 1 Cor. 15:10).[47] It all begins with the actor's inner preparation, or what Paul calls the "renewing of your minds" (Rom. 12:2). The Spirit renews our minds by efficaciously ministering God's word, in particular the Father's verdict in the Son, the forgiveness of sins: "Conscience is thus eschatological, oriented to that which I have been made through Christ and which, through the power of the Holy Spirit, I am becoming."[48]

What is remarkable is how spiritual formation is a ministry of the word. Jesus' description of the Spirit's work suggests less the image of a causal power than a communicative presence. The Spirit "will teach" (John 14:26), "bear witness" (15:26 RSV), "guide you into all truth," and "declare to you the things that are to come" (16:13). Spiritual formation is the Spirit's internal ministry of the word, whose purpose is to re-create in disciples the image of their Lord (Rom. 8:29). What the Spirit ministers is not generic holiness but concrete Christlikeness. As the Spirit's testimony to the Lord's word guarantees its geographic expansion (Acts 13:49), so the Spirit enables the word to capture our every thought and imagining (2 Cor. 10:4-5). For it is not the body as much as it is the human heart that is the crucial site of dramatic conflict, both in Scripture and in the contemporary world.[49] Spiritual formation, whereby Christ's heart and mind are transplanted into us, is perhaps the last chapter in the "conquest narrative" of the word of the Lord that Luke recounts in the book of Acts (19:20).

Prayer is also a way of active participation in the Son's fellowship with the Father. Praying "Our Father" with Jesus and asking for God's kingdom to come is one of the chief means of centering our hearts and minds on the truly real. Prayer is also linked to the efficacy of the word, especially in situations of spiritual warfare where the dramatic conflict for hearts and minds takes place. To put on Christ is to put on "the whole armor of God" (Eph. 6:11), and in his inventory of this armor Paul juxtaposes the "sword of the Spirit" ("the word of God") with praying "in the Spirit" (Eph. 6:17–18). It was through prayer that Jesus himself had the strength to say, "Not my will but yours be done" (Luke 22:42).[50]

---

47. John Webster, *Word and Church: Essays in Christian Dogmatics* (Edinburgh: T&T Clark, 2001), 265.
48. Ibid., 259.
49. See further my *Remythologizing Theology*, 380, 488.
50. On the role of prayer as a means of sanctification, see further ibid., 378–86.

Praying with the Son to the Father for the kingdom's coming is perhaps the best example of how the Spirit ministers the word in order to form little Christs. For disciples see themselves as they truly are, in Christ, most clearly when they pray the Scriptures in the Spirit. To participate, through prayer, in the Son's fellowship with the Father has nothing to do with pretending or playacting a role; on the contrary, it is the enactment of our core identity in Christ. Sanctification, the project of putting on Christ, often requires tearing off the social masks that we think define us. What we often take to be our true self is largely a fictive construction. According to C. S. Lewis, it is through prayer that we come to perceive our true identity. Prayer is a powerful tonic of reality, exposing our constructions to be no more than a theater of shadows: "Now the moment of prayer is for me . . . the awareness, the re-awakened awareness, that this 'real world' and 'real self' are very far from being rock-bottom realities."[51] The Spirit's internal ministry of the word that attests to our identity in Christ is ultimately an internal ministry of reality.

RECAPITULATION: THE PAULINE IMPERATIVE

Every drama involves memorable characters, persons who say and do striking things. The drama of redemption is no exception. And yet the protagonist of this story is also its playwright-producer. The creator God not only sets the stage but also enters into the drama. But this is not all. What is even more marvelous is not that God enters into human history to become one of us but that, through the work of the God-man, the triune God makes human beings into "little Christs," who embody and enact God's image in accord with God's will.

We began this chapter by confronting head-on what is perhaps the most serious objection to the theatrical model, namely, that it encourages disciples to playact their faith. That way lies madness and hypocrisy. The way forward, we suggested, is to take the theatrical metaphor with all seriousness and encourage actors to *become* the role they play, the part to which they have been cast. This is not a matter of pretending. For, as we have seen, the New Testament affirms that we have indeed "put on" Christ. What we might call the Pauline indicative is just this announcement: "As many of you as were baptized into Christ have clothed yourselves with Christ" (Gal. 3:27). That the saints have put on Christ's righteousness is, for Paul, a fait accompli.

Christ is more than a costume, more than something that Christians hide behind. Nor is Christ an external (moral) example that disciples must emulate. On the contrary, throughout this chapter I have been at pains to insist that disciples act out only what is first inside them. To "put on" Christ is to acknowledge that the life of Christ has been conceived within us. In acting out

---

51. C. S. Lewis, *Letters to Malcolm: Chiefly on Prayer* (New York: Harcourt, Brace & World, 1964), 81.

Christ we are, through the Spirit, letting Christ live in and through our lives. I then suggested that, in an era where the issue of personal identity is more confusing than ever, we view ourselves first and foremost in terms of our union with Christ and all that it entails.

The *Pauline imperative* follows from the Pauline indicative: it is only because disciples have already put on Christ (Gal. 3:27) that Paul can then exhort his readers to "put on the Lord Jesus Christ, and make no provision for the flesh, to gratify its desires" (Rom. 13:14). The preacher of the gospel walks a fine line, both reminding disciples what is already the case and encouraging them to conform their lives to what is in Christ. Realizing one's identity "in Christ" is both gift and task. The chosen "in Christ," those who have been elect/cast to play the part of saints, have the privilege and responsibility of playing the role of persons made new in Christ: that of persons destined to be remade in the image of Jesus Christ (Rom. 8:29). The divine call is decisive because it determines our identity. At the same time, our response to the call matters, for it determines whether we will embrace our God-given identities or seek to forge our own.

Only in Jesus Christ is there a perfect identity between person and role.[52] In everyone else, there is a certain gap or tension between identity (who we are, our personhood) and role (what we say and do, our persona), between what we are called to be "in Christ" and what we are actually able to realize of our destiny in this life. The tension in question is eschatological: at the present moment disciples have one foot in the past (in Adam's fallen nature) and one in the new (in Christ). It is precisely the saints' eschatological position that generates the dramatic tension: Will we become in actuality what we are in reality? Will we conform to who we truly are in Christ? Hence the importance of the Pauline imperative: *put on Christ*; bring your life into conformity with *what is in Christ*.

To speak of the Pauline indicative and imperative, the *is* and the *ought*, is to begin to perceive how Christian ethics (i.e., moral theology) follows from doctrine (i.e., dogmatic theology). Ethics is not about struggling to act like Jesus, as if Jesus were an external ideal; it is rather about acting Jesus out, because our life participates in his. Dietrich Bonhoeffer puts it well: "The place that in all other ethics is marked by the antithesis between ought and is . . . [here] is occupied in Christian ethics by the relation between reality and becoming real, . . . the relation between Jesus Christ and the Holy Spirit."[53] The disciple's character development, the saint's sanctification, is a matter of living out the heart and mind of Jesus Christ that, by grace through faith, is inscribed and impressed upon our minds and hearts by God's word and Spirit. In brief: "little Christs" are to act out their new natures, their being in Christ. Spelling out what being "in Christ" involves is the descriptive, indicative task of theology; encouraging us to conform to or act out our new natures is theology's, and the

---

52. As Hans Urs von Balthasar puts it: "Only in the drama of the God-Man do we find identity between the sublime actor and the role he has to play" (*Theo-drama*, 1 [1988]: 646).

53. Bonhoeffer, *Ethics*, 49-50.

church's, imperative task: "To act well is to act in accordance with my nature and so to move toward perfection, that is, the entire realization of my nature."[54]

No person can act well without knowing who one is or the part one has to play. Doctrine is an aid to forming disciples because it tells them who they are and how to live: because we have been raised with Christ, we are to "seek the things that are above, where Christ is" (Col. 3:1). This too is the Pauline imperative. Paul is not saying, "*Pretend* to be in Christ." On the contrary, he is telling us to act out what we truly are. Theology is not only about living to God but also about living out what Christ is. To seek what is "above" is not to deny our embodied existence in the world but to act out the kingdom of God "on earth as it is in heaven" (Matt. 6:10).

Doing these things does not make a person good; on the contrary, the good that we have to do is to live out the good that we have from being in Christ. Ethics is simply action prompted by what is in Christ: "[Christian ethics] unfolds the *is*, the new situation, the new world, which *is* as a result of Christ's saving activity."[55] Christ's saving activity is not only past but also present: Christ now reigns, and it is the disciple's privilege and responsibility to participate in this reign by acting out or *actualizing* what Christ has made real, and therefore really possible: "[Christ] is the 'is' and, in the Spirit, the 'ought.'"[56]

Jesus Christ, the second Adam, defines the new humanity that disciples are to act out: "Jesus Christ is the human response to God in which we participate by faith."[57] The more we lose ourselves to gain Christ, the more we find our true selves, for we were created for no other purpose than to be "little Christs." But wait: is this not to live boringly forever in a world where everyone is the same as everyone else? By no means! Peter, Paul, and John are each Jesus' disciples, but not his clones. C. S. Lewis goes further: "There is so much of Him that millions and millions of 'little Christs,' all different, will still be too few to express Him fully."[58] There is deep mystery here, and high paradox, but no silliness or contradiction. What we can say is that disciples are persons who live lives that are *simul mimesis et authenticos:* simultaneously imitative (i.e., true to Christ) and authentic (i.e., true to oneself).

---

54. John Webster, "'Where Christ Is': Christology and Ethics," in *Christology and Ethics*, ed. F. LeRon Shults and Brent Waters (Grand Rapids: Wm. B. Eerdmans Publishing Co., 2010), 39.
55. Christopher R. J. Holmes, *Ethics in the Presence of Christ* (London and New York: T&T Clark International, 2012), 2.
56. Ibid., 12.
57. Ibid., 15.
58. Lewis, *Mere Christianity*, 190.

Chapter 6

Forming the Company, Doing Church

Doctrinal Directions for Acting Out Life Together in Christ

> *The whole world is a theater for the display of the divine goodness, wisdom, justice, and power; but the church is the orchestra, as it were—the most conspicuous part of it.*
> —Calvin, *Commentary on Psalms*, on 135:13–14

> *I believe in . . . the holy catholic church.*
> —The Apostles' Creed

Disciples are "little Christs," but the Pauline imperative ("Put on Christ") refers to more than the costuming of individuals. Imitating Christ is not like impersonating Elvis. Christian identity, the role disciples have been called to play, requires being with others. It takes two or three gathered in Christ's name fully to represent him. It takes a company.

It takes a company of players to represent the good news of Jesus Christ. The gospel is not primarily an escape clause by which individuals make their getaway to heaven but rather an announcement that God has done something in Christ to change the world, together with the implicit summons to conform our lives to this new reality. *Observance* is the key term. Disciples first observe what God has done in Christ. Second, disciples observe this reality in the sense of obeying or conforming to it. Third, as disciples submit their wills to the will of God as revealed in Christ, they in turn are observed by the world. For, as William Ames puts it, "Observance is the submissive performance of the will of God for the glory of God."[1] The Lord's Prayer is answered as disciples gather to do God's will on earth as it is in heaven.

---

1. Ames, *Marrow of Theology*, 219.

Doing God's will on earth as it is in heaven is not something disciples undertake lightly or with their own resources only. It is not easy, perhaps not even possible, for humans to achieve true community by their own devices. "Communification by works" (to coin a phrase and a term) has proved to be an elusive ideal, as amply attested by everything from denominational divisions to the demise of communism.[2] It is for this very reason that the gospel is good news, for it announces something wonderful, perhaps even unprecedented, in human history: the creation of a new kind of community that transcends the boundaries of time, space, race, gender, and class.

The present chapter continues to unpack *what is in Christ* by considering the church, the gathered company of disciples that together comprise the body of Christ. This body is animated by Christ's Spirit, whose task is to conform disciples to the new reality coming into being in Christ. We cannot rehearse everything that is in Christ: all the treasures of wisdom are hidden in him. This chapter focuses on the *people* in Christ: the church as company of those committed to working out and walking in the way of Jesus Christ. It follows that people, the company of Christ's disciples, are a theater of the gospel, or rather, a theater of triune operations.

The "things into which angels long to look" (1 Pet. 1:12) that pertain to the gospel of salvation are being realized in, through, and as the company of Jesus' disciples. As theater of the gospel, the church is both the company of actors and the staging area in which the action is being played out.[3] In chapter 2 I described the church as the "domain of doctrine." The gathered people of God is the best place to see the love of God and the truth of Jesus Christ lived out in the fellowship of the Holy Spirit. Disciples gather both to conform to the gospel and to celebrate it.

The church makes known "the plan of the mystery hidden for ages in God" (Eph. 3:9) not only by proclaiming the gospel, but just as important, instantiating it. According to Paul, the church is the culmination of the plan and the means through which "the wisdom of God in its rich variety might now be made known to the rulers and authorities in the heavenly places" (Eph. 3:10). The church may be the orchestra of the theater of the gospel, but the angels apparently have front-row seats in the balcony.

The present chapter focuses on the church's "inner world": its life together *ad intra* (in itself), its domestic ministry. The underlying theme is *rehearsing*. Disciples gather to rehearse: to retell and remember the main action of the play, to study their roles, to learn their lines until they know them by heart, to prepare for witness/performance in the world. To be sure, theology is still

---

2. For the latter, see esp. Jean-Luc Nancy, *The Inoperative Community* (London and Minneapolis: University of Minnesota Press, 1991). Nancy argues that community is neither a collection of separate individuals nor a collective substance: "The community that becomes *a single thing* (body, mind, fatherland, Leader . . .) necessarily loses the *in* of being-*in*-common" (xxxix).

3. In the next chapter I will further treat the importance of the concept "place" in the local church's witness to its environs.

required: disciples gather to seek, speak, and show understanding of the riches that are in Christ. We shall examine the church's life together *ad extra* (toward the outside world) in the next chapter. The immediate aim of the present chapter is to appreciate the edifying role doctrine plays in the church itself.

COMMUNIO SANCTORUM: DISCIPLES' GATHERING AS COMMAND PERFORMANCE—"DO THIS"

"The church is God's new will and purpose for humanity."[4] When Peter explains to the Jews of Jerusalem that the Pentecost phenomenon is a consequence of God raising Jesus from the dead in fulfillment of the Davidic covenant, giving the status of "Lord" and "Christ" to the one they had crucified, the people responded: "Brothers," they asked, "what should we do?" (Acts 2:37). We can paraphrase Peter's answer, "Repent, and be baptized every one of you in the name of Jesus Christ so that your sins may be forgiven; and you will receive the gift of the Holy Spirit" (Acts 2:38), in two words: "*Do church!*" What is "church"? How are we to do church?

The church is the gathering of repentant sinners whom the Spirit constitutes as saints by uniting them to Jesus Christ. On this, the Puritan William Ames and the Lutheran Dietrich Bonhoeffer agree. Ames rightly perceives the church as both the object and effect of redemption: it is the object, because Christ loved the church and gave himself for the church (Eph. 5:25); it also is the effect, because the church was constituted by being called and united to Christ, through the word of the gospel and the power of the Spirit. The faith that grants individuals union with Christ also brings communion with others; hence "the church can be defined at once as a company of believers, a company of those who are in Christ, and a company of those who have communion with him"[5] and, as we shall see, with one another.

A Company of the Baptized: Participating in the Drama of the Christ

Jesus' public ministry begins with his baptism by John. Mark's account, though typically brief, says enough to indicate that something dramatic and Trinitarian is indeed happening, for when Jesus came out of the water, "he saw the heavens torn open and the Spirit descending on him like a dove," and he heard a voice from heaven saying "You are my Son, the Beloved; with you I am well pleased" (Mark 1:9–11). Matthew lingers longer on the event, noting John's initial reluctance to baptize the one who should be baptizing him, and Jesus' assurance that "it is proper for us in this way to fulfill all righteousness" (Matt. 3:15).

---

4. Dietrich Bonhoeffer, *Sanctorum Communio: A Theological Study of the Sociology of the Church*, vol. 1 of *Dietrich Bonhoeffer Works* (Philadelphia: Fortress Press, 2009), 141.
5. Ames, *Marrow of Theology*, 176.

John's baptism with water signified the repentance that sinners need to prepare themselves for the coming judgment associated with the kingdom of God. It is a symbolic act, fairly dripping with meaning. Some scholars link it to Jewish proselyte baptism, an initiatory rite; others link it to ritual cleansing. That John was calling Jews to be baptized meant that their inclusion in ethnic Israel was not enough to be right with God. That Jesus, who is sinless and thus needs no purification, presents himself for baptism suggests that he here begins to act as our representative. That he receives a special anointing of the Spirit suggests that he is equipped to undertake his messianic task, with all the prophetic, priestly, and kingly rights and responsibilities appertaining thereunto.

John contrasts his water baptism with the Messiah's baptism "with the Holy Spirit and fire" (Matt. 3:11). John's baptism sought to prepare disciples for the coming kingdom; Jesus' baptism effectively transfers them into that kingdom (cf. Col. 1:13). Jesus nevertheless commands his disciples to make more disciples precisely by "baptizing them in the name of the Father and of the Son and of the Holy Spirit" (Matt. 28:19). This is the first half of the Great Commission, the dominical charge to form a company of Christ-followers.

The most striking thing about Christian baptism is the way in which it inserts whole persons, body and soul, into the story of Jesus, and in a very public manner. Jesus' disciples do not follow a particular set of teachings; rather, they follow and identify with Jesus Christ. Especially in Luke–Acts, the disciples are believers who confess Jesus as Messiah and Lord and commit to following him as the "Way" (Acts 9:2). Baptism is a symbolic action that marks one's setting out on Jesus' way by ritually enacting the death of the old self and the birth of the new. Baptism is the actor-disciple's port of entry into the evangelical action. It is a potent précis of the climax of Jesus' messianic mission, signifying his death, burial, and resurrection. In Paul's words: "Do you not know that all of us who have been baptized into Christ Jesus were baptized into his death?" (Rom. 6:3; cf. Col. 2:12). The baptism of adults by immersion is a particularly concrete and realistic reenactment of Jesus' death and resurrection: the going under the water (often in Scripture a symbol of chaos or judgment) and the rising up from the water (a symbol of deliverance).

Baptism by water is a public declaration of an individual's initiation into the drama of redemption as an active participant, an outward expression of the inward grace of baptism by the Spirit, which effectively (albeit mystically) joins a person to Jesus' history. Water baptism is the fitting response of those who, by faith, accept the gospel and identify themselves as followers of Jesus. So, for example, when the Jews who heard Peter's explanation of Pentecost repented and believed, they were also baptized (Acts 2:41). Similarly, the Ethiopian eunuch, upon realizing that his life was implicated in the story of Jesus, demonstrates his understanding, and his acceptance of this new reality, by demanding of Philip, "Look, here is water! What is to prevent me from being baptized?" (Acts 8:37).

Calvin comes close to appreciating the theatrical dimension of baptism (i.e., its symbolic reenactment of Jesus' death and resurrection) when he says that it represents God's promise of forgiveness "as painted in a picture from life."[6] To be sure, Calvin regarded baptism as involving words and actions, a dramatic token of our mortification, cleaning, and renewal in Christ. As the Spirit came upon Jesus in his baptism, so baptism by water signified one's baptism with Christ's Spirit. Calvin views baptism first and foremost as a dramatic token of our union with Christ, and hence of the new life that we have in him. Indeed, Calvin says that baptism is "the firmest bond of the union and fellowship that he has deigned to form with us."[7] One of the implications of being united to Christ is that one is united to all those who similarly participate in his death and resurrection. Here is Calvin again: "Baptism is the sign of the initiation by which we are received into the society of the church."[8] The church is the company of the baptized.

Discipleship, then, begins with baptism. Baptism enables disciples to participate in the drama of the dawning of the "new creation" in Christ (2 Cor. 5:17) in the context of the old creation. It is one thing to join the company of the redeemed, quite another to know what to do next. In this regard the connection between baptism and teaching is striking. To return once more to Peter's Pentecost sermon: immediately after the three thousand were baptized, Luke tells us that those in the newly constituted Jerusalem church "devoted themselves to the apostles' teaching [*didachē*] and fellowship [*koinōnia*], to the breaking of bread and the prayers" (Acts 2:42). In devoting themselves to teaching, the church is but responding to the second part of Jesus' Great Commission: "teaching [*didaskō*] them to obey everything that I have commanded you" (Matt. 28:20).

It is not surprising that disciples baptized into the triune name of God should require teaching or instruction: "making disciples" requires both baptizing and teaching. Teaching is necessary because it is not immediately obvious how one is to join with others and act out what is in Christ. And this is precisely the purpose of doctrine: to provide instruction, call it theatrical direction, for disciples newly initiated into the drama of the Christ.

Directing the Company: The Pastor as Catechist, Dramaturge, and Theologian

Catechism: Instruction by Word of Mouth

Though the Bible is not, strictly speaking, a play script, there is much therein for disciples to learn and perform. The Bible is the primary text from which disciples learn how to act as disciples, because it is from the Bible that they learn about the divine protagonist and the nature of the triune action, the drama "behind" the doctrine, which doctrine helps us better to understand: "To learn how to

---

6. Calvin, *Inst.* 4.14.9.
7. Ibid., 4.15.6.
8. Ibid., 4.15.1.

interpret these scripts well by playing them out in one's life is to learn how to be a disciple."[9] Disciples must learn not only to tell the story of Jesus so as to identify him and say what he has done but also to live out the story and act out what is in Christ. To follow Jesus is to walk his way: "Learning how to act shapes a person into a disciple."[10]

The early church put a premium on preparing disciples for their new life in Christ. In this regard, it is most significant that for centuries in the early church, the baptism of new believers was preceded by a one-to-three-year period of instruction, or catechesis (from the Gk. *katēcheō* = to instruct orally). It is no easy thing to be baptized in the name of the Father, Son, and Spirit: What is one supposed to do after that? What began as informal teaching developed into a formalized system, the "catechumenate," complete with instruction manuals.[11] Catechesis helped new converts become disciples who could enter with understanding into the dramatic story of God and the church, an entry onto a new stage marked by one's baptism.[12]

Catechesis enjoyed two golden ages, one in the patristic era (fourth and fifth centuries), the other at the time of the Reformation. In the early church, such luminaries as Cyril of Jerusalem, Ambrose, and Chrysostom regularly gave catechetical addresses during Lent in order to prepare catechumens for baptism at Easter, at which time the successful catechumen would profess the faith and, for the first time, participate in the Eucharist, occasionally to great applause.[13] Augustine's handbook for catechists is particularly noteworthy in its focus on salvation history as the framework for the disciple's instruction and for its aim not only to teach but also to evoke a loving response from those being catechized.[14] Augustine conceived of catechism as an apprenticeship in Christian discipleship. What is all the time of catechesis for, he asks, "except to hear what the faith and pattern of Christian life should be?"[15] The implication is that good catechism prepares disciples to participate in the theodrama with all their hearts, souls, minds, and strength.

Catechesis declined after the Roman Empire became Christian and infant baptism became the norm. In an age where being a Christian was the default convention in which one was simply socialized into the faith, it no longer seemed

---

9. Terrence W. Tilley, *The Disciples' Jesus: Christology as Reconciling Practice* (Maryknoll, NY: Orbis Books, 2008), 73.

10. Ibid.

11. The best-known early instruction manuals include Hippolytus's *Apostolic Tradition*, Augustine's *Catechizing the Uninstructed*, and Gregory of Nyssa's *Catechetical Oration*.

12. See L. Gregory Jones, "Baptism: A Dramatic Journey into God's Dazzling Light: Baptismal Catechesis and the Shaping of Christian Practical Wisdom," in *Knowing the Triune God: The Work of the Spirit in the Practices of the Church*, ed. James J. Buckley and David S. Yeago (Grand Rapids: Wm. B. Eerdmans Publishing Co., 2001), 147–77.

13. See Maxwell E. Johnson, "Christian Initiation," in *The Oxford Handbook of Early Christian Studies*, ed. Susan Ashbrook Harvey and David G. Hunter (Oxford: Oxford University Press, 2008), 705. The classic study is by Michel Dujarier, *A History of the Catechumenate: The First Six Centuries* (New York: Sadlier, 1979).

14. Augustine, *Catechizing the Uninstructed* 4.8; 6.10.

15. Augustine, *Faith and Works*, 6.9.

necessary to set aside a special period for Christian instruction. Everything changed again with the Reformation, however, which from one perspective was a restoration of the vision of the church as a learning community. Both Luther and Calvin, and many of their followers as well, composed catechisms for children and adults alike.[16] The primary purpose of these Reformation catechisms was to help pastors prepare the company of the baptized to walk the Christian way. Here I want to focus on Calvin's *Catechism of the Church of Geneva* (1541).

Calvin thought it vital to recover the ancient practice of catechism: "The church of God will never preserve itself without a catechism."[17] He therefore agreed to return to Geneva only on the condition that magistrates make catechetical instruction mandatory. Calvin recovered not only the practice but also the ancient form of catechism, which consisted of questions and answers organized around the Ten Commandments, the Apostles' Creed, the Lord's Prayer, and the sacraments.[18] The catechism was used in churches and homes, and public recitations from the catechism took place four times a year, just before celebrations of the Lord's Supper. It consisted of 373 pairs of questions and answers on matters concerning faith, obedience, spirituality, and church life. The first question provides an orientation for the others: "What is the chief goal of human life?" (Answer: "It is to know God").

Though the Geneva Catechism became a teaching norm in the church, Calvin intended to do more than transmit knowledge. To know God rightly is to respond in worship, and the way rightly to worship God is "to put our whole trust in him; to serve him by obedience to his will, . . . to call upon him in all our necessities, . . . and finally, to acknowledge, both in heart and with the mouth, that he is the sole author of all blessings."[19] Accordingly, it is best if we think of Calvin's Catechism as instruction for disciples in doctrine, duty, and devotion alike.[20] Catechetical instruction ultimately served a pastoral purpose: to give disciples the requisite understanding for right participation not only in the Lord's Supper but also in all aspects of the Christian life. Karl Barth was a great admirer of Calvin's Geneva Catechism precisely for this reason: "Christian dogmatics, when it really speaks, is just as alive and intelligible as anything else in the world."[21]

---

16. Of these, perhaps the most influential was Luther's Small Catechism of 1529.

17. Calvin, letter to Edward Seymour, October 22, 1548 (cited in Scott M. Manetsch, *Calvin's Company of Pastors: Pastoral Care and the Emerging Reformed Church, 1536–1609* [Oxford: Oxford University Press, 2013], 266).

18. Calvin reordered things, putting the Ten Commandments after the Apostles' Creed instead of before it.

19. John Calvin, *Catechism of the Church of Geneva*, Q. 7 (Hartford, CT: Sheldin & Goodwin, 1815), 10. Cf. J. I. Packer's definition: "Catechesis is the communicating of Christian fundamentals of doctrine and ethics for personal spiritual response" ("The Return to Catechesis: Lessons from the Great Tradition," in *Renewing the Evangelical Mission*, ed. Richard Lints [Grand Rapids: Wm. B. Eerdmans Publishing Co., 2013], 116).

20. The Apostles' Creed norms our thoughts, the Lord's Prayer our hearts, and the Ten Commandments our habits.

21. Karl Barth, *Theology of John Calvin*, trans. Geoffrey W. Bromiley (Grand Rapids: Wm. B. Eerdmans Publishing Co., 1995), 284.

Dramaturgy: The Nature of "Sound Doctrine"

Jesus too was a catechist of sorts, and what he taught was how to recognize, and live out, God's reign on earth. Specifically, Jesus taught his followers *how to live toward God*, to cite again William Ames's fine definition of theology. Stated provocatively: Jesus taught theology, and his pedagogy took the form not only of question and answer but also of parable, prayer, and practice (to name but a few).[22] Further, among the gifts the ascended Christ gives the church are "pastors and teachers [*didaskalous*]" (Eph. 4:11). This is not the place to enter into the discussion of whether Paul had one office in mind or two. Calvin was content to view pastors as "doctors" (those who teach doctrine) as long as we acknowledge another kind of doctor who superintends the education of pastors and preserves the purity of doctrine (Calvin, *Commentary on Ephesians*, on 4:11).

Doctrine (Lat. *doctrina* = teaching) is the operative term. It is significant that the Pastoral Epistles (1–2 Timothy, Titus) repeatedly link doctrine, as instruction in living toward God, to both right confession and right conduct.[23] At its best, doctrinal instruction exercises pastoral functions: correcting error, deepening understanding, fostering wisdom, funding endurance, and encouraging godliness. Indeed, this is why doctrine is "sound" (Gk. *hygianousē* = health-giving [Titus 2:1]): right teaching steers disciples in the life-giving way of Jesus Christ, as opposed to false doctrines that are toxic or noxious, inimical to an individual's or community's well-being. Sound doctrine gives rise to salutary habits of life.

Pastor-theologians exist to help disciples learn and play their parts in a fitting manner. Here catechism resembles theatrical rehearsal, where would-be disciples not only learn their lines but also new reflexes, thus enabling them spontaneously to glorify God and do the right thing, precisely because they understand the nature and telos of the drama of redemption and their place in it. Pastor-theologians are dramaturges (workers of drama) charged with preparing the company of the baptized to put feet on their doctrine, walking the way of Jesus Christ with not only theoretical but also practical understanding. The dramaturge is the person who makes drama work by helping the actors better to understand the (trans)script and play their respective parts. It is the dramaturge's responsibility to research the play, keep it historically accurate, think about the playwright's intent, and study the play's production history.[24] In sum: the pastor-theologian teaches people of faith to speak and act with right understanding. Disciples understand the drama of redemption when they are able to explain it to others in their own words and when they are able to participate rightly in the play's action.

This, I submit, is the nature and purpose of Christian doctrine: to provide a special kind of instruction, akin to theatrical direction, for fitting participation

---

22. See Robert H. Stein, *The Method and Message of Jesus' Teaching* rev. ed. (Louisville, KY: Westminster John Knox Press, 1994).
23. Cf. the earlier discussion in chap. 1 above.
24. For more on theology as dramaturgy, see my *Drama of Doctrine*, 244–54.

in the drama of redemption. "Fittingness" is the key term. Theological fittingness requires more than logical coherence. It involves right thinking, desiring, and doing alike, involving all the disciple's faculties: cognitive, affective, and dispositional. Fitting participation requires what we might call dramatic consistency, *theodramatic* coherence, for the whole into which everything else fits is none other than the history of Jesus Christ, the concrete embodiment of the wisdom of God. Fittingness with what God has said and done must be the disciple's supreme criterion for discerning truth, goodness, and beauty alike inasmuch as these are functions of *what is in Christ*.

Doctrine, then, is the means by which the company of the baptized comes to understand better the drama of the gospel and their new role in it. It is a matter not only of education but also of character and spiritual formation. Doctrine offers directions for both theoretical and practical understanding, direction for *seeing* and *doing* the kingdom of God on earth as it is in heaven. Doctrine, then, is not simply a body of knowledge, but an active bodily doing. In particular, doctrine provides the grammar for the "body language" of the church, the body of Christ. Doctrine provides direction for what the body of Christ is to say and do in his name and for his sake. Church without doctrine to direct it is blind; yet doctrine without the church to embody it is empty. Doctrine makes explicit what we need to know to participate *understandingly* in what God is doing to renew all things in Christ. We need to know, for example, who the principal actors are, and this is precisely what the creeds of Nicaea and Chalcedon provide: identity descriptions for the triune God and for Jesus Christ, respectively.

Local, Regional, and Masterpiece Theater: Creeds and Confessions

It is the pastor's responsibility to oversee the formation of the company of the baptized. Pastors do this by providing oral instruction and, in so doing, resemble dramaturges who give theatrical direction about the meaning of the drama of redemption and how rightly to take part in it. This is a heavy responsibility, though the burden is lightened considerably when pastors attend to the great tradition of Christian dramaturgy, especially the seven ecumenical councils of the early church.[25]

As we have seen, catechisms in the early church and Reformation regularly gave attention to the Apostles' Creed that, like the ancient rule of faith, was essentially a summary of the apostolic teaching. The rule of faith has a narrative form and identifies the creator God with the covenant God of Israel and ultimately with the Father of Jesus Christ: the one who brought Israel out of Egypt is also the one who raised Jesus from the dead. This rule thus identifies the divine dramatis personae and serves as a synopsis of the Christian metadrama: the story that links cosmos, covenant, and Christ. As such, it also provided a quick way for disciples to orient themselves as the people of God in the world.[26]

---

25. See Carl R. Trueman, *The Creedal Imperative* (Wheaton, IL: Crossway, 2012), 90–102.
26. For further discussion of the rule of faith, see my *Drama of Doctrine*, 203–7.

The more one understands about what the drama of redemption is about, the more effective and fitting one's participation will be. Creeds and confessions are important and offer the pastor precious resources for deepening disciples' understanding of God and the gospel. As persons of faith, disciples want to speak with understanding. To the extent that they do speak and act, they are performing. The only question is whether they are speaking understanding or misunderstanding, performing competently or incompetently. Of course, the disciple's goal should be speaking understanding not merely with competence, but also with excellence.

The heretic chooses for oneself (Gk. *hairesis* = choice, that which is chosen) how to speak and act, even if it means speaking and acting contrary to the rest of the company of the baptized. There is thus little place for *catechesis* in *hairesis*. It is not for this kind of independence (i.e., of autonomous choice) that Christ has set us free. On the contrary, disciples are free from sin but "enslaved to God" (Rom. 6:22). Furthermore, disciples are not autonomous individuals but live together in Christ: "There is one body and one Spirit, . . . one Lord, one faith, one baptism" (Eph. 4:4–5). Pastors of local churches must do what they can to express solidarity with other local churches and, if possible, with the church universal.

Local churches would do well to attend to the performance practice of the historic catholic church. Reciting the Apostles' Creed is one way to do this. And there are other instances of creedal theology, "masterpiece theater," of which local churches ought to be aware. The Nicene Creed, for example, was not merely a local instance of faith speaking understanding, but a permanent insight into the nature of God, as well as "a guide to correct reading of Scripture and an adequate expression of belief and identity."[27] The Nicene Creed, along with the other creeds associated with the seven ecumenical councils of the ancient church, were "officially adopted to be binding on the universal church rather than merely on a local or a regional church."[28] The purpose of the creeds is to direct disciples into a deeper understanding of the meaning of the drama and the divine dramatis personae. After all, local churches are not the first to have struggled to understand the Bible. When the company of the baptized participates in the drama of redemption, they enter into a centuries-long tradition about how best to put on Christ and serve the kingdom of God.

Creedal theology gives "catholic" direction, general directions for the church at all times and places to follow; then the confessions of post-Reformation Protestantism expressed the particular identity of companies of the baptized in specific geographical regions who faced particular theological problems. As such, confessional theology originally gave direction not for the whole church nor for

---

27. Philip Turner, "Introduction," in *Nicene Christianity: The Future for a New Ecumenism*, ed. Christopher R. Seitz (Grand Rapids: Brazos Press, 2001), 11.

28. Jaroslav Pelikan, *Credo: Historical and Theological Guide to Creeds and Confessions in the Christian Tradition* (New Haven, CT: Yale University Press, 2003), 9.

individual churches but rather for churches that shared a particular history and geography, churches that became *regional* theaters of the gospel.²⁹

Pastors do well to relate the local churches under their care and instruction to creedal and confessional theology. When doing local theater, it is important to be aware of the masterpiece theaters of the past (i.e., the seven ecumenical councils) as well as the "great performances" that have given rise to the various churches of the Reformation (i.e., the historic confessional traditions of Protestantism). Creeds and confessions are more than occasional statements or ephemeral performances, more than knee-jerk responses to the immediate context. On the contrary: in speaking understanding to their own historical contexts, creeds and confessions contain lessons not only for their own times and places but also for the church today. In such manner may the Spirit guide the church "into all the truth" (John 16:13).

Catechisms, creeds, and confessions are important pedagogical devices in the pastor-dramaturge's repertory of disciple making. All too often, however, they are associated with making not disciples but divisions (i.e., denominational splits). While doctrine should divide truth from falsehood, it ought not divide Christians from their common theodramatic cause. Like all other aspects of creation, creeds and confessions too can be used to further human pride or the lust for power. They are human responses to revelation, not the revelation itself. Yet their purpose is to serve as binding indications of the church's understanding of and commitment to the God of the gospel: to the truth of *what God has done in Christ*. No one confession, tradition, or denomination exhausts or expresses everything that is in Christ, but this is no reason to despise them. For, even though they display the signs of the time in which they were first formulated, they nevertheless yield precious and permanent insights into some aspect of the drama of redemption.

A Theater of Reconciliation: Exhibiting the Peace of Christ

What is in Christ? The Nicene Creed discovered the eternal Son, the second person of the Trinity, in Christ. The Council of Chalcedon discovered that in Jesus Christ there is one person (the eternal incarnate Son) with two natures. Thus in Christ there is perfect deity and perfect humanity. But there is more, much more. There is the relationship of the triune God and the human creature. There is, in a word, *reconciliation*: "In Christ God was reconciling the world to himself" (2 Cor. 5:19). Reconciliation is itself a multifaceted reality. My focus here is on the church as a theater of reconciliation that displays the reconciliation in Christ. For there is also in Christ the company of the baptized, the body of which Christ is head (Eph. 5:23; Col. 1:18; 2:19). Hence a crucial doctrine

---

29. Interestingly, many of the 16–17th-century Protestant confessions bear national or regional titles, such as The First Helvetic Confession (1536), The Scots Confession (1560), The Belgic Confession (1561) and The Westminster Confession (1647).

that directs disciples to act out what is in Christ is the doctrine of the church: ecclesiology.

The church is both a character in the drama of redemption and, in a real sense, the drama's goal. This dual character stems from its being the harbinger of the new age in the midst of the old, the vanguard of the kingdom-city of God amid the kingdom of this world. Here, too, doctrine provides direction for understanding and performance. Consider the doctrine of the church in Calvin's *Catechism of the Church of Geneva*. To the question "Is this article necessary to be believed?" the proper response is, "Yes, truly, unless we would render the death of Christ without effect, and account all that we have said, for nothing. For this is the sole purpose of all, *that there should be a Church*."[30] At this point the skeptic will no doubt object: Surely the primary effect of Christ's death was to provide a means for sinners to escape judgment and go to heaven? Disciples need understanding of this point: Is the point of the drama to get up to heaven or to bring heaven down to earth? And then, however one answers that, what is the role of the church?

Alfred Loisy, the Roman Catholic modernist, famously observed, "Jesus foretold the Kingdom, and it was the Church that came."[31] In context, Loisy's point was that Jesus did not seem concerned with questions of the church's organization. Yet the question remains: is the church a mere parenthesis, or intermission, in the drama of redemption rather than its end and objective, as Calvin apparently thought? A good case can be made that the church, understood as the society of believers in Christ, is indeed the purpose for which God created the heavens and the earth. Though God does not live "in shrines made by human hands" (Acts 17:24), he does indwell a structure made *of* men and women: the church is the house and household of God (Eph. 2:19; cf. 1 Tim. 3:5; 3:15; Heb. 3:6; 10:21; 1 Pet. 2:5; 4:17).[32] The church is the temple of God, the place of God's special covenant presence (2 Cor. 6:16; Eph. 2:21).

The church as the "house" or "temple" of God has nothing to do with physical buildings, institutions, or organizations. The church is first and foremost the company of the baptized, and God is visibly present primarily in those reconciliatory practices that take place *between* the members of this company. It is easy to overlook the significance of Jewish-Gentile relations in the early church, but precisely there we see the firstfruit of Jesus' death on the cross. Paul is addressing Gentiles when he speaks of those who were once "far off" from "the covenants of promise" but have now been "brought near by the blood of Christ" (Eph. 2:12–13). In Christ "there is no longer Jew or Greek" (Gal. 3:28) but rather reconciliation: "For he is our peace; in his flesh he has made both groups into one and has broken down the dividing wall, that is, the hostility between us" (Eph. 2:14). In short: *what is in Christ* is nothing less than

---

30. Question 94, emphasis added.
31. Alfred Loisy, *The Gospel and the Church* (New York: Charles Scribner's Sons, 1912), 166.
32. See also Gary Badcock, *The House Where God Lives: The Doctrine of the Church* (Grand Rapids: Wm. B. Eerdmans Publishing Co., 2009).

peace and reconciliation, "one new humanity in place of the two" (2:15). In Christ there is a racially and ethnically diverse company of the baptized, growing into a holy temple, the firstfruit of the heavenly temple glimpsed by John that is the Lord God (Rev. 21:22).

The church is the vanguard of God's kingdom: the fellowship of the Spirit; the peace of Christ. These predications are also indications: to say what the church *is* already hints at what the church is to *do*. The church is a theater of reconciliation, and this is also its vocation: the church's "ministry of reconciliation" (2 Cor. 5:18) is a mandate not to bring reconciliation about—only God can do that—but rather to bear witness to the reconciliation already won through the cross of Christ. To do church is to display what is in Christ and therefore to bear witness to reality.

It takes a company of the baptized to be a theater of reconciliation, to exhibit the new reality "in Christ" by embodying Spirit-empowered ways of being with one another. Yet to be church is to "do the truth" (John 3:21; 1 John 1:6): "Truthful human action is action which is in conformity with the reality which is established in the resurrection of Jesus from the dead."[33] Again, the purpose of doctrine is to instruct disciples in patterns of truthful living. The church must act out what is in Christ. Alas, the company of the baptized is not entirely free of sin; the church too bears false witness. It has been fifty years since Martin Luther King Jr. declared Sunday 11:00 a.m. to be the most segregated hour of the week in Christian America. To the extent that this is still the case, the church has failed to act out what is in Christ.

The doctrine of the church tells us what the church is in Christ. Described theologically rather than sociologically or historically, we can say that the church is the *communio sanctorum*: the company of saints that have communion with the triune God and with one another because of their common union, through faith and the Holy Spirit, with Christ (1 John 1:3). It is no small thing to confess with the Apostles' Creed, "I believe . . . in the communion of saints"; for in every age it seems that there is all too much evidence to the contrary. Yet this confession also speaks understanding of what God has done in Christ: "In him, broken and divided humanity has become one."[34] Bonhoeffer had an especially keen grasp of the communion that is in Christ inasmuch as he viewed church as the presence and activity of Christ himself, existing as community: "My brother or sister is . . . that other person who has been redeemed by Christ. . . . Our community consists solely in what Christ has done to both of us."[35]

We now see that the company of the baptized gathers not only to do God's will together but also, precisely in and through its life together, to witness to God's kingdom come. Stated differently: the church is not simply to *do* God's will on earth as it is in heaven but also to exist *as* God's will, as the embodiment

---

33. John Webster, *Word and Church*, 224.
34. Dietrich Bonhoeffer, *Life Together*, vol. 5 of *Dietrich Bonhoeffer Works* (Minneapolis: Fortress, 2005), 32.
35. Ibid., 34.

of God's will-to-communion. The church is a company of the baptized gathered to be one body of Christ. The body of Christ, like human bodies, is the means by which persons act and make a difference in the world. It follows that in large measure the common life of disciples will consist of acting out in many and various ways the reality of our union and communion in Christ.

SCENES OF CONGREGATIONAL LIFE

The communion of saints is the life of Christ in the world, the embodied public presence and activity of the church's head (Christ). In the next chapter we shall consider ways in which the church should engage the broader society and world. Here the concern is to ask how the church, as a theater of reconciliation, ought to order its own communal life as what Calvin calls the "society of Christ."[36] How does the church, as the communion of saints, order its own life around, and practice, the truth, goodness, and beauty of the gospel? What makes the doings of the church specifically *christological* rather than merely ethical?

The Godless Congregation: Community without Christ?

Not every gathering has for its aim "acting out what is in Christ." There are many would-be theaters of reconciliation, from grassroots volunteer groups like the Guardian Angels to official governmental initiatives like the Truth and Reconciliation Commission of South Africa. One noteworthy trend is the rise of so-called "godless congregations," communities of secular social activism. The watchword of the Humanist Community at Harvard is "I believe in community." This community and others like it hold Sunday morning meetings geared toward attracting the part of the population that responds to surveys regarding institutional religious affiliation by choosing "none."

There are more than one hundred chapters of Humanist Communities nationwide. The upswing in communities of like-minded "nones" is a fascinating development, raising anew certain questions: What makes a community? Whence our desire to form communities? Interestingly enough, the new humanist communities are coming increasingly to resemble Christian churches, except that they are trying to make do, or rather to do community, without God and without Christ.

The "Houston Oasis" bills itself as "a community grounded in reason, celebrating the human experience."[37] The community meets Sunday mornings at 10:30 to provide fellowship and support. Their Web page proudly states, "There is no doctrine to follow," yet the community has something like a confession of faith, even if it begins not with *Credo* (I believe) but *Cogito* (I think).

---

36. Calvin, *Inst.* 4.1.3.
37. See http://www.houstonoasis.org/.

The tenets of their thought system include the following: that reality is known through reason rather than revelation; that meaning in life comes from making a difference; that everyone should be accepted wherever they are and whatever they are doing as long as they are accepting in return. Meanwhile, in London, the "Sunday Assembly" meets to hear talks, listen to music, and celebrate the wonders of life: "It's a service for anyone who wants to live better, help often, and wonder more." These godless congregations gather to help people who have been hit by disasters, to make music, to enjoy fellowship, and to discuss the issues of life: call it "Communal Activistic Atheism." A forthcoming book *The Godless Congregation* asks, "How are congregations even possible without God? Might such communities be even better than traditional churches? How does one build a community dedicated to the highest human values, God not included?"[38]

The first thing to be said, by way of evaluation, is that even godless congregations act out doctrine even if it is not clear what ideological superstructure is holding up the secular edifice. Second, such communities force the church to think more carefully about its distinct nature, identity, and mission. What makes the church a distinct and unique theater of reconciliation? Or ought we to think of these godless congregations as "anonymous churches" that inadvertently participate in the practices and politics of Jesus?

The three case studies below correspond to the theological virtues of faith, hope, and love, thereby representing paradigmatic ways that Christian disciples do community. My working hypothesis is that Christian discipleship is distinct and unique because the practices of Jesus, and the politics of the kingdom of God, are distinct and unique by being hypermoral and eschatological rather than merely moral and ethical. This is another way of saying that the way disciples do community has everything to do with the particular drama in which they are participating as a company of the baptized.

The key difference between the communion of saints and godless congregations is that the former are not trying to bring reconciliation about as much as bear witness to what God has already done. The basis for the reconciling practices that constitute the Christian community is the cross of Christ. One wonders what, if anything, grounds the community of godless congregations. My fear is that such companies gather around nameless and faceless ideals that, like idols, do nothing for those who admire them. Bonhoeffer dismisses the notion that what Christians ultimately have in common is only piety of common vision. Goodwill alone cannot constitute community; only the gospel can create one out of many: "Christian community is not an ideal we have to realize, but rather a reality created by God in Christ in which we may participate."[39] This is exactly right: disciples gather, in the Spirit, to act out the communion that is already a reality in Jesus Christ. How do disciples live out together their reconciliation in Christ? Let us count the ways.

---

38. James Croft and Greg Epstein, *The Godless Congregation* (New York: Simon & Schuster, forthcoming).

39. Bonhoeffer, *Life Together*, 38.

The Godly Congregation (1): Fidelity

It requires faith to live out what is in Christ. Faith is the trusting response to the proclamation of the gospel. It is the living in and living out of trust in God's word. God is faithful in the sense that he is true to his word; God can be relied on to stand by his words, come what may. Furthermore, while Jesus never stood in need of justification, the faith that implicitly trusts God's word to the limit may be predicated of Jesus as well.[40] It is precisely the obedience of faith that is at issue when, faced with the cup of divine judgment, Jesus declares "Your will be done" (Matt. 26:42). In so saying, Jesus displays perfect humanity (i.e., obedient answerability to God), just as Mary's "Let it be with me according to your word" (Luke 1:38) displays the paradigmatic reflex of the disciple.[41]

Those who are united to Christ by his Spirit are enabled by the Spirit to participate in, and witness to, the faith of Jesus Christ through their own patterns of patient and enduring faithfulness. Jesus as second Adam has made possible a new way of doing humanity, characterized this time by deep trust and covenant faithfulness. Of all people, disciples ought to know that faithfulness is necessary for community: "Let your 'Yes' be yes" (Jas. 5:12) is another way of saying, "Let your word be your bond."

One of the most important ways disciples act out the reconciliation that is in Christ is by practicing marital fidelity. Jesus prohibits divorce because God, in ordaining marriage, has provided for the two, male and female, to again become one: "So they are no longer two, but one flesh. Therefore what God has joined together, let no one separate" (Mark 10:8-9; cf. Gen. 1:27; 2:24). Marriage begins with a promise of union and communion: "forsaking all others." This was precisely the covenant promise that God gave Israel, and the pledge expected in return. As we saw in chapter 4, a covenant is a personal relationship founded on an oath-bound commitment. Both the Old Testament prophets and the New Testament apostles readily employ marriage as a metaphor and model to describe God's relationship to Israel and Christ's relationship to the church respectively (Jer. 31:32; Eph. 5:25-33).

God instructed Hosea to marry Gomer, a "wife of whoredom" (Hos. 1:2), to symbolize Israel's unfaithfulness to its covenant vows to have no other gods but Yahweh (cf. 3:1). It is precisely the unfaithfulness of Israel that puts God's covenant faithfulness into such sharp relief. God is constant even in the face of his people's inconstancy: "I will heal their disloyalty; I will love them freely" (14:4). God's covenant love overcomes spiritual adultery. If Christian marriage

---

40. For an excellent discussion of the issues surrounding the right interpretation of the Pauline phrase "faith of Jesus Christ" (Rom 3:22, 26; Gal. 2:16; Phil. 3:9), see R. Michael Allen, *The Christ's Faith: A Dogmatic Account* (London and New York: T&T Clark, 2009). Allen argues that the faith of Christ is "the economic echo of eternal filiation which marks the Son in relation to his Father" (180).

41. On Mary as a model of discipleship, see further "Do Whatever He Tells You: The Blessed Virgin Mary in Christian Faith and Life. A Statement of Evangelicals and Catholics Together," *First Things*, no. 197 (November 2009): 49-59.

is to be an outward sign of Christ's relationship to the church (Eph. 5:32), then the expectation is that we will see the same covenant constancy.

In his treatise *The Excellence of Marriage*, Augustine says that marriage creates a unique social bond: "The first natural bond of human society . . . is that of husband and wife," which is then extended, possibly for generations, through children.[42] Precisely as a symbol of union with Christ, marriage signifies not only the union of husband and wife but also the indissolubility of that union as well.[43] Indeed, the second of the three goods of marriage that Augustine lists is the good of mutual fidelity (*fides*), that is, commitment to the exclusiveness of their particular one-flesh communion (i.e., to abstain from adultery).

Christian marriages participate in the drama of redemption when they model the covenant faithfulness that characterizes Christ's relationship to his bride, the church. Christian marriage is a microcosm of the communion of saints. Just as the church is called to live out that union in covenant faithfulness to God and one another, so married couples act out compelling scenes of covenant faithfulness whenever conflict is peacefully resolved. In the final analysis, the communion of saints is mirrored by the indissolubility of marriage: "I believe in the communion of man and wife." It is significant that Paul so often moves from discussing the covenant faithfulness of God to exhorting his readers to sexual purity and fidelity, a sign of the church's holiness: "If marriage is the New Testament's final symbol of eschatological redemption, then divorce cannot be consonant with God's redemptive will."[44]

If Christian marriage can be a "school for character"[45] (and sanctification), then it can, and also should be, a theater of reconciliation. Doctrine provides direction for disciples to act out that covenant fidelity that is in Christ: "We must recover the New Testament's vision for marriage as an aspect of *discipleship* and as a reflection of God's unbreakable *faithfulness*."[46]

The Godly Congregation (2): Generosity

Sharing what one has with others in the family of God is another concrete way of acting out union with Christ and the communion of the saints. Paul's appeal to the cross as doing away with the hostility that had separated Jews and Gentiles (Eph. 2:14–15) is well known. Less appreciated is Paul's concern with "the collection for the saints": the monetary offering to the Jerusalem church that Paul relentlessly solicited from Gentile churches. The collection for the saints at Jerusalem was every bit as dramatic as the Jerusalem Council (Acts 15), where

---

42. Augustine, *Marriage and Virginity*, trans. Ray Kearney (New York: New City Press, 1999), 33.
43. Elsewhere Augustine calls marriage "the sacrament of an inseparable union" (*Marriage and Concupiscence* 1.23).
44. Richard B. Hays, *The Moral Vision of the New Testament: A Contemporary Introduction to New Testament Ethics* (San Francisco: HarperCollins, 1996), 366.
45. Roland H. Bainton, *Here I Stand: A Life of Martin Luther* (Peabody, MA: Hendrickson, 2009), 307.
46. Hays, *Moral Vision of the New Testament*, 372.

Jewish Christians led by Peter and James gave their blessing on Paul's mission to the Gentiles, acknowledging that God's covenant included those previously thought to be "not my people." Indeed, the collection is a mirror image of the council inasmuch as each demonstrates in its own way the unity of the church and the communion of saints.

It is important not to underestimate the importance of this Pauline theme for, as we shall see, the collection is intimately connected to Paul's gospel. Indeed, the collection for the Jerusalem saints was "Paul's *obsession* for nearly two decades."[47] How shall we understand this apostolic passion for fundraising, Paul's magnificent obsession? First, the details: Paul makes mention of the collection in several of his epistles (Rom. 15:25–32; 1 Cor. 16:1–4; Gal. 2:9–10), most extensively in 2 Corinthians 8–9. Paul uses different terms to describe the collection, including "grace" (*charis*, 1 Cor. 16:3; 2 Cor. 8:6–7), "service" (*diakonia*, Rom. 15:25, 31; 2 Cor. 8:20; 9:12–13), "fellowship" (*koinōnia*, Rom. 15:26), and a "service that you perform" (*diakonia tēs leitourgias*, 2 Cor. 9:12 NIV). The collection involved Gentile churches in three different provinces (Macedonia, Achaia, and Galatia). It was not a tax: on the contrary, Paul insists that "they voluntarily gave according to their means, and even beyond their means, begging us earnestly for the privilege of sharing in this ministry to the saints" (2 Cor. 8:3–4).

On one level, this generous giving is the way disciples witness to and participate in the generous self-giving of the triune God, and in particular the Son: "For you know the generous act of our Lord Jesus Christ, that though he was rich, yet for your sakes he became poor, so that by his poverty you might become rich" (2 Cor. 8:9). Paul encourages the Corinthians similarly to share out of their abundance with those who are in need "in order that there may be a fair balance [Gk. *isotēs* = equality]" (2 Cor. 8:14; cf. Rom. 15:27). At another level, however, the collection is a powerful display of how disciples act out their union in Christ. The Gentile churches' financial contribution to the Jewish Jerusalem church puts money where Paul's mouth is: it is a tangible expression of what Paul has been saying all along about the equality of Jews and Gentiles in Christ. In a family, economic fellowship is par for the course. The Gentile churches are not loaning funds but giving money to the *one* communion of saints: by loving the saints in Jerusalem, they are merely loving their own body (cf. Eph. 5:28). This helps explain Paul's obsession: the credibility of his very mission to the Gentiles was at stake. The collection went a long way in demonstrating that there was indeed one Lord, one faith, one baptism, and one church.

Generous giving is one way the church acts out not only the communion of saints but also the doctrine of providence. In giving to others, the church trusts God to provide for basic needs, as Israel trusted God to provide manna for their daily bread (see Exod. 16): "God is able to provide you with every blessing

---

47. Scot McKnight, "Collection for the Saints," in *Dictionary of Paul and His Letters*, ed. G. F. Hawthorne, R. P. Martin, and D. G. Reid (Downers Grove, IL: InterVarsity Press, 1993), 143, emphasis original.

in abundance, so that by always having enough of everything, you may share abundantly in every good work" (2 Cor. 9:8). The fear of scarcity, that there is never "enough," prevents people from sharing what they have. The saints act out ("perform") the doctrine of divine providence as well as the *communio sanctorum* when they have "all things in common" (Acts 2:44). Belief in divine providence casts out the fear of scarcity.[48]

The generosity that characterizes the church as a theater of reconciliation also explains why the Apostles' Creed lists "the forgiveness of sins" immediately after "the communion of saints." For, of the many treasures that are in Christ, perhaps the greatest is forgiveness. This, at least, is the basis of Paul's appeal for disciples to act out what God has given them by giving to (i.e., forgiving) others: "Forgive each other; just as the Lord has forgiven you, so you also must forgive" (Col. 3:13; cf. Eph. 4:32). Indeed, *not* to forgive one another is both to deny the explicit dominical command (Matt. 6:14-15; 18:21-22) and, in an important sense, to deny the gospel itself (i.e., the communion we have in Christ). A failure to act out the forgiveness that is in Christ is a tacit admission of either disbelief or disobedience: one way or another, the failure to reconcile with those who have injured you is a refusal to acknowledge the reconciliation that is in Christ. Christians witness to the truth of what is *in* Christ by acting it *out*.

Forgiveness presupposes sin. Sin is that inward curvature of one's existential spine that creates alienation between oneself and others. In sinning "against" others, the sinner creates distance and division. Forgiveness is a necessary reconciling practice that restores communion to the company of the saints: "Forgiveness serves not primarily to absolve guilt but as a reminder . . . of what communion with God and with one another can and should be."[49] Disciples are never more authentic than when they ask for forgiveness and forgive others. Unlike the genuine communion of saints, the sanctimonious community conceals rather than confesses their sins to one another (Jas. 5:16). Bonhoeffer says that in confession of sins to other saints, there is a "breakthrough to community": unacknowledged sin short-circuits reconciliation, but those who confess their sin, and hence their inability to justify themselves, live out the grace of God (2 Cor. 5:19) "and in this very act find community for the first time."[50]

Is it rational to believe in the communion of saints and the forgiveness of sins? Some skeptics wonder whether gifts can truly be given without incurring some obligation on the part of the recipient or if such a thing as forgiveness truly exists.[51] Only God can ultimately forgive sin because all sin is ultimately against God ("Against thee, thee only, have I sinned" [Ps. 51:4 RSV]). But

---

48. See further, Scott Bader-Saye, *Following Jesus in a Culture of Fear* (Grand Rapids: Brazos Press, 2007), chap. 10, "The Risk of Generosity," 133-47.

49. L. Gregory Jones, *Embodying Forgiveness: A Theological Analysis* (Grand Rapids: Wm. B. Eerdmans Publishing Co., 1995), xvi.

50. Bonhoeffer, *Life Together*, 110.

51. See Jacques Derrida, *On Cosmopolitanism and Forgiveness* (London and New York: Routledge, 2001); and John D. Caputo, Mark Dooley, and Michael J. Scanlon, eds., *Questioning God* (Bloomington: Indiana University Press, 2001), esp. 1-149.

God has forgiven, thereby enabling ways of righting relationships that do not involve "an eye for an eye and a tooth for a tooth" (Matt. 5:38). Disciples are called to forgive one another as a sign and acting out of the divine forgiveness already abundantly poured out on the cross of Christ.[52] When saints forgive one another as they have been forgiven in Christ, they enter into the dramatic movement of God's own triune generosity.[53]

The Godly Congregation (3): Hospitality

Hospitality is the fundamental gesture of God's grace, the opening up of God's "household" (*oikos*), his own triune life, to "strangers and aliens" (Eph. 2:19). Hospitality is also "at the heart of Christian life, drawing upon God's grace and reflecting God's graciousness."[54] Hence Christian disciples ought "to regard hospitality to strangers as a fundamental expression of the gospel."[55] The entire drama of redemption may be viewed from the perspective of hosts and guests. Ancient Israel was to show hospitality to strangers, for they had been strangers in Egypt (Deut. 10:19). In the Gospels, Jesus sometimes appears as stranger or guest (e.g., Luke 7:36–50; 10:38–42; 19:1–10) and at other times as host (Luke 9:10–17; 22:7–23; 24:30). Mention has already been made of how Jesus' death on a cross makes room for "others" (i.e., Gentiles).

Hospitality hardly seems to qualify as a reconciling practice that characterizes disciples of Jesus. After all, there now is an entire hospitality industry outside the church where strangers are welcomed. There are also hospitals that "welcome" the sick. All three terms—*hospitality*, *hotel*, and *hospital*—derive from the Latin *hospes*, meaning either "host" or "guest."[56] Hospitality concerns the host-guest relationship. Our particular concern is how disciples live out union with Christ by inviting others into their home and family and what makes Christian hospitality a characteristic scene of congregational life.

The roots of hospitality as a distinctive Christian practice go back to Jesus' teaching. Jesus subverts ancient conventions when he challenges his hosts to offer hospitality not only to those who can return it but also to those who cannot: "Invite the poor, the crippled, the lame, and the blind" (Luke 14:13). Offering

---

52. "If forgiveness does take place, it will be but an echo of the forgiveness granted by the just and loving God—the only forgiveness that ultimately matters, because, though we must forgive, in a very real sense no one can either forgive or retain sins 'but God alone' (Mark 2:7)" (Miroslav Volf, *Exclusion and Embrace: A Theological Exploration of Identity, Otherness, and Reconciliation* [Nashville: Abingdon Press, 1996], 124–25).
53. Kelly M. Kapic and Justin L. Bolger, *God So Loved, He Gave: Entering the Movement of Divine Generosity* (Grand Rapids: Zondervan, 2010).
54. Christine D. Pohl, *Living into Community: Cultivating Practices That Sustain Us* (Grand Rapids: Wm. B. Eerdmans Publishing Co., 2012), 159.
55. Christian D. Pohl, *Making Room: Recovering Hospitality as a Christian Tradition* (Grand Rapids: Wm. B. Eerdmans Publishing Co., 2009), 5.
56. For a bittersweet account of the last almshouse in the United States, see Victoria Sweet, *God's Hotel: A Doctor, a Hospital, and a Pilgrimage to the Heart of Medicine* (New York: Riverhead Books, 2012). What was once God's house of care has become a den of chargemasters (and red tape).

hospitality to those who are unable to return the favor mirrors the unconditional hospitality of God. The hyperethical quality of Christian hospitality comes into even greater focus in Jesus' teaching about the kingdom of heaven, where the invitees are those who fed him when he was hungry, gave him to drink when he was thirsty, clothed him when he was naked, and took care of him when he was sick. Few people have had occasion to minister in these ways to Jesus himself. But that is precisely the point: "Truly I tell you, just as you did it to one of the least of these who are members of my family, you did it to me" (Matt. 25:40).

Hospitality to strangers acts out the gospel, for it is an expression of the love shared for all the members of the body of Christ: "Early Christian writers claimed that transcending social and ethnic differences by sharing meals, homes, and worship with persons of different backgrounds was a proof of the truth of the Christian faith."[57] There is perhaps no more startling example of the radical implications of the communion of saints than what Paul asks Philemon to do: not only to welcome a former slave back into his household as a brother in Christ but also, by implication, to grant him his freedom (Phlm. 16). Paul does not command Philemon to do this but urges Philemon to act toward Onesimus as he would toward Paul himself: "Welcome him as you would welcome me" (v. 17). Welcoming those who are in Christ is a dramatic expression of one's welcome into the household of God by Christ (Rom. 15:7).

The example of Philemon reminds us not to romanticize early Christian *koinōnia*, as if each gathered community was a kind of first-century hippie commune. The early church worked hard to demonstrate the reconciliation that existed in Christ (the modern age does not have a monopoly on biases based on sex, race, and class). Yet work they did, striving in particular to distinguish Christian hospitality from Greek and Roman practices: "For Chrysostom, Lactantius, Jerome, and other leaders of the ancient church, hospitality was a significant context for transcending status boundaries and for working through issues of respect and recognition."[58]

Disciples act out their union with Christ by practicing hospitality in the name of Christ in the quiet quotidian scenes of their own homes and also corporately as the household of God. There is reluctance, perhaps even fear, of having others into our homes, even when those others are fellow Christians: "Welcome is one of the signs that a community is alive. To invite others to live with us is a sign that we aren't afraid, that we have a treasure of truth and of peace to share."[59] Hospitality, like fidelity and generosity, is a way of demonstrating the truth that is in Christ Jesus. It is a way of not only saying but *doing* grace: "More than anywhere else, when we gather as church our practice of hospitality should reflect God's gracious welcome. God is host, and we are all guests of God's grace."[60]

57. Pohl, *Making Room*, 5.
58. Ibid., 18–19.
59. Jean Vanier, *Community and Growth*, 2nd rev. ed. (New York: Paulist Press, 1989), 266.
60. Pohl, *Making Room*, 157.

REHEARSING COMMUNION: THE SUPPER AS SUMMA OF THE GOSPEL

Theater involves word and bodily actions. On a regular basis the church gathers as a company of the baptized to celebrate—in words, acts, and body—the words, acts, and body of Jesus Christ. In celebrating the Lord's Supper, the church represents the body of Christ, and Christ presents, makes present, his body. Divine and human agents are both active in this rehearsal of a key scene in the drama of redemption. In rehearsing this dominical scene, the church receives spiritual nourishment and strength for the morrow's performance.

In what follows we shall see that, though the first Lord's Supper is a central scene in act 3, it also echoes scenes from act 2, scripts the church's present performances in act 4 and, furthermore, anticipates the play's end (for the numbered acts, see chap. 4 above). In addition to this intermingling of past, present, and future, the Lord's Supper also encapsulates the three dynamic marks that characterize the communion of the saints we have just examined: fidelity, generosity, and hospitality. For all these reasons, the Lord's Supper represents a condensed summary or summation of the climax of the drama of redemption—the creation of a new, unified body of Christ, the prime exhibit of God's kingdom on earth—and hence a summa of the gospel.

The Table as Set (Apart) Piece

Earlier we asked how the church does reconciliation differently in light of the many other social organizations committed to community. In the present context the question becomes even more acute in view of the many other societies that break bread together. Something as pedestrian as a meal surely cannot be the crucial scene in the theater of the gospel! After all, even the godless congregations we considered in the last section occasionally get together for dinner.

Not every dinner that invokes the Lord's name is a bona fide celebration of the Lord's Supper. First Corinthians 10–11 contains important doctrinal direction for the church's right performance of what commentators acknowledge is not only a Passover (cf. 1 Cor. 5:7) but also a covenant-renewal meal (Exod. 24:11). At Passover meals, it was the custom for the youngest son to ask, "Why is this night different from other nights?" (Exod. 12:26–27). One can similarly inquire of the Lord's Supper, "What makes this meal different from other meals?" In the case of the Passover, the host would rehearse the story of Israel's deliverance from Egypt, the gospel scene of the Old Testament. In the case of the Lord's Supper, Christians rehearse the story of the host himself.

According to Paul, the bread and the wine of which Christians partake at the Lord's Supper are important props that, when ingested, insert disciples into the drama of redemption: "The cup of blessing that we bless, is it not a sharing [*koinōnia*] in the blood of Christ? The bread that we break, is it not a sharing [*koinōnia*] in the body of Christ?" (1 Cor. 10:16). However, Paul also criticized the way in which the saints at Corinth were sharing or participating in the Supper, declaring their performance "unworthy" (11:27) and going so far as to suggest that the Corinthians were participating not in the Lord's Supper but in some other kind of meal: "When you come together, it is not really to eat the Lord's supper" (1 Cor. 11:20).

Apparently the nature and purpose of the Lord's Supper had been lost on the Corinthians. They seem to have confused this sacred feast with profane banquets. No doubt there was a certain desire, as in ancient Israel, to be like everyone else. Israel, for example, wanted a human king "like other nations" (1 Sam. 8:5, 20). At the very least, the Corinthians' behavior indicated a lack of understanding about the nature of the kingdom that Jesus had proclaimed and inaugurated by his death. The way the church at Corinth ate together displayed their divisions, a far cry from demonstrating oneness in Christ (1 Cor. 11:18–19). The basic problem probably had to do with the logic of worldly kingdoms, that is, the status barrier that divides the rich from the poor. Somehow, what should have been a compelling depiction of new humanity in Christ had become, instead, a scandalous display of ongoing inequities: "One goes hungry and another becomes drunk" (11:21). In Calvin's words: "It was, therefore, an unseemly spectacle, and not in accordance with the Lord's Supper."[61]

Direction for Fitting Participation in Jesus' Death

Paul's rebuke to the Corinthians for their terrible table manners (so to speak) is as sharp as his rebuke to Peter's similar discrimination against fellow Christians (Gal. 2:11–14) that we examined in the preceding chapter (5). In both cases, a table—one an ordinary dining table, the other the Lord's Table—that was to have symbolized fellowship in Christ had become a symbol of disunity and discord. No wonder that, in each case, Paul speaks of the condemnation that ensues (1 Cor. 11:32, *katakrinō*; Gal. 2:11, *kataginōskō*).

Paul wants the Corinthians to examine themselves before celebrating the Lord's Supper so that they can participate fittingly (1 Cor. 11:28–29). Once again we see that doctrine is necessary for disciples to act out the truth that is in Jesus Christ. For there is an ever-present possibility of inappropriate performance: ways of speaking and acting that go against the grain of *what is* in Christ. The company of the baptized does well to consider the doctrine of the Lord's Supper inasmuch as it is a kind of summation of what is in Christ, namely, Christ's body and blood. Accordingly, we shall examine Paul's explanation of Jesus' institution of his Supper in order to gain a better sense of what Communion means and how disciples should act it out.

---

61. John Calvin, *Commentary on the Epistles of Paul to the Corinthians*, vol. 1 (Edinburgh: Calvin Translation Society, 1848), 370–71.

"This Is My Body, Which Is Given for You" (Luke 22:19)

If baptism is our port of entry into the drama of redemption, the Lord's Supper is the port where we obtain provisions for the journey. Each of these sacraments both solicits and signals our participation in the theodrama in an intense and instructive fashion. The bread and wine are tangible reminders of the climactic scene where God fulfilled his messianic promise and acted decisively to reconcile all things to himself: the cross of Christ. The blood poured out for many is a graphic sign of the new covenant ministered by Christ (1 Cor. 11:25; cf. Jer. 31:31–34), better than Israel's covenant because it involved a better blessing (the Holy Spirit) and a broader scope (Gentiles as well as Jews). The bread and the wine thus represent Jesus' self-giving for the sake of the church. Jesus here is both host and meal.[62]

"Do This in Remembrance of Me" (Luke 22:19)

The church gathers at the Lord's Table not as onlookers but as actors, active participants in the eating and drinking. There is not only something past to remember but something in the present to be done. Doctrine provides direction for participating in the Lord's Supper fittingly. The questions are, What exactly are we doing? Is the action entirely ours? This is not the place to develop a full-scale theology of the Lord's Supper. Here I want only to point out how "remembering" involves more than a motion of the intellect. To "do this in remembrance" is to rehearse: it is a matter of doing something in the present that recalls something done in the past in preparation for something yet to be performed in the future.

"Until . . . the kingdom of God" (Mark 14:25)

Jesus told his disciples that he would not drink wine with them again until that day when he would "drink it new in the kingdom of God," presumably in a covenantal meal of cosmic scope: the marriage supper of the Lamb (Rev. 19). This is why Paul tells his readers at Corinth that each time they break bread and drink the cup they "proclaim the Lord's death until he comes" (1 Cor. 11:26). The Lord's Supper thus commingles past, present, and future: the Lord's death has already happened; the church is now remembering it; the Supper itself is a harbinger of the heavenly feast that will follow the return of the King. In breaking bread, the church is actually celebrating the inbreaking of God's kingdom, something that takes place first in the person and work of Jesus; then subsequently in his body, the church; and finally and definitively at the drama's end. The Lord's Supper is thus a symbolic act laden with theodramatic significance: "eating together, ritualized in the Lord's Supper, continually

---

62. "The connection between bread and body, wine and blood, rests in Christ's word. . . . Everything here depends on the reliability of his promise, on the efficacy and the authority of his words" (Herman N. Ridderbos, *The Coming of the Kingdom* [Philadelphia: P&R, 1962], 438).

reenacts the center of the gospel."⁶³ Christ communicates in his Supper, and what he communicates is communion with the triune God and all the saints.

Breaking Bread, Discerning the Body

The church's raison d'être is to be a theater of the gospel: not merely the place where the gospel is exhibited, but the exhibition itself. The church exhibits the good news of what God is doing in Christ by participating in the Lord's Supper fittingly. To do this, one needs to have some idea of what is going on: What do the elements stand for? What do the words mean? Something important is clearly at stake for Paul. I believe it is the gospel itself, and I believe it has something to do with his enigmatic statement: "For all who eat and drink without discerning the body, eat and drink judgment against themselves" (1 Cor. 11:29).

With Calvin, I lament the "unhappy contests" that have (ironically enough) divided Christians over the interpretation of Jesus' words "This is my body."⁶⁴ My own approach tries to be integrative and conjunctive rather than exclusive and disjunctive: "body" has two related yet distinct senses, and only disciples who rightly "discern the body" in both senses are able to act out the truth of the body of Christ.

The Real Presence of Christ

Doing the Lord's Supper in remembrance of Christ is not playacting. The church is not pretending that the bread is Christ's body, nor is it simply going through the motions in an attempt to reenact a past event. On the contrary, the church is now celebrating something that is in one sense already past (Christ's death) but in another sense not yet fully realized (the marriage supper of the Lamb). Most important: what the church does in breaking bread is not a mere human projection or representation but a participation in the triune God's communicative action. A brief review of Calvin's theology of the Lord's Supper helps us better understand how the church celebrates the real presence of Christ.⁶⁵

For Calvin, it is not the elements but the whole event of the Lord's Supper that communicates Christ.⁶⁶ Jesus' words and actions in instituting the Supper remind us that the meal is a gift of God to the people of God, a means of nourishing the church's faith by communicating Christ and his benefits. The gift of God in question, then, is nothing less than union with Christ; the Lord's

---

63. Pohl, *Making Room*, 30.

64. See Thomas J. Davis, *This Is My Body: The Presence of Christ in Reformation Thought* (Grand Rapids: Baker Academic, 2008), esp. chap. 9, "Discerning the Body: The Eucharist and the Christian Social Body in Sixteenth-Century Protestant Exegesis," 149–68.

65. See Thomas J. Davis, *The Clearest Promises of God: The Development of Calvin's Eucharistic Teaching* (New York: AMS Press, 1995).

66. Cf. Peter T. Forsyth: "It was the *action* that was symbolical, the breaking rather than the bread, the outpouring rather than the wine. 'This' is not this object but this act" (*The Church and the Sacraments*, 3rd ed. [London: Independent Press, 1949], 234.

Supper is a banquet "wherein Christ attests himself to be the life-giving bread, upon which our souls feed unto true and blessed immortality."[67] To eat the bread and drink the wine are embodied actions that dramatically symbolize the church's participation (*koinōnia*) in the body and blood of Jesus (1 Cor. 10:16).

Calvin affirms the ascension of the risen Christ and thus denies that the bread and the wine are localized instantiations of his resurrection body. At the same time, the elements really communicate (i.e., make common, make personally present) Christ and nourish the soul by virtue of the Spirit, who raises communicants up to fellowship with Christ in heaven. The Lord's Supper is thus a concentrated form of the ministry of Word and Spirit that enlivens and strengthens faith. The Lord's Supper thus involves both divine and human actors: the risen Lord offers himself in the word of the gospel by his Spirit, and the human communicants participate by eating and drinking in faith. In Calvin's words: "We eat Christ's flesh in believing, because it is made ours by faith."[68] Again, this is no playacting (pretending) but a theater of real operations, gracious operations, for "by true partaking of him, his life passes into us and is made ours."[69]

This, then, is the first sense in which "discerning the body" (1 Cor. 11:29) is a condition for right participation in the Lord's Supper: communicants rightly discern the body when they acknowledge the real spiritual presence of Christ, the real presence of Christ's risen/spiritual body. To be sure, he is not "on" but "at" the table, thanks to the Spirit that unites guests to host.[70] The Lord's Supper is thus much more than "dinner theater." It is rather a theater of the gospel that efficaciously enacts the eschatological *is* in "This is my body": in participating in the Supper, communicants remember what is already past, remember in the right now of the present, and anticipate the not-yet of the feast in the future (the marriage supper of the Lamb).

The Real Presencing of Christ

This is only half the story of how the Lord's Supper is a theater of the gospel. We catch a glimpse of the second part of the story, and of how the two parts are related, in one of Calvin's observations: "Inasmuch as he [Christ] makes himself common to all, [he] also makes all of us one in himself."[71] In addition to the *risen/spiritual body* of Christ, in the Lord's Supper we also discern the *gathered/ social body*. The company of the baptized gather "in Christ" in order to "Do this" not only to remember or re-present Christ but also to *presence* Christ (to display his presence in their midst). The Lord's Supper is a theater of the gospel

---

67. Calvin, *Inst.* 4.17.1.
68. Ibid., 4.17.5. By "flesh" Calvin is thinking of Jesus' humanity.
69. Ibid., 4.17.5.
70. See the discussion in John Jefferson Davis, *Worship and the Reality of God: An Evangelical Theology of Real Presence* (Downers Grove, IL: InterVarsity Press, 2010), chap. 4, "The Eucharist," 113–70, esp. 164.
71. Calvin, *Inst.* 4.17.38; cf., "For we must first of all be incorporated (so to speak) into Christ, that we may be united to each other" (Calvin, *Commentary on Corinthians*, 335).

inasmuch as it communicates this twofold *communio*: union with Christ and communion with one another in Christ.

The church theater of the gospel is not a building or even a company of players but the embodied interaction among the actors who together communicate the main idea of the Great Play of the Word: the "spiritual blessing[s] in the heavenly places" (Eph. 1:3) summed up in Christ. Included among these spiritual blessings, and enjoying first rank, are union and communion. "Discerning the body" rightly (1 Cor. 11:29) means seeing not only the real presence of Christ at the table but also the real presence of Christ in the *communio sanctorum*, in the present communion of saints. It is precisely by being/doing church—realizing the communion of saints, not least in fellowship around the Lord's Table—that the community "presences" Christ, in its own life displaying the life of Christ.

One way to fail to discern the body, then, is to fail to discern what is in Christ, namely, the communion of the saints. "Without discerning the body" means failing to discern the real presence of Christ and hence the oneness the church enjoys in him. This was precisely why Paul confronted Peter at Antioch: for failing to discern the body by drawing back from eating with the Gentiles, and thus "not acting consistently with the truth of the gospel" (Gal. 2:14). By way of contrast, those who fittingly participate in the Lord's Supper discern the body, for the right doing is the discerning. To cite Calvin again: "For Christ invests us this honor, that he wishes to be discerned and recognized, not only in his own Person, but also in his members."[72]

In a highly condensed and concentrated form, the Lord's Supper is a theatrical presentation of the redemption won by Christ. When the church celebrates the Lord's Supper, it also enacts the very purpose of Christ's coming, namely, the new reconciled humanity that exists in Christ, in whom there are no racial or social or economic divisions. In celebrating communion, the church not only proclaims but also performs its unity. Better: by enacting the words and the sacramental actions, we are *really* drawn into the ongoing theodramatic action by the Spirit.

In breaking bread together, the company of the baptized becomes a unified company of faith. Participating in the Lord's Table makes strange "bread fellows" (companion = *com* [with] *panis* [bread]). The present-day church must take every opportunity to discern the body, especially in multiethnic and socially diverse communities. Doing so not only nourishes faith (reconciliation in Christ is real!) but is also a compelling witness to the power of the cross. It is difficult to rebut a reconciled community.

Local churches would do well to give it an even greater role and prominence to the Lord's Supper, perhaps by celebrating it on a weekly basis. If preaching is weekly, why not also the Lord's Supper, a visible word of the gospel, especially when we have an explicit dominical command, "Do this" (Luke 22:19)? Indeed,

---

72. Calvin, *Commentary on Corinthians*, on 1 Cor. 12:12; cited in Thomas J. Davis, *This Is My Body*, 161.

regular celebration of the Lord's Supper may also be a means of responding to another dominical command, "Make disciples of all nations" (Matt. 28:19), since Communion can be a powerful means of spiritual formation: "It focuses the church's attention on the core realities of the Christian faith: the incarnation, the cross, the resurrection, and the return of Jesus Christ."[73] To get the Lord's Supper right is thus to grow in understanding of the whole drama of redemption.

RECAPITULATION:
THE CATHOLIC-EVANGELICAL IMPERATIVE

The Lord's Supper is a doctrine and a doing, both a theory about the presence of Christ in the elements as well as a theater for presenting Christ. As such, the Lord's Supper is a gathering point for the life of the church, the place where the church comes into its own as a theater of the gospel, and it serves as a microcosm, an embodied précis, of the whole drama of redemption. The Lord's Supper is the conspicuous display not only of the high point of the drama, the death of Jesus, but also of the drama's end, the perfection of God's kingdom on earth as it is in heaven.

The Lord's Supper is a response to the dominical command ("Do this"), which reminds us that the church is a creature of God's word: an assembly that gathers to remember, proclaim, and celebrate God's promise made good. The Supper is the gift of God for the people of God, which is why in many traditions it is called the Eucharist (Gk. *eucharisteō* = I gave thanks). Giving thanks is surely the proper response to the gospel (*euangelion* = good news, gospel) that the Son of God has given up his life so that we could live in him. Eating the bread and drinking the cup are themselves recapitulations of the whole gospel action. By gathering in Jesus' name to "do" communion, the church rehearses the gospel, not only the death of Jesus on the cross but also the creation of a new people in Christ.

"He is risen!" This is the evangelical thesis, the good news that the crucified Jesus is now risen Lord, that he is alive, and that we are alive in him as well through faith. "To live is Christ" (Phil. 1:21 ESV). Nevertheless, as Tertullian says, "One Christian is no Christian" (*Unus Christianus, nullus Christianus*). The gospel is the good news that, as Lord, Christ has formed a kingdom people. To be in Christ is to be part of his kingdom, a member of the communion of those who have been set apart as his followers (i.e., saints). The gospel is therefore simultaneously the proclamation of a new Lord and a new people. The good news is that I have union with Christ *and* communion with other saints. This is the catholic qualifier of the evangelical thesis (from Gk. *kata + holos* = by the whole). Hence the catholic-evangelical imperative: *live out union with Christ in communion with other Christians.* This is a mandate for individual Christians and

---

73. John J. Davis, *Worship and the Reality of God*, 165.

for local congregations alike: act out what is in Christ in your common life, with other Christians and with other churches.

The church acts out the gospel, and its new life in Christ, when at the Lord's Supper communicants communicate communion. In one sense, we can commune only with those who are physically present, those who share our immediate space and time. In another sense, we commune with those who are physically distant precisely by participating in the same symbolic action as others: "Because there is one bread, we who are many are one body, for we all partake of the one bread" (1 Cor. 10:17). What Calvin says about the presence of Christ in the bread goes for the presence of the saints to one another: "the Spirit truly unites things separated in space."[74]

The catholic-evangelical imperative is actually a twofold directive. Our emphasis has been only on the first part, that because union with Christ implies the communion of the saints, the gospel therefore implies the church. There is, however, a second implication and imperative: it takes many churches to communicate the gospel. While the local church is a true church, it is not the whole church. It may feel like a blow to our ecclesial pride to admit it, but the truth of the matter is that no single Christian community communicates the fullness of the gospel or of what is in Christ. Local churches (and even denominations) would thus do well to consult the broader communion, historical and geographic, of the saints to see how other communities are acting out what is in Christ.[75]

This chapter has explored one important aspect of *what is in Christ*: the fellowship that believers who find themselves "in him" have with one another, across space and time. The next chapter continues our analysis of *what is in Christ*, but with a view to the church's work *ad extra*, its mission to demonstrate the reality of being in Christ to a world whose own material reality is fading away (1 Pet. 1:4).

---

74. Calvin, *Inst.* 4.17.10.

75. The parenthetical reference to denominations raises a host of questions that are beyond the present work, the most important of which concerns the problem of the one and the many: how much diversity in doctrinal and practical matters can there be before not simply bread but also unity is broken? On this important question, see Ephraim Radner, *A Brutal Unity: The Spiritual Politics of the Christian Church* (Waco: Baylor University Press, 2012); Paul M. Collins and Barry Ensign-George, eds., *Denomination: Assessing an Ecclesiological Category* (London and New York: T&T Clark International, 2011).

Chapter 7

Staging the Play in Ten Thousand Places

How the Company of the Gospel Enacts Parables of the Kingdom

Preach the gospel at all times, and use words only when necessary.
—Francis of Assisi

Theology is the church's continuing communal effort to think through her mission of speaking the gospel.
—Robert Jenson, *Systematic Theology*, 1:22

Acts in God's eye what in God's eye he is—
Christ—for Christ plays in ten thousand places.
—Gerard Manley Hopkins, "As Kingfishers Catch Fire"

Disciples gather to break bread for the sake of nourishment in Christ and mutual fellowship. Yet these dress rehearsals also serve the purpose of preparing the company for its corporate task: to minister the reconciling word of the gospel in speech and action in the interactive theater of the world. As the Father sends the Son into the world, so the Son sends his disciples (John 17:18). God has given the church the dignity of participating in his own triune mission to the world. Indeed, in an important sense the various local churches that Paul founded were to embody the gospel. Each local church was to witness to the gospel through word, deed, and suffering: proclamation, practice, and passion. Accordingly, the present chapter deals with the church's mission in, to, and for the world. The focus is still ecclesiology, but now with an eye to the church's outreach in particular places and new contexts. How does the church do life together in Christ *ad extra*?

The theatrical model here comes into its own, in the notion of the church as the theater of the gospel, as a performance practice, gathered to act out the new creation in Christ in the midst of the old. The church is the place not only where the gospel is heard but also where it is seen. For the meaning of the gospel can ultimately be learned only through a demonstration of what the proclamation means in practice. Hence the importance of the testimony of disciples who can both speak and show understanding, who understand the length and breadth, the ground and grammar of the gospel. Doctrine, we have argued, transcends the theory/practice dichotomy inasmuch as it yields both theoretical and practical understanding. Doctrine not only indicates what is in Christ but also implicitly directs us to conform to this new reality. Disciples need to understand not only the event of Jesus Christ but also the situation in which the church now finds itself. Doctrine illumines this as well.

To speak and act with understanding is to engage in communicative action. As finite human beings, we speak and act from particular embodied positions. Embodiment is not a curse but instead is a means of making a difference in the world. The church, precisely as the body of Christ, has been appointed by God to make a difference in the world. The church is apostolic because it continues to follow the teaching and way of the apostles even as it enters new cultural territory. *Doctrina*, lived understanding, ultimately involves not only concepts but also the church's whole way of life: beliefs, values, and everyday practices. In the final analysis, doctrine enables the church to *do* the truth and thus fulfill its vocation "to live as Jerusalem in the midst of Babylon."[1]

The world is all the places where the companies of the baptized gather to perform the drama of doctrine, to speak and act with theodramatic understanding. The drama of doctrine refers to the process by which the church attempts to work out yet another aspect of *what is in Christ*, namely, the freedom and love of God. Disciples "do church" whenever and wherever they enact shapes of love and freedom (as well as shapes of truth, goodness, and beauty), for which Christ has set us free. The purpose of doctrine is to make us wise unto Christ: the center, climax, and central content of the theodrama. Doctrine helps the church to move forward with its script by providing answers to the following questions:

1. Where are we in the theodrama? What act and scene are we playing?
2. Who are we? In what kind of plot are our lives entangled?
3. What is happening? What is God doing?
4. What should we be saying and doing in response?[2]

Together, these add up to a single, comprehensive question: *Why are we, the church, here?*

The church performs the drama of doctrine when it embodies and enacts the way of Jesus Christ in the various concrete situations that comprise the world.

---

1. William Stringfellow, *An Ethic for Christians and Other Aliens in a Strange Land* (Waco, TX: Word Books, 1973) 152.

2. I am modifying N. T. Wright's four questions: (1) Who are we? (2) Where are we? (3) What is wrong? (4) What is the solution? (*The New Testament and the People of God*, 122–23).

We begin by examining further the notion of the body of Christ, in particular, its locatedness in the world. The second section explores the way in which the church is in the world but not of it. The chapter concludes with a consideration of how the church, as a localized communicative agency, embodies the heart of God and the wisdom of Jesus Christ in (at least) ten thousand places and times.

LOCAL CHURCH, LOCAL THEATER: WHERE IS "IN CHRIST"?

So if you have been raised with Christ, seek the things that are above, where Christ is, seated at the right hand of God.

—Colossians 3:1

The church is the performance of the gospel word in the power of the gospel Spirit. In the preceding chapter we saw that the church is itself an element of the gospel: the reality of the church is a sign that social reconciliation is not a merely utopian idea. In a world full of the weeping of the wounded, it is good to know that there is a place characterized by justice and peace. Not so fast: where exactly is this place? It is one thing to say that God is at work, creating a multinational, multicultural, and socioeconomically diverse community; it is quite another to locate it.

While the church may be most itself in sharing the Lord's Supper, it is not always *at* Table. On the contrary, the company of the baptized is also *in* the world, playing Christ in ten thousand and more places. Gerard Manley Hopkins's poem makes an important ontological point in a memorable way: each thing in creation is what it is as it is doing what it was created for. So with humanity, and the new humanity that is the church. We are created *in* Christ to act Christ *out*. And we can play Christ in ten thousand ways and in ten thousand places.

Corpus Christianum or *Corpus Christi*: Where in the World Is the Church?

The church is a theater of the gospel in a double sense: the space designed for the performance of plays (place), and the lived presentation of dramatic action (people). We must not be misled into thinking that the theater of the gospel is the physical church building or into thinking that the world is always "outside" the church. The church-world relationship is more complicated than that. Further, some performances fail to participate in the theodrama: "On that day many will say to me, 'Lord, Lord, did we not prophesy in your name, and cast out demons in your name, and do many deeds of power in your name?' Then

I will declare to them, 'I never knew you'" (Matt. 7:22–23). There are thus two challenges: to clarify the position of the church vis-à-vis the world and to distinguish true from false churches.

"I believe in the holy catholic church." So far, so orthodox. But ought we also to believe in the *local* church? We all have reasons not to believe in local congregations, for they are always made up of less-than-perfect individuals, many of whom may have offended us. The alternative, however, is to believe in a utopian church, that is, a church that presently exists nowhere (i.e., in no particular place). Indeed, there are many today who, all too aware of various church scandals and shortcomings, regard the church, as they do the world generally, in *dystopian* terms, as a "bad place." Indeed, outside the church societies are caught between the Charybdis of modern utopianism and the Scylla of postmodern dystopianism.

Here too, doctrine directs disciples in the way and truth of Christ, especially as this concerns his body, for doctrine directs us to see the local church as a particular representation of the church universal. So it has been from the beginning, which explains why Paul speaks of "the churches of the Gentiles" (Rom. 16:4), "the churches of Galatia" (1 Cor. 16:1), "the church of the Thessalonians" (1 Thess. 1:1), and most interesting of all, "the churches of Judea that are in Christ" (Gal. 1:22). Everything depends, however, on the way the local represents the universal: each local body bears the responsibility of instantiating, in its space and time, the whole body of Christ. Specifically, each local congregation is charged with living out the way of Jesus Christ, in the power of the Spirit and in its particular location. This becomes particularly apparent in the letters written to the seven churches in the book of Revelation. The church of Ephesus, for example, receives a commendation for its patient endurance (2:2–3), a warning for abandoning its first love (2:4), and an exhortation to repent and reprise its mission (2:5).

That these churches have regional designations is not inconsequential. The church is neither everywhere (in which case it would be identical to the world) nor no place (= utopia). Instead, the church is always someplace. The Greek term *ekklēsia* (assembly, gathering) for church implies locatedness (i.e., gathered *here*, not *there*). The church is thus a concrete reality, not an abstract ideal. Despite the rise of "global Christianity," if we are to speak about the church the way the New Testament does, we shall view it first and foremost as a local gathering.

The mission of the local church is thus to represent the universal church. It is also "to represent the reign of God."[3] In chapter 4 we suggested that the drama of redemption is the story of how God makes good on his covenant promise to David and establishes a king that brings justice and peace to the nations. We also saw that baptism symbolizes the saints' transference from the prince of this age to the kingdom of the Son (Col. 1:13). The question that remains is how saints are to act out their new citizenship in heaven (Phil. 3:20). Put differently: How

---

3. George R. Hunsberger, "The Newbigin Gauntlet," in *The Church between Gospel and Culture: The Emerging Mission in North America*, ed. G. R. Hunsberger and Craig Van Gelder (Grand Rapids: Wm. B. Eerdmans Publishing Co., 1996), 15.

does the church "put on" the kingdom of God amid the kingdoms, tyrannies, and democracies of the world?

In the era of Christendom, when the church wielded political power, the question was moot, for the whole world supposedly was Christian. The problem with Christendom, as Lesslie Newbigin and John Yoder have pointed out, is that the church easily loses sight of mission when church is fused (or confused) with world.[4] There was nothing for the local church prophetically to present, nor was there an audience to observe it: "The sense that the Church is a body sent into the world, a body on the move and existing for the sake of those beyond its borders, no longer played an effective part in men's thinking."[5] Newbigin contrasts Christendom's fusion of church and world (*corpus Christianum*) with the present situation, where the church is a minority contrast community (*corpus Christi*).

The mission of the local church is to constitute itself as a theater of the gospel, walking the way of Jesus Christ across the stage of the world. When the company of the baptized does church, it theatrically presents the kingdom of God to the world. At the same time, it would be presumptuous simply to identify the visible church with the kingdom of God. It is preferable to view the church as an enacted parable of the kingdom. What comes to the fore in considering local church as local theater is the importance of "locale."

Church as Place: The Scene of Meaningful Action and Interaction

"Christ plays in ten thousand places"—but what is *place*, and is Hopkins in this line thinking of local churches? Bodies have location: position and extension in space and time. The church is not an ethereal idea but an embodied presence in a particular place. As we have seen, the church is a community that gathers in the name of Christ in a particular region (e.g., Galatia). Theater, likewise, occurs in particular spaces, for the medium of theater is embodied persons. A theater, like a church, is "a communication between live actors and live spectators within a given space."[6] The mention of space brings us back to the question of the church-world relationship. One way of explaining how the church is in the world would be to locate various church building on the map, with fixed spatial coordinates. But this is not the way to locate the body of Christ. The "church of the Thessalonians" does not refer to a single geographic location. Even though it is embodied, a local church does not simply occupy space but rather cultivates it. The local church is a placemaking endeavor.[7]

Fully to appreciate the local church, the localized body of Christ, as a form of local theater means distinguishing space from place. We can start with

---

4. See Michael W. Goheen, "'As the Father Has Sent Me, I Am Sending You': Lesslie Newbigin's Missionary Ecclesiology," *International Review of Mission* 91 (2002): 345–69.
5. Lesslie Newbigin, *A Faith for This One World?* (London: SCM Press, 1961), 110.
6. Gay McAuley, *Space in Performance: Making Meaning in the Theatre* (Ann Arbor: University of Michigan Press, 1999), 3–4.
7. On the importance of placemaking, see Craig G. Bartholomew, *Where Mortals Dwell: A Christian View of Place for Today* (Grand Rapids: Baker Academic, 2001), part 3.

Isaac Newton's distinction: "Place is a part of space which a body takes up."[8] There is nothing particularly dramatic about space. Space can be either empty (a "formless void" of undifferentiated pure physical extension [Gen. 1:2]), or structured ("Let the waters under the sky be gathered together into one place, and let the dry land appear" [1:9]). By and large, however, space is impersonal and abstract. It is harder to make a personal connection to an arbitrary point on a graph than it is to a point on a map that names a particular place evoking memories or associations. That a particular point in space has a name means that someone has been there and had some kind of experience. And this is, indeed, what separates "space" from "place": place is "a meaningful location."[9]

What turns nondescript space into a particular place is what embodied persons experience or do there. A patch of earth becomes holy ground when Moses there experiences the self-revelation of God (Exod. 3:4–6). Jacob falls asleep at "a certain place," dreams of a ladder ascending to heaven, and after waking names it "Bethel" ("house of God"): "Surely the LORD is in this place" (Gen. 28:11–17). The new discipline of human geography has helped to explain why place matters: "If we think of space as that which allows movement, then place is pause; each pause in movement makes it possible for location to be transformed into place."[10] How space becomes place has everything to do with what people take time to do in a particular location. Space is thus the theater for social interaction; place is what those gathered make of it.

The rediscovery of "place" goes some way in helping us to understand the sense in which a local church is a local theater: "Fundamental to the idea of place would seem to be the idea of an open and yet bounded realm within which the things of the world can appear and within which events can 'take place.'"[11] Place and theater have this in common: each depends on persons interacting in a particular space and time. Theater-place makes embodied human communicative action and interaction possible: "To exist at all . . . is to have a place—*to be implaced*, however minimally or temporarily."[12]

The church is local in that whenever the community gathers, it does so to demonstrate in its embodied life a particular way of being-in-the-world. In an age increasingly marked by displacedness, where fewer and fewer people feel that they belong to any place, much less "a land flowing with milk and honey" (Exod. 13:5), the company of the baptized have a remarkable opportunity to put on

---

8. Isaac Newton, Andrew Motte, Florian Cajori, and R. T. Crawford, *Sir Isaac Newton's Mathematical Principles of Natural Philosophy and His System of the World*, vol. 1, *The Motion of Bodies* (Berkeley: University of California Press, 1934), 6.

9. Tim Cresswell, *Place: A Short Introduction* (Oxford: Blackwell, 2004), 7. Cf. Eric Jacobsen: "Place, in contrast to space, is a context-specific, meaning-rich concept" (*The Space Between: A Christian Engagement with the Built Environment* [Grand Rapids: Baker Academic, 2012], 55).

10. Yi-Fu Tuan, *Space and Place: The Perspective of Experience* (Minneapolis: University of Minnesota Press, 1977), 6.

11. J. E. Malpas, *Place and Experience: A Philosophical Topography* (Cambridge: Cambridge University Press, 1999), 33.

12. Edward Casey, *Getting Back into Place: Toward a Renewed Understanding of the Place-World* (Bloomington: Indiana University Press, 1993), 13, emphasis original.

hospitality and, furthermore, to become "*the place of meeting and activity in the interaction between God and the world.*"[13] What makes the church "holy" is not the ground on which it stands but rather what those who are gathered do there.

One of the marks of the church is the celebration of the Lord's Supper. Typically this happens in a space (at the Table) that is sealed off from the outside world. In this regard, what often appears as the least important elements of the service, the dismissal, is from a missiological perspective the most significant: "Go in peace to love and serve the Lord" or "Let us go forth into the world in the name of Christ." Hence the church, the company of the baptized, leaves the church building but continues to exist as church in the world. The "local" church is therefore a complex notion. It exists in a particular place, but that place is not fixed in space. Rather, the church exists in the "space" between its members, in the space of meaningful interaction.

How many Christians need to gather in order to constitute a church? Jesus' words may provide an answer: "where two or three are gathered in my name" (Matt. 18:20). It takes at least two people to interact, and it is disciples speaking and acting in the name of Christ that turn a pairing, or a crowd, into a church: the body of Christ. A gathering of two or three is sufficient to continue the drama of redemption. Two or three participants can thus be a localized church, a space that, thanks to its being the location where social identity is enacted, becomes a stage for playing Christ—not an empty place but a storied place, a place that has meaning because of the drama enacted there.[14]

The local church acts out its life as the body of Christ when what happens between its members makes apparent or brings to appearance the presence and activity of God. The church is the place where scenes (parables) of the kingdom of God become enacted. The gathering of disciples forms a storied or dramatized place that comes to acquire a particular meaning based on what is typically done there: "Place is a gathering of meanings that endures through practices."[15] Disciples gather together to continue the way of Jesus Christ, to pass on beliefs and practices alike by carrying on a living tradition. As a local theater of the gospel, the gathering of disciples is a historically extended, socially embodied, dramatized argument about the good news of Jesus Christ.

The Gathering of Disciples "in Christ"

The church's mission is different from that of Israel. The people of Israel were to observe all the words of the law so that they could "live long in the land" that God gave them "to possess" (Deut. 32:47; cf. Gen. 15:7). But there is no place

---

13. John Inge, *A Christian Theology of Place* (Aldershot, UK: Ashgate, 2003), 52, emphasis original.
14. Cf. Walter Brueggemann, *The Land: Place as Gift, Promise, and Challenge in Biblical Faith*, 2nd ed. (Minneapolis: Augsburg Fortress, 2002), 198.
15. Mary McClintock Fulkerson, *Places of Redemption: Theology for a Worldly Church* (Oxford: Oxford University Press, 2007), 36.

on earth that the church aspires to possess or to call home. On the contrary, the church desires "a better country, that is, a heavenly one" (Heb. 11:16). Augustine speaks for many when he says, "Our hearts are restless until they find rest in You."[16] This sense of restlessness is closely related to the modern sense of placelessness and lostness. Nevertheless, the church's mission is not to conquer territory or even to Christianize society; that way Christendom lies. The church is called rather to make disciples and present Christ.

The church is charged with participating in the drama of redemption, a drama at whose center is Christ the king and the reign of God. Yet the church does not stage the kingdom by capturing more space for Christ. On the contrary: the standing challenge is to play Christ in ten thousand places, and this means *placemaking*. Specifically, it means acting out the life of Christ in particular places or, stated differently, acting out the place of Christ in particular situations: "For where two or three are gathered in my name, I am there among them" (Matt. 18:20). The church is a local theater, a place in which Christ comes to be present. Christ is "between" the saints ("in the midst of them"), in the dynamic interaction that characterizes loving relationships empowered by the Holy Spirit. Disciples act out the presence of Christ whenever and wherever they enact their own existence "in Christ."

There are no spatial coordinates for determining one's position "in Christ." Or are there? After God raised Jesus from the dead, says Paul, he "seated him at his right hand in the heavenly places" (Eph. 1:20). God has also blessed all those in Christ "with every spiritual blessing in the heavenly places" (1:3). Even more to the point, and most startling of all, is Paul's claim that believers who have been made alive in Christ have themselves been raised up and seated "with him in the heavenly places in Christ Jesus" (2:6). "In the heavenlies" is thus the place of Christ's exaltation at God's right hand as well as the location of the company of the baptized. What is this place?

"Heaven" is the place where God dwells (Ezra 1:2). "In the heavenlies" must be nearby, because Christ is there seated at God's right hand, "far above all rule and authority and power and dominion" (Eph. 1:21).[17] God's "right hand" links to Psalm 110, a royal psalm understood as referring to Christ's position of honor in God's kingdom. The "place" where Christ is thus is not strictly spatial but rather palatial: the right hand of God is the place where God reigns, the domain in which God's will is done. "In the heavenlies" thus designates a very special kind of location that is less physical than personal: "in Christ."

What does it mean to be "in Christ"? How can the church be in Corinth, or in Chicago, and at the same time be seated with Christ "in the heavenlies"? That believers can simultaneously be "in Christ," "in the heavenlies," and "in Chicago" actually helps us to triangulate our position. It is not a matter of having

---

16. Augustine, *Confessions* 1.1.

17. M. Jeff Brannon contends that "heaven" and "in the heavenlies" are synonymous expressions. See his *The Heavenlies in Ephesians: A Lexical, Exegetical, and Conceptual Analysis* (London and New York: T&T Clark International, 2012).

one foot on earth and the other in heaven: as embodied creatures, human actors cannot be in two places at once. But we can be in overlapping domains: we can be in Chicago, Illinois, the United States, and North America at the same time. Similarly, we are "in the heavenlies" in the same way that we may be said to be "in Christ," namely, in the domain that Christ personally rules.

Disciples are people who have been made new in Christ. Our new being is manifest in new action: "To act well is to act in accordance with my nature and so to move toward perfection, that is, the entire realization of my nature."[18] It is thus in the nature of discipleship to act out one's being in Christ. This "acting out" and "being in" are, I believe, mutually illumining. Similarly, the concept "place" as we developed it above helps us better to understand what it means for the church to be "in Christ," as I now hope to show.

The phrase "in Christ" (*en Christō*) occurs seventy-three times in Paul's letters. One scholar of Greek prepositions claims, reasonably enough, that "spatial meanings evolve into non-spatial ones but not vice-versa."[19] It is worth noting, however, that none of the major New Testament studies of union with Christ interact with the emerging literature on place. Be that as it may, many New Testament scholars focus on the spatial or locative meaning of "in Christ." Yet this does not mean that disciples are "in Christ" the way coins are in a piggy bank or milk is in a carton. Rather, disciples are "in the sphere of Christ's control."[20] The preposition *en* thus denotes "the sphere within which some action occurs"[21]—in short, theater![22]

Neither heaven nor the church is utopian. However, the local church is indeed a *eutopia* (lit., "a good place") because it is the place where disciples gather as the domain of Christ: "our citizenship is in heaven" (Phil. 3:20).[23] We become citizens of heaven when, as baptized saints, we are transferred into the kingdom of Christ (Col. 1:13): "To be baptized seems to mean to be transferred in[to] a sphere or space determined by Christ, in Christ as a

---

18. John Webster, "'Where Christ Is': Christology and Ethics," in *Christology and Ethics*, ed. F. LeRon Shults and Brent Waters (Grand Rapids: Wm. B. Eerdmans Publishing Co., 2010), 39.

19. Pietro Bortone, *Greek Prepositions: From Antiquity to the Present* (Oxford: Oxford University Press, 2010), xii.

20. Stanley E. Porter, *Idioms of the Greek New Testament*, 2nd ed. (Sheffield, UK: Sheffield Academic Press, 1994), 159. See further Constantine R. Campbell, *Paul and Union with Christ: An Exegetical and Theological Study* (Grand Rapids: Zondervan, 2010), 68–73.

21. Murray J. Harris, "Appendix: Prepositions and Theology in the Greek New Testament," in *New International Dictionary of New Testament Theology*, ed. Colin Brown, vol. 3 (Carlisle: Paternoster Press, 1976), 1191.

22. The idea of place as a location associated with certain activities helps us to understand how being "in Christ" involves both union with Christ (a "being" word) and participation in Christ (a "doing" word). See the discussion in Campbell, *Paul and Union with Christ*, 413.

23. *Eutopia* fits nicely with other *eu-* terms associated with the drama of redemption, such as *euangelion* itself (= good news, gospel), *eucatastrophe*, and *Eucharist*. In an earlier work, I referred to the church as a "Christotope": a spatiotemporal manifestation of the new order "in Christ" (see *Drama of Doctrine*, 358).

space or sphere."[24] *Eutopia* refers to the disciples' "place" in the drama of redemption: the local church is empowered by Christ's Spirit to enact scenes now of the not-yet kingdom of God. Put differently: the church's "place" is the space between two ages, the old age and the age to come. And this leads to the church's mission: to serve as a living preview of a coming "attraction," the "new heavens" and "new earth" (2 Pet. 3:13; Rev. 21:1), where God will be "all in all" (1 Cor. 15:28).

For the moment, the church is to "seek the things that are above, where Christ is" (Col. 3:1). As we have seen, this is not a matter of wanting to be anywhere but here, on earth (or in Chicago). No, the church's mission is not to seek utopia but to be a *eutopia*: a good place in which the good news of reconciliation in Christ is exhibited in bodily form. The church participates in Christ not by partaking of his substance but by continuing his history and by exhibiting the history of his effects (spiritual blessings): "Truly to seek what is above is not to flee embodied social existence but to see it as caught up in the entire reorientation of created life in the kingdom of Christ."[25]

It therefore turns out that eutopia, the place where Christ is present and presents himself, *is* the people, disciples in communicative action and interaction. This is true of the new Jerusalem as well, which describes place in terms of people (Rev. 21:2–22:5): "The new Jerusalem is a dwelling place, to be sure. But it is God's dwelling place in the saints rather than their dwelling place on earth."[26] As to the dwelling of the saints, Jesus tells his disciples, "I go to prepare a place for you" (John 14:2). That place is in Christ, but where Paul speaks of being "in Christ," John typically speaks of "abiding in" Christ (6:56; 15:4–7). Interestingly, disciples are said to abide in Christ when they (1) eat his flesh and drink his blood (6:56), (2) abide in his words (15:7), and (3) obey his commands (15:10), which is to say, when disciples gather to do church.

The local church is charged with turning every space where two or three are gathered into a *eutopia*: a place that practices and thus exhibits the reign of God. This is not the same thing as taking land, for the kingdom of God is ultimately not of this fallen world. Rather, the church's placemaking mission means taking every word, thought, and activity captive to the broader drama of redemption (2 Cor. 10:4–5). Doing church means living out, in all the activities of everyday life, our identity in Christ. When disciples act out their being in Christ, the church enacts God's reign and thus becomes an enacted parable or theater of the kingdom of God. Where is Christ? He is in individual disciples and in the space between disciples, the "place" where scenes of his peaceable kingdom are played out.

---

24. Hans Burger, *Being in Christ*, 206.
25. Webster, "Where Christ Is," 51.
26. Robert H. Gundry, "The New Jerusalem: People as Place, Not Place for People," in *The Old Is Better*, 401.

AN INTERACTIVE THEATER OF RESIDENT EXILES AND HOLY FOOLS

While the church's most important location is "in Christ," the company of saints also inhabits particular geographic locations (e.g., Corinth; Chicago). One frequently hears the phrase "in the world but not of it" to describe the church-world relationship, even though this precise wording is not found in the Bible.[27] What we do find in Scripture is Paul's exhortation "Do not be conformed to this world" (Rom. 12:2), John's command "Do not love the world or the things in the world" (1 John 2:15), and Jesus' statement to his disciples "You are not of the world, but I chose you out of the world" (John 15:19 RSV; cf. 17:14).

What bearing does this negative prepositional phrase "not of" have on our understanding of the church and its mission? The answer is straightforward: the church is "in" the world in a spatial sense but not "of" it in the sense that it is not under its sway; it is not "in" the world in the sense of being under the sphere of its control. The term "resident exile" captures the awkwardness, and the challenge, of this uneasy situation. The church in the world is like Israel in exile (1 Pet. 1:1): a minority "holy nation" (1 Pet. 2:9), living amid other kingdoms and empires.

What is a resident exile to do? The course of least resistance is to blend in, to become like the other nations: to learn the language and the practices of the dominant culture. The danger here is to lose one's status as a holy ("set apart") nation, and hence one's very identity. Another possibility is sectarianism: living as a people set apart with as little contact as possible with the surrounding society. The danger here is to lose one's status and role as salt and light (Matt. 5:13–16), and hence the church's mission. Or one could apply Karl Marx's eleventh thesis on Feuerbach, originally intended for intellectuals, to the church: "The philosophers have only *interpreted* the world in various ways; the point is to *change* it."[28]

To Change the World: The Exiles' Errand?

Does performing the drama of doctrine, living out *what is* in Jesus Christ, require the church not merely to interpret the world differently but to change it? Specifically, does it require the church to redeem not only the time but also the "spirit of the times," that is, the cultural Zeitgeist? Paul uses imagery of military triumph to communicate Christ's victory over the powers and principalities: "He [Christ] disarmed the rulers and authorities and made a public example

---

27. I did find something close in Herman Melville's *Moby Dick* (1851): after viewing the great whale, Ishmael says, "Do thou, too, live in this world without being of it" (chap. 68). Cf. John 17:11–13, where Jesus speaks of being "in the world," and 17:14, 16 where he speaks of being "not of the world" (KJV).

28. Karl Marx, *The German Ideology* (Amherst, NY: Prometheus Books, 1998), 571.

of them, triumphing over them in it [the cross] (Col. 2:15). At various times in history, the church has indeed employed the sword (the power of the State) to change the world, by force if need be, thus rewriting (and radically departing from) St. Francis's maxim: "Preach the gospel at times, and use words only when necessary."

Paul also deploys the imagery of military triumph in quite different fashion: "For I think that God has exhibited us apostles as last of all, as though sentenced to death, because we have become a spectacle [*theatron*] to the world" (1 Cor. 4:9). The likely reference here is to the pageant in which gladiators, with prisoners bringing up the rear, process into the arena, ultimately to die. This too is theater. Jesus clearly states that his kingdom is not "from" or "of" this world; if it were, he adds, "my followers would be fighting" (John 18:36). Is the company of the baptized therefore on the side of the victor or the victim?

The situation of the church being in but not of the world cannot be reduced to a simplistic either-or, but that has not stopped some from trying to do so. The tendency of "Christendom" is to transform the world, perhaps by force, so that culture and society are ordered along explicitly Christian lines. This remains the hope of those who would wield influence by political rather than military means, making God's law the law (or morality) of the land by the ballot box rather than the sword. At the other end of the spectrum are churches who have little or no interest in dominating culture or changing the world but wish only to devote themselves to distinct church ministries (life together *ad intra*), as in the beginning of the church: "They devoted themselves to the apostles' teaching and fellowship, to the breaking of bread and the prayers" (Acts. 2:42).

James Davison Hunter has recently examined three paradigms for conceiving the church's posture vis-à-vis the world: "relevance *to*," "purity *from*," and "defensive *against*," to which we could add "transformative *of*."[29] In one way or another, each of these paradigms fails either to preserve the church's distinct identity, to encourage the church's mission to be salt and light, or to distinguish the nature of the church's public influence from other types of political power. Each of these ways overlooks what Hunter takes to be the main problem: the institutions of contemporary post-Christian culture are shaping disciples rather than the other way around. To change the world, Hunter suggests, one must change the world's social imaginary, the way culture structures our perception and experience of everyday reality. This is a tall order at any time, but especially at the present moment, which Hunter describes as one of "dissolution," which is characterized by the (post)modern doubt "that what is said has anything to do with what exists 'out there.'"[30]

Hunter's analysis is germane to the present project insofar as it raises questions about the capacity of doctrine to effect transformation. It is one thing to know the right propositional truths or system of orthodox belief, quite

---

29. James Davison Hunter, *To Change the World: The Irony, Tragedy, and Possibility of Christianity in the Late Modern World* (Oxford: Oxford University Press, 2010), 213–19.
30. Ibid., 205.

another to transform the social imaginary, that set of symbols and stories that shape a society's common life.³¹ The lived experience of many Christians, sadly enough, is that the Christian doctrines to which they notionally subscribe neither illumine their experience of "real life" nor are corroborated by that "real life." There is a performative contradiction between the official Christian curriculum and the lived curriculum implicit in the practices of everyday life.

Is it possible, however, that the problem is less with doctrine per se than with a picture of doctrine that has held us captive? The whole thrust of the theatrical model presented here is to tear down the fourth wall that separates doctrine from life. Doctrine is the attempt to set forth in language *what is in Christ* and to summon people to participate in it. Doctrine directs our attention to what God is doing, yields understanding, and then directs us to demonstrate our understanding in our performance (i.e., our acting out the truth of Jesus Christ). Hunter's own model ("faithful presence") moves in this direction too, calling disciples "to live in fellowship and integrity with the person and witness of Jesus Christ."³² He sees the central ministry of the church as that of forming disciples "to live the alternative reality of the kingdom of God within the present world order faithfully."³³

Hunter's model is congenial to the present proposal, though I prefer to speak of faithful presence *and activity*. Wherever two or three disciples are gathered, they are to engage themselves and others in ways that participate fittingly with what is and is coming to be in Christ. In sum: faithful presence, truthful witness, and loving and just action should mark the church's engagement with the world. Yes, the question of criteria looms large: Who/what determines what counts as fidelity, truth, love, and justice? It is here that the theatrical model can move the discussion forward. The fundamental criterion for discerning these things is not theoretical but theatrical: it is the diagnostic question: "Do these words and deeds accord with what God is doing in Christ?"³⁴

Words are cheap. Discipleship is costly because it requires the word's enactment. The church exists to witness to the true, utterly reliable word and faithfulness of God, namely, Jesus Christ: "For all the promises of God find their Yes in him" (2 Cor. 1:20 RSV). God has already acted, reconciled the world, and proved himself faithful. The church does not need to redeem society as much as indicate that redemption has already taken place. The company of the baptized is charged simply with living out this evangelical reality: what is in Christ. The vocation of the church is to live out the already/not-yet kingdom of God amid the kingdoms of this world. Christian doctrine directs the church not to seize earthly kingdoms or political fiefdoms, especially not by force, but rather

---

31. "The culture-producing institutions of historical Christianity are largely marginalized in the economy of culture formation in North America" (ibid., 89).
32. Ibid., 197.
33. Ibid., 236.
34. To be sure, we need subordinate criteria to determine whether we have correctly understood what God is doing in Christ. Of these subordinate criteria, conformity to the testimony of the prophets and apostles (i.e., *sola scriptura*) is chief.

to perform parables of the kingdom inaugurated in Christ. Living out the truth of what is in Christ is a compelling way to testify to another social imaginary, one rooted in the real itself (thus providing balm for the wound of dissolution mentioned above). Staging parables of the kingdom of God puts the accent on the church's prophetic witness, not kingly rule. In particular places and times the church "realizes" the reality given in Christ for all times and places.[35] In Bonhoeffer's words, the Church of Jesus Christ "is the place—that is, the space—in the world where the reign of Jesus Christ over the whole world is to be demonstrated and proclaimed."[36]

The church is called not to lord it over, escape from, or even transform culture (and especially not to be transformed by it!), but rather to *communicate* to it. Specifically, the church is to communicate Christ, and what is in Christ, in everything that it says and does. In doing so, the church cannot help but communicate the meaning of life and the hope of life eternal. The church's part in the theodrama is to attest its climax and anticipate its denouement. The Holy Spirit equips the church for this ambassadorial task (2 Cor. 5:20). The church enacts parables of the kingdom of God when it participates in the reality of the kingdom by speaking the truth in love, calling for justice, forgiving rather than judging, and creating a place for undistorted communication by lifting up every voice. Against such things there is no law (Gal. 5:23).

A Public Faith: Local Church as Interactive Theater

The church's mission is to present Christ, not to extend Christendom. The beginnings of the modern missionary movement arose from this distinction. While the Crusaders were "prepared to compel," missionaries chose instead to "demonstrate, invite, explain, entreat, and leave the result with God."[37] While the Crusaders could rely on coercion, missionaries had to learn how to communicate, and this meant learning the language and custom of their new cultural situation: "Mission involves moving out of one's self and one's accustomed terrain, and taking the risk of entering another world. It means living on someone else's terms."[38] After Christendom, disciples often find themselves in the minority even in Western countries; they are resident exiles, missionaries in their own land.

The challenge is to communicate in a compelling way what is in Christ. How can the church persuade others that it is following the way of truth and life? This question is so important that Augustine devoted the fourth book of *On*

---

35. According to Bonhoeffer, the church's mandate is "the commission of allowing the reality of Jesus Christ to become real in proclamation, church order, and Christian life" (*Ethics*, 74).

36. Ibid., 63.

37. Andrew F. Walls, "Afterword: Christian Mission in a Five-Hundred Year Context," in *Mission in the Twenty-First Century: Exploring the Five Marks of Global Mission*, ed. A. F. Walls and Cathy Ross (London: Darton, Longman & Todd, 2008), 196.

38. Ibid., 197. The phrase "living on someone else's terms" occurs repeatedly in Walls's writings as a kind of shorthand for missionary existence.

Christian Doctrine to answering it. In the first three books, Augustine discusses his approach to understanding the Bible, but in the fourth he focuses on helping ministers of the word to communicate the results of their biblical interpretation to others. One should either teach (*docere*), delight (*delectare*), or persuade (*flectere*) one's listeners. The goal of biblical interpretation is obedient listeners who are persuaded to live according to the double love command (Mark 12:29–31). Preachers should persuade their congregations both to assent to Christian doctrine and to act it out. Faith speaking understanding means, for Augustine, that pastors must not only teach their congregations the truth but also persuade them of it and enable them to live it out.

We here return to the discussion in chapter 3 about the challenge of getting one's message across in an experience economy. Gilmore and Pine say that if a business wants to create interest, then guests (their term for customers) ought to experience the offering "in a place so engaging that they can't help but pay attention.... Stop *saying* what your offerings are ... and start creating places ... where people can experience what those offerings ... *actually* are."[39] The contention of the present chapter is that the local church is such a place. The company of the baptized plays Christ in ten thousand spaces, spaces *between* disciples and also between disciples and the watching world. The missionary (as opposed to crusading) task of the church—the discipling of the nations, playing Christ in ten thousand places—is essentially a matter of interactive theater.

According to Miroslav Volf, there is no one way that the church ought to relate to contemporary culture, though the goal in every cultural situation is to bring its vision of the good life into the public sphere: "A vision of human flourishing and the common good is the main thing the Christian faith brings into the public debate."[40] We can go further: the company of Christ's followers renders this vision *visible* in their speech and action. In the experience of many churchgoers, the theatrical analogy works out differently. All too often, the clergy are the main actors, sometimes even the stars, with the congregation a mainly passive audience. Not so in the perspective offered here, where it is the whole company's responsibility to perform the drama of doctrine, at the Table, yes, but also when out and about (in public). Mere spectators do not need to be involved in what is happening. By way of contrast, disciples are active participants in the theodrama, not least in the role of witnesses.

What we might term the *playerhood* of all believers is an aspect of the priesthood of all believers: it involves the privilege and responsibility of interpreting the Bible and of living out one's interpretations with others. The church is that company whose vocation is to perform the drama of doctrine: to live out, together, the truth of what is in Christ. Clothed with new natures by the Spirit-dresser, disciples are costumed interpreters whose common life puts arms, legs, and feet on the gospel: "The most authentic Christian biblical

---

39. Pine and Gilmore, *Authenticity*, 149.
40. Miroslav Volf, *A Public Faith: How Followers of Christ Should Serve the Common Good* (Grand Rapids: Brazos Press, 2011), xvi.

interpretation is human enactments of God-informed life.... What we do as the people of God is our interpretation of the Bible."[41] The most compelling presentation of Christianity is a community of Christians acting out Christ.

"Costumed interpretation" is a common practice in so-called "living museums" like Old World, Wisconsin, or Colonial Williamsburg. Costumed interpreters take on historical roles and dress in order to communicate what life was like at a particular place and time. Visitors to these sites often agree that it was the presence of costumed interpreters that made their time memorable. It is not the acting that impresses (the players are motivated by a higher calling than Oscar fever) but rather the passion and knowledge of the costumed interpreters. Many, if not most, are volunteers who have thoroughly researched the period and person they are rendering. These living museums are actually forms of interactive theater. The costumed interpreters do not only embody their roles; they also draw the "guests" into the play: "Creating relationships with the guests, thereby involving them in the story, is the primary focus of the interactive genre."[42]

The Bristol Renaissance Faire is a good example of interactive theater. Each year it attracts thousands of visitors to its unlikely Midwest site. Guests (the preferred term for "audience" in the context of interactive theater) enter the gates of a decent facsimile of Bristol, England, on a summer's day in 1574. It is a festival day, and the whole village awaits the arrival of Queen Elizabeth I and her court. Eighty players assume various roles, from members of the queen's court to members of the clergy, military, minstrels, and general populace (including thieves). These costumed interpreters mingle and engage with the guests throughout the grounds in a manner that parallels the way in which the church interacts with the world. Of course, Christians are performing not some strange old world (the world behind the biblical text) but the strange new world of the Bible (the world "in front of" the text)), and they are celebrating the return not of a queen but of the King.

Interactive theater is the work of an ensemble, "a group that shares three things mutually and in abundance: trust, play, and joy."[43] The company of the baptized is an ensemble that shares these things and more: union with Christ and the Spirit of communion. What makes interactive theater unique is its goal of drawing those *outside* the company into the play as well. What happens in the church should attract others. This is what Tertullian wanted the church to do in his third-century context: "'Look,' they say, 'how they love one another' (for they themselves hate one another); 'and how they are ready to die for each other' (for they themselves are readier to kill each other)."[44] We

---

41. David Scott, "Speaking to Form: Trinitarian-Performative Scripture Reading," *Anglican Theological Review* 77 (1995): 144–45.
42. Gary Izzo, *The Art of Play: The New Genre of Interactive Theatre* (Portsmouth, NH: Heinemann, 1997), 188.
43. Ibid., 136.
44. Tertullian, *Apology* 39.7.

need not share Tertullian's pessimism about the world outside the church to see his point: what happens in and among the company of the baptized must be qualitatively distinct from what happens in other social groups. Those in the watching world are guests that the company invites into places created by the interaction. In the interactive theater of the gospel, the entire world's a stage, and everyone is a potential guest. There is no overarching plot that the players must follow, only a series of "floating scenes" that give the guests a taste of what is being communicated: "It is not so much a story being told, but a reality being explored."[45]

The mission of the church is to communicate the riches and the good that are in Christ. The best-costumed interpreters are not those who have memorized their lines but those who so understand what is going on, and their own part in it, that they invariably say and do what is fitting and fascinating. Indeed, one of the most important qualifications of costumed interpreters is the ability to intrigue the guests: "The character must be extraordinary. . . . The theatre is a sanctuary for the display of the extraordinary."[46] Just so. As Jesus' parables used everyday scenes to communicate something extraordinary, so the church enacts everyday scenes that communicate the extraordinary nature of the kingdom of God. The floating scenes that the church ensemble stages are enacted parables of the kingdom of God, the reality in question. Like Jesus' parables themselves, the church is an extended metaphor, a storied drama. The church is extended in time like a dramatic scene; it is extended in space in that it is an encroachment of the sphere where Christ reigns onto the stage of the world.[47]

A Foolish Faith? Power in Weakness

What does the kingdom of God look like in the twenty-first century? What should the local church be saying and doing in order to communicate what is in Christ? These are contested questions at present, and we can only indicate the right direction. The present-day challenge is to do church in a post-Constantinian age. It is easier to rule out the wrong strategies. For example: local churches should not view themselves as part of a "holy American Empire," as if one could lord the way, truth, and life over the rank and file of unbaptized society. Nor should the church serve as a rubber stamp to the social status quo. The church falls short of its commission to enact parables of the kingdom when it simply blesses moral-therapeutic action, like so much frosting on the cake of civic religious life. Although the church works for the common good and advocates for forms of life that are conducive to human flourishing, its vision as

---

45. Izzo, *The Art of Play*, 34.
46. Ibid., 61–62.
47. Not everything the church does is parabolic; the saints that make up the company of faith are still sinners. It is only by God's grace that what the church does is not more often *unlike* the kingdom of God.

to what these consist in may vary greatly from the prevailing cultural paradigms. God's *shalom* is not quite Plato's *Republic* or liberal democracy.[48]

The church's mandate is to enact scenes not merely of the good life but also of the gospel life. To restate the central theme of the present work: doctrine directs disciples to live out their new reality in Christ. The goal is to perform parables that demonstrate in coordinate action what "living well with others in Christ" looks like in particular places in the twenty-first century. To enact parables of the kingdom is to enact scenes of Christian wisdom, where the players speak and show "an integrated *way of life* that enables the flourishing of persons, communities, and all creation."[49] One of the most important ways to communicate God's covenant faithfulness is for disciples to make sure that their word is their bond. For example, Paul contrasts his own promise making, rooted in God's promise, with the fickleness which is the way of the world: "Do I make my plans according to ordinary human standards, ready to say 'Yes, yes' and 'No, no' at the same time?" (2 Cor. 1:17; cf. Matt. 5:37).

There is often a fine line, however, between the extraordinary and the eccentric. It is likely that the church's lived convictions will strike many observers as not only odd but also foolish, especially if the scenes that disciples play out are as socially subversive as Jesus' parables. Though Jesus is the wisdom of God incarnate, some of those who observed him (John. 10:20), including his own family (Mark 3:21), regarded him as out of his mind. Jesus' table fellowship with sinners and people of ill repute was particularly damaging to his social standing. Indeed, disciples who follow Jesus' way must be prepared to endure a similar loss of status, to lose symbolic capital or social power.

Status anxiety is a perennial threat to the church's faithful performance. The Philippians to whom Paul wrote his epistle knew all about it. They lived in a Roman colony but did not take part in pagan festivals, especially those that honored the Roman emperor. Local churches today no longer fear the Roman Empire, but another kind of empire, the global communications-marketing technocracy, may have taken its place.[50] Ancient Rome is small potatoes compared to today's postindustrial-business-entertainment complex. As in Philippi, so today's church struggles with status anxiety in the face of the new empire of popular culture. Like status-anxious individuals, some churches may be tempted to employ tools of this empire, such as mass marketing, to achieve larger numbers and be reckoned a success in the eyes of the world. Success, what sells, is indeed the ultimate indicator of high status in today's empire.

---

48. Nicholas Wolterstorff notes the requirement of liberal democracy that people of faith not bring their religious convictions to debates in the public square: "The Role of Religion in Decision and Discussion of Political Issues," in *Religion in the Public Square: The Place of Religious Convictions in Political Debate*, by N. Wolterstorff and Robert Audi (London: Rowman & Littlefield, 1997), 67–120.

49. Volf, *A Public Faith*, 101.

50. See Michael Hardt and Antonio Negri, *Empire* (Cambridge, MA: Harvard University Press, 2000).

The message of the cross, from the time of the apostle Paul to the present, has consistently been a hard sell. It is difficult to connect the dots between Jesus' crucifixion and human flourishing. Yet this is precisely Paul's message: this horrific death is, by God's amazing grace, the means by which a new creation has come and a new community has been formed. Paul is under no illusion as to the scandal of this announcement, especially to a Corinthian audience that valued the conventional marks of social status. The crucified Christ had none of the marks that society associates with greatness: power, income, education, and a noble family. Paul nonetheless decided not to employ the techniques of a professional rhetorician in order to exercise "spin" control. He refused to "market the gospel as a consumer commodity designed to please the hearers and win their approval."[51] Instead, he opted to play the low-status role of the weak and dishonorable fool (1 Cor. 4:10; cf. 1:17).

Paul's cruciform foolishness has nothing to do with silliness or irrationality. On the contrary, it is part of a long tradition of the "wise fool," as in Shakespeare's *King Lear*. The fool in *Lear* speaks truth but has no political power; the fool is not a king but a prophet who questions conventional wisdom. Paul plays the role of the fool because in this way he can participate in God's own foolishness (1 Cor. 1:25): "Because . . . in the cross of Christ God has affirmed nothings and nobodies, he [Paul] is able to embrace the role of the fool as the authentic mode of his own existence."[52] Note that the scandal of the cross has less to do with its supposed irrationality than with its "stupidity" as concerns social status.

Paul cared nothing for social status. The only status that mattered to him was his status as justified: declared righteous "in Christ." The cross overturns all the status logics of this world. Accordingly, members of the company of faith, like Paul, will be perceived to be holy fools who march to the beat of a different kingdom drummer. To live out one's new status in Christ means enacting parables of God's own foolishness, for example, the "foolishness" of forgiving others at great cost to oneself.[53] As a theater of holy fools, the company of faith is charged with acting out the socially subversive new reality brought into existence in Christ. Accordingly, we could say that the church is charged both with enacting parables of the kingdom and with performing the apocalypse: the end of the (old) world.

The church is a dramatization of life in Christ "between the times." Consider the subversive, world-destroying nature of the word of the cross: "These people who have been turning the world upside down have come here also. . . . They

---

51. Anthony Thiselton, *The First Epistle to the Corinthians: A Commentary on the Greek Text* (Grand Rapids: Wm. B. Eerdmans Publishing Co., 2000), 20–21.

52. L. L. Welborn, *Paul, the Fool of Christ: A Study of 1 Corinthians 1–4 in the Comic-Philosophical Tradition*, JSNTSup 293 (London and New York: T&T Clark International, 2005), 250.

53. Some New Testament scholars think that the popular theater is "the most plausible social context for understanding Paul's language about the 'folly' of the message of the cross" (ibid., vii). Some even go as far as to suggest that Paul's employment as a *skēnopoios* (Acts 18:3) is best translated not "tentmaker" but "maker of stage properties" (see further ibid., 11).

are all acting contrary to the decrees of the emperor, saying that there is another king named Jesus" (Acts 17:6–7). To be sure, the proclamation of the cross and its implications, faith speaking understanding, creates not only cognitive but also existential dissonance. That Christ had to die in order to establish right relationships between humanity and God and between oneself and others means that none of the worldly stratagems for making things right actually works. All the socially sanctioned things we do to "gain" our life turn out to be futile and ineffective.

Paul plays the role of the fool in order to subvert the powers that be and the prevailing status logic. God, through the cross, has reversed the status wisdom of the world. He has made "nobodies" and "not a people" into his sons and daughters, a treasured possession. As Luther says, with only slight overstatement, the cross reveals for the first time who God is. At the same time, the deep wisdom of God continues to look foolish, whether on the school playground or in the realm of geopolitics. We know what happens there: Insulted? Talk back. Struck in the face? Hit back. Wronged? Return evil for evil. By way of contrast, disciples who follow Christ do everyday life with a subversive difference: Insulted? Keep silent. Struck in the face? Turn the other cheek. Wronged? Forgive.

The vocation of the company of faith is to perform the drama of the doctrine of the cross, speaking and showing what it means to have died and been raised with Christ. To perform the doctrine of atonement (so to speak) is to participate rightly in his death. Please note: this does *not* mean that we ought literally to repeat the passion on Good Friday, as the *Penitente* Brotherhood (Lat. *paenitentes* = penitents) does, by staging ritual crucifixions to do penance. To do that is seriously to misunderstand the definitive once-for-all nature of Christ's death and hence to deny rather than continue the theodrama. Only Christ's death takes away the sins of the world (John 1:29; Heb. 9:26; 1 John 2:2). Bearing testimony to the truth of the cross may not require us literally to die, then, though it does require us to "die daily," which for Augustine means doing charitable works, pouring oneself out for others. The company of faith must not only speak understanding as concerns the cross but also demonstrate a willingness to align their hearts and lives to the new status order in Christ. Indeed, Paul's overarching goal in writing to the Corinthians, and to us, is to get us to understand and participate in the drama of redemption to the point of being able to say, "But we have the mind of Christ" (1 Cor. 2:16).

IMPROVISATION: EMBODYING THE MIND OF CHRIST ALWAYS, EVERYWHERE, AND TO EVERYONE

Displaying the mind of Christ at every moment in every situation is the disciple's ultimate goal. To perform the drama of doctrine is, finally, to perform or embody the gospel wisdom of God, made known definitively in the incarnation. To act out what is in Christ is another way of saying, Embody the mind of

Christ! Here, too, we see that a theatrical model best orients theology toward wisdom, because it insists both on understanding the drama of redemption and on demonstrating that understanding in practice: speech and action.

Disciples are to imitate, but not replicate, Christ. To replicate is to make an exact copy, a duplicate. To imitate means to continue a pattern.[54] Paul appeals to the Corinthians to imitate him: "For this reason I sent you Timothy, . . . to remind you of my ways in Christ Jesus, as I teach them everywhere in every church" (1 Cor. 4:17). Imitation requires both fidelity and, in some cases, creativity if one is to continue the *same* pattern in a *different* situation. And this is precisely the role of theology: to hand on the truth, once delivered to the saints, further to disciples in new times and places; to continue the tradition by keeping it vital and vibrant (1 Cor. 11:2; 15:3; Jude 3).

Christ is alive: his Spirit continues to blow (John 3:8), and the gospel is infinitely translatable, able to penetrate every cultural joint and marrow. To continue the ways of Christ Jesus is to translate not only Scripture but also the theodrama itself into other languages and cultures. Here, too, the challenge is to preserve (biblical) sameness while respecting (cultural) difference. This requires not only fidelity to the text, but also attention to the context, as well as flexibility, even creativity, on the part of those charged with continuing the same pattern/drama in new cultural scenes.

Disciples who play Christ in new places must therefore be not replicators or innovators but improvisers: those who can express and enact theodramatic understanding in new situations. Indeed, this is what it finally means to be "biblical" in performing the drama of doctrine. The aim of doctrine is to discipline the believer's mind, heart, and imagination to think, desire, see—and then *do*—reality as it is in Jesus Christ, and we come to understand this reality by having minds, hearts, and imaginations nurtured by the canonical Scriptures.

Being biblical is therefore not a matter of reproducing the culture "behind" the biblical text. In this, Christianity differs from Islam: for Muslims, "obedience to Allah lies in faithful reproduction of conditions that obtained at the time the Qur'an was revealed."[55] By way of contrast, the challenge for the Christian disciple is to display the same dramatic pattern (God's revelation and redemption in Christ, the reign of God) under new conditions, in different times and places. Hence the performative understanding of faith is not a replication of the biblical authors' situation (the world behind the text) *but of unfolding what the authors say about the theodrama in one's own situation (the world in front of the text)*. To be sure, the church sometimes demonstrates faith in ways that speak misunderstanding as well as understanding. That is because the company of the baptized is still on the way, seeing through a glass, and acting on a stage, dimly. If the church sounds an uncertain note or performs less than charitable actions,

---

54. Jason B. Hood, *Imitating God in Christ: Recapturing a Biblical Pattern* (Downers Grove, IL: InterVarsity Press, 2013), 12.

55. Andrew F. Walls, *The Cross-Cultural Process in Christian History* (Maryknoll, NY: Orbis Books; Edinburgh: T&T Clark, 2002), 74.

it is a sign not of a flaw in the drama itself but in the company: the church at present has only the firstfruits of the Spirit, which is why its performances are *parables* of the kingdom rather than its final realization.

"Just Say *Yes*": The Freedom of the Christian and the Spirit of the Improvisatory Disciplines

The church did not have long to wait before it was confronted with new linguistic challenges, cultural conundrums, and conceptual puzzles. Disciples today have much to learn by studying how saints in the past spoke understanding with both freedom and fidelity.

Improvising at Nicaea

One of the first theological crises in the early church had to do with the identity of Jesus. Was the Son of God literally "of God" (sharing his divine nature and status)? The "Arians" argued that the Son of God was subordinate to God in being: the "firstborn of all creation" (Col. 1:15), to be sure, but a creation nevertheless, mutable rather than immutable, and thus to be put on the "creature" side of the Creator/creature ledger.[56] In a monotheistic framework such as Judaism, there were few conceptual resources to help resolve this issue, and there were no "scripted" answers in the Bible either. To speak forth biblical understanding requires more than rote memorization of one's line: the Arians had proof texts too (e.g., "the Father is greater than I" [John 14:28]).

Theological necessity was the mother of doctrinal invention, and Athanasius devised (or dare I say, *improvised*) a way forward with the word *homoousios* (same substance). This new, nonbiblical term faithfully captures what Scripture says about the Son's being "one" (John 10:30) yet "begotten" of the Father (Heb. 1:5) and of having the "exact imprint of God's very being" (Heb. 1:3) yet not regarding this "equality with God" (Phil. 2:6) something to be held tight. Athanasius improvised the concept of *homoousios* not out of the blue, but out of the canonical script and the conceptual resources at hand in his fourth-century context. Athanasius therefore exemplifies what it means for faith to speak understanding.

The company of faith is not always able to address contemporary issues and disputes by reciting Scripture, much less the Nicene Creed. Sometimes, to be faithful, we need to be creative. When disciples find themselves in strange new territory, they will spontaneously *extend* the pattern. It is but a small step from the notions of performing the world implied by the text and extending the pattern of Jesus Christ to that of improvising with a canonical transcript.

---

56. The dispute over how to think about the relation of Father and Son is only tangentially related to Arius himself. The real issue was over how to conceive the generation of the Son, and hence the extent to which the Son is the "same" or "different" from the Father in being and status. For further discussion, see Lewis Ayres, *Nicaea and Its Legacy: An Approach to Fourth-Century Trinitarian Theology* (Oxford: Oxford University Press, 2004), esp. chaps. 1–2 and 5.

Marks of Improvisatory Discipleship

The church always has to improvise. It does so out of a desire, not to be original, but rather to minister the gospel in new contexts, to speak and show its understanding of the drama of redemption. Improvisation hardly seems an inspired choice as an image for embodied theological wisdom. Is not improvisation a matter of impromptu innovation rather than of faithful performance? Whose line is it anyway? These are important questions, yet we must not be held captive by misleading pictures of improvisation. Improvisation has nothing to do with glibness or cleverness, much less laziness or wit: "A good improviser is someone who is awake, not entirely self-focused, and moved by a desire to . . . give something back, and who acts upon this impulse."[57]

Genuine improvisation is a matter of freedom and fittingness. Disciples improvise each time they exercise Christian freedom fittingly, in obedient response to the gracious word of God that set it in motion. Improvising to the glory of God is ultimately a matter simply of being who one has been created to be in Christ, so that one responds freely and fittingly as if by reflex or second nature: "Where the Spirit of the Lord is, there is freedom" (2 Cor. 3:17). Free improvisation is a matter of training (formation) and discernment (imagination). It is a matter of being able to say and do things that are consistent with the canonical script and advance the dramatic action, even when, like Athanasius, we find ourselves in uncharted intellectual and cultural territory.

Christian doctrine is an important ingredient in forming faithful disciples to be effective improvisers, but not because doctrines tell us exactly what to say and do. Their purpose is not merely to give us "answers" but to instill in us habits of seeing, judging, and acting in theodramatically appropriate manners. This is how doctrine nurtures understanding: "But solid food is for the mature, for those who have their powers of discernment trained by constant practice to distinguish good and evil" (Heb. 5:14 ESV). The key thing is to understand what God is doing in Christ so well that one can participate fittingly in the action even when the setting and scenery look completely different. In addition to helping the players understand the divine play, doctrine encourages disciples to acquire three habits or dispositions that characterize good improvisatory wisdom.[58]

1. *Spontaneity* ("Don't make plans"). Improvisers have to learn to be spontaneous. Most people, disciples included, tend to be utterly predictable, usually because of status anxiety: we are afraid to be thought strange. We therefore follow conventional wisdom: "Play by the rules. Follow the recipe. Do it like everyone else." The problem with this strategy is that we become unremarkable, ordinary players in an extraordinary drama. "Deadly theater" is

---

57. Patricia Ryan Madson, *Improv Wisdom: Don't Prepare, Just Show Up* (New York: Bell Tower, 2005), 15.

58. For more on improvisation, see Keith Johnstone, *Improv: Improvisation and the Theatre* (New York: Routledge, 1989). For an intriguing application of improvisation to Christian ethics, see Samuel Wells, *Improvisation*.

the theater of predictability, clichés, and stock effects. The problem with deadly theater, however, is that it fails to be interactive. The company of faith must beware of status anxiety and the temptation to betray our Lord by staging dull, socially conventional scenes. Patricia Ryan Madson, the author of a book on improvisation, played by the rules until she lost her academic post, at which point she made the following resolution: "I promised myself that whatever happened I would never again make choices simply to impress others or to gain status."[59]

Learning spontaneity means casting out the fear of failure. One of the most typical obstacles to spontaneity is "preplanning," thinking out a course of action in advance, usually out of a concern with losing control of the situation. The most common stratagem for maintaining control of a scene or situation is "script writing." This happens whenever an actor has a blueprint for how one wants the action to develop. However, script writing is actually an attempt to manipulate one's scene and fellow actors, ensuring that everything proceed according to one's preplanned mental flow chart. Instead of going with the flow, scriptwriters want to micromanage things.[60]

A second obstacle to spontaneity, at the other end of the spectrum, is the temptation to ad-lib or display originality. The desire to be original often comes at the expense of fidelity, however: "Ad lib is individual cleverness, not evolved dialogue."[61] Ad-libbing is the theatrical equivalent of heresy, where one person stubbornly insists on going their own way instead of playing the game. As in theater, so in music: improvisation is the work of an ensemble, and each player's freedom is a variation on a given theme: "soloists elaborate upon what the structure of the piece has to say."[62] The structure of the Christian piece, as we have seen, is a five-act play (see chap. 4 above). Christian theology is faithful improvisation on a theodramatic gospel theme.

Spontaneity thus has nothing to do with arbitrary invention or random action. On the contrary, it has everything to do with the disciple's readiness to spring into action, knowing that whatever scene is being played is part of an overarching theodrama. Disciples have the added advantage of knowing about divine providence. That doctrine directs us to employ our freedom in the faith that God will weave our actions and reactions into the drama in his own good time and in his own wise way. It is trust in God, not the ability to control, that allows for spontaneity.

2. *Accepting offers* ("Say 'yes'"). A second improvisational virtue is a willingness to throw oneself into the action. Every improvisation begins with a basic premise or assumption about what is happening ("We're stranded on a desert island

---

59. Madson, *Improv Wisdom*, 13.
60. The history of Christian missions has had its fair share of scriptwriters. The best missionaries knew how to improvise, as we shall see in the next section.
61. Viola Spolin, *Improvisation for the Theatre*, 3rd ed. (Evanston, IL: Northwestern University Press, 1999), 355.
62. Tommy Flanagan, jazz pianist, cited in Paul F. Berliner, *Thinking in Jazz: The Infinite Art of Improvisation* (Chicago: University of Chicago Press, 1994), 170.

with a Ping-Pong table"). No matter how absurd the premise, it represents an "offering" to the other actors that they can either take up or ignore. An "offer" is an invitation to accept the premise, extend the action, and keep the play going. Offers can either be accepted or "blocked." To accept an offer is to respond in a way that maintains and develops the initial premise. In accepting an offer, the improviser says *yes* to the basic premise. In contrast, blocking the offer prevents the scene from developing. Actors who say *no* to offers reject the premise of the play, halting the action and hence the improvisation.

The connection to Christian discipleship is direct, and striking, not least because the entire theodrama is filled with examples of people either accepting or blocking divine offers. Consider God's promise to Abraham, "I will make of you a great nation" (Gen. 12:2). This promise sets up the basic premise of the divine-human drama of redemption. The whole theodrama is essentially the history of divine improvisation on this covenantal theme. There are also further offers: "Here is the Lamb of God" (John 1:29). "Repent, and be baptized" (Acts 2:38). "Take up your cross and follow me" (Mark 8:34). Scripture is filled with examples of persons either accepting or blocking these divine offers. The most striking example is perhaps Mary's response to the "offer" of bearing the Son of God: "Here am I, the servant of the Lord; let it be with me according to your word" (Luke 1:38)—in other words, *yes*!

Does doctrine more often direct disciples to accept or to block offers? Much depends on who is doing the offering. Disciples ought to follow their Lord's example in blocking satanic offers (i.e., temptations). On the other hand, even life's trials can be "offerings" that enable disciples to say *yes* in the sense that they are willing to endure them (Jas. 1:2). Here, too, the question is whether actors are willing to enter into situations over which they have no control: those who say *yes* "are rewarded by the adventures they have, and those who say 'No' are rewarded by the safety they attain."[63] This desire for worldly safety and security is the opposite of faith. Sin, the will to worldly power, is the ultimate blocking strategy.

If everyday improvisers can accept and affirm the events of daily life, how much should Christians, those who believe in the goodness of a sovereign God, be able to do so? Of all people, Christians ought to be bold improvisers, for they know "all things work together for good for those who love God" (Rom. 8:28). The doctrines of creation and providence combine to direct disciples to say *yes* to the divine offers that fill our every waking hour: "Every person you meet is a gift of God, every circumstance you will meet is a gift of God."[64]

3. *Remembering the story; continuing the plot* ("Stay on course"). The third habit of good improvisation is the narrative skill of remembering what has gone on before and being able to continue the story line and theme. Surprisingly enough, memory is more important for improvisation than originality. The

---

63. Johnstone, *Impro*, 92.
64. Bloom, *Beginning to Pray*, 76–77.

improviser is like someone walking backward who sees only where he has been, not where he is going.[65]

Improvisers use narrative competence to keep the full story in mind as they respond to new offers in order to move the story forward effectively. One key story-making skill is the ability to reincorporate earlier material in order to provide both continuity and closure. Reincorporation is about bringing back past elements of the story into the present scene in order to form a unified drama. Improvisers also need to be attentive to what is happening in the moment, for the future is formed out of the past and present: "The salient difference between acting from a script and improvising is that [in improvising] one has to be not less but far *more* keenly attentive to what is given by the other actors and the situation."[66]

As we have seen, the aim of the theodrama is to create a new people of God and a new earth. But how on earth does God accomplish this plan conceived "before the foundation of the world" (Eph. 1:4; 1 Pet. 1:20)? When viewed "from below"—from the perspective of the developing historical action—the triune God appears to be the paradigm improviser, making good on his promise to Abraham in faithful, yet unexpected, ways. For example, the eternal Word, the Son of God, takes on Israel's role, and accepts the Father's offer to be sent into the world, and into exile (i.e., the cross), for the world's salvation. The triune economy is itself a master class in narrative reincorporation: Jesus did not come to abolish the law but to fulfill it. He played the role of Israel, not to mention prophet, priest, and king. He even played the role of certain key props like the manna from heaven, the sacrificial lamb, and the temple. Finally, he reincorporated (Irenaeus would say "recapitulated") the story of Adam, yet with a significant new twist: he resisted temptation and consistently responded in obedience to God's word. Hence Jesus' history as the second Adam was in continuity with the earlier story, but it was not a literal repetition.

God was in Christ, improvising the Abrahamic covenant. Indeed, we might say that the New Testament improvises on the Old. Jesus' work was both creative ("new") yet entirely in keeping (faithful) with what God had done in Israel previously. The apostle Paul similarly "improvised" the gospel for non-Jewish listeners in Asia Minor and Rome. Good improvisers know how to continue the same action in new situations. This is the disciples' charge too: we are to reincorporate our life stories into Christ's life story, acting in creative new ways, in new cultural contexts, that are entirely in keeping with (i.e., faithful to) what went on before: *his* story.

Illustrative Vignettes

Improvisation is the freedom of the Christian to continue the story of the Christ in new situations. Luther's description is apt: "As our heavenly Father has in

---

65. Johnstone, *Impro*, 116. This is a good image for disciples who walk in faith, for divine providence is best seen in retrospect.

66. Martha C. Nussbaum, *Love's Knowledge: Essays on Philosophy and Literature* (New York: Oxford University Press, 1990), 94.

Christ freely come to our aid, we also ought freely to help our neighbor through our body and its works, and each one should become as it were a Christ to the other that we may be Christs to one another and Christ may be the same in all, that is, that we may be truly Christians."[67]

We begin with a negative illustration, the celebrated "From Jerusalem to Jericho" study, also known as The Good Samaritan Experiment. In 1973 two psychologists devised a test for seminary students that effectively inserted them into a modern-day reenactment of the parable of the Good Samaritan (Luke 10:30–37).[68] The seminarians were randomly divided into two groups. Each student was charged with preparing and delivering a sermon at a specified time and place. The first group was asked to write on the parable of the Good Samaritan, the second group on other texts. Upon arrival at the designated place, each student was told that the location was changed and that they had only a certain amount of time (enough, not much, or hardly any, respectively) to get there. The variables thus set, the students then encountered the test: along the way to their new venue, the students encountered a person slumped against an alley wall; as each student passed, the person would cough and groan. So which students would stop and help?

The Good Samaritan Experiment put three hypotheses to the test: (1) in light of the ministry calling of the seminary students, most would stop. (2) The students with the story of the Good Samaritan in their heads would be more likely to stop. (3) Those in less of a hurry would be more likely to stop. What this scenario was testing was each seminarian's IQ (Improvisation Quotient): would they spontaneously accept the "offer," remember the story of Jesus that as followers they are pledged to extend, and participate fittingly in the divine drama of redemption? The answer was not particularly encouraging: of those in a low-hurry condition, 63 percent stopped and offered aid, but only 10 percent of those in a high-hurry condition did so—and a few of the latter literally stepped over the groaning person as they hastened to deliver their sermon on the Good Samaritan!

One of the best biblical examples of the right kind of Christian improvisation is found in Paul's shortest epistle. Paul asks Philemon to act in a way that was as shocking to the Romans as it was fitting to his new situation as a member of the company of faith. Paul wants Philemon to receive Onesimus, his escaped slave, back into his household, not as a fugitive to be punished, but as a brother in Christ to be welcomed. Paul is at pains not to command Philemon's obedience (though he has the right to do so), expressing instead the hope that his good deed "might be voluntary and not something forced" (Phlm. 14). Paul is confident that Philemon will freely do even more than Paul asks as a demonstration of his

---

67. Martin Luther, "The Freedom of a Christian," in *Three Treatises*, 2nd ed. (Philadelphia: Fortress Press, 1970), 305.
68. J. M. Darley and C. D. Batson, "'From Jerusalem to Jericho': A Study of Situational and Dispositional Variables in Helping Behavior," *Journal of Personality and Social Psychology* 27, no. 1 (1973): 100–8.

theodramatic understanding. Nothing is as refreshing to the heart as free and fitting Christian improvisation (Phlm. 20).

Even more impressive are spontaneous ensemble improvisations. Some years ago I met with a theology student at a nearby Starbucks to discuss his plans for the future. The discussion turned from possible doctoral programs, to the state of systematic theology, and to specific doctrinal issues. After an hour or so, a woman seated nearby broke in: "Excuse me. I couldn't help overhearing. So many ideas! But in the end, isn't your faith merely intellectual? Does any of your academic theology make one bit of difference in the way you live?" It was, and is, an excellent question—one to which this book attempts an answer. What was remarkable, however, was what happened next.

Another woman who had been waiting in line for her coffee stepped out and professed her faith in Christ, adding that her belief in certain Christian truths had a decisive bearing on the way she lived. The woman who had interrupted me then disclosed that she was in an abusive relationship with her husband, and that her daughter was struggling with a crippling illness. How could there be a God? By this time two other people had entered the store. The young man volunteered that he had struggled with severe doubts about the faith even though his father was an evangelical pastor, but that he had returned to the faith with more conviction than ever. At this point the skeptic inquired whether we were all part of the same group. We were not, we had never met one another, and we attended different churches (Presbyterian, Roman Catholic, independent, and charismatic). The last bystander now entered the discussion and said that she too was a Christian but attended a church of yet another denomination.

At this point my heart sank: surely such a disparate and ramshackle group as ours would soon break ranks over doctrinal differences or, worse, compete for her attention in a show of ecclesiastical one-upmanship. O me of little faith! Instead, and to my pleasant surprise, what was played out—in Starbucks, of all places!—was nothing less than the *communion sanctorum*. Almost instinctively, each of us knew that it was more important to present a unified front, with the good news of the gospel, than it was to magnify our differences. A scene that had opened with a rather cynical offering closed with impromptu hugs and the exchange of phone numbers. I do not know whether or not that doubter is now part of the company of faith. I only know that the incident refreshed my heart.

We turn now from incidental events to what the British call "major incidents." How ought the company of faith respond to natural hazards (e.g., floods, fires) and human-caused disasters (e.g., terrorism, accidents), to the groans not just of isolated persons at the side of the road but also to the cries of suffering throngs? This was what confronted the Rev. Roger Abbott in 1989 when a Boeing 737 crashed into the nearby village of Kegworth, England. His initial reaction was hesitation, but after two hours he offered his services as a pastoral caregiver. He did not save lives, but he did work with the bereaved, injured, and traumatized. And years later, still wondering about his initial hesitation, he wrote a book.[69]

The book is not a theodicy: Abbott does not try to "explain" catastrophes. His focus is rather on the church as a local community that has gathered to live under the authority of Scripture and to live out what is in Christ: "The evangelical catholic Christian community possesses enormous divinely endowed human resources for pastoral care in major incidents."[70] He also came to see that the church should be making disciples in the sense of preparing church members to reach out and embrace traumatized persons, irrespective of their particular faith. It is the desire to display the compassion of Christ that inclines disciples spontaneously to respond to disasters.

Does doctrine actually help disciples to become the sort of people who will respond with theodramatic fittingness in situations where propositional theology is tested to the limit? Yes, though its primary purpose is not to provide an "answer" to the problem of evil as much as it is to equip disciples to become "answerable" agents, persons who improvise Christlike, compassionate responses to all who cry out in the wildernesses of pain, emotional trauma, and existential angst. Disciples can acknowledge both that the drama of redemption is larger than any major incident and that in certain situations lament may be the best response. Disciples will respond differently than other caregivers because the Spirit of Christ has formed them, not least by means of the big theodramatic picture. So Rev. Abbott reports, "I decided my primary role was to represent Christ as a compassionate presence and listener."[71]

A final vignette. The 2011 monsoon season in Thailand produced a hundred-year flood, the fourth most expensive natural disaster in human history, affecting over 12 million people. A Thai theologian, taking on the role of theater-critic, later asked how well the church had performed.[72] In particular, how integral was its sense of mission (i.e., how integrated was its *demonstration* with its *proclamation* of God's love)? The Micah Network (from Mic. 6:8) is a global community of Christians (local congregations, aid organizations, academic institutions, etc.) committed to integral mission: "Integral missions is . . . a way of calling the church to keep together, in her theology as well as in her practice, what the Triune God of the biblical narrative always brings together: 'being' and 'doing,' the 'spiritual' and the 'physical,' the 'individual' and the 'social,' . . . 'preaching truth' and 'practicing the truth.'"[73]

---

69. Roger Philip Abbott, *Sit on Our Hands, or Stand on Our Feet? Exploring a Practical Theology of Major Incident Response for the Evangelical Catholic Christian Community in the UK* (Eugene, OR: Wipf & Stock, 2013). Coincidentally, Abbott adopts the canonical-linguistic method I propose in *The Drama of Doctrine*.

70. Ibid., 7.

71. Ibid., 78.

72. Natee Tanchanpongs, "How Deep Was It? Plumb Lining the Commitment to Integral Mission," *Common Ground Journal* 9, no. 2 (2012): 32–47.

73. Vinoth Ramachandra, "What Is Integral Mission," http://www.micahnetwork.org/library/integral-mission/what-integral-mission-vinoth-ramachandra.

What did most Thai churches do when confronted with their own, large-scale version of the Good Samaritan Experiment? Most churches prayed for the flood victims, but few became involved in relief efforts, community stabilization, or economic revitalization. Of those that did, some did so as a means of evangelism. Yet Christian improvisation, if it is to be fitting, requires more than right proclamation: rightly to participate in the theodrama requires disciples to embody the mind of Christ, and this means ministering to the whole person and to whole communities: integral mission.

Contextualization: Improvising the Faith in New Places

Mission is the operative word. Ultimately mission is the work of Son and Spirit to incorporate people into the church and the church into the life of the triune God. Christ sends the church into the world to be his ambassadors (2 Cor. 5:20; Eph. 6:20): communicative agents authorized to speak and act on his behalf. Mission is always local: disciples are to embody the mind of Christ *here* and *now*, in this particular place and situation. Mission cannot always be preplanned. Indeed, the story of the history of the church and of the transmission of the faith can be told under another maxim for improvisation: "Start anywhere."

Disciples must always, everywhere, and to everyone improvise what to say and do such that they continue the same theodramatic action in different contexts. There must be fittingness to the biblical text and to the cultural context, fidelity to biblical language, yet intelligibility to the language of the day. The challenge for the company of faith is to perform the *same* drama under radically *different* conditions, the same apostolic design for living in a post-Christendom scene, for there is no *other* gospel than the one associated with the "one Lord, one faith, one baptism" (Eph. 4:5).

There is one canon but many cultures. Consequently, there is no one culture to which all disciples must conform. Unity of faith is not the same as uniformity. Faithfulness may look different under different cultural contexts. Scripture is the supreme authority for the disciple, but what is of transcultural significance is not the world behind the text but the theodrama of which the Bible is sometimes transcript, sometimes script, and sometimes prescript. The salient point is that the vocation of the disciple—to faithfully enact the theodrama everywhere and at all times—involves mission, improvisation, and contextualization alike, and that these are all different ways of thinking about the same thing: the transmission of faith.

Andrew Walls rightly relates transmission and translation, and he roots the latter in the divine act of translation at the heart of the theodrama: "And the Word became flesh and lived among us" (John 1:14).[74] The challenge for disciples is to translate not only the biblical words but also the actions that

---

74. See Andrew F. Walls, "The Translation Principle in Christian History," in *The Missionary Movement in Christian History: Studies in the Transmission of the Faith* (Maryknoll, NY: Orbis Books; Edinburgh: T&T Clark, 1996), 26–42.

bear the theodrama along. The company of faith transmits the faith not only by translating Scripture but also by performing the gospel: living out what is in Christ, speaking and displaying understanding. Doing church becomes nothing less than a matter of world-for-world translation, that is, of unfolding and continuing the world in front of (not behind) the biblical text in new cultural contexts. The purpose of such translation is not to replicate the past but to enact the way of truth in new settings, to make Christ live in new contexts.

Local churches are ultimately charged with representing the church universal in particular places. The challenge is to translate not only the biblical words but also the whole understanding of the drama of redemption. This is what it takes to display the mind of Christ in twenty-first-century North America or Africa: the ability to translate a way of speaking, doing, and being from the New Testament to the present.[75] It may therefore be better to speak not of *translating* but of *transposing*. Dramatic transposition, like its musical counterpart, is a matter of preserving the same melodic line (speech) and harmony (action) in a different key (culture). To transpose or modulate is to change from one mode, key, or form to another while preserving the same subject matter. The mode of gesture, dress, and so forth may be different when *Romeo and Juliet* is transposed into the twentieth-century New York City setting of *West Side Story*, for example, but the story is the same.

Improvising Discipleship, Enlarging Understanding: Doctrine as Rule and Result

How do we know whether a given performance or improvisation—a speech or act—is actually a translation or representation of the drama rather than a mistranslation or misrepresentation? How can we tell whether disciples are going on in the same apostolic way, rightly participating in the good work that God began in Christ, rather than losing their way? If the purpose of theology is "to make or clarify Christian decisions,"[76] then the ability to make sound judgments about theodramatic fidelity and fittingness is the acid test of theological wisdom.

Christology as Norm

Sound judgment begins with sound doctrine, that is, with a sure grasp of the truth concerning Jesus Christ. For example, the docetic idea that the Son only appeared to assume humanity (because gnostics associated matter with evil) runs afoul of John's criterion: "Every spirit that confesses that Jesus Christ has come in the flesh is from God, and every spirit that does not confess Jesus is not from God" (1 John 4:2–3). We can generalize the point: everything we say

---

75. In the next section we shall see that the historical process of transmission is vital. Those who try to jump directly from the New Testament to the present, without the mediation of church history—the story of the church's mission—will have an impoverished understanding of the gospel and of Christ.

76. Walls, *The Cross-Cultural Process*, 79.

about God, Christ, and the theodrama must minimally be consistent with the testimony of the prophets and apostles.

In addition to the explicit statements in Scripture, there are numerous instances of how God's people should speak and act. Indeed, Paul refers to the entire Old Testament along these lines: "These things happened to them [Israelites] to serve as an example, and they were written down to instruct us" (1 Cor. 10:11). Richard Hays suggests that Scripture serves as a norm for the church today because it has paradigmatic authority: disciples today can discern "imaginative *analogies* between the stories told in the text and the story lived out by the community in a very different historical setting."[77] It is a matter of what I have been calling world-for-world translation or theodramatic transposition, namely, the ability to imaginatively view one's current situation as caught up in the very same story as that of ancient Israel or, more to the point, the early church. The names and faces and weapons that oppose the church may have changed, but the principalities and powers they represent are constant. The church continues to enact the same plot in different parts of the world stage. The scenery may have changed, but the play is still the same.

In addition to the propositional and paradigmatic instruction transcribed in the Scriptures, disciples may also look to the deliverances of catholic tradition as a normative guide for contemporary performance. We cannot answer the question "Who is Jesus Christ for us today?" as if we were the first Christians to pose it. There is a tradition of faithful wrestling with this question. Moreover, if the Spirit is indeed leading the church into all truth, it is possible that some of these earlier struggles produced insights that have transcultural significance, beyond their originating contexts. This may be the best perspective on what happened at the Council of Chalcedon in 451.

After Nicaea declared the Son divine (325), it fell to later generations to work out the relationship of Jesus' divinity and his humanity. Chalcedon expressed this relationship with the vocabulary available at the time: "truly God and truly man, . . . one [person] in two natures, without confusion, without change, without division, without separation."[78] This "formula" provided a way of making sense of what Scripture says about Jesus Christ. It therefore represents not only a report on what fifth-century Christians were thinking but also a deeper insight into the meaning of what Scripture says. We should no more relativize the Chalcedonian formula simply because it is culturally situated than we would relativize Newton's Second Law of Motion, that force = mass x acceleration ($F = ma$), just because he was a seventeenth-century Englishman.

Chalcedon speaks the truth about Christology, nothing but the truth, but not the *whole* truth. There is more to be said about Jesus Christ. However, what new things the company of faith say must be consistent with the truth as it has been expressed in earlier times, in different contexts, with different vocabularies.

---

77. Richard B. Hays, *The Moral Vision of the New Testament*, 298.

78. Translation from Henry Bettenson, *Documents of the Christian Church* (Oxford: Oxford University Press, 1947), 73.

The ancient rule of faith, essentially a brief summary of the theodrama, does not work against Christian freedom but enables it to flourish. Scripture is the supreme rule of Christian speech and action, but tradition serves as a subordinate rule. Disciples thus improvise the way forward via a process of "ruled creativity."

Let me be clear. Disciples today do not need to use the same vocabulary as the Greek-speaking Christians did at Chalcedon. What is paradigmatic, and authoritative, is the judgment underlying the language and concepts of Chalcedon. Chalcedon's "two natures in one person" language is faithful to biblical discourse, not because it repeats the same biblical words or concepts (it does not), but because it renders in *different* terms the *same* underlying judgments concerning the identity and nature of Jesus Christ. *Judgment* is the key term, for it refers to what the mind does when it decides how to speak and act. The judgments we make in particular situations demonstrate whether or not we have the mind of Christ.

Chalcedon does not define for all time what a person is or what comprises a nature; instead, it *provides direction, and a concrete example, for the kinds of things all Christians ought to say about Jesus Christ.* Chalcedon is thus a showcase for improvisatory wisdom. Although the Bible alone has magisterial authority, the early catholic consensus has ministerial authority insofar as it displays biblical judgments. It thus provides pedagogical direction and an important opportunity for global theology to display catholic sensibility, a concern for doing theology in communion with the saints.

The challenge of improvising discipleship is that of going on in the same way as Chalcedon, but not in a slavish or repetitive manner (i.e., dead theater). Yet one way to remain authentically Christian is to strive for continuity with the great performances of the past. Chalcedon is a "great performance," an improvised response to a particular historical context that contains lessons and guidelines for the rest of the church as well. Yes, disciples in other contexts will find new things to say about Jesus that speak understanding (see below), yet these new things must "go on in the same way" as that indicated by Chalcedon.

Improvisatory wisdom means knowing how to go on (i.e., to continue the theodrama) in the *same* way, but *differently*. The company of faith plays the same drama, but in ten thousand different places, each with its own particular social setting and cultural scenery. Everything thus depends on the ability to make judgments about *sameness*. Scripture is the disciples' ultimate authority, for it is the means by which God's word rules the church. In addition to the explicit and implicit judgments inscribed in Scripture, we have suggested that creedal formulas are a subordinate authority and means for forming good improvisatory judgment. Theodramatic wisdom, judgments about what to say and do in order to continue the theodrama, can also be gleaned through an apprenticeship to certain practices, such as the celebration of the Lord's Supper, which we examined in the preceding chapter.

Despite the variety of contexts in which disciples live out what is in Christ, there are certain convictions and practices that remain constant. Disciples everywhere and at all times (1) worship the one God who brought Israel out of Egypt and Jesus out of the tomb; (2) confess Jesus as Lord and Savior; (3) acknowledge the Spirit of Christ, and hence the presence and activity of God, in believers; (4) recognize that each local group of believers is related, in Christ through the Spirit, to every other local group, thus creating a multiethnic, multicultural people that transcends time and space; (5) read, preach, and teach the Scriptures, especially for their authoritative testimony to Jesus; and (6) use water, bread, and wine in the special way that Jesus commanded in order to participate in his story.[79]

How do we know how to carry on these convictions and practices fittingly in new situations? Are there clear criteria for assessing fitting performance, what is true speech and right action? The short answer is yes, there are, though their implementation is not always easy or straightforward. Then again, neither is the Christian life. One criterion is *theodramatic correspondence*: our confidence that we are performing the same gospel in different contexts should be in proportion to our ability to establish continuity with the canonically attested history of salvation. Does what we say and do correspond to what God has said in Scripture and done in Jesus Christ? A related criterion is *theodramatic coherence*: Is what we are proposing to say and do at least congruent with the catholic tradition, the ways in which Christians from other times and places have participated in the drama of redemption in their own words and in their own contexts? A final criterion is *theodramatic conductivity*: Does what we say and do transmit the faith to others and lead them, and us, to a greater understanding of and obedience to the Lord Jesus Christ? Stated differently, does it expand Christ's sphere of influence and thus advance the kingdom of God?[80] In the final analysis, however, using these criteria and discerning how to embody the gospel in new contexts requires not methodical procedures but sanctified persons whose minds, hearts, and imaginations are captive to the word and intent on theodramatic understanding.

Christology as Outcome

Doctrine develops as the church encounters new challenges and seeks to say and do what is theodramatically fitting. This insight puts a new spin on the notion of "performing the drama of doctrine." To this point, we have focused on how doctrine provides direction for right and fitting enactments of what is in Christ, but this is only half the story. The "drama of doctrine" also refers to the new and exciting insights into doctrine that the church discovers as it tries to perform the theodrama in new situations. Indeed, theology often begins when Christians who want to speak and act with understanding ask, "What does discipleship look like here?" The question is especially acute when the company of faith encounters new problems or crosses new cultural frontiers.

79. Walls, *The Missionary Movement*, 23–24.
80. See the discussion of criteria for assessing the expansion of Christianity in Walls, *The Cross-Cultural Process*, 8–25.

Theology is always dramatic, "an act of adoration fraught with the risk of blasphemy."[81] Think, again, of Nicaea and Chalcedon. There is a sense in which the church does not fully grasp what the Scriptures mean in all their fullness until we begin to speak and act on their basis. In other words, performing the world in front of the biblical text enriches our understanding of it: "As Paul and his fellow missionaries explain and translate the significance of the Christ in a world that is Gentile and Hellenistic, that significance is seen to be greater than anyone had realized before. It is as though Christ himself actually grows through the work of mission."[82] In this sense, then, the development (of doctrine) *is* the drama.

It is a delightful paradox: the church discovers even more of the mind of Christ as it seeks to translate and embody the wisdom that it has into various forms of life and thought. The Holy Spirit uses the very process of *demonstrating* understanding as a means to *enlarging* the church's understanding. What this means is that no single translation or performance or inculturation of the gospel is definitive. We can learn not only from the masterpiece theater of the past but also from current productions in different places, perhaps especially from the global South. How can this be? How can acting out doctrine give us fresh insight into it? Andrew Walls thinks he knows why, and he explains with a theatrical analogy.

All the world's an auditorium, and everyone can see the stage of world history, but no one sees the whole of it. Even those closest to the action are unable to perceive what is happening further away. The most important thing that happens onstage is the Jesus Act. Note that it happens onstage. It is part of the play, and thus it has a specific location, as does each person in the audience: "Culture is simply a name for a location in the auditorium."[83] Though the Jesus Act is visible to all, each person sees it from their own particular place in the great interactive theater of the world: "the very universality of the Gospel, the fact that it is for *everyone*, leads to a variety of perceptions and applications of it."[84] These perceptions multiply when one factors in variation of time as well as space.

Some of us regard the Jesus Act from a distance of two thousand years. And yet (and this is the afore-mentioned paradox), instead of becoming harder to see, more and more aspects of this Act have come into focus, though we continue to see as through a mirror, dimly (1 Cor. 13:12). The best place from which to understand the cross may be the crossroads of Christian history. For, from the start, new disciples have had to act out their life in Christ in new cultural situations. A certain diversity (e.g., Jewish, Gentile) was constitutive of the church's unity: "Christ, the new Adam, incorporated all human diversity and

---

81. "Notes of Recent Exposition," *Expository Times* 64, no. 11 (1953): 322.
82. Walls, *The Missionary Movement*, xvii.
83. Ibid., 44.
84. Ibid., 46.

was manifested in different cultural forms as people who were formed by these cultures put their faith in him, and he was formed among them."[85]

The "Ephesian moment" is Walls's term for the coming together of people from two cultures to experience Christ. The original Ephesian moment was quite brief: once the Roman Empire came under Christian rule (and became Christendom), disciples began to perform the faith in a somewhat monocultural way. However, in our own day we are experiencing another Ephesian moment: globalization and multiculturalism mean that there are now several major cultures in the church. That, and the increasing secularization of the West, has made life challenging for local churches everywhere.

The more the Spirit forms Christ in local Christian communities, many of whom act out their union with Christ in ways far different from our own, the more we come to understand the full meaning and implications of the gospel: "Translation did not negate the tradition, but enhanced it. The use of new materials of language and thought . . . led to new discoveries about Christ that could not have been made using only the Jewish categories of messiahship."[86] The way, truth, and life of Jesus Christ is universal, not because it is suspended in some timeless, cultureless realm but because it can be played out in myriad times, cultures, and place. Just as the local church is a concrete instantiation of the universal church, so local performances of the theodrama really participate in the universal thing that God is doing in Christ. To perform the drama of doctrine, with others, in ten thousand places is to come closer to attaining "the measure of the full stature of Christ" (Eph. 4:13). The children of faith need the diet of doctrine, and considerable performance practice, if they are to develop into "grown-up" disciples.

RECAPITULATION: THE SAPIENTIAL IMPERATIVE

Calvin envisions sacred assemblies of angels for whom the church is "a theater in which they marvel at the varied and manifold wisdom of God."[87] Calvin here recalls Paul's description of the church's role in the revelation of the mystery of God's plan of salvation, whereby "the wisdom of God in its rich variety might now be made known" (Eph. 3:10). All too often, however, the church is less a theater of divine wisdom than it is a showcase for foibles all too human.

Doctrine gives direction for the church's increase of understanding. Theology exists to minister understanding and educate desire and to do this with the aim of edifying the church. Yes, theology informs, but it is much more than the accumulation of knowledge. Rather, like the Scriptures themselves, theology's aim is "to make [us] wise for salvation" (2 Tim. 3:15 ESV). Disciples need more than knowing *that* (knowledge); they need to know *how* to live out their

---

85. Walls, *The Cross-Cultural Process*, 77.
86. Ibid., 80.
87. Calvin, *Inst.* 3.20.23. Cf. 1 Cor. 4:9; 1 Tim. 3:16.

knowledge of Jesus Christ (wisdom). Wisdom is lived knowledge, the ability to transpose what we know here to that problem over there. Theology exists not to increase the church's inventory of doctrinal knowledge but to cultivate doctrinal wisdom: the ability to make right theodramatic judgments, to know what to say and do in order to advance the main action of the play, and to do so in a contextually fitting way that effectively communicates to others.

We can formulate the sapiential imperative for disciples as follows: seek wisdom, get understanding, and have the mind of Christ Jesus. Of course, in this context, *mind* means more than intellect alone. Doctrine yields more than habits of cognition. Disciples need more than the right answers in order to heed Paul's exhortation "Be careful then how you live, not as unwise people but as wise" (Eph. 5:15).

When it comes to discipleship, there are no geniuses. Having the mind of Christ has nothing to do with one's IQ. Rather, to live out what is in Christ takes time, practice, and role models. The best way to learn theology is to begin living the Christian life in community. The course of discipleship is participation in the drama of doctrine, the best way by which we learn who we are in Christ: "learning—taken to be a transformation of knowing—can be characterized as a change in the alignment between experience and competence."[88] The ultimate aim of theology, however, is to form not simply competent (i.e., knowledgeable) but also excellent (i.e., wise) actors in the drama of redemption. *The wise disciple is the one who discerns and enacts in new, contextually appropriate ways the same truth, goodness, and beauty that is God's reconciling love in Jesus Christ.*

Can wisdom be taught? How can the company of faith learn the mind of Christ? This is an issue of ongoing concern, and a full response would take us beyond the scope of the present work. It must therefore suffice to summarize the findings of the present and preceding chapters. In sum, we learn wise judgments about how to live out the transcultural truth of Jesus Christ in new situations by learning doctrine, and this in three ways:

1. *As catechumens of the canon.* Everything begins with acquiring biblical, literary, and canonical competence (canon sense). Disciples need to understand the overall story line of the Scriptures and especially the nature and role of the church.

2. *As apprentices of catholicity.* It is by studying and perhaps imitating paradigmatic performances in both Scripture and tradition that disciples learn the deep patterns of biblical judgment about how to speak and act so as to continue the same story of Christ in different contexts (catholic sensibility).

3. *As alchemists of contextuality.* We have seen how in church history the company of faith improvised with the conceptual resources at hand in particular contexts, appropriating them for gospel purposes, thereby transforming the

---

88. Etienne Wenger, *Communities of Practice: Learning, Meaning, and Identity* (Cambridge: Cambridge University Press, 1998), 139.

dross of secular ideas and cultural materials into the gold of theological concepts that minister understanding (contextual sensitivity).[89]

To be "in Christ" is to belong to "the sphere of life and action created by the extension of the universal mission of Jesus."[90] The mission of the company of faith is to embody and enact parables of the kingdom of God. The church, in order to communicate Christ to the world and grow up into Christ, must learn to "speak the truth in love" (Eph. 4:15) everywhere, at all times, and to everyone. This is the work of wisdom and the goal of theological formation. Yet the church must also *suffer* the truth in hope, and it is to this final aspect of its vocation that we now turn.

---

89. Another way of thinking about the church as using contextual resources for its own purposes (i.e., plundering the Egyptians) is in terms of "excorporation," the process by which consumers resist cultural hegemony by using products contrary to their producers' intent. John Fiske, the sociologist who first came up with the idea, explains that excorporation is "the process by which the subordinate [folks] make their own culture out of the resources and commodities provided by the dominant system" (*Understanding Popular Culture* [Boston: Unwin Hyman, 1989], 13).

90. Hans Urs von Balthasar, *Theo-drama*, 3 (1992): 246.

Chapter 8

(Torn) Curtain

On Earth as He Is in Heaven

> *A man, when he suffereth for Christ, is set upon a hill, upon a stage, as in a theatre, to play a part for God in the world.*
> —John Bunyan, *Seasonable Counsel: or, Advice to Sufferers* (1684)

> *The martyrs are God's witnesses.*
> —Augustine, *Homily on the First Epistle of John* 1.2

We are approaching the end, both of the drama of redemption and our study of the role of doctrine in making disciples. We began part 2 with a focus on the disciples' task of walking on the stage of the world in the light of God's word. There we set forth the nature of the triune drama of redemption in which disciples take part (chap. 4) and examined the actor-disciple's inner preparation (chap. 5) as well as the way in which the church's life together, especially its celebration of the gospel in the Lord's Supper, serves as a dress rehearsal for the church's mission to the world (chap. 6). Next we considered the way the local church in various places acts out what is in Christ, and we suggested that performing the theodrama leads to an increase in theodramatic wisdom (chap. 7). What remains to be seen is how disciples strike a balance between celebrating the play's climax (during the Lord's Supper) and continuing to participate in the action (always performing!).

Perhaps it is premature to speak of the play's end. However, if the climax is not the end, then what scene are present-day disciples playing? If the really decisive events of the drama of redemption have already taken place, what is left for the church to do? Is everything the church says and does *anticlimactic*? How does the climax of the play relate to its ending? However we formulate the question, we are asking about the doctrine of last things: eschatology. What might it mean for disciples to perform in the drama of *this* doctrine? Does the church enact parables of the kingdom as a sign that the play has, for all soteriological intents and purposes, ended? Or is there something still at stake and, if so, what?

What is at stake in such questions is the gospel, for the gospel is nothing less than the proclamation that the climax of the divine drama has taken place. What exactly is the good news that the church has to proclaim to the world? After all, the nations still rage. Cancer cells still multiply. Justice miscarries. Couples divorce. Too many parents shout with angry voices at their children. What, then, has Jesus done to change the world? A brief examination of Stephen's discipleship will help us gain a purchase on our question, and thereby on our own vocation as disciples today.

Luke introduces Stephen as "a man full of faith and the Holy Spirit" (Acts 6:5) whose wisdom was intimidating to the Jews (6:10) and whose message was taken to be detrimental to the temple, and thus to the whole religious establishment (Acts 6:11–14). Stephen is not an apostle but a disciple, yet like the apostles he is made to give an account of himself before the high council (6:12–15). Like his Lord, Stephen stands trial for his faith. Stephen's lengthy speech (7:2–53) is essentially a summary of Acts 2–3 of the theodrama, told so as to highlight Israel's persecution of God's prophets and its opposition to the Holy Spirit, who speaks through the prophets (7:51–52). Stephen is simply one more example (though the first known *Christian* example) of the suffering martyrdom that often follows the world's refusal of God's Spirit. Stephen uses the same language that led to the verdict of blasphemy against Jesus: "I see the heavens opened and the Son of Man standing at the right hand of God!" (Acts 7:56; cf. Mark 14:62). Stephen's death occurs not long after Luke's editorial comment: "The word of God continued to spread; the number of the disciples increased greatly in Jerusalem, and a great many of the priests became obedient to the faith" (Acts 6:7). On one level, there is victory, but on another level, something that looks like defeat. In any case, Stephen is a "little Christ."

Stephen is the model disciple, a personification of "faith speaking understanding." His martyrdom, too, is paradigmatic: present-day disciples must boldly proclaim the gospel and display the same patient endurance. Stephen's example helps us grasp the importance of acknowledging the climax as the decisive turning point of the drama even while persevering to the drama's end. Everything depends on rightly understanding the significance of Stephen's vision of the exalted Christ: "But filled with the Holy Spirit, he gazed into heaven and saw the glory of God and Jesus standing at the right hand of God" (Acts 7:55). Calvin says that it was precisely by this looking up into heaven and beholding Christ that Stephen was able to gather the courage to endure, so "that by dying he may triumph gloriously, having overcome death."[1]

---

1. John Calvin, *Commentary upon Acts of the Apostles* (Grand Rapids: Wm. B. Eerdmans Publishing Co., 1949), 313.

CLIMAX: "SITS AT THE RIGHT HAND OF GOD THE FATHER ALMIGHTY"

The climax is a high point, the most important moment in the play, the key turning point that makes all the difference. According to Gustav Freytag's famous analysis, however, the climax is only the third moment in a five-part dramatic structure: (1) exposition, (2) the "rising action" that builds toward the climax, (3) the climactic turning point in the action, (4) the "falling action" that unravels the conflict between protagonist and antagonist, and (5) the denouement, where the last vestige of conflict is finally resolved and the last vestige of anxiety released.[2]

Most Christians, if pressed, would probably identify the cross and resurrection of Jesus as the climax of the drama of redemption. Indeed, Jesus himself points to the cross as the high point when, in a phrase heavy with dramatic irony, he refers to his being "lifted up from the earth" as the means of drawing people to himself (John 12:32) and bestowing eternal life (3:14–15). Though "lifted up" connotes exaltation, John leaves us in no doubt as to what Jesus had in mind: "He said this to indicate the kind of death he was to die" (12:33).

If Stephen's death was a glorious triumph, how much more was Christ's death so. The Scriptures leave us in no doubt that Jesus defeated the powers and principalities (death, demons, devil) on the cross. The Roman soldiers may have stripped Jesus of his clothes, but Paul says that Jesus "disarmed the rulers and authorities and made a public example of them, triumphing over them" through his death on the cross (Col. 2:15). The cross and resurrection belong together, of course: the latter demonstrates the efficacy of the former as well as the Father's role in the Son's victory over sin and evil. Yet the nexus of events that comprise the gospel, the high point not only of act 3 but also of the whole drama, includes other, lesser-known moments as well, such as the tearing of the temple curtain and the ascension. The tearing is a particularly rich event and provides an important clue as to why what happens to Jesus is the climax of the theodrama, namely, that Jesus' death and resurrection represents a tearing of the curtain that separates heaven and earth, and opens up the place where Christ is revealed as cosmic Lord.

Scission

Paul's prayer for the Ephesian Christians—that God would open their eyes to see the heavenly realities so that they could know their glorious hope (Eph. 1:17-21)—recalls Stephen's vision: "I see the heavens opened and the Son of Man standing at the right hand of God" (Acts 7:56). Clearly we are no longer in Kansas or in Ephesus. Somehow, local congregations, zip codes and all, have

---

2. Gustav Freytag, *Technique of the Drama: An Exposition of Dramatic Composition and Art*, trans. Elias J. MacEwan, 3rd. ed. (Chicago: Scott, Foresman & Co., 1900).

been caught up in a story of universal scope, where earthly events have heavenly parallels. To be "in Christ" is to be part of a cosmic drama, and disciples need doctrine rightly to understand and perform it.

Our immediate concern is with Stephen's claim: "Behold, I see the heavens opened" (Acts 7:56). The opening of heaven allows for commerce and communication between the two realms of divine and human habitation. On earth, the preeminent place of divine-human commerce and communication had been the temple, at least until Jesus' appearance on the world stage. Stephen mentions the temple in his speech, pointedly observing, "The Most High does not dwell in houses made with human hands" (Acts 7:48). In what we can only call a "wondrous exchange," the people of God, who in the Old Testament could only approach the holy God via the sacrificial system of the physical temple in Jerusalem, are in the New Testament declared to be God's temple themselves (1 Cor. 3:16–17; Eph. 2:21). The climax of the drama is indeed a turning point that sets in motion tectonic shifts in the very relationship of heaven and earth.

"And the curtain of the temple was torn in two, from top to bottom" (Mark 15:38; cf. Matt. 27:51; Luke 23:45). There are actually three "curtains": Jesus' flesh (Heb. 10:20), the one in the earthly temple at Jerusalem, and the celestial barrier that prevents fallen men and women from entering God's presence (i.e., the heavenly sanctuary).[3] The climax of the drama is the moment when all three curtains are torn simultaneously. Hebrews 10:19–25 describes this climactic moment when Jesus' death opens up a new and better access to life in God's presence (it also stands at the climax of the book of Hebrews).[4] It is the capstone of the author's exposition of the person and work of Jesus Christ as definitive sacrifice and superior high priest and also a transition to the exhortations that comprise the rest of the book. This passage identifies *what is in Christ* and how disciples should *act it out*.

Incarnate Curtain

There is no shedding of blood without the tearing of skin. We know that one of the Roman soldiers pierced Jesus' side with a spear and that blood and water poured out (John 19:34). This is the very same blood that serves as the basis of the new covenant and by which Jesus was able to enter into the Holy Place of the "true tent," into the presence of God in heaven itself (Heb. 9:24). "In Christ" there is a new and better covenant, sacrifice, and high priest (8:1–9:15). The climax of the theodrama is the act that constitutes Jesus as both lamb and high priest of this new and better covenant, namely, his self-offering on the cross (10:14). This is the turning point that gives all who are in Christ the means and the confidence to enter into God's presence. Jesus' blood opens up a new and

---

3. Gregory K. Beale argues that the temple is "a small model of the entire cosmos" and so points forward to a cosmic temple where God's presence will be all in all (*The Temple and the Church's Mission*, 48).

4. See the discussion in Peter O'Brien, *The Letter to the Hebrews* (Grand Rapids: Wm. B. Eerdmans Publishing Co., 2010), 360–61.

living way to approach God, a way "opened for us through the curtain (that is, through his flesh)" (10:20).

Temple Curtain

In three places (6:19; 9:3; 10:20) Hebrews mentions the curtain that kept the Holy of Holies cordoned off. Hebrews depicts "the area behind the curtain spatially by identifying it with heaven (9:24) and temporally by linking it with the age to come (9:6–10)."[5] The tearing of the curtain is a sign that Christ's once-for-all sacrifice of his body makes obsolete the law's provisions for dealing with sin. The torn curtain represents both the passing of the old covenant and the new opening into the heavenly temple made possible through the blood of Jesus. The tearing of the physical curtain signifies that God's majestic presence is no longer veiled or distant but rather shines forth from the crucified and risen Christ. The torn curtain on earth makes sense if indeed Jesus is the locus of a new, more intimate relationship to God. The tearing of the curtain thus signals that point in the drama where the greatest obstacle—the barrier between sinners and a holy God, earth and heaven, this age and the age to come—is confronted and removed: "The *velum scissum* reveals, in part, the eschatological nature of Jesus' death. It serves to reveal (in the special material) that Jesus' death inaugurates a turning of the ages depicted graphically in Ezekiel 37."[6]

Celestial Curtain

The high point of Jesus' mediatorial work is arguably his unique entry into the heavenly sanctuary (Heb. 9:23–27). Jesus' sacrificial work tears the curtain separating the earthly from the heavenly sanctuary, allowing him to enter the latter as the unique priest-king after the order of Melchizedek (6:20). Only the crucified Christ penetrates the celestial curtain, the place where God is enthroned: "His entrance into the 'throne' of the temple 'in the heavens' is yet another way of stating who he is and what he has done."[7] In penetrating the celestial curtain, Christ becomes mediator of a new and better (because permanent) covenant. Christ's entry into the heavenly throne room is the climax not only of the theodrama but also of the book of Hebrews: "Now the main point in what we are saying is this: we have such a high priest, one who is seated at the right hand of the throne of the Majesty in the heavens" (Heb. 8:1).

Session

"The Lord says to my lord, 'Sit at my right hand until I make your enemies your footstool'" (Ps. 110:1). Jesus cites this enthronement psalm in connection with his own person and work (Matt. 26:64). There are over thirty quotations or

---

5. Ibid., 242.
6. Daniel Gurtner, *The Torn Veil: Matthew's Exposition of the Death of Jesus* (Cambridge: Cambridge University Press, 2007), 183.
7. D. Stephen Long, *Hebrews* (Louisville, KY: Westminster John Knox Press, 2011), 134.

allusions to Psalm 110 throughout the New Testament, and all point to Jesus' being seated at the right hand of God (Rom. 8:34; Eph. 1:20; Col. 3:1; Heb. 1:13; 1 Pet. 3:22; etc.).[8] The early church rightly understood that the drama of the Christ includes his ascension, entry into heaven, and heavenly session (Lat. *sessio* = sitting down) at the right hand of the Father. Jesus' session was an important part of apostolic teaching, figuring prominently in both the Apostles' Creed and the earlier Old Roman Creed: *sedet ad dexteram patris*.

Various Reformation confessions and catechisms affirm Christ's heavenly session, usually in connection with the resurrection and ascension, under the general heading of his exaltation. Most take the phrase "sits at the right hand of the Father" to indicate Christ's exaltation to participation in God's majesty. For example, the Heidelberg Catechism says that Christ's sitting on the right hand of God signifies that he is head of the church, the one through whom the Father governs all things.[9] For our purposes, what is most significant is the way the heavenly session of Christ serves as the climax of the drama, and in particular how the session is connected to the scission, that is, the tearing of the curtain that separated humanity from God. The Leiden Synopsis (1625) states: "The fruits of Christ's ascension are many and great. By his entry the heavenly holy place was opened to us."[10] The same document goes on to distinguish the sovereignty that the divine Son enjoyed from eternity with the "economic" kingship proper to the God-man Jesus Christ.[11] Other documents view the session as the climax of the story of the crucified one but go further in stressing the benefits of Christ's ascended humanity: first, that Christ is our advocate in heaven; second, as pledge that our humanity too will be restored to the image of God and thus fit for life in God's presence; third, that as Lord he can give his Holy Spirit to his people on earth in order to preserve them against all enemies. In the words of Calvin's Geneva Catechism: "For in as much as Christ has entered into heaven in our name, as he descended to the earth for our sakes, he has opened to us also that door, which, on account of sin, was before shut. Secondly, he appears in the presence of God, as our Intercessor and Advocate."[12]

To say that Jesus sits at the right hand of the Father is another way of confessing Jesus as Lord. "Jesus is Lord" is an announcement of his enthronement in the heavenly places. Yet, according to Hebrews 8:1, the one who enters the throne room and sits down is none other than the high priest. Jesus Christ, the

---

8. See David M. Hay, *Glory at the Right Hand: Psalm 110 in Early Christianity* (Nashville: Abingdon Press, 1973).

9. Heidelberg Catechism, Q. 50. Cf. Richard Bauckham: "The potent imagery of sitting on the cosmic throne has only one attested significance: it indicates his participation in the unique sovereignty of God over the world" ("The Divinity of Jesus Christ in the Epistle to the Hebrews," in *The Epistle to the Hebrews and Christian Theology*, ed. R. Bauckham et al. [Grand Rapids: Wm. B. Eerdmans Publishing Co., 2009], 33).

10. Cited in Heinrich Heppe, *Reformed Dogmatics* (Grand Rapids: Baker, 1978), 502.

11. See ibid., 504–5.

12. Calvin, Geneva Catechism, Q. 77.

crucified one, is both High King and high priest.[13] The coronation of the high priest is also the crowning of his high-priestly work. That this is the high point of the drama of redemption is brought out exceptionally well by Karl Barth's commentary on the Apostles' Creed, and in particular on the line "and sitteth on the right hand of God the Father Almighty."[14]

The first thing Barth notes is that, with this line, we approach the goal of Jesus' work. Many articles in the Apostles' Creed rehearse events in Jesus' story that have already happened (e.g., conceived, born, suffered, crucified, buried, descended, rose again). However, when we come to "sits on the right hand," there is "suddenly a present."[15] Jesus *now* sits at the right hand of God. We are no longer in the realm of history but in *now* time, which is also *new* time: the end time inaugurated by the drama of the Christ. That Jesus sits at the right hand of the Father means that the climax has been reached: all the other events pertaining to Jesus lie in the past, but his ruling from on high is present and ongoing. That the incarnate, crucified, and risen Jesus has entered the heavenly sanctuary also signals the exaltation of humanity: "We with Him beside God" (cf. Eph. 2:6).[16]

Jesus' heavenly session is a fitting climax because, as we saw in chapter 4, the rising action of the theodrama had everything to do with the covenant promise and kingdom of God. As true prophet after the order of Moses, Jesus makes God known. As Lamb of God and high priest after the order of Melchizedek, Jesus fulfills the covenant plot by revealing the mystery of God's grace. As High King in the line of David, Jesus completes the kingdom plot as the Son of Man. It is precisely as High King and high priest that Jesus gives content to divine omnipotence and divine grace. Barth therefore characterizes Christ's heavenly session as "the beginning of the end-time, that is, the time in which the Church has to proclaim to all the world the gracious omnipotence and the omnipotent grace of God in Jesus."[17]

Christ's heavenly session is climactic because it is the end point to which the drama has been moving since the opening act of creation, namely, the establishment of God's dwelling place, a palace-temple, on earth. Ancient Near Eastern kings typically built temples to commemorate victory in battle, and Yahweh does something similar, creating a garden temple in Eden after subduing the watery chaos.[18] That garden temple becomes corrupt. There thus begins a

---

13. Note that Ps. 110:4 speaks of the "my lord" (v. 1) as "a priest forever according to the order of Melchizedek."

14. Cf. Douglas Farrow's similar claim that Jesus' ascension is the climax of the entire drama of redemption, the act "in which the link between our fallen world and the new creation was fully forged" (*Ascension and Ecclesia: On the Significance of the Doctrine of the Ascension* [Edinburgh: T&T Clark, 1999], 39).

15. Karl Barth, *Dogmatics in Outline* (London: SCM Press, 1949), 124.

16. Ibid., 125.

17. Ibid., 124.

18. For an extended treatment and exegetical justification of this point, see Beale, *The Temple and the Church's Mission*, 60–80. See also Tremper Longman III and Daniel G. Reid, *God Is a Warrior* (Grand Rapids: Zondervan, 1995), 83–88.

long restoration project that involves Israel's tabernacle and temple, climaxes with the temple of Jesus' flesh and Jesus' entry into the heavenly sanctuary, and concludes only with the establishment of a new heaven and a new earth: God's cosmic garden-temple-palace.

Jesus' heavenly session gives us the necessary perspective from which to see how Jesus' life was a divine improvisation on a plethora of Old Testament persons, places, events, and ideas (e.g., Adam, Eden as garden-temple, the Day of Atonement, kingdom). All are ingredients in the forward action leading to the theodramatic climax, the complex of events concerning Jesus that culminate with his heavenly session. We can now see how the Old Testament story of God reestablishing his new creational kingdom out of the chaos of covenant rebellion is taken up and transformed by the New Testament story of Jesus. The missions of Son and Spirit, and before them, the divine promise to Abraham and David—all conspire to move the theodrama forward toward an eschatological goal: the new creational reign of Jesus Christ.[19] The climax of the theodrama is eschatological, a matter of heaven-space and end time breaking into the historical here and now.[20]

What is in Christ thus embraces the beginning (Col. 1:16–17) and the beginning of the end: a new covenant, new humanity, and new covenant people.[21] To be "in Christ" is to be part of the kingdom of God and new creation. That Jesus is now sitting at the right hand of the Father is, literally and figuratively, the high point of the divine action, the point at which God the Father exalts the Son, gives him the name above every name, and makes him ruler of heaven and earth (Phil. 2:9–11).[22] Stephen saw it all in his final moments on earth, and it was this vision that emboldened his witness and sustained its integrity.

CONFLICT: POSTVICTORY THEATER OF THE OPPRESSED

Jesus Christ, the High King, has been enthroned in heaven, yet trials remain for citizens of his kingdom on earth. Stephen beheld the heavenly throne room, then suffered for his witness (Acts 7:55–58). His discipleship is emblematic.

---

19. Beale, *A New Testament Biblical Theology*, 16. Beale further observes: "The end-time new-creational kingdom has not been recognized sufficiently heretofore as of vital importance to a biblical theology of the NT" (19). I agree, and I submit that theodrama goes a long way to remedying this deficiency in systematic theology.

20. Cf. Beale: "The apostles understood eschatology not merely as futurology but as a mind-set for understanding the present within the climaxing context of redemptive-history" (ibid., 18).

21. Beale attends particularly to themes that figure prominently at both the Bible's beginning (Gen. 1–3) and end (Rev. 21–22): the (complex) notion of the new-creation-temple-kingdom (ibid., 23).

22. Biblical theologians tend to champion either the kingdom of God or new creation as the broader biblical theme. Beale seeks to be at peace with as many biblical theologians as possible by advocating the notion of "movement towards the new-creational reign" (ibid., 23). I have tried to cover the same ground with the rubric "being in Christ."

Stephen is a paradigm for what it means to live out what is in Christ: for living on earth as Christ is in heaven.

V-E Day

Unlike Paul Revere, the apostle Paul announced not the coming of hostile forces but rather their complete downfall and utter destruction: "Paul is a *herald of the kingdom of God and of the victory and Cosmic Lordship of Jesus Christ.*"[23] As a result of the cross, resurrection, ascension, and heavenly session, Christians now celebrate and confess "the forgiveness of sins, the resurrection of the body, and the life everlasting."[24] Call it V-E Day, for Victory over Enemies (e.g., sin, Satan, death) or Victory over Evil. The more familiar V-E Day (May 8, 1945) marked the unconditional surrender of the armed forces of Nazi Germany and thus the end of the Third Reich. In the case of Jesus' victory, however, there was defeat but not surrender, hence the ongoing conflict. The Allied forces won a historical victory in Europe, but Jesus' victory is both historical and eschatological, for the powers and principalities he defeated are not merely earthly but also cosmic.

There is conflict in each and every act in the theodrama. Though the climax of the play, the victory of the one lifted high on the cross and his subsequent enthronement as High King, happened in act 3, the powers and principalities have not surrendered. The church is still playing the closing scenes of act 4, participating both in the heralding of Christ's victory and in the mop-up operation. The church is also the theater or "arena in which God displays his cosmic triumph over the powers that rule the present evil age."[25] Thanks to Christ's victory, Christians are "more than conquerors" (Rom. 8:37). And yet the mode of Christian victory, like the kingdom of God itself, is not what we might have expected. Jesus is Lord, to be sure, but the postvictory church is in no position to lord it over others.

Local churches are "outposts of new creation existence where the power of the coming age is fully present."[26] The power in question, however, is cruciform: the peculiar power of Jesus' self-giving that culminated on the cross. The church, as a living parable, embodies the kingdom of God to the extent that it participates in the power of Jesus' suffering love. Indeed, disciples wage warfare "through persistent acts of love and the enjoyment of *shalom* by the power of God's Spirit."[27] As we have seen, to enact the reign of God is to live out one's reality "in Christ," to live in such a way that demonstrates Jesus' pervasive influence on our way of life. Disciples are to inhabit their physical places in a way that displays their true citizenship in the kingdom of heaven.

---

23. Gombis, *Paul: A Guide for the Perplexed*, 23, emphasis original.
24. The last three lines of the third paragraph ("I believe in the Holy Spirit") of the Apostles' Creed.
25. Gombis, *Paul: A Guide for the Perplexed*, 58.
26. Ibid., 55.
27. Gombis, *Drama of Ephesians*, 58.

This will involve companies of the faithful living in ways that subvert the for-profit logic of worldly powers.

Timothy Gombis's *The Drama of Ephesians* has for its theme the church's participation in the triumph of God. On his view, Ephesians 1:20–2:22 recounts the climax of the theodrama—God's setting the world right in Christ—with the metaphor of divine warfare. Just as many ancient narratives of conquest end with the triumphant king building a temple to commemorate the victory, so God manifests his victory by creating the church, a living temple (2:21–22).[28] Paul says that the company of saints has been raised with Christ "and seated . . . with him in the heavenly places" (2:6). The church is thus simultaneously seated in the heavens but also standing on earth. Better: the local church is a piece of heaven on earth. In Gombis's words: "God has triumphed by opening up a sphere within creation that is the beginning of God's work of making all things new."[29]

Doctrine gives disciples directions on living for God in this postvictory moment when the satanic powers have been defeated but nevertheless refuse surrender. What is in Christ is *victory*, and the church is called to be a standing witness to Christ's triumph over sin and death. Ephesians 3:1–14 shows us how Paul acts out V-E Day in Christ, even from his prison cell. Paul's mandate is "to make everyone see what is the plan of the mystery hidden for ages in God" (3:9). He does so by planting churches, theaters of reconciliation that live out the new humanity created in Christ (2:15). God defeats the powers by creating in Christ "one unified, multiracial body consisting of formerly divided groups of people."[30] It is enough to make Screwtape turn in his grave.

To do church is to live out, with others before God, the truth that is in Christ. There is no more authentic way of living, or witness, than that. Disciples must not only speak the truth but also live it out; or as Gombis puts it, disciples must be "truthing in love" (cf. Eph. 4:15, 21).[31] Doctrine directs disciples to live to God in all situations; this means living out the truth that is in Christ everywhere, at all times, with everyone. The company of the faithful must inhabit and enact the victory that God has already accomplished by cultivating "patterns of thought, speech, and action that are characteristic of the new humanity."[32] This is what it means to do the truth, peace, justice, righteousness, and all else that is in Jesus (Eph. 4:21): "We perform vital roles in God's drama of redemption—we wage our warfare—when we resist idolatrous and destructive patterns of life."[33] The saints participate in Christ's victory over the powers and principalities by witnessing to the power of the cross: "They have conquered him [Satan] by the blood of the Lamb and by the word of their testimony" (Rev. 12:11).

28. Ibid., 86.
29. Ibid., 105.
30. Ibid., 117.
31. Ibid., 57.
32. Ibid., 167.
33. Ibid., 183.

A Theater of Martyrdom

We ... [know] that suffering produces endurance.
—Romans 5:3

Followers of Christ must do more than observe his story from a safe distance. There is a difference between an onlooker and a witness. The onlooker (*homo spectans*) observes but does not take part in the action. By way of contrast, the one giving witness (*homo particeps*) is an active participant.[34] Stephen was a witness: one who did not try to keep the action at arm's length but became involved, giving eloquent personal testimony in life, with words, and in death.

Disciples today are heralds of God's kingdom too, evangelists who, like Stephen, proclaim the good news that Christ has offered his life for the sins of the world and entered the heavenly temple-palace of God. That's the good news. The bad news is that those who spread the good news are often reviled, sometimes persecuted. For the good news is subversive, overturning conventional wisdom, not least about the way to wield power and ensure peace and justice. Christians make love by making war, though the way they participate in the divine warrior's work of setting the world aright is cruciform and weak in the world's eyes. The church's mission is to be a company of faith that speaks the truth in love and, when necessary, suffers this speaking in hope.

The English term "martyr" comes from the Greek *martys*, "witness." Søren Kierkegaard defines witness as "someone who directly demonstrates the truth of the doctrine he proclaims—directly, yes, partly by its being the truth within him, ... partly by his volunteering his personal self and saying: See, now, if you can force me to deny this doctrine."[35] Alas, the powers that be are only too willing to try. What begins with testimony ends with trial. Martyrs are witnesses who are willing to die for their belief. Christian martyrs form the company of faith who would speak understanding, testifying to *what is in Christ* no matter what the cost. In becoming a place where others might perceive the presence and activity of the living Christ, the witness tacitly agrees to "take responsibility for God's believability."[36] Doctrine directs disciples to play the role of martyr: one who testifies in various ways—speaking, acting, and suffering—to the truth that is in Jesus Christ. Though the witness may die, the doctrine triumphs: "This is the constant practical [dramatic!] proof of the truth of the doctrine."[37]

Jesus Christ is the chief martyr, "the faithful and true witness" (Rev. 3:14), and Kierkegaard took Christ's passion to be the normative pattern for Christian

---

34. I owe this distinction to Gabriel Marcel, *The Mystery of Being*, vol. 1, *Reflection and Mystery* (Chicago: Henry Regnery, 1960), 121-24.
35. Søren Kierkegaard, *Papers and Journals: A Selection* (London: Penguin Books, 1996), 492.
36. Rowan Williams, *Tokens of Trust: An Introduction to Christian Belief* (Louisville, KY: Westminster John Knox Press, 2007), 23.
37. Kierkegaard, *Papers and Journals*, 492.

witness in general. Jesus warns his disciples that they too will undergo trials for their testimony, for "a disciple is not above the teacher" (Matt. 10:24). The church participates in God's mission to the world by speaking, doing, and suffering the truth. Actions speak louder than words, and disciples' *passions*—not active doing but passive being done to—sometimes speak louder than acts. A willingness to suffer and the ability to endure are the criteria of authentic witness. When the church bears faithful witness, it not only proclaims but also becomes the gospel.

Suffering for one's testimony can be a means by which disciples are conformed to Christ's image, if indeed the suffering produces endurance. Enduring adversity—more specifically, cruciformity—is for Luther one of the marks by which we recognize an authentic church: "They must endure every misfortune and persecution, all kinds of trials and evil from the devil, the world, and the flesh."[38] *Foxe's Book of Martyrs* (1563) recounts only a fraction of these trials, those suffered by sixteenth-century Protestants in England and Scotland. Andrew Walls makes a similar survey but focuses on African Christian witness from the second century to the twentieth century: "The test of discipleship is suffering; and Africa, which has known so much suffering, has often been a furnace for the testing of Christian quality."[39] A Christian Dinka poet, referring to her native Sudan, has penned a haunting line: "Death has come to reveal the faith."[40]

Dying well, whether on stage or in real life, is perhaps the supreme challenge for the actor-disciple. Disciples must be prepared to give all for the sake of their testimony. Doctrine ultimately gives direction both for speaking understanding and for dying well, for the latter is part of one's witness too. The company of the faithful comprises a theater of martyrdom, a place of exemplary action and exemplary suffering. The author of Hebrews 10:32–33 asks his readers to remember their previous endurance of sufferings, which included "being publicly exposed [*theatrizō*] to abuse and affliction." This is the martyrdom of Christian life, a spectacle of faith.

There is nothing distinctly Christian about physical suffering: "If you prick us, do we not bleed? . . . If you poison us, do we not die?"[41] However, when Christians suffer for their testimony to the truth of what is in Christ, or suffer as a Christ for others, they participate in the sufferings of Christ (1 Pet. 2:21; 4:13) and so make the reality of Christ visible. The church makes disciples in order to form a company of faith, a theater of martyrdom. For, in its life together, the church is more than a theater of morality. The gospel message concerns not just morals but overwhelming mercy: it is the good news that God has overlooked our corruption and has poured out his own life to inaugurate a new creation,

---

38. Martin Luther, *On Councils and the Church, Part III* (1539), in *Luther's Works*, vol. 41 (St. Louis, MO: Concordia Publishing House, 1986), 164.
39. Andrew F. Walls, "The Cost of Discipleship: The Witness of the African Church," *Word & World* 25, no. 4 (2005): 434.
40. Cited in ibid., 442.
41. William Shakespeare, *The Merchant of Venice*, act 3, scene 1.

over which Christ has become king. The church is "the actualization of the realm of God/Christ in the 'here' . . . and 'now.'"[42] In everything that it says and does, the church enacts a martyrdom of new life. Doctrine directs disciples in this new way of being-toward-resurrection.

What does one give the God who has everything? Augustine answers that we must render unto God his own image: our humanity, ourselves.[43] Is it realistic to think that disciples should be willing and able to give their lives, in life and possibly death, for the sake of their Christian witness? It is if disciples locate their deepest identity in Christ. For martyrdom is nothing less than "the outward enactment . . . of the identity of every Christian person."[44] Whatever the situation, the vocation of the disciple is to embody Christ. "I am who I am *in Christ*" must be the disciple's constant confession.

Doctrine is never more dramatic than when, in the face of various internal and external trials, individuals must decide in freedom whose story to enact, which plot to develop. Unlike temptation (*tentatio*), a trial (*probatio*) is an external and public event—hence "theater of martyrdom."[45] What counts as victory in the trial of discipleship, the theater of martyrdom? It is the disciple's love for the truth that is in Jesus Christ and that produces endurance through suffering. Our endurance is our "show" of strength, though of course our strength is not our own, but Christ's. Rather, the object of our witness is not our own strength but the victory that Christ won in his flesh, a victory seen with the eyes of faith. Christian martyrs are ultimately witnesses to Christ's victory on the cross; bearing witness, speaking and living out what faith sees in Christ, is the very way disciples participate in that victory.[46]

Ultimately it is the disciples' belief in God's providence that enables them to endure the trials of faith. The doctrine of providence directs disciples to trust that all things in the theodrama "work together for good for those who love God, who are called according to his purpose" (Rom. 8:28). The doctrine of providence depicts God as the supreme improviser, able to incorporate even the evil that humans do in ways that serve his purposes and subvert theirs. Precisely because disciples know that Jesus has won the decisive victory, they can trust God's wisdom and goodness in the postvictory theater of oppression. Still, trials are a test of faith and understanding alike: the questions "How long?" and "Why, O Lord?" resound throughout the canon (Exod. 5:22; 1 Sam. 14:41; Pss. 10:1; 88:14; Isa. 63:17; Hab. 1:2; Rev. 6:10).

Whether or not it is correct to describe it as a lifestyle, martyrdom is perennially out of fashion inasmuch as it throws into question Everyman's

---

42. James G. Samra, *Being Conformed to Christ in Community: A Study of Maturity, Maturation and the Local Church in the Undisputed Pauline Epistles* (London and New York: T&T Clark, 2006), 134.

43. See Carole Straw, "Martyrdom," in *Augustine through the Ages: An Encyclopedia*, ed. Allen D. Fitzgerald (Grand Rapids: Wm. B. Eerdmans Publishing Co., 1999), 538.

44. Michael Jensen, *Martyrdom and Identity: The Self on Trial* (London and New York: T&T Clark International, 2010), 159.

45. Ibid., 166.

46. Ibid., 173.

everyday assumptions about the meaning of life and human flourishing. Be that as it may, fitting performances of Christian doctrine will always have something of the martyrological about them insofar as they acknowledge the rule of Christ, enacting new-creation practices amid the detritus of the old. The company of the faithful testifies to the nonultimacy of worldly power and to the penultimacy of worldly goods. Indeed, martyrdom "is part of the *missio dei* to the world, and shows how Christian discipleship in general is to be oriented to the world."[47] In participating in the interactive theater of martyrdom, disciples witness to the truth that is in Christ but may also draw guests into the world that the martyr attests. What the church as a theater of martyrdom finally demonstrates is a way of truth and life that endures everything—ridicule, persecution, death—for the sake of being, doing, and suffering like Christ (Jas. 1:4).

CATHARSIS: PURIFICATION OF THE HEART

Endurance produces character, and character produces hope.
—Romans 5:4

According to Aristotle, the aim of tragic drama is to produce catharsis. Watching someone else (i.e., an actor in a theater) experience tragedy has a beneficial, purifying effect on the audience, cleansing or releasing them of and from negative emotions like pity and fear or, at the very least, restoring them to their proper place and balance.[48] Pity and fear are the appropriate responses to tragedy because spectators not only sympathize but also identify with the characters: these things could happen to us! For centuries commentators have debated whether Aristotle had in mind a medical, religious, or intellectual sense of this cleansing effect. Nevertheless, the basic idea is that the hearts of the audience are somehow purified as a result of their vicarious experience in the theater. Martha Nussbaum goes further, arguing that catharsis is educative: a means by which spectators gain a deeper understanding of certain emotions and of the ways these emotions attune us to human existence, enabling us to make better moral judgments in light of our finitude and vulnerability.[49] In one way or another, then, Aristotle seems to be suggesting that watching tragic drama is good for the heart, resulting in a state of greater emotional maturity.

Nothing in my appropriation of the theatrical model suggests that watching plays is conducive to our sanctification or that theatergoing is the best way to

---

47. Ibid., 195.
48. Aristotle, *Poetics* 1449b28.
49. Martha Nussbaum, *The Fragility of Goodness: Luck and Ethics in Greek Tragedy and Philosophy*, rev. ed. (Cambridge: Cambridge University Press, 2001), 388–90.

make disciples of all nations. On the contrary, my concern has been with how doctrine helps disciples participate rightly in the action; the players themselves *are* a holy theater. Performing the drama of doctrine may nevertheless be cathartic inasmuch as doctrine not only informs disciples about *what is* and urges them to conform to it, but also because, in so doing, it builds up their character and affects their emotions as well. If disciples are to become Christlike, they must not only participate in the actions exemplified by Christ but also in his attitudes and dispositions. These too comprise the "mind of Christ" (1 Cor. 2:16; Phil. 2:5). Indeed, it is precisely because discipleship involves more than doing things (activism) that we may speak of a *catharsis* of doctrine. In short: while doctrine informs the mind and directs our acts, performing doctrine—participating in *what is* in Christ—purifies our affections.

Doctrine directs God's people to speak and show understanding of what God has done in Christ. Because actions speak louder than words, and passions louder than actions, one way the company of faithful speaks and shows their understanding is by doing good and undergoing suffering. Suffering is not a particularly popular or attractive strategy for human flourishing. Churches on the lookout for effective marketing strategies for Christian discipleship would therefore be advised to look elsewhere. However, it is precisely through suffering, participating in the drama of the passion of Christ by witnessing to it, that the saints experience a distinctly Christian catharsis best summed up by the apostle Paul: "Suffering produces endurance, and endurance produces character, and character produces hope" (Rom. 5:3–4).

Steadfast: Patient Endurance

Neither the drama of redemption in which Christians participate nor the understanding they speak is tragic. Suffering accompanies Christian witness, to be sure, but the overarching context is not tragic or ethical but rather eucatastrophic and eschatological. Hence there is a distinctly Christian catharsis that involves not the purging of pity and fear but the purification of ungodly desires and the acquisition of the mind of Christ, including his attitudes and disposition—in a word, his *heart*. Disciples grow in Christlikeness as they learn, rehearse (in worship), and perform the character of Christ with works of love. Christian catharsis (the traditional term is *sanctification*) comes about when disciples take up their cross and change from being merely spectators, admiring Christ from afar, to actors who live in the new creation inaugurated by Jesus, embodying and enacting *what is in Christ*.

What is in Christ? Of the many answers, the most compelling in the context of suffering for one's witness may be *covenant faithfulness*: the steadfast love and faithfulness of God associated with the name he proclaimed to Israel (Exod. 34:5–7). God's steadfast love (*hesed*) and faithfulness (*'ĕmet*) refer to God's utter constancy and reliability. Love is patient and endures all things (1 Cor. 13:4–7), and God *is* this love (1 John 4:8). It is this conviction of God's steadfast love, a love in Christ from which nothing in creation can separate us (Rom. 8:39), that allows Stephen to stand fast in his witness. Thanks to God's steadfastness, the church too is able to stand fast and to *withstand* until the end.

In Christ there is not only God's love but also his majesty. Jesus' transfiguration, that dramatic moment when the voice from heaven declares Jesus to be the beloved Son (Matt. 17:5), anticipates his heavenly enthronement. The apostles beheld Jesus' glory (Luke 9:32), including his face shining like the sun (Matt. 17:2). The apostles were thus "eyewitnesses of his majesty" (2 Pet. 1:16). If we connect the canonical dots, the most likely explanation of Jesus' transfiguration is that it was "a revelation of his *eschatological enthronement* and ultimate divine sovereignty and authority over all things."[50] In short, the transfiguration was an apocalypse, a key moment in the theodrama when heaven breaks through to earth. Jesus' transfiguration is a preview of the climax of the whole theodrama, that moment when the beloved Son enters God's cosmic palace-temple in heaven and occupies his place as Lord. We may recall that this is precisely what Stephen saw: the Son of Man standing at the right hand of God (Acts 7:56). No doubt this partly accounts for his spirit of boldness and calmness. The former is obvious throughout Stephen's speech. The latter is evidence by Luke's observation that "his face was like the face of an angel" (6:15).

To fittingly perform the drama of redemption, disciples must not merely go through the external motions, doing right; they must also have the right inner dispositions of the heart. Doctrine affects the affections too when disciples follow its directions. We must taste to see that the Lord is good (Ps. 34:8). Following doctrine's directions is cathartic, purifying our hearts of the self-pity and fear that impede bold and calm witness.

If there is a secret to discipleship, it is the messianic secret: the mystery, now revealed, that Jesus Christ is indeed the Son of Man who reigns in heaven. And if the transfiguration was the preview of this heavenly enthronement, then the book of Revelation is the feature-length film. Revelation is a compelling account of the *denouement* of the historical and cosmic drama of redemption, aiming to produce a particular effect on its readers: the distinctly Christian catharsis that results in the disciple's steadfastness (and, as we shall see in the next section, thankfulness). Whereas tragedies deal with the downfall of the protagonist, the drama of redemption deals with the overthrow of the antagonist: Satan, the great dragon (Rev. 12:9). The book of Revelation was written to encourage faithful witnesses at risk of feeling the effects of this dragon's breath, meaning Caesar's sword.

The book of Revelation, like other apocalyptic discourse, was written to encourage disciples facing the prospect of social or political persecution by various earthly powers. The book enables local companies of the faithful to see themselves as part of a great cloud of witnesses who display patient endurance under fire (1:9; 2:2; 3:10). By revealing the end of the conflict, Revelation

---

50. Harink, *1 and 2 Peter*, 154.

communicates strength for the journey. In particular, assurances that Christ has defeated the evil powers and that God will preserve his saints through times of tribulation enable saints to persevere: "Feelings of fear and resentment are released by the book's repeated presentations of the destructions of the hearers' enemies."[51]

Rejoicing: Joyful Hope

Nothing saps disciples of the strength necessary for faithful perseverance more than despair. Actors would indeed be performing tragedies if the gateway to the world stage (rather than Dante's hell) were inscribed with the fateful words "Abandon all hope, ye who enter here."[52] The modern response to tragedy, exemplified in the thought of Friedrich Nietzsche and Martin Heidegger, is courage in the face of nonbeing. This, however, gets us no further than Kierkegaard's "knight of infinite resignation,"[53] a Stoic attitude suitable for actors performing the drama of dread (i.e., finite human existence).

Disciples who follow the directions of Christian doctrine perform a very different play, however, in which being-toward-resurrection features more prominently than being-toward-death. To be sure, there is suffering in the triune comedy, and disciples must learn to endure it, yet they do so with the mind of Christ, in confident and even joyful hope that "all manner of things shall be well"[54] when God is all in all (1 Cor. 15:28). That disciples have been born into "a living hope through the resurrection of Jesus Christ" (1 Pet. 1:3) is no idle bit of information but rather one that ought to color one's attitude to daily life. That disciples have "an inheritance that is imperishable" (1:4) ought likewise to dominate one's inner world, which is why Peter goes on to say, "In this you rejoice, even if now for a little while you have had to suffer various trials" (1:6).

Rejoicing is not a mere emotional add-on to discipleship but rather belongs to its very essence. As we have seen, having the mind of Christ means having his same attitudes and dispositions as well as his beliefs. I agree with Martha Nussbaum that emotions too have a cognitive aspect: "Love, pity, fear, and their relatives—all are belief-based in a similar way: all involve the acceptance of certain views of how the world is and what has importance."[55] Disciples must not merely assent intellectually to doctrine but also rejoice emotionally, knowing that it leads us deeper into the one who is the ultimate source of all truth, goodness, and beauty, and the sum total of our desire and delight. The proper response to discovering the riches that are in Jesus Christ, including the resources for coping with both finitude and fallenness, is neither resentment nor a shrug of

---

51. Adela Yarbro Collins, *Crisis and Catharsis: The Power of the Apocalypse* (Philadelphia: Westminster Press, 1984), 154.
52. Dante, *The Divine Comedy*, vol. 1, *Hell*, canto 3.
53. Søren Kierkegaard, *Fear and Trembling/Repetition*, trans. Howard V. Hong and Edna H. Hong, vol. 6 of *Kierkegaard's Writings* (Princeton: Princeton University Press, 1983), 42–46.
54. Julian of Norwich, *Revelations of Divine Love*, 32.
55. Nussbaum, *Love's Knowledge*, 41.

the shoulders but joyful embrace. The truth and goodness of God that doctrine explicates in describing *what is in Christ* are the disciple's delight.

"Rejoice in the Lord always; again I will say, Rejoice" (Phil. 4:4). This imperative is not burdensome for disciples assured of life with Christ in the heavenly realms. Again, by "heavenly" we mean the sphere of Christ's rule, which is already present on earth, as it is in heaven. The church is the community "on whom the ends of the ages have come" (1 Cor. 10:11). Paul says that participating in Christ's kingdom more than compensates for whatever disciples may have to suffer for bearing witness to the lordship of Christ before the powers and principalities (including public opinion) of this world: "So we do not lose heart. Even though our outer nature is wasting away, our inner nature is being renewed day by day. For this slight momentary affliction is preparing us for an eternal weight of glory beyond all measure" (2 Cor. 4:16–17).

Disciples are "protected by the power of God through faith" (1 Pet. 1:5). Protected from what, and how? Luther's commentary on this passage is worth pondering. He first points out that people undergoing suffering for their faith need to know the hope to which they have been called (Eph. 1:18). Faith gives us this knowledge, and faith itself is evidence of God's power: "For when God creates faith in man, this is as great a work as if He were to create heaven and earth again."[56] Faith is God's protecting power because it gives us a true and clear understanding of everything that pertains to salvation (i.e., the theodrama) so that we are able to discern between true and false doctrine.[57] Luther reminds us that the trials of faith may be not only physical but also ideological. In the face of these threats, disciples have the assurance that God will protect "their spiritual ability to make judgments in accordance with the truth of Christ."[58]

Disciples need right hearts as well as right beliefs in order to rightly participate in the drama of redemption. Indeed, in one sense the human heart is the principal site of the dramatic conflict. Put differently, discipleship is to a large extent a matter of cultivating right dispositions in the heart. Doctrine has a role to play in this work too inasmuch as its explication of *what is in Christ* not only orients the mind but also enraptures the heart.

Disciples speak and show the kingdom of God on earth, not least through their suffering witness, provided "that they have their hearts in the right place," to cite a familiar idiom. In this case, however, proverbial wisdom fails: it is not enough to have good intentions. On the contrary, the only "right place" for one's heart to be is fixed on Christ, resting in God. This is the distinctly Christian catharsis that comes from performing the drama of doctrine: "But even if you do suffer for righteousness' sake, you will be blessed. Have no fear of them, nor be troubled, but in your hearts reverence Christ as Lord" (1 Pet. 3:14–15 RSV). There is no place for self-pity, or fear of the world, in the hearts of those who acknowledge Jesus Christ as Lord, the one set apart, high above all

---

56. Martin Luther, *The Catholic Epistles*, vol. 30 of *Luther's Works* (St. Louis: Concordia, 1967), 14.
57. Ibid., 15.
58. Harink, *1 and 2 Peter*, 46.

earthly powers: "It is this 'holy fear,' or respectful awe focused on Christ, that drives out other fears."[59] The "fear of the LORD" (cf. Ps. 111:10; Prov. 1:7) is thus the wellspring of the disciple's joyful hope, the beginning of witness, wisdom, and worship alike.

RECAPITULATION: THE DOXOLOGICAL IMPERATIVE

Rejoice in hope, be patient in suffering, persevere in prayer.
—Romans 12:12

The vocation of the disciple is to become like Christ, an embodied witness to a new reality: the coming of God's kingdom on earth as it is in heaven. The present work has emphasized what disciples have to do—the nature of their participation in the drama of redemption—in terms of faith speaking and showing understanding. This is a critical point: contra Marx, it is not the task of the disciples to transform the world, only to bear witness to its transformation through Christ in the Spirit. The late Metropolitan Anthony Bloom, archbishop of the Russian Orthodox Church in Great Britain, effectively dispatches all exaggerated activist impulses by citing a Russian proverb: "If you do not die first, you will have time to do it. If you die before it is done, you don't need to do it."[60]

Stephen's discipleship is again exemplary. He faithfully spoke what he saw and understood (Christ is Lord). Stephen patiently endured the stones and insults of unbelieving opposition. His joy and hope were not in his own accomplishments but in the love and mercy of Jesus. Disciples today would do well to emulate Stephen. Like Stephen, we cannot control even our immediate context, much less change the world. What we can and must control, however, are our own tongues and hands. As people of faith, our overarching concern ought to be with speaking and showing our understanding of what is in Christ. In the words of Archbishop Bloom: "The basic thing is that I never ask myself what the result of any action will be—that is God's concern. The only question I keep asking myself in life is: what should I do at this particular moment?"[61] In each and every moment, doctrine directs disciples to speak and show forth understanding of what is in Christ. It is important to keep in mind, however, that our speaking and doing are secondary and responsive. Doctrine is first and foremost an indication of what God has said and done before it is a direction for the disciple's speech and action.

---

59. J. Ramsey Michaels, *1 Peter*, Word Biblical Commentary (Waco, TX: Word, 1988), 187.
60. Bloom, *Beginning to Pray*, 89.
61. Ibid., 14.

The doxological imperative, "Rejoice in the Lord always" (Phil. 4:4), is tied to another, on which it depends: "Pray without ceasing" (1 Thess. 5:17). Prayer is what enables disciples to patiently endure and joyfully hope in the face of hostility or indifference. For prayer reminds us, as nothing else can, that it is God's words and acts that determine the final result of what takes place on the stage of world history: "You meant evil against me; but God meant it for good" (Gen. 50:20 RSV). Finally, in reminding us that we are part of God's drama (theodrama) rather than the other way around, prayer reorients us to reality (i.e., the Creator/creature distinction).

Stephen's witness was emboldened by his direct address to God when, as he stood dying, he prayed, "Lord Jesus, receive my spirit" (Acts 7:59). His final prayer echoed the words of Jesus on the cross: "Lord, do not hold this sin against them" (Acts 7:60; cf. Luke 23:34). Disciples are able to "rejoice in the Lord always" only as they "pray without ceasing." Because prayer acknowledges what is in Christ—consolation, hope, wisdom, reconciliation, and so forth—it should be the disciple's first response and reflex in every situation. Prayer is what we do on earth to be drawn higher up and further into heaven. Disciples are never more like Christ than when they pray, especially when they repeat the words that Jesus taught the first disciples: "Our Father who art in heaven."

Prayer is an example both of faith speaking understanding and of the divine-human dialogical action that propels the drama of redemption. In praying, disciples do not merely observe the theodrama but also assume speaking parts. Furthermore, in praying "Our Father" with Jesus, disciples participate in his filial relationship with God as adopted sons and daughters. Prayer thus embodies the gospel inasmuch as those who pray acknowledge (1) themselves as dependent creatures and covenant servants, (2) Jesus as Lord, and (3) the covenant blessing of fellowship with God the Father made possible by the risen Christ and the Spirit of adoption.

Prayer is what enables disciples affectively to experience what they believe in the intellect and confess with their lips. Prayer is the key to understanding God, ourselves, and the prerequisites for right participation in the triune mission to the world. As Jesus' prayer in Gethsemane led to his strengthened resolve ("Not my will but yours be done" [Luke 22:42]), so our prayers may be a means of grace by which our thoughts and desires are realigned to conform with Christ's. Through prayer, disciples gain a renewed sense of their mission and the source of their strength. In prayer, disciples offer to the Lord all that they have, all that they do, and all that they are. If speaking is a form of doing, then prayer is the quintessential act of the disciple, a precious means, like theology, of learning to live well to God.[62] Prayer aids disciples to live on earth as Christ is in heaven.

The new in Christ is something to celebrate: "The blind receive their sight, the lame walk, . . . the deaf hear, the dead are raised, the poor have good news brought to them" (Luke 7:22). These are the tangible tokens of the light, life,

---

62. For further discussion of this point, see my *Remythologizing Theology*, 381–84.

and love of God poured out in Christ for us and our salvation. Perhaps, then, we should view doctrine as directing people of faith to sing rather than merely speak understanding. The company of faith would then be a Chorus of the Rock, not only praying but also *praising* without ceasing, setting forth in song the wonders that are in Christ: "The first and constitutive act of God's people is to praise God."[63]

The appropriate response to recognizing and undergoing experience of God's grace (*charis*) is gratitude (*eucharistia*). The greatest doxological act that disciples make is offering their lives as wise witnesses to the gospel, expressing their love for Jesus Christ by obeying his commands and walking his way in holiness, justice, and love. Disciples who attain Christlikeness do not perform the drama of doctrine for their own honor but for Christ's. For the drama is, at root, the unfolding of the mystery of God's love for an unloving world. Disciples are not the stars of the show, only the little lights who reflect, in word and deed, the brightness of him who is alone their light, life, and love. Doctrine helps disciples grow in understanding and equips us for the good work of conforming our minds and hearts to Christ; yet all right performance calls attention not to ourselves but to Christ alone. He alone is the one to whom all glory belongs (Heb. 13:21).

"I celebrate myself, and sing myself,"[64] declared Walt Whitman, but he got it wrong: his doxology was misdirected. Those who act, suffer, and sing as disciples do so "lost in wonder, love, and praise" not of themselves but of their Redeemer.[65] Disciples respond rightly to the doxological imperative when, in performing the drama of doctrine, they prayerfully acknowledge God as the author of all good gifts, respond in faithful obedience to the grace of God made word and flesh, and with grateful hearts sing spiritual songs to the Lord (Eph. 5:19; Col. 3:16).

---

63. Harink, *1 and 2 Peter*, 42.
64. Walt Whitman, "Song of Myself."
65. From Charles Wesley's hymn "Love divine, all loves excelling."

Conclusion:
Tell and Show

Exhibiting the Gospel in Company with Christ

I believed, and so I spoke.

—2 Corinthians 4:13

Come, I will show you the bride, the wife of the Lamb.

—Revelation 21:9

In his study of early Christianity, Robert Louis Wilken makes an important observation about patristic theologians: "All the figures portrayed in this book prayed regularly, and their thinking was never far removed from the church's worship."[1] This is why theology is best pursued in company with Christ, in both senses of the term: in Christ's own presence and with others who belong to his company. Wilken later cites the famous definition of the desert monk Evagrius: "A theologian is one who prays, and one who prays is a theologian." I want only to add "and acts": a theologian is one who prays and acts, or as C. S. Lewis prefers to put it, one who prays and *works*.[2] For Lewis, work and prayer are on a par: both are divine gifts that endow human creatures with the "dignity of causality."[3] Both praying (worshiping) and acting (working) are ways in which

---

1. Robert Louis Wilken, *The Spirit of Early Christian Thought: Seeking the Face of God* (New Haven, CT: Yale University Press, 2003), 25.
2. C. S. Lewis, "Work and Prayer," in *God in the Dock: Essays on Theology and Ethics* (Grand Rapids: Wm. B. Eerdmans Publishing Co., 1970), 104–7.
3. According to Blaise Pascal, God has established prayer "in order to communicate to His creatures the dignity of causality" (*Pensées* no. 513 [1670]).

disciples participate fittingly in the drama of redemption and contribute to it. Praying and acting are two ways of getting things done in the world.

The present work is a wake-up call about the importance of following the direction of doctrine for disciples who wish to play their parts to the glory of God. I have argued that doctrine tells us what is in Christ and exhorts us to conform to what is. I have also argued that doctrine must be acted on from the inside out: it is not enough merely to go through the external motions; mimicking is not mimesis. True disciples live out what is in Christ, and this means embodying Christ's heart and mind alike.

A theologian is one who prays—and stays awake. This is easier said than done. On the night he was betrayed, on the eve of the drama's climax, Jesus went out to pray with his disciples at the Garden of Gethsemane. The matter at hand was a matter of life and death (and not Jesus' only), and through prayer Jesus was reminded of his identity and received the strength to complete his mission. His prayer was the means of aligning his heart, mind, and will to God's will (to the theodrama). Unfortunately, the disciples fell asleep; they were as good as dead to the strange new world that Jesus was inaugurating. Jesus encouraged them, saying, "Keep awake and pray" (Mark 14:38). They fell asleep again.

The church's Great Commission is to make disciples and teach them to obey everything that Jesus has commanded. A prerequisite for learning this Great Curriculum is that disciples stay awake. "The dog ate my homework" is at least a semblance of an excuse, but when Jesus returned to the disciples and found them sleeping a second time, Mark informs us, "They did not know what to say to him" (Mark 14:40). There are no alibis for disciples. Hence Paul exhorts the church at Colossae, "Continue steadfastly in prayer, being watchful in it with thanksgiving" (Col. 4:2 RSV). To be "watchful" is to stay awake, and to be awake is to be aware of and alert to what is happening around us, and especially of what we ourselves are doing. When disciples are awake and praying, they are aware of and alert to the constant presence and activity of the triune God and to the big theodramatic picture in which they have been given the dignity to play scenes small and large.

Neither Christian doctrine nor prayer has anything to do with wish fulfillment. Disciples are not playing pretend games, lost in myth, fantasy, and science fiction. To be "lost in wonder, love, and praise" when contemplating what is in Christ is a far cry from losing touch with reality. Performing the drama of doctrine is serious play. What is ultimately at stake in such play is the nature of ultimate reality and human flourishing, God and the good life. Contrary to what Friedrich Nietzsche thought, Christian doctrines do not deny life in a misguided attempt to suppress natural instinct. That way lies the drama of Darwin's doctrine. Biology, however, will not save us, nor will evolutionary theory give disciples direction for right participation in the play of human history.

Christian doctrine is for grown-ups who have childlike imaginations, trusting stories in general only because one story, the gospel of Jesus Christ, happens to be true (and true because it happened: "He is risen"). Christian doctrine is a dose of reality, a slap in the face that wakes up the bleary-eyed and hungover, all those who cannot open their eyes (or prefer to keep them shut) to the new thing God is doing in Christ through the Spirit. To see with the eyes of the heart what Stephen saw, the risen Christ reigning from his heavenly palace temple, is to be fully awake to the theodrama that frames our lives, our brief but momentous stints onstage the great theater of the world.

Doctrine gives disciples directions for what really matters: for making the most of their place and time, living with others to God in ways that lead to human flourishing and divine glory. The present book has focused on doctrine as an indication of "what is" in Jesus Christ: the name, the person, the work, and the wondrous result of the work—covenant fellowship with God. Jesus says, "I am the way, and the truth, and the life" (John 14:6). Christian doctrine does not distract disciples from the "real" world but, on the contrary, ministers reality by indicating and explicating the truth about Jesus, thereby directing disciples on his way. There are no armchair disciples: followers of Jesus deal not with theoretical abstractions but with concrete realities, acting out his way, new life, at all times and places. Performing the drama of doctrine is ultimately about being in Christ and about demonstrating one's understanding in quotidian acts of wisdom and devotion. One can only rightly perform the drama of doctrine, of course, if one is rightly related to Jesus Christ, its subject matter. Disciples rightly relate to Christ precisely by participating fittingly with others, through the Spirit, in his body and his reign. This is what it means to keep company with Christ.

Performing the drama of doctrine ultimately means conforming to Christ, displaying in embodied human speech and action "what is" in Christ. Doctrine must be done; otherwise, our understanding of the theodrama will remain merely theoretical. It is by following doctrine's directions, making every effort to conform our minds and hearts to the new reality in Christ, that disciples become mature and attain "the measure of the full stature of Christ" (Eph. 4:13). On second thought, disciples are not so much grown-ups as growing-ups, actors who mature as they learn to communicate understanding, both in words (speaking truth in love) and deeds (doing works of love).

One phrase in particular recurs throughout the present work: *what is in Christ*. In philosophy, metaphysics is the study of ultimate reality: what is. Theology too focuses on ultimate reality, though I call the study of what is in Christ not metaphysics but theodramatics: God, creatures, and their relationship. We have seen that what is in Christ includes the reconciliation of God to humanity (2 Cor. 5:19) and the communion of the saints (Eph. 2:14–20). To do justice to what is in Christ, therefore, requires both dogmatic and moral theology: the indicative (what is) implies the imperative (do this), at least if one seeks wisdom, which is the ability to flourish by participating fittingly in the created order. To live well with others is to live to the glory of the Son of God, "the Author of life" (Acts 3:15) and the "perfecter of our faith" (Heb. 12:2).

The Great Curriculum of Christian doctrine involves humanity and divinity, the creature and the Creator, and the Creator-creature relation, especially as it subsists in Christ. In studying Christian doctrine, the disciple's course objective is clear: to get real, which means getting right—with God, oneself, and others. The drama of doctrine is the challenge to disciples to live in the real world, that is, as new creation (2 Cor. 5:17) in the new creational kingdom inaugurated in Christ.

Doctrine focuses on reality, though it is best to construe theology (as opposed to the natural sciences) as a *grateful* (rather than critical) *realism*. Yes, there is evil, suffering, and injustice in the world, but these things have only penultimate reality. In contrast, ultimate reality, the new creation in Christ, is a matter (for humans) of a new embodied existence of eternal life and blessedness. The Christian's blessed hope is to participate in this new "eutopian" reality. In fostering deeper theodramatic understanding—a greater appreciation for the identity of the players and the meaning of the play—doctrine informs and directs the disciple's witness, wisdom, and worship alike.

EXEUNT: THE DISMISSAL

Go into all the world and proclaim the good news.
—Mark 16:15

Worship services typically end with a dismissal, usually a benediction, sometimes accompanied by the sign of the cross. This *dismissio* is itself a kind of mission: a "sending away." Disciples ought to leave the daily or weekly worship service with the mind-set of graduates at commencement, ready to contribute to society and confront the tests of life. A graduate understands things (at least something about what they majored in) and knows how to do certain things. Graduates should also be able to articulate what they understand. Philosophy students, for example, ought to have a response to the age-old question "Why is there something rather than nothing?" In similar fashion, disciples should be prepared to respond to the somewhat more recent question "Why are we, the church, here?"

The church is a herald of the gospel and harbinger of the new creation. The vocation of the church is to proclaim the gospel and publish the majesty of Christ, in words of truth and works of love. This is abstract, to be sure, which is precisely why we have an extended transcript that tells us what God and the people of God have actually done: "For whatever was written in former days was written for our instruction" (Rom. 15:4; cf. 1 Cor. 10:11). Scripture is full of scenes of improvised wisdom that repay careful study among those who would learn the mind of Christ. Why is the church here? "You are there to be the presence of the Lord God, the presence of Christ, the presence of the Spirit, the presence of the Gospel—this is your function on this particular day."[4]

The church is a company of grateful realists who acknowledge what is in Christ with thankful hearts that overflow in praise, proclamation, and obedient practice. As realists, the believing community is under no illusion that followers of Christ walk rose-strewn paths. No, the way is often rocky, yet the company is convinced that Christ is present and active as Savior and Lord. As the grateful, the company of faith thankfully accepts the gift of the Holy Spirit, the one who unites disciples to Christ and communicates the power of Christ's new life. The company further rejoices in the assurance that nothing can separate those who are in Christ from their Lord's steadfast love. Finally, the company freely acknowledges that the proper return for God's acts of grace is the offering of a grateful life: "Let them thank the LORD for his steadfast love, for his wonderful works to humankind. And let them offer thanksgiving sacrifices, and tell of his deeds with songs of joy!" (Ps. 107:21–22).

The church exists to form and train grateful realists (i.e., disciples) to understand the theodrama and their roles in it so they can communicate and continue God's wonderful works for the sake of the world. There is theater whenever one person meets another. Every encounter with another person constitutes a small scene, and whether disciples will say and do the right thing is what makes for drama: "Every human meeting is judgment, is crisis, is a situation in which we are called either to receive Christ or to be Christ's messenger to the person we are meeting."[5] We have seen how doctrine helps disciples learn their parts and acquire habits of right judgment and right practice. One of the most important tasks disciples have is to tell others about the theodrama, its implications, and in particular its climax and end: the gospel that Jesus Christ is Lord.

Doctrine serves the church by nurturing its understanding of the truth, goodness, and beauty that subsist in Jesus Christ. The church is indeed a "living Bible" when it lives out what Scripture tells us God is doing in and through Christ. What the church does in Christ's name, its "body language," is proclamation too. In particular, the church enacts the drama of redemption when it plays its role as the body, and bride, of Jesus Christ. For in Christ, we know God as we are known—in that deep, relational, and covenantal way of knowing that characterizes the "two becoming one flesh" (Eph. 5:31–32). This was the aim of Jesus' mission, which had everything to do with disciples coming to know God, enjoying eternal life, publishing the truth of Christ to the world, and becoming one (John 17:21).

The church is to go out into the world to enact parables of God's kingdom, loving the world with an extraordinary outpouring of its own life as Christ poured out his life for the church. The church is to enact the love and justice of God at

4. Bloom, *Beginning to Pray*, 76.
5. Ibid., 75.

all times, in ten thousand places, and to everyone. In sum: the church exists to be a living exhibit of the reality of the gospel. It is a trifle to dismiss outmoded and archaic doctrines; it is something else altogether to ignore scenes that enact the doctrine of God's love through racial reconciliation, familial forgiveness, social justice, and ecclesial communion. This too is gospel proclamation.

ENCORE: THE GLORIA

Do everything for the glory of God.
—1 Corinthians 10:31

While doctrine sets forth in speech the truth of what is in Christ, worship sets forth this same truth in symbolic action in the church's corporate life and does so in the form of a response or offering addressed to God. To respond is to offer something in return. Everything the company of disciples does in the name of Jesus Christ is ultimately a liturgical response, a word or song or act of gratitude that answers a prior grace of God. The company of the faithful gathers, usually on Sundays, for worship services to make formal response. Discipleship does not end, however, with the dismissal from traditional church worship. On the contrary, disciples are called to make informal responses each day, in all situations. Because the grace of God envelops those who are in Christ, gratitude must be the disciple's default gesture: "Thanks be to God!" is to be one's constant mind-set and habitual expression.

Sacrifices of thanksgiving, unlike Christ's once-for-all sacrifice (Rom. 6:10; Heb. 7:27), are to be offered repeatedly. The most important sacrificial gift disciples offer is themselves: "Present your bodies as a living sacrifice, holy and acceptable to God, which is your spiritual worship" (Rom. 12:1) and your theology and doctrinal performance. Consider that in speaking of a "living" sacrifice, Paul is urging his readers to see their entire embodied existence as an offering to God. The "bodied" nature of our sacrifice reminds us that it is not enough to "think good thoughts." To be Christlike is also to desire right desires, and to do good deeds. Moreover, our embodied existence must be "holy and acceptable" to God. This is another way of saying that disciples must live to God, which recalls William Ames's definition of theology: "living to God" is both our "spiritual worship" (Rom. 12:1) and our theological vocation (see chap. 1 above). Doxology and doctrine may diverge in a yellow wood, but in the strange new world of the Bible they converge, and disciples must travel both simultaneously, which will make all the difference.

Throughout this work I have insisted that the purpose of doctrine is to increase the disciple's understanding of the theodrama in order rightly to participate in it. Each day affords disciples a plethora of opportunities to present their bodies as living sacrifices. Doctrine gives disciples direction for fitting sacrificial acts and, furthermore, for understanding their entire lives as thanksgiving offerings to God. Disciples perform doctrine throughout the day and in their day-to-day activities (in "ordinary time") as well as in those rare moments where one's acts may become the stuff of song and story (in "extraordinary time"). However, the real heroes may be those whose heroics go unsung yet who remain steadfast in matters great and small. Sometimes faith's performance is prosaic rather than epic. This too is the drama of doctrine.

For the disciple, all of life is liturgical, a public offering of gratitude whereby one gives everything one has, does, and is to the one who has given it. These quotidian offerings of thanksgiving are condensed versions, small-scale summary scenes, of the great drama of redemption. Again, there is no merit in simply going through external motions. The antidote to such empty ritualism (deadly theater) is worship "in spirit and truth" (John 4:23), whereby one's embodied life is animated by the Spirit and oriented by the Scriptures. Disciples should approach all of life with the intention of offering their time and talents as living sacrifices that celebrate, and correspond to, the reality of the already/not-yet reign of Christ on earth.

If men and women are indeed "eucharistic animals,"[6] then presenting embodied daily sacrifices of thanksgiving to God is an instance not of role-playing but of achieving the true ends of human personhood. That human beings are created for praise should come as no surprise; it is only fitting that creatures worship their Creator. What else but praise can one give the God who has and is every perfection? A good portion of the Scriptures is made up of praise (see the Psalms), and there is strong scriptural warrant for thinking that the supreme goal of the whole theodrama is nothing less than the glory of God (see esp. Eph. 1).[7] As we have seen, each of the five acts that comprise the theodrama features a gracious act of God: creation (act 1); election (act 2); incarnation and crucifixion (act 3); resurrection, ascension, Pentecost, and heavenly session (act 4); and consummation (act 5). Each of the doctrines that correspond to these respective acts ministers understanding of the theodrama as a whole. Disciples participate in these gracious acts by bearing witness to them, in many and various ways, in particular through the corporate life of the body of Christ.

The church, precisely as the body of Christ, presents itself as a living sacrifice. Its spiritual worship is to perform the drama of doctrine for, as we have seen, both doctrine and doxology have a common end: glorifying who God is and what God has done in Christ. The church plays a complex role: it is "the body of Christ" (1 Cor. 12:27), "the fellowship of the Holy Spirit" (2 Cor. 13:14

---

6. Kallistos Ware, *The Orthodox Way*, rev. ed. (Crestwood, NY: St. Vladimir's Seminary Press, 1995), 53–54.

7. Cf. Beale: "The glory of God is the grand goal of the entirety of redemptive history" (*A New Testament Biblical Theology*, 958). See also James M. Hamilton, *God's Glory in Salvation through Judgment: A Biblical Theology* (Wheaton, IL: Crossway, 2010).

RSV), and "the temple of God" (1 Cor. 3:16 NASB). The church is God's dwelling place on earth, the living temple of the new creation.[8] The church not only calls for but in a certain sense also constitutes the divine "Encore": the reappearance as it were of Christ on earth after his definitive historical performance. The company of the faithful is a living theater that remembers, celebrates, meditates upon, and reenacts God's wonderful works. The church is God's encore performance: the place, in Christ, where grace and gratitude meet again and again and again.

The common aim of both theology and doxology is God's glorification. It is also, according to the well-known words of the Westminster Larger Catechism, the answer to its first question: "What is the chief end of man? Man's chief and highest end is to glorify God and enjoy him forever." The church is the doctrinal and doxological "encore" where the company of faith prays and praises without ceasing, speaking and showing its understanding of God and the gospel in ways, small and large, that glorify God.

"Glory to God in the highest, and peace on earth to people of goodwill." Gloria in Excelsis Deo is an ancient hymn, based on Luke 2:14, whose Latin words were probably translated by Hilary of Poitiers. The hymn is thoroughly biblical, robustly Trinitarian, and clearly christocentric. It is at once fully doctrinal and fully doxological, without confusion, division, or separation. This is the disciples' theme song for performing the drama of doctrine. When disciples in their life together act out what is in Christ, they perform or express what we would call a *eucharistic realism*: a living thanks offering for the *eucatastrophe* (Gk. *eukatastrophē* = good outcome]), *euangelion*, and *eutopia* in Christ. For it is only when disciples enact the new creational kingdom in Christ, praising without ceasing, that we begin to catch a glimpse, by way of eschatological anticipation, of the way things are (and will be) in Christ. When disciples display faith and hope by the way they endure and rejoice in their sufferings, they become "an apocalypse of Jesus Christ, an intrusion of the messianic era into the time of the world."[9] Their worship is their witness, and vice versa.

Doctrine and doxology are equally dangerous.[10] To make disciples is to awaken sleeping images of God and let them loose on the world. Enacting and celebrating what is in Christ has ego- and world-shattering power. To live out doctrine in grateful response to God's grace and the praise of his glory (Eph. 1:12, 14) is to subvert the social logics and cultural conventions of this world. For disciples must do more than simply talk about God's perfections to glorify God; they must also participate in, embody, and enact them. We glorify God when we show the world the goodness of his attributes. Imitation is the sincerest form of glorification, which is why the Lord requires us to "do justice, and to

---

8. See Beale, *A New Testament Biblical Theology*, 958–60.
9. Harink, *1 and 2 Peter*, 49.
10. I want here to acknowledge the influence of Mark Labberton's *The Dangerous Act of Worship: Living God's Call to Justice* (Downers Grove, IL: InterVarsity Press, 2007) on this point of my argument.

love kindness, and to walk humbly with [him]" (Mic. 6:8). Our performances invariably fall short. Even at our best, we image God only dimly, through the veil of our flesh. God nevertheless remains faithful.

Whenever disciples gather in groups of two or three (Matt. 18:20), they should present their bodies and their activities as exhibits of the gospel, the new reality under the lordship of Christ Jesus. This is their spiritual worship, performance of doctrine, and glorification of God. Rightly to perform the drama of redemption is the disciples' chief mandate, the index of their wisdom, witness, and worship alike. Doctrine is a vital aid to right performance. The drama of doctrine thus refers both to the process by which disciples acquire understanding of the theodrama and to the requirement to demonstrate that understanding daily by, for example, speaking truth, making peace, doing justice, and loving mercy.

Doctrine directs the company of faith to speak and show what is in Christ. The church keeps company with Christ in heaven, not least as his theatrical exhibit on earth. The best defense of the faith is its compelling (lived) demonstration: the action by which disciples exhibit the reality of God and the gospel, *theos* and theodrama. Everything I have said here about the importance of doctrine for discipleship pertains not only to theology and doxology but also to apologetics. To demonstrate the theodrama is to show its truth, goodness, and beauty—the truth, goodness, and beauty that is in Christ. Everything that the church has, is, and does is in, for, and through Christ. To exhibit Christ is the church's raison d'être and what we might call its "martyring orders"—which is to say, its commission to witness to what is in Christ by embodying his mind and, if necessary, suffering in the body: "My Father is glorified by this, that you bear much fruit and become my disciples" (John 15:8).

When the company of faith follows doctrinal directions, it lives up to its name and becomes a society of Jesus: an earthly body in which God's light and love circulate in truth-speaking, right-doing, and life-giving ways. The church is a performance aimed not at earning but at exhibiting the righteousness of God, the life eternal, and the hope of the world. To perform the drama of doctrine is to do and become a constant display of faith and faithfulness, grace and gratitude, mercy and love. *This* glorious show must go on.

Appendix

What Has Broadway to Do with Jerusalem?

Doctrines are directions not only for understanding but also for demonstrating one's understanding of the gospel, its truth, goodness, and beauty alike. Hopefully by this point readers will not need more convincing that the theatrical analogy is remarkably helpful in thinking about the way in which disciples enact doctrine. However, even those who value the analogy may appreciate having answers to potential objections. Hence we present a review of some historical and contemporary objections, together with my responses.

THE ANTITHEATRICAL PREJUDICE: RESPONDING TO HISTORICAL OBJECTIONS

How wise is it to employ a model based on something that has for centuries been the object of such ecclesial criticism and disdain? In order to answer this, it may help to know something about the origins of the so-called antitheatrical prejudice.[1]

---

1. For a fuller account, see Jonas S. Barish, *The Antitheatrical Prejudice* (Berkeley: University of California Press, 1981).

Since Paul cautions against being taken captive by the "empty deceit" of philosophy (Col. 2:8), and since Plato regarded the theater as inferior to philosophy, then surely theology must be even more wary of confusing theology with things theatrical. To be sure, philosophy has often been a boon to theology as well. The challenge, with respect to philosophy and the theater alike, is to enlist each in the service of theology while vigilantly avoiding the errors of their respective ways.

It is easier, of course, simply to have nothing to do with them at all. This was Tertullian's strategy in the third century when he dismissed philosophy with his famous rhetorical question, "What has Athens to do with Jerusalem?"[2] Tertullian was also the first church father to write a treatise against going to plays (*De spectaculis* = *The Shows*), in large part because he was alarmed at the extent to which the church was conforming to the surrounding pagan culture.[3] The "spectacles" he had in mind included gladiatorial games in the arena, horse races in the "circus," as well as plays in the theater. Tertullian had three main arguments against all the Roman shows with which he would have been familiar in his hometown of Carthage: (1) They are steeped in idolatry, either originating in or deriving from the worship of false gods (e.g., rituals in a temple devoted to Venus). (2) They excite unholy passions (e.g., "frenzy" is "the ruling spirit" of the arena). (3) Attending them is implicitly forbidden by Scripture. Tertullian acknowledges that the Bible never says, "Thou shalt not enter the theater" as clearly as it says, "Thou shalt not kill." He nevertheless appeals to Psalm 1:1 "Happy is the man who has not gone to the gathering of the impious. Happy are those who do not follow the advice of the wicked ... or sit in the seat of scoffers."

Tertullian's main concern is the adverse affect of Roman spectacles on would-be disciples. Why, he asks, should Christians want to watch what they would never do themselves? If the theater is an ecclesia of the devil, then disciples ought have no part of it (he mentions instances of people becoming demon possessed while attending spectacles). Tertullian then turns the tables, suggesting that the pagans will have a ringside seat at the greatest show above earth, namely, Christ's second coming, at which time dancers will display even more agility as they leap in the flames of hell. The sarcasm is palpable when he states that if spectators enjoy watching people die, they will have a wonderful time at the Last Judgment, when they can "enjoy" not just death but also damnation.

Tertullian's reasons for avoiding theater are not quite Plato's, whose general critique of poetry and the arts in *The Republic* is the root of the long-standing antitheatrical prejudice in Western philosophy and theology.[4] Plato, too, worries about the power of the theater to arouse irrational and immoral passions and to give children inappropriate role models. Even today many voice similar

---

2. Tertullian, *De praescriptione haereticorum*, chap. 7.
3. See Reginald Melville Chase, "De Spectaculis," in *The Classical Journal* 23, no. 2 (1927): 107–20; and Victor Power, "Tertullian: Father of Clerical Animosity toward the Theater," *Educational Theatre Journal* 23, no. 1 (1971): 36–50.
4. See esp. Plato, *The Republic*, 10.

concerns about the violence in film and on television. In addition to Plato's pragmatic concern is a deeper, epistemological concern that the arts, and theater in particular, are only reflections of reflections of truth (i.e., the Forms that exist above the historical flux). Plato contrasts God's idea of a bed (the Platonic ideal), a bed made by a carpenter (a shadow of the ideal), and a theatrical prop (a painter's imitation of the carpenter's bed).[5] The prop is twice removed from the truth: the theater is, for Plato, a poor imitation of what is already an imitation.

Augustine inherited all these concerns about the theater. With Tertullian, Augustine held that the theater is so rooted in pagan religion that Christians cannot support it. When Roman authorities sought to cope with a plague by offering theatrical displays to appease the gods, Augustine shrewdly noted that evil spirits, foreseeing the end of one plague, "took the opportunity to introduce another, far graver one, not into the bodies of the Romans but into their morals."[6]

Augustine speaks from personal experience: as a former pagan, he had firsthand knowledge of the moral debauchery of the theater and of its power to incite lust, admitting that "stage-plays . . . carried me away."[7] Looking back on his former self, he can only marvel: "Why does man like to be made sad when viewing doleful and tragical scenes, which yet he himself would by no means suffer? And yet he wishes, as a spectator, to experience from them a sense of grief, and in this very grief his pleasure consists. What is this but wretched insanity?"[8] To make matters worse, the emotions that the theater incites are not even genuine. It is one thing passively to experience grief in the theater, quite another to act out real Christian compassion when someone suffers real loss.

Augustine shared with Plato an even deeper concern, that the language of the theater is "as a sign system inadequate for representing Christian things."[9] This is a serious charge, one that, if true, would effectively undermine the proposal of the present book. It is therefore worth investigating further. When we do, we see that Augustine is reacting specifically to the content of Roman theater, which he saw as mirroring the false content and bad morals issuing from pagan religion. In the words of one commentator: "The craft of acting is thus an overtly false mode of signification: actors deliberately impersonate a false pantheon and present it as real, then undercut the sanctity of the reality by lampooning their gods. Theater is distinguishable from pagan rituals only because priests, as opposed to actors, take the gods seriously and try to represent them with dignity. Yet the priests are ultimately no better than stage actors."[10]

What is interesting, but beyond the scope of the present work to tell, is the story of how subsequent Christian thinkers come eventually to see parallels

5. Ibid., 10.597–99.
6. Augustine, *City of God* 1.33; ed. R. W. Dyson (Cambridge: Cambridge University Press, 1998), 47.
7. Augustine, *Confessions* 3.2.
8. Ibid.
9. Donnalee Dox, *The Idea of the Theater in Latin Christian Thought: Augustine to the Fourteenth Century* (Ann Arbor, MI: University of Michigan Press, 2004), 12.
10. Ibid., 13.

between the theater and the liturgy and how the church itself gradually came to employ theater for evangelistic and other purposes in the medieval mystery and passion plays. The salient point is Augustine's failure to redeem Greco-Roman theater as he had critically appropriated Greco-Roman rhetoric and other aspects of pagan culture (including philosophy). For some reason, most likely because he was so repelled by the only concrete example of which he was aware, when it came to drama and theater, Augustine was unable to plunder the Egyptians (cf. Exod. 12:36). For good or for ill, Augustine saw no resources for Christian thought in classical theater as he had in classical rhetoric and philosophy.

Fast-forward a millennium. By the time of the Reformation, Calvin could use the theatrical model to speak of God's good creation. Everyday life takes place in the "dazzling theater" of God's glory,[11] and men and women are spectators in this glorious theater in order to view God's works (i.e., creation and providence).[12] Calvin clearly had a more positive, or at least neutral, conception of the theater than did Augustine. Yet in large swaths even of the Reformed tradition, theater remained guilty by association. When, in his famous *Lectures on Calvinism*, Abraham Kuyper turns to consider the relationship of Christ, culture, and religion, he rightly urges Christians not to withdraw from the world but rather to view all of life as set under the lordship of Christ. However, Kuyper also identifies three no-fly zones for Calvinists: dancing, card playing, and theaters. He does not object to dance per se, only to the impurity that is often associated with social dancing. He objects to card playing not because it is a game, nor because there is something demonic in the cards themselves, but rather "because it fosters in our heart the dangerous tendency to look away from God, and to put out trust in *Fortune* or *Luck*."[13]

Kuyper's complaint against theater is of a different order. There is nothing sinful in fiction, including dramatic fiction ("the power of the imagination is a precious gift of God"),[14] nor is the problem Plato's concern about the low epistemic value of theatrical representations. What, then, is the difficulty? Kuyper's main objection is that theater exercises a bad influence not on the audience but on the actors: "The constant and ever-changing presentation of the character of another person finally hampers the moulding of your personal character."[15] This is a fascinating line of attack with which we dealt in chapter 5.

The present book is neither an apology for theatergoing nor a plea to include drama in worship services. I am therefore not concerned to rebut each of the above objections point by point. My principal claim is that the theater, alongside philosophy, ought to be one of theology's bridesmaids. In particular, I am commending *dramatization* as a framework for understanding

---

11. Calvin, *Inst.* 1.5.8.
12. Ibid., 1.6.2.
13. Abraham Kuyper, *Lectures on Calvinism* (Grand Rapids: Wm. B. Eerdmans Publishing Co., 1931), 74.
14. Ibid.
15. Ibid., 75.

the nature and function of doctrine in the church. Philosophy and science are each important, and each has its place. However, when philosophy and science become controlling paradigms for theology, I must protest, not least because they fail to appreciate the poetic and dramatic aspects of theological truth. The picture of theology as a science has held the church captive for too long, and this view is partly responsible for the default assumptions that doctrine, like philosophy, has little to do with the life of the church and that theology, like science, is best left to the "professionals."[16]

Augustine himself points the way past his critique of theater. In his work *Christian Instruction*, he says, "We should not avoid music because of the associated pagan superstitions if there is a possibility of gleaning from it something of value for understanding Holy Scripture."[17] Quite sensibly he adds, "We were not wrong to learn the alphabet just because they say that the god Mercury was its patron."[18] In book 4 he issues a rousing appeal for Christians to employ the tools of classical rhetoric in defense of the faith. Apparently he thinks it possible to redeem Cicero's teaching with regard to the three aims of the orator—to teach, to delight, and to move—as long as Christian speakers remember to use eloquence not merely to persuade but rather to minister truth. We can apply everything Augustine says about music and rhetoric to dramatics too, even if Augustine himself saw no reason to do so.[19] We, however, do have good reason: not only is the subject matter of Christianity essentially dramatic, but (so I am arguing) the search and display of Christian understanding has everything to do with theatrical presentation. What disciples say and do in space and time constitutes a system of earthly signs that ultimately refer to heavenly things.

"THE PLAY'S NOT THE THING": RESPONDING TO CONTEMPORARY OBJECTIONS

We turn now to consider some reasons why present-day Christians may continue to harbor an antitheatrical prejudice.[20] Unpacking, and more importantly, responding to these objections may provide an opportunity to clarify what is

---

16. Besides, it is no longer clear which philosophy best serves as theology's handmaiden. See the various essays that debate this question in Oliver Crisp, Gavin D'Costa, Mervyn Davies, and Peter Hampson, eds., *Theology and Philosophy: Faith and Reason* (London: T&T Clark International, 2012).

17. Augustine, *Christian Instruction* 2.18.28.

18. Ibid.

19. See Dox, *Theater in Latin Christian Thought*, for an account of how medieval Christian thinkers were able to see the theater as a model for human life before God. See also James K. A. Smith, "Staging the Incarnation: Revisioning Augustine's Critique of Theatre," *Literature and Theology* 15, no. 2 (2001): 123–39. Smith reconsiders Augustine's critique of the theater in light of Augustine's affirmation of the goodness of creation, the centrality of the incarnation, and the hope of resurrection, each of which gives reason for a positive assessment of embodied witness.

20. Readers who harbor no particular prejudice against the theatrical model may wish to skip this section.

at stake and, perhaps, reduce the possibility of misunderstanding. Fending off criticisms is also a way of demonstrating the theatrical model's superiority. Here, then, are six more objections, together with my considered responses.

1. "*The dramatic metaphor risks making theology less biblical* by imposing an external model (i.e., the theater) onto Scripture."

Yes, there is a risk, but as Bilbo Baggins knew, there is a risk each time we leave the house ("It's a dangerous business, Frodo, going out your door"). This serious charge, if shown to be true, would lead me to abandon the metaphor altogether. Whenever any model becomes the driving force behind or the focus of theology, rather than an aid to understanding, we risk losing the ministerial nature of the model and are in danger of creating an idol. Metaphors can be wonderful ministerial aids, but they make terrible masters. Theologians must therefore employ any model in an ad hoc rather than reductionist manner.

Interestingly enough, the dramatic model may bring less risk of doing violence to the subject matter of Scripture than other possibilities. Christianity is more like a drama than it is a philosophy of life, a science, geometry, or even a system of morality. If drama involves a unified action specified by a script, then this seems to be exactly what the Bible, and Christianity, are all about. The history of redemption involves human actors in embodied relationships responding in covenant-keeping or covenant-breaking ways to God's covenant-making, self-presenting initiatives on the stage of history. Christian theology is all about being caught up into the life and activity of God: Father, Son, and Spirit.

The most important reply to the objection that drama is a foreign imposition, then, is that Christianity is intrinsically dramatic. The model of theology proposed here, my framework for thinking how doctrine bears on discipleship, thus corresponds to what is being modeled. Also in its favor is the dramatic model's capacity to be expansive rather than reductionist. In the beginning of my exploration of the drama model, I was thinking only about the church's life as a kind of biblical interpretation (as the performance of a script). Then I began to see doctrine in terms of theatrical direction for the church's participation in the ongoing drama of redemption. Though I was often on the verge of saying to the dramatic analogy, "Thus far shall you come, and no farther" (Job 38:11), I have been repeatedly surprised by the expansive fecundity of the model. Thinking of history as the theater of the gospel allows me better to explain and explore, in edifying ways, God's relationship to the world and the believers' relationship to God.

2. "*The Bible is not dramatic literature.*"

The Bible as a whole does not resemble a play script, though certain parts do so more than others.[21] Still, the overall story line of Scripture traces the

---

21. I am thinking in particular of Job and several prophetic books in the Old Testament and of the Fourth Gospel in the New. See William Doan and Terry Giles, *Prophets, Performance, and Power: Performance Criticism of the Hebrew Bible* (Edinburgh: T&T Clark, 2005); and Jo-Ann A. Brant, *Dialogue and Drama: Elements of Greek Tragedy in the Fourth Gospel* (Peabody, MA: Hendrickson, 2004).

interpersonal interaction between God and his human creatures. This interaction is scripted in the sense that there is a plot with a beginning, middle, and end, making the Bible's story into a single unified action. The plot concerns how God executes his eternal decree in time (see chap. 4).

Strictly speaking, the theodrama, God's actions in history, is "behind" the Bible. The theodrama is the drama that Scripture describes and that gave rise to the Scriptures themselves. There is also drama *between* biblical texts. For example, at the beginning of his public ministry, Jesus stood up to read in the synagogue and selected a passage from Isaiah 61:1–2. After the reading he sat down and, according to Luke, "the eyes of all in the synagogue were fixed on him" (Luke 4:20). Jesus' dramatic pause made for riveting theater. The next moment is theatrical as well, for Jesus presents himself as the fulfillment of Scripture (4:21).

While a few parts of the Bible (e.g., the Lord's Prayer) resemble lines that one might find in a dramatic script, most do not. But this is not part of my claim. What is dramatic is not the explicit form of the Bible itself but the matter to which it bears witness. Each part of Scripture contributes to our understanding of the whole theodrama, both the meaning of what God has said/done and what we must say/do in response.

3. *"The Bible is not a script."*

This objection is closely related to the preceding one. What do scripts and Scripture have in common? Both are forms of writing that prescribe forms of action (e.g., celebrating the Lord's Supper). It is tempting, however, to press the dramatic analogy even further, insisting that Scripture is the divine playwright's inspired script. For example, the Christian ethicist Allen Verhey likens the Christian life to a performance of the biblical script.[22] Strictly speaking, however, scripts are written *before* a play, not after the play. The Israelites who were brought out of bondage in Egypt were following Moses, not a script. Moreover, the people were not performing a script (i.e., following a blueprint) when first the Israelites and later their kings "did what was evil in the sight of the LORD" (Judg. 2:11; 1 Kgs. 11:6; 2 Kgs. 13:11; etc.) or when the people forsook the covenant.

I accept these disanalogies. Yet throughout Israel's history there was a text, covenant discourse put into writing, that served as a reminder of the people's unique relationship as God's "treasured possession" (Deut. 7:6). *Ideally*—that is, if the people had been obedient—the "book of the covenant" (Exod. 24:7; 2 Kgs. 23:21) would have functioned as a script, and not simply as a failed prescript. As it so happened, however, much of the Old Testament in particular is a transcript recording Israel's failure to conform to the law.

In what sense, then, could we take Israel's history, the narrative from the exodus to the exile and back again, as a script for the church today? Does it

---

22. Allen Verhey, "Scripture as Script and as Scripted," in *Character Ethics and the New Testament: Moral Dimensions of Scripture*, ed. Robert L. Brawley (Louisville, KY: Westminster John Knox Press, 2007), 19.

make any sense to speak in terms of "performing" the exodus, or the conquest of Canaan, or King Omri's doing evil in the sight of the Lord? Should we reinstitute slavery just because it existed in New Testament times? It is not always clear what it means to be biblical in brave new worlds and bold new contexts. The examples above reinforce the point: the Bible is not a script in the sense of a blueprint that maps out in advance our exact lines and movements. Eugene Peterson is closer to the mark when he describes biblical interpretation as the process of inhabiting the world displayed by the biblical text.[23] For this is the way in which the Bible "scripts" the theodrama: not by specifying in advance what each player is to say and do in every context, but rather by communicating the deep meaning of the theodrama itself. What is God up to?

The Bible is the divinely authorized account, the normative specification, of the theodrama. "In many and various ways" (Heb. 1:1) God speaks in Scripture, in ways that witness to the unified theodrama script-urally but not, strictly speaking, as a script. The Bible is rather a collection of authoritative scenarios: normative descriptions (and sometimes interpretations) of the action, divine and human dialogues that advance the action, or monologues that reflect on it. As a means by which God continues to speak to his people, the Bible is also a part of the ongoing theodramatic action. The canon is thus a collection of various scenes from the one theodrama that, taken together, communicate the meaning and significance of what God is doing as well as what we are to do in response. It follows that *what the church indwells and performs is not the script per se but rather the past, present, and future theodrama that the script transcribes, describes, and prescribes and anticipates.*

The analogy is not exact, but the point is clear. The Bible may not technically be a script, but it is Scripture: the authoritative word that transcribes, describes, and prescribes the church's participation in the drama that the Bible presupposes and implies. The point bears repeating: Scripture gives us not a script in the narrow sense of the term—a detailed template for speech and action—but in the broader sense of a collection of authoritative scenarios that serve as lessons, positive and negative, for us (1 Cor. 10:6-11). We are to speak and act in situations today *as* faithful prophets and apostles did in theirs. (This "as" will open up the possibility, indeed the necessity, of improvising with a transcript.) What is on offer is not merely information to be mastered but concrete wisdom to be deployed in a variety of situations. Learning how to be biblical has more to do with what an intern (or pastor) has to do in morning hospital rounds than it does with learning something like the multiplication table. "All Scripture is inspired by God and profitable" (2 Tim. 3:16 RSV) for governing our understanding of the theodrama and for training in right participation.

---

23. See Eugene H. Peterson, "Scripture as Script: Playing Out Part," in *Eat This Book: A Conversation in the Art of Spiritual Reading* (Grand Rapids: Wm. B. Eerdmans Publishing Co., 2006).

4. *"The dramatic model does not do justice to propositions."*

This objection contains two concerns: first, that the focus on action leads to a disregard of revealed truth; second, that the emphasis on theater as handmaid to theology suggests that doctrine aims at right performance (orthopraxis) rather than right opinion (orthodoxy).[24] These are important points, and I am grateful for the opportunity to correct possible misunderstandings and to distinguish my theodramatic realism from inadequate forms of theological pragmatism.

To the extent that the dramatic view of doctrine aims to cultivate godly disciples, it is concerned with practice. As I hope these pages have shown, however, the practice in question is that of responding to and fitting in with what God has done, is doing, and will do, all of which are susceptible of true, though not exhaustive, description (see John 21:25). Actions, too, have propositional content. The cross of Christ is a particularly eloquent statement of God's love for the world. Moreover, the cross of Christ specifies the meaning of what Scripture says elsewhere about God's love. At the very heart of Christianity is the proclamation of the gospel of the coming reign of God, matched by another proposition: "He has risen" (Matt. 28:6 RSV). This proposition describes something that God has done (Acts 3:15), and its full meaning presupposes an acquaintance with the broader drama of redemption (as in Stephen's speech in Acts 7). The dramatic model reminds us that biblical statements about God are often either descriptions of key moments in the theodrama or generalizations based on one or more previous divine acts.

The dramatic model *is* action-oriented, but not exclusively so. It serves as a partial corrective to the prevailing view of theology as the science of God, with its emphasis on organizing systems of revealed truths. Yet too hard a dichotomy between knowing and doing only falsifies the nature of Christian faith, which is the disposition to stand by one's words and act them out. Indeed, in a cultural situation marked by agnosticism and apathy, one is hard pressed to say which deserves more attention today: propositions or actions. Theologians would do well to emphasize both, hence my emphasis on speaking and showing understanding.

Does the theatrical model lead to a neglect of revealed truths (i.e., propositions)? This might be the case if we restricted God's revelation to something *behind* the biblical text. This was the position of certain mid-twentieth-century thinkers associated with the Biblical Theology Movement who gave theological pride of place to God's mighty acts in history.[25] For them, revelation was always and only a matter of God's actions in salvation history. That is not my understanding.

---

24. So Randall Rauser: "Vanhoozer seems to believe that a sentence is true in virtue of prompting one to appropriate action" (*Theology in Search of Foundations* [Oxford: Oxford University Press, 2009], 261). Rauser worries that the theodramatic model entails a quasi-pragmatic definition of truth, where the true is either merely "what works" or "what incites to good works." He goes on to contrast his own realist view of doctrine as "descriptive" with my allegedly nonrealist "directive" view (261–64).

25. See, e.g., G. Ernest Wright, *God Who Acts* (London: SCM Press, 1952).

Theologians who equate revelation with history have a hard time moving from action to theology, drama to doctrine. How do we formulate doctrine on the basis of God's mighty acts in history? The answer, I believe, is straightforward: only *speech* can disambiguate behavior, and only divine speech can disambiguate divine behavior. But this is precisely what we have in Scripture: God's speech, divine discourse. God is both producer and primary actor. God takes on a speaking part. Indeed, divine statements and pronouncements form some of the high point of the drama. Consider, for example, Exodus 20:2 ("I am the LORD your God, who brought you out of the land of Egypt") or the voice that spoke from heaven at Jesus' baptism in Matthew 3:17 ("This is my Son, the Beloved, with whom I am well pleased"). These divine pronouncements are every bit as theatrical, in the sense that we have defined it, as are the divine actions.

The theodramatic model includes and even features divine speaking. This is vital. For it is the particular vocation of the theater to explore the dual intuitions "to do is to say" (action is the language of the theater) and "to say is to do" (speech is a form of acting). God's mighty speech acts punctuate, galvanize, and reorient the theodramatic action through the Scriptures, from Genesis and the Prophets to the Gospels and Revelation.

The theatrical model emphasizes both aspects of the divine speaking: the *saying* itself (which is a kind of doing) and *what is said* (the propositional content). God's word is not empty. The Lord proposes something specific for his people's consideration: the propositional content that makes up the substance of the covenants, the commandments, and the testimony to Jesus Christ. The notion of a "speech act" highlights the performative nature of language, yet what speakers do with language has propositional content too. According to the Pastoral Epistles, one of the most important things pastor-theologians do with language is preserve a specific message ("Guard what has been entrusted to you" [1 Tim. 6:20]) and pass it on to the next generation ("Proclaim the message [the gospel]" [2 Tim. 4:2]). Christian theology concerns a series of very particular events, connected to the very particular history of a specific people (Israel), and culminating in the very specific apostolic testimony to the life, death, resurrection, and ascension of Jesus Christ and the sending of the Holy Spirit.

In addition to describing what God has said and done, the theatrical model views Scripture itself as a collection of divine speech acts, the product of God's speak-acting through the prophets and apostles. To invoke Scripture's inspiration is to accord to the canonical discourse a supremely authoritative status.[26] The apostle Paul, for example, substitutes "Scripture" for "God," thereby lending credence to the notion that "what Scripture says, God says": "For the Scripture says to Pharaoh . . ." (Rom. 9:17). Assertions and creedal statements—claims

---

26. For an extended treatment of the doctrine of Scripture, see my "Triune Discourse: Theological Reflections on the Claim That GOD Speaks, Parts 1 and 2," in *Trinitarian Theology for the Church: Scripture, Community, Worship*, ed. David Lauber and Daniel Treier (Downers Grove, IL: InterVarsity Press, 2009), 25–78.

like "God is spirit" (John 4:24); "God is one" (Rom. 3:30); "God is light" (1 John 1:5); "God is love" (1 John 4:8)—are therefore very much part of the theodramatic action.[27]

Furthermore, though I claim that doctrine gives direction for discipleship and that disciples display their understanding by their actions, I am not commending a theodramatic pragmatism according to which something is true simply because it leads to right doing (good works). On the contrary, I am contending for a theodramatic realism, where what counts is believing *into* the truth in the sense that one is disposed not only to assert its truth but also to bring one's life into conformity with it. To "direct" understanding is to orient one's thinking according to a model of reality so that we gain a purchase on what is real, the better to engage (participate in) it. Doctrine is directive even in its indicative mood. After all, indicatives *indicate*: they direct our beholding attention to what God has said and done. How we are to participate in the theodrama (the imperatives) depends on what the theodrama is (the indicatives). "Theater" is not only a place for doing but also a place for beholding (*theōreō* = behold), and what we behold in the theater of the gospel is God and God's ways (Exod. 34:6–7). The dramatic model overlooks neither *what is said* nor *what is* but rather roots its imperatival directives ("Do this") in its directives to attend to what God has already done ("Behold"; "Taste and see").

There is one more twist, an ironic footnote. Several Christian psychologists who have interacted with the theodramatic model have come to the opposite conclusion. They worry that my approach is overly propositional, a cognitivism too far.[28] In their view, it is misleading to expect *any* theory of doctrine actually to change lives. One does not acquire new habits simply by thinking orthodox thoughts. In the view of these counselors, my proposal errs by exaggerating the role of cognition and action to the detriment of being, desire, and relationality. They believe that doctrine is a necessary, but not sufficient, condition for personal transformation.

These contrary assessments of my theodramatic proposal from philosophers and psychologists respectively are telling. They rightly remind us that it is not enough for disciples merely to *know* the truth: they must also *desire* to be conformed to it. In response, I affirm that precisely this insight allows the theodramatic model to come into its own, because the biblical theodrama not only informs the mind but also seeks to take every imagination captive to the picture—or rather, the person—of Jesus Christ. The directive account of doctrine employs propositions to address minds, wills, and hearts alike. For

---

27. Paul Helm mistakenly thinks that general or creedal statements are "not part of the action. . . . They are in the drama but not of it" ("Analysis 17—Unexpected Help," August 1, 2008, http://paulhelmsdeep.blogspot.com/2008/08/analysis-17-unexpected-help.html). Why not? It is a severe (and wholly unnecessary) restriction on what lines playwrights can write to forbid them from having characters make statements. It is also a demonstrably false claim; there are myriad counterexamples of characters in plays that state truths (e.g., the "wise sayings" of the fool in Shakespeare's *King Lear*).

28. See the essays by Chuck deGroat, Charles Hackney, and Theresa Clement Tisdale in *Edification* 4 (2010): 5–46.

doctrine directs us not to an abstract theoretical truth (Who cares?), but rather to a concrete truth that concerns us, a truth that is good for us ("He is risen"). Scripture indicates not only the truth, but also the goodness and beauty of Jesus Christ. And the drama derives from the question with which Christ confronts us: Will we be transformed by, and united to, the one who is truth?

5. *"An emphasis on Scripture as script, prescript, and transcript unhelpfully downplays the role of the Holy Spirit."*

This objection comes not from philosophers or psychologists but from certain theologians concerned by the apparent marginalization of the person and work of the Holy Spirit. Once again, there are two distinct concerns: (1) that the Spirit's person and work not be bound to the task of ministering or actualizing a text; and (2) that the dramatic model's emphasis on *performing* the theodrama entails the Pelagian assumption that doctrinal direction (*ought*) implies ecclesial ability (*can*), independent of the regenerating and sanctifying work of the Holy Spirit.

At least one Pentecostal theologian, though appreciative of my emphasis on the imagination and improvisatory freedom, worries that the idea of performing the biblical text stifles our playful participation in the theodrama.[29] If we are to be transformed into the image of Jesus (the point of the play), we need the *energia* of the Spirit more than we do the *scientia* associated with textual exegesis: "The Spirit is not the director of a scripted drama but the moral and eschatological imagination of the story itself and of its performance in the world."[30]

We can commend this concern not to make the Spirit so subservient to the script, so that the Spirit becomes a mere means to an end. Many Protestants may demur, however, from the alternative suggestion that we view revelation as more dynamic, "as the interplay of Spirit, Word, and community."[31] On this view, the community's performance is part and parcel of a "revelatory synergism."[32] It's a fine point. One way to view the difference is to distinguish *theatrical* play governed by a dramatic scenario (the Protestant *sola scriptura*) from *game* play in which the players become so absorbed into the play of God as to become revelatory themselves (Spirit, word, community).[33]

Of course, one need not be a Pentecostal theologian to come to the aid of pneumatology or to decry the alleged tendency of Western theology to marginalize the Holy Spirit. But must the notion that theology aids the disciples' performance of the biblically attested theodrama minimize the Spirit? It might, if the only thing disciples needed for right performance was a pinch of (theoretical) knowledge and a dash of goodwill. If it were, then Israel would have been able to secure its own righteousness, in the sense of right performance, by following the

---

29. See Wolfgang Vondey's *Beyond Pentecostalism: The Crisis of Global Christianity and the Renewal of the Theological Agenda* (Grand Rapids: Wm. B. Eerdmans Publishing Co., 2010), esp. 34-40, 71-77.
30. Ibid., 39.
31. Ibid., 71.
32. The expression is Rickie Moore's, cited in ibid., 71.
33. Ibid., 76-77.

law. God's law is, after all, the ultimate (pre)script: "Do this, and you will live" (Luke 10:28; cf. Lev. 18:5). But it is not enough.

The Bible as the transcript and prescript of the theodrama may be a necessary condition of right performance, but it is not a sufficient condition. The theatrical model views the Holy Spirit not only as the *director* but also as the *enabler* of the obedience of faith and the *prompter* who incites the players toward wisdom and holiness. The Spirit is also the *giver* of life, and this is the crucial point. For a script is lifeless without a company of actors to perform it. The church, a company that performs parables of the kingdom of God, is the creation of the Holy Spirit. The Spirit not only dresses the players (in Christ's righteousness) but also unites them to Christ. It is no slight to the Spirit to acknowledge his twofold ministry of the Word. It is the Holy Spirit who "spoke by the prophets," inspiring the Scriptures in the first place. Second, in providing illumination, the Spirit does not simply give glosses on the biblical text (as if Scripture were the problem). Rather, the Spirit brings about understanding by reviving our very being, renewing our minds, and reordering the desires of our hearts. Christian performance is anything but Pelagian, as Paul declares: "I can do all things through him who strengthens me" (Phil. 4:13).

6. *"Drama is a term less appropriate than story or narrative."*

"Story" we know, and "narrative" we know, but who, "Drama," are you? Why make things more complicated when we already have serviceable terms, especially if these terms do a better job of representing theology's subject matter? To respond to this objection, we need to draw a few more distinctions and connections.

The "narrative" turn in philosophy and theology is well documented.[34] Paul Ricoeur is representative of philosophers who have come to appreciate the singular power of narrative to articulate human action, identity, historicity, and especially temporality.[35] Theologians too, since the 1980s, have focused their attention on the way in which biblical narrative depicts the identities of God and Jesus Christ and shapes Christian identity. The power of narrative derives largely from the power of story.

A story is a sequence of events with a beginning, middle, and end. The plot is what accounts for relationships between these events, the unifying pattern that holds them together.[36] Stories are much more than rhetorical devices that give color to what we say. Rather, they are the means by which most of us explain and explore our everyday reality. As such, they are essential to the toolbox that is our

---

34. See Stanley Hauerwas and L. Gregory Jones, eds., *Why Narrative? Readings in Narrative Theology* (Grand Rapids: Wm. B. Eerdmans Publishing Co., 1989); and Kevin J. Vanhoozer, *Biblical Narrative in the Philosophy of Paul Ricoeur: An Essay in Hermeneutics and Theology* (Cambridge: Cambridge University Press, 1990).

35. Paul Ricoeur, *Time and Narrative*, 3 vols. (Chicago: University of Chicago Press, 1984.

36. See the definition in Peter Brooks's seminal work, *Reading for the Plot: Design and Intention in Narrative* (Cambridge, MA: Harvard University Press, 1984): "Plot is the principle of interconnectedness and intention which we cannot do without in moving through the discrete elements—incidents, episodes, actions—of a narrative" (5).

interpretive framework or worldview, "the grid through which humans perceive reality."[37] Humans are storytelling creatures;[38] stories are ways of making sense of either bits or the whole of reality. When people disagree about things, it is often because they perceive things through different story-spectacles. (I am assuming that stories can be *true* as well as fictional, that some story-spectacles may enable us to view the world *as it is*).

We can clarify matters considerably by distinguishing "story" as an object of discourse (*what is told*) from "narrative" and "drama" as modes of discourse (*how one presents the story*).[39] The same basic sequence of events (e.g., boy meets and marries girl) can be told or narrated in different ways (such as comedy, romance, even tragedy if it is the wrong girl). The story is the raw material on which discourse sets to work.

Though both narratives and dramas share a common story shape, they represent stories differently. Narratives use narrators and typically recount their stories in the third person (he, she, they) and thus can be kept at arm's length. Dramas, by way of contrast, *show* rather than *tell* and are typically enacted in the first person and second person, the language of personal interaction (e.g., "You shall be holy, for I am holy" [1 Pet. 1:16; cf. Lev. 19:2]). And this is perhaps the most important difference, the element that makes drama more suitable than narrative to serve as handmaid to theology: though stories can entrance us and invite us into their worlds, dramas insert us into the action and demand that we say or do something.[40] When we enter the biblical story, we are entering into real history—the only history there is, the history of God's outreach to the world. Drama is *story made flesh*. The point is not so much that drama is the most appropriate literary analogue but rather that history is itself dramatic. The word of God has entered into human history and is even now awaiting our response.

---

37. N. T. Wright, *The New Testament and the People of God*, 38.

38. See Jonathan Gottschall, *The Storytelling Animal: How Stories Make Us Human* (New York: Houghton Mifflin Harcourt, 2012).

39. I am adopting and adapting this distinction from Seymour Chatman, *Story and Discourse: Narrative Structure in Fiction and Film* (Ithaca, NY: Cornell University Press, 1980).

40. See my "Once More into the Borderlands: The Way of Wisdom in Philosophy and Theology after the 'Turn to Drama,'" in *Transcending Boundaries in Philosophy and Theology: Reason, Meaning, and Experience*, ed. K. Vanhoozer and Martin Warner (Aldershot, UK: Ashgate, 2007), 31–54, esp. 43–46, where I relate drama to practical wisdom, or *phronēsis*—the process of deliberating well in particular situations.

Selected Bibliography

Abbott, Roger Philip. *Sit on Our Hands, Or Stand on Our Feet? Exploring a Practical Theology of Major Incident Response for the Evangelical Catholic Christian Community in the UK*. Eugene, OR: Wipf & Stock, 2013.

Ames, William. *The Marrow of Theology*. Latin, 1656. ET repr., Grand Rapids: Baker, 1968.

Augustine. *City of God against the Pagans*. Translated by R. W. Dyson. Cambridge: Cambridge University Press, 1998.

———. *Confessions*. Translated by Henry Chadwick. Oxford: Oxford University Press, 1998.

———. *On Christian Teaching*. Translated by. R. P. H. Green. Oxford: Oxford University Press, 1997.

Ayres, Lewis. *Nicaea and Its Legacy: An Approach to Fourth-Century Trinitarian Theology*. Oxford: Oxford University Press, 2004.

Badcock, Gary. *The House Where God Lives: The Doctrine of the Church*. Grand Rapids: Wm. B. Eerdmans Publishing Co., 2009.

Balthasar, Hans Urs von. *Theo-drama: Theological Dramatic Theory*. Vol. 1, *Prolegomena*. San Francisco: Ignatius Press, 1988.

———. *Theo-drama: Theological Dramatic Theory*. Vol. 2, *Dramatis Personae: Man in God*. San Francisco: Ignatius Press, 1990.

———. *Theo-drama: Theological Dramatic Theory*. Vol. 3, *Dramatis Personae: Persons in Christ*. San Francisco: Ignatius Press, 1992.

Barish, Jonas A. *The Antitheatrical Prejudice*. Berkeley: University of California Press, 1981.
Barth, Karl. *Church Dogmatics*, I/1. Translated by Geoffrey Bromiley. 2nd ed. Edinburgh: T&T Clark, 1975.
———. *Church Dogmatics*, II/1. Translated by Geoffrey Bromiley. Edinburgh: T&T Clark, 1957.
———. *Church Dogmatics*, III/3. Translated by Geoffrey Bromiley. Edinburgh: T&T Clark, 1961.
———. *Dogmatics in Outline*. London: SCM Press, 1949.
Bartholomew, Craig G. *Where Mortals Dwell: A Christian View of Place for Today*. Grand Rapids: Baker Academic, 2011.
Bartholomew, Craig G., and Michael W. Goheen. *The Drama of Scripture: Finding Our Place in the Biblical Story*. Grand Rapids: Baker Academic, 2004.
Batey, R. A. "Jesus and the Theatre." *New Testament Studies* 30 (1984): 563–74.
Bavinck, Herman. *Reformed Dogmatics*. 4 vols. Grand Rapids: Baker Academic, 2003–8.
Beale, Gregory K. *A New Testament Biblical Theology: The Unfolding of the Old Testament in the New*. Grand Rapids: Baker Academic, 2011.
———. *The Temple and the Church's Mission: A Biblical Theology of the Dwelling Place of God*. Downers Grove, IL: InterVarsity Press, 2004.
Beckerman, Bernard. *Dynamics of Drama: Theory and Method of Analysis*. New York: Alfred A. Knopf, 1970.
Billings, J. Todd. *Union with Christ: Reframing Theology and Ministry for the Church*. Grand Rapids: Baker Academic, 2011.
Bloom, Anthony. *Beginning to Pray*. New York: Paulist Press, 1970.
Bonhoeffer, Dietrich. *The Cost of Discipleship*. Translated by R. H. Fuller et al. New York: Touchstone, 1995.
———. *Ethics*. Vol. 6 of *Dietrich Bonhoeffer Works*. Minneapolis: Augsburg-Fortress, 2005.
———. *Life Together*. Vol. 5 of *Dietrich Bonhoeffer Works*. Minneapolis: Fortress, 2005.
———. *Sanctorum Communio: A Theological Study of the Sociology of the Church*. Translated by Reinhard Krauss and Nancy Lukens. Vol. 1 of *Dietrich Bonhoeffer Works*. Minneapolis: Fortress Press, 1996.
Borg, Marcus J. *Speaking Christian: Why Christian Words Have Lost Their Meaning and Power—and How They Can Be Restored*. New York: HarperOne, 2011.
Bouchard, Larry. *Theater and Integrity: Emptying Selves in Drama, Ethics, and Religion*. Evanston, IL: Northwestern University Press, 2011.
Boulton, Matthew Myer. *Life in God: John Calvin, Practical Formation, and the Future of Protestant Theology*. Grand Rapids: Wm. B. Eerdmans Publishing Co., 2011.
Brannon, M. Jeff. *The Heavenlies in Ephesians: A Lexical, Exegetical, and Conceptual Analysis*. London and New York: T&T Clark International, 2012.
Briggs, Richard S. *Words in Action: Speech Act Theory and Biblical Interpretation: Toward a Hermeneutic of Self-Involvement*. Edinburgh: T & T Clark, 2001.
Brook, Peter. *The Empty Space*. New York: Atheneum, 1968.
Burger, Hans. *Being in Christ: A Biblical and Systematic Investigation in a Reformed Perspective*. Eugene, OR: Wipf & Stock, 2009.
Calvin, John. *Commentary on a Harmony of the Evangelists*. Edinburgh: Calvin Translation Society, 1866.
———. *Institutes of the Christian Religion*. Edited by John T. McNeill. Translated by Ford Lewis Battles. Philadelphia: Westminster Press, 1960.
Campbell, Constantine R. *Paul and Union with Christ: An Exegetical and Theological Study*. Grand Rapids: Zondervan, 2010.

Clarke, W. Norris. *Explorations in Metaphysics: Being—God—Person.* Notre Dame, IN: University of Notre Dame Press, 1994.
Clowney, Edmund P. *Preaching Christ in All of Scripture.* Wheaton, IL: Crossway, 2003.
Cox, Harvey. *The Future of Faith.* New York: HarperCollins 2009.
Cresswell, Tim. *Place: A Short Introduction.* Oxford: Blackwell, 2004.
Davidson, Richard M. "The Divine Covenant Lawsuit Motif in Canonical Perspective." *Journal of the Adventist Theological Society* 21 (2010): 45–84.
Davis, John Jefferson. *Worship and the Reality of God: An Evangelical Theology of Real Presence.* Downers Grove, IL: InterVarsity Press, 2010.
Dean, Kenda Creasy. *Almost Christian: What the Faith of Our Teenagers Is Telling the American Church.* New York: Oxford University Press, 2010.
Dox, Donnalee. *The Idea of the Theater in Latin Christian Thought: Augustine to the Fourteenth Century.* Ann Arbor: University of Michigan Press, 2004.
DuBay, Thomas. *Authenticity: A Biblical Theology of Discernment.* San Francisco: Ignatius Press, 1997.
Ebeling, Gerhard. *The Word of God and Tradition: Historical Studies Interpreting the Divisions of Christianity.* Philadelphia: Fortress Press, 1968.
Edmonds, David, and John Eidinow. *Wittgenstein's Poker: The Story of a Ten-Minute Argument between Two Great Philosophers.* New York: HarperCollins, 2001.
Farrow, Douglas. *Ascension and Ecclesia: On the Significance of the Doctrine of the Ascension.* Edinburgh: T&T Clark, 1999.
———. *Ascension Theology.* London and New York: T&T Clark, 2011.
Ford, David F. *The Future of Christian Theology.* Oxford: Wiley-Blackwell, 2011.
Fulkerson, Mary McClintock. *Places of Redemption: Theology for a Worldly Church.* Oxford: Oxford University Press, 2007.
Gentry, Peter J., and Stephen J. Wellum. *Kingdom through Covenant: A Biblical-Theological Understanding of the Covenants.* Wheaton, IL: Crossway, 2012.
Goffman, Erving. *The Presentation of Self in Everyday Life.* New York: Doubleday, 1959.
Goheen, Michael W. "'As the Father has sent me, I am sending you': Lesslie Newbigin's Missionary Ecclesiology." *International Review of Mission* 91 (2002): 345–69.
Gombis, Timothy. *The Drama of Ephesians: Participating in the Triumph of God.* Downers Grove, IL: InterVarsity Press, 2010.
———. *Paul: A Guide for the Perplexed.* London: T&T Clark International, 2010.
Gundry, Robert H. *The Old Is Better: New Testament Essays in Support of Traditional Interpretations.* Tübingen: Mohr Siebeck, 2005.
Gurtner, Daniel. *The Torn Veil: Matthew's Exposition of the Death of Jesus.* Cambridge: Cambridge University Press, 2007.
Hahn, Scott. *Kinship through Covenant: A Canonical Approach to the Fulfillment of God's Saving Promises.* New Haven: Yale University Press, 2009.
Harink, Douglas. *1 and 2 Peter.* Brazos Theological Commentary on the Bible. Grand Rapids: Brazos Press, 2009.
Hays, Richard B. *The Moral Vision of the New Testament: A Contemporary Introduction to New Testament Ethics.* San Francisco: HarperCollins, 1996.
Heide, Gale. *System and Story: Narrative Critique and Construction in Theology.* Eugene, OR: Pickwick Publications, 2009.
Heppe, Heinrich. *Reformed Dogmatics.* Grand Rapids: Baker, 1978.
Herdt, Jennifer. *Putting on Virtue: The Legacy of the Splendid Vices.* Chicago: University of Chicago Press, 2008.
Holmes, Christopher R. J. *Ethics in the Presence of Christ.* London and New York: T&T Clark International, 2012.
Hood, Jason B. *Imitating God in Christ: Recapturing a Biblical Pattern.* Downers Grove, IL: InterVarsity Press, 2013.

Hunsberger, George R., and Craig Van Gelder, eds. *The Church between Gospel and Culture: The Emerging Mission in North America.* Grand Rapids: Wm. B. Eerdmans Publishing Co., 1996.

Hunter, James Davison. *To Change the World: The Irony, Tragedy, and Possibility of Christianity in the Late Modern World.* Oxford: Oxford University Press, 2010.

Izzo, Gary. *The Art of Play: The New Genre of Interactive Theatre.* Portsmouth, NH: Heinemann, 1997.

Jacobsen, Eric. *The Space Between: A Christian Engagement with the Built Environment.* Grand Rapids: Baker Academic, 2012.

Jensen, Michael P. *Martyrdom and Identity: The Self on Trial.* London: T&T Clark, 2010.

Johnson, Marcus Peter. *One with Christ: An Evangelical Theology of Salvation.* Wheaton, IL: Crossway, 2013.

Johnstone, Keith. *Impro: Improvisation and the Theatre.* 1981. New York: Routledge, 1989.

Kierkegaard, Søren. *Purity of Heart Is to Will One Thing.* San Francisco: HarperOne, 1956.

Klink, Edward W., III, ed. *The Audience of the Gospels: Further Conversation about the Origin and Function of the Gospels in Early Christianity.* London: T&T Clark International, 2010.

Kuyper, Abraham. *Lectures on Calvinism.* Grand Rapids: Wm. B. Eerdmans Publishing Co., 1931.

Labberton, Mark. *The Dangerous Act of Loving Your Neighbor: Seeing Others through the Eyes of Jesus.* Downers Grove, IL: InterVarsity Press, 2010.

Lakoff, George, and Mark Johnson. *Metaphors We Live By.* 2nd ed. Chicago: University of Chicago Press, 2003.

Lauber, David, and Daniel Treier, eds. *Trinitarian Theology for the Church: Scripture, Community, Worship.* Downers Grove, IL: InterVarsity Press, 2009.

Lee, Sang Hyun. *The Philosophical Theology of Jonathan Edwards.* Princeton: Princeton University Press, 1988. Expanded ed., 2000.

Lewis, C. S. *God in the Dock: Essays on Theology and Ethics.* Grand Rapids: Wm. B. Eerdmans Publishing Co., 1970.

———. *Letters to Malcolm: Chiefly on Prayer.* New York: Harcourt, Brace & World, 1964.

———. *Mere Christianity.* New York: Touchstone, 1996.

Lincoln, Andrew C. *Truth on Trial: The Lawsuit Motif in the Fourth Gospel.* Peabody, MA: Hendrickson Publishers, 2000.

Long, D. Stephen. *Hebrews.* Louisville, KY: Westminster John Knox Press, 2011.

Madson, Patricia Ryan. *Improv Wisdom: Don't Prepare, Just Show Up.* New York: Bell Tower, 2005.

Manetsch, Scott M. *Calvin's Company of Pastors: Pastoral Care and the Emerging Reformed Church, 1536–1609.* Oxford: Oxford University Press, 2013.

Moran, Gabriel. *Showing How: The Act of Teaching.* Valley Forge, PA: Trinity Press International, 1997.

Muller, Richard A. "Toward the *Pactum Salutis*: Locating the Origins of a Concept." *Mid-America Journal of Theology* 18 (2007): 11–65.

Natanson, Maurice. "Jean Paul Sartre's Philosophy of Freedom." *Social Research* 19 (September 1952): 364–80.

Nussbaum, Martha C. *The Fragility of Goodness: Luck and Ethics in Greek Tragedy and Philosophy.* Rev. ed. Cambridge: Cambridge University Press, 2001.

———. *Love's Knowledge: Essays on Philosophy and Literature.* New York: Oxford University Press, 1990.

O'Brien, Peter. *The Letter to the Hebrews*. Grand Rapids: Wm. B. Eerdmans Publishing Co., 2010.
Peterson, Eugene H. *Eat This Book: A Conversation in the Art of Spiritual Reading*. Grand Rapids: Wm. B. Eerdmans Publishing Co., 2006.
Pine, B. Joseph, II, and James H. Gilmore. *Authenticity: What Consumers Really Want*. Boston: Harvard Business School, 2007.
———. *The Experience Economy: Work Is Theatre and Every Business a Stage*. Boston: Harvard Business School Press, 1999.
Pohl, Christian D. *Making Room: Recovering Hospitality as a Christian Tradition*. Grand Rapids: Wm. B. Eerdmans Publishing Co., 2009.
Ramm, Bernard. *Special Revelation and the Word of God: An Essay on the Contemporary Problem of Revelation*. Grand Rapids: Wm. B. Eerdmans Publishing Co., 1961.
Rauser, Randall. *Theology in Search of Foundations*. Oxford: Oxford University Press, 2009.
Rowe, C. Kavin. *World Upside Down: Reading Acts in the Greco-Roman Age*. Oxford: Oxford University Press, 2009.
Samra, James G. *Being Conformed to Christ in Community: A Study of Maturity, Maturation and the Local Church in the Undisputed Pauline Epistles*. London and New York: T&T Clark, 2006.
Sanders, Fred. *The Deep Things of God: How the Trinity Changes Everything*. Wheaton, IL: Crossway, 2010.
———. *The Image of the Immanent Trinity: Rahner's Rule and the Theological Interpretation of Scripture*. New York and Frankfurt: Peter Lang, 2005.
Sayers, Dorothy. *Creed or Chaos?* New York: Harcourt, Brace & Co., 1949.
Schweitzer, William M. *God Is a Communicative Being: Divine Communicativeness and Harmony in the Theology of Jonathan Edwards*. London: T&T Clark, 2012.
Smith, Christian. *Soul Searching: The Religious and Spiritual Lives of American Teenagers*. New York: Oxford University Press, 2005.
Spolin, Viola. *Improvisation for the Theatre*. 3rd ed. Evanston, IL: Northwestern University Press, 1999.
Stanislavski, Constantin. *An Actor Prepares*. New York: Routledge, 1964.
Steiner, George. *After Babel: Aspects of Language and Translation*. London and New York: Oxford University Press, 1975.
Stewart, James S. *A Man in Christ: The Vital Elements of St. Paul's Religion*. Grand Rapids: Baker, 1975.
Swain, Scott R. *Trinity, Revelation, and Reading: A Theological Introduction to the Bible and Its Interpretation*. London: T&T Clark, 2011.
Taylor, Charles. *A Secular Age*. Cambridge, MA: Belknap Press of Harvard University Press, 2007.
Thiselton, Anthony C. *The First Epistle to the Corinthians: A Commentary on the Greek Text*. Grand Rapids: Wm. B. Eerdmans Publishing Co., 2000.
———. *The Hermeneutics of Doctrine*. Grand Rapids: Wm. B. Eerdmans Publishing Co., 2007.
Tilley, Terrence W. *The Disciples' Jesus: Christology as Reconciling Practice*. Maryknoll, NY: Orbis Books, 2008.
Trueman, Carl R. *The Creedal Imperative*. Wheaton, IL: Crossway, 2012.
Turner, Victor. *Drama, Fields, and Metaphors: Symbolic Action in Human Society*. Ithaca, NY: Cornell University Press, 1975.
Vander Lugt, Wesley. *Living Theodrama: Reimagining Theological Ethics*. Farnham, Surrey, UK: Ashgate, 2014.

Vanhoozer, Kevin J. "At Play in the Theodrama of the Lord: The Triune God of the Gospel." In *Theatrical Theology: Explorations in Performing the Faith*, edited by Trevor Hart and Wesley Vander Lugt. Eugene, OR: Cascade, 2014.

———. *The Drama of Doctrine: A Canonical-Linguistic Approach to Christian Theology*. Louisville, KY: Westminster John Knox Press, 2005.

———. "Once More into the Borderlands: The Way of Wisdom in Philosophy and Theology after the 'Turn to Drama.'" In *Transcending Boundaries in Philosophy and Theology: Reason, Meaning, and Experience*, edited by Kevin J. Vanhoozer and Martin Warner, 31–54. Aldershot, UK: Ashgate, 2007.

———. *Remythologizing Theology: Divine Action, Passion, and Authorship*. Cambridge: Cambridge University Press, 2010.

———. "The Voice and the Actor: A Dramatic Proposal about the Ministry and Minstrelsy of Theology." In *Evangelical Futures: A Conversation on Theological Method*, edited by John G. Stackhouse, 61–106. Grand Rapids: Baker Books, 2000.

Volf, Miroslav. *A Public Faith: How Followers of Christ Should Serve the Common Good*. Grand Rapids: Brazos Press, 2011.

Vondey, Wolfgang. *Beyond Pentecostalism: The Crisis of Global Christianity and the Renewal of the Theological Agenda*. Grand Rapids: Wm. B. Eerdmans Publishing Co., 2010.

Walls, Andrew F. "The Cost of Discipleship: The Witness of the African Church." *Word & World* 25, no. 4 (2005): 433–43.

———. *The Cross-Cultural Process in Christian History*. Maryknoll, NY: Orbis Books; Edinburgh: T&T Clark, 2002.

———. *The Missionary Movement in Christian History: Studies in the Transmission of the Faith*. Maryknoll, NY: Orbis Books; Edinburgh: T&T Clark, 1996.

Walls, Andrew F. and Cathy Ross, eds. *Mission in the Twenty-First Century: Exploring the Five Marks of Global Mission*. London: Darton, Longman & Todd, 2008.

Webster, John. "God's Perfect Life." In *God's Life in Trinity*, edited by Miroslav Volf and Michael Welker. Minneapolis: Fortress Press, 2006, 143–52.

———. "'It Was the Will of the Lord to Bruise Him': Soteriology and the Doctrine of God." In *God of Salvation: Soteriology in Theological Perspective*, edited by Ivor J. Davidson and Murray A. Rae, 15–34. Farnham, UK: Ashgate, 2011.

———. "'Where Christ Is': Christology and Ethics." In *Christology and Ethics*, edited by F. LeRon Shults and Brent Waters. Grand Rapids: Wm. B. Eerdmans Publishing Co., 2010, 32–55.

———. *Word and Church: Essays in Christian Dogmatics*. Edinburgh: T&T Clark, 2001.

Welborn, L. L. *Paul, the Fool of Christ: A Study of 1 Corinthians 1–4 in the Comic-Philosophical Tradition*. JSNT Supplement Series 293. London and New York: T&T Clark International, 2005.

Wells, Samuel. *Improvisation: The Drama of Christian Ethics*. Grand Rapids: Brazos Press, 2004.

Wenger, Etienne. *Communities of Practice: Learning, Meaning, and Identity*. Cambridge: Cambridge University Press, 1998.

Wenkel, David H. "The Most Simple and Comprehensive Script for the Theo-drama of Scripture: Three Acts or Four?" *Scottish Bulletin of Evangelical Theology* 30 (2012): 78–90.

Wilken, Robert Louis. *The Spirit of Early Christian Thought: Seeking the Face of God*. New Haven: Yale University Press, 2003.

Willard, Dallas. *The Great Omission: Rediscovering Jesus' Essential Teachings on Discipleship*. San Francisco: HarperCollins, 2006.

Williams, A. N. *The Architecture of Theology: Structure, System, and Ratio*. Oxford: Oxford University Press, 2011.
Williams, Rowan. *Tokens of Trust: An Introduction to Christian Belief*. Louisville, KY: Westminster John Knox Press, 2007.
Williamson, Paul R. *Sealed with an Oath: Covenant in God's Unfolding Purpose*. Downers Grove, IL: InterVarsity Press, 2007.
Wittgenstein, Ludwig. *Philosophical Investigations*. Translated by G. E. M. Anscombe. 3rd ed. Oxford: Blackwell, 1958.
Wolfe, Alan. *The Transformation of American Religion: How We Actually Live Our Faith*. New York: Free Press, 2003.
Wright, N. T. *How God Became King: The Forgotten Story of the Gospels*. New York: HarperOne, 2012.
———. *The New Testament and the People of God*. Vol. 1 of *Christian Origins and the Question of God*. Minneapolis: Fortress Press, 1992.
———. *Surprised by Hope: Rethinking Heaven, the Resurrection, and the Mission of the Church*. New York: HarperCollins, 2008.

Index of Scripture References

OLD TESTAMENT

Genesis

1:2	27, 52, 174
1:3	63
1:9	174
1:17	91
1:20	91
1:26–28	100
1:27	154
2:16–17	84
2:24	154
3:1	87
3:4	87
3:5	87
3:9	84
3:15	42, 86, 98
12:2–3	85, 103
12:2	193
14:13	101
15:7	175
17:6–8	86
22:1–2	105
22:1	84
28:11–17	174
31:44	101
46:2	84
50:20	226

Exodus

3:4–6	174
3:4	84
3:7–8	92
3:14	67, 84
5:22	219
6:7	103
12:26–27	160
12:36	242
13:5	174
16	156
16:4	91
19:5	92
19:5–6	85
19:6	7, 92
20:2	92, 248
20:3	103
24:7	104, 245
24:11	160
34:5–7	221
34:6–7	249
34:6	86

Leviticus

18:5	251
19:2	252

Deuteronomy

4:1–40	103
4:26	103–4
7:6	245
7:18	95
8:2	95
10:19	158
18:15–16	108

Deuteronomy (continued)
20:1	92
29:21	104
30:19	103–4
31:28	103–4
32	105
32:47	175
34:10–11	108

Joshua
9:6	101
24:1–18	95

Judges
2:11	245
2:17	104
17:6	59
21:25	59

1 Samuel
3:4	127
3:6	84
8:5	161
8:20	55, 161
14:41	219
20:14–17	101

2 Samuel
7:8–16	100
7:12–14	86

1 Kings
11:16	245
15:19	101
18	106

2 Kings
1:12	91
13:11	245
23:21	245

Ezra
1:2	176

Job
23:1–7	105
38:11	244
40:1–9	105

Psalms
9:1	95
10:1	219
14:2	91
19:1	66
34:8	222
40:7	84
51:4	157
78	95
88:14	219
89:3–4	103
93:1	100
96:4–10	100
106	95
107:21–22	233
110	176, 212
110:1	211
110:4	79, 108
111:10	225
119	63
119:105	63
119:130	64, 132
135:13–14	139

Proverbs
1:7	225
4:23	46

Isaiah
1:2	104
6:8	84
40–55	106–7
43:10	109
51:22	91
53:5	5
53:10–12	79
53:10	79
60:2	27
61:1–2	245
63:17	219
65:17	5
66:22	5

Jeremiah
3:8	104
11:4	103
19	45
31:31–34	162
31:31–33	101
31:32	154
31:33	5, 134
34:8–10	101

Ezekiel
4	45
20	95
33:30–33	19
36:26	5
36:28	103
37	211

Daniel
4:31	91
7:13–14	100

Hosea
1:2	154
3:1	154
4–5	105
4:1	104
14:4	154

Amos
2:6–8	105
3:9–10	105

Micah
6:1–8	105
6:8	197, 237

Habakkuk
1:2	219

Zechariah
3:1	103

Malachi
2:14	101

NEW TESTAMENT

Matthew
3:11	142
3:15	141
3:17	76, 91, 248
4:1–2	107
5:13–16	179
5:14	65
5:16	18
5:37	186
5:38	158
6:1	18
6:5	117
6:9	124
6:10	2, 6, 138
6:14–15	157
7:22–23	172
7:23	104
7:24	19
7:26	19
12:28	92
12:30	42, 131
12:42	108
16:15	105
17:1–7	64
17:1–5	76

Index of Scripture References

17:2	222	3:38	107	1:9	64
17:5	222	4:4	88, 108	1:10	108
18:20	175–76, 237	4:8	88	1:14	42, 68, 86, 91, 198
18:21–22	157	4:10	108	1:15	107
21:19	108	4:12	88, 108	1:18	38
22:42	29	4:16–22	132	1:27	107
23:27–28	117	4:20	245	1:29	107, 188, 193
24:5	59	4:21	245	1:32–34	107
25:40	159	4:41	111	2:13–22	45
26:6–13	43	7:19	92	3:8	189
26:10	43	7:21–22	92	3:13	91
26:13	44	7:22	226	3:14–15	209
26:39	91	7:36–50	43, 158	3:14	76, 79
26:42	154	8:30	87	3:16	77
26:64	211	9:10–17	158	3:21	25, 40, 151
27:51	210	9:20	105	3:31–35	107
28:5–7	86	9:23	36, 125	4:10	39
28:6	247	9:28–36	76	4:19	107
28:19	142, 166	9:31	26, 92	4:23	235
28:20	3, 143	9:32	222	4:24	249
		10:28	251	4:29	107
Mark		10:30–37	195	5:18	106
1:9–11	141	10:37	44, 123	5:19–20	73
1:11	76	10:38–42	158	5:26	77
3:21	186	11:20	92	5:33	107
4:15	87	11:23	131	5:37	107
5:9	87	14:13	158	5:45–46	107
7:6	117	17:20	45	6:31–35	91
8:29	105	17:21	45	6:38–40	79
8:34	193	19:1–10	158	6:38	78
9:2–8	76	22:7–23	158	6:46	106
10:8–9	154	22:19	162, 165	6:56	178
12:29–31	183	22:20	101	6:63	77
12:29	45	22:28	88	8:12	64
12:30	1	22:28–30	79	8:28	76, 79
13:22	98	22:28–29	109	8:31	44
14:3–9	43	22:42	80, 135, 226	8:32	39
14:6	123	23:34	226	8:44	87–88
14:9	44	23:45	210	8:45	106
14:25	162	24:4–7	86	9	65
14:38	230	24:13–27	132	9:5	64–65
14:40	230	24:18	111	9:17	107
14:62	208	24:27	90, 132	9:24–26	107
15:38	210	24:30	158	10:17–18	94
16:15	42, 232	24:48	109	10:18	78–79
		24:34	92	10:30	190
Luke		24:51	93	11:41	76
1:3–4	31			12:1–8	43
1:32–33	103	**John**		12:5	43
1:38	127, 154, 193	1:1	38, 75	12:27–28	75
2:10–11	86	1:5	27	12:28	76
2:14	236	1:6	107	12:32–33	76, 79
3:22	76	1:7	107		

John (*continued*)

Ref	Page
12:32	209
12:33	209
12:36	64
12:49	79
13:2	88
14:1	125
14:2	178
14:6	106, 231
14:7	106
14:10	106
14:26	135
14:28	190
15:4–7	178
15:4	44
15:7	178
15:8	237
15:9	44
15:10	178
15:13	39
15:19	179
15:23	106
15:26	135
16:7	93
16:13	135, 149
16:14	76
17:1–4	30
17:1	76
17:4	79
17:5	76
17:11	39
17:14	179
17:18	169
17:21	233
17:24	30, 79
18:14	107
18:30	106
18:36	180
18:37	106
18:38	40
19:5	40
19:6	106
19:7	106
19:12	106
19:15	106
19:34	210
20:31	35, 108
21:24	108
21:25	247

Acts

Ref	Page
1:8	70
1:10–11	86
1:11	42, 93
2	93
2:14–36	95
2:23	5, 97
2:24	5
2:33	5
2:37	141
2:38	5, 141, 193
2:41	142
2:42	143, 180
2:44	157
3:15	77, 231, 247
3:22	108
5:3	88
5:19	86
6:5	208
6:7	208
6:10	208
6:11–14	208
6:12–15	208
6:15	222
7	247
7:2–53	95, 208
7:48	210
7:51–52	208
7:55–58	214
7:55	208
7:56	208–10, 222
7:59	226
7:60	226
8:26	86
8:38	142
9:2	142
9:4	84
9:10	84
10	119
10:22	86
11:26	113
13:49	135
15	155
16:9	86
17:6–7	188
17:6	6, 95
17:7	6
17:24	150
18:12–23	106
18:24–27	107
18:28–19:16	107
19:20	135
22:20	110
20:27	102

Romans

Ref	Page
1:1–6	132
1:3	91
1:18	91
1:25	87
3:19–28	122
3:30	249
4:17	51, 116
5:3–4	221
5:3	217
5:4	220
5:8	39
5:12–6:8	121
5:12–21	108
6:3–4	128
6:3	142
6:10	234
6:22	148
8:5	124
8:13	124
8:20–22	80
8:28	45, 193, 219
8:29	135, 137
8:34	212
8:37	215
8:39	222
9:17	248
11:36	132
12:1	234
12:2	135, 179
12:12	225
13:12	121
13:14	120–21, 137
15:4	232
15:7	159
15:25–32	156
15:25	156
15:31	156
16:4	172

1 Corinthians

Ref	Page
1:17	187
1:25	187
2:2	17
2:16	188, 221
3:16–17	210
4:9	23, 28, 180
4:10	187
4:13	124
4:16	23, 123–24
4:17	189
5:7	160
6:20	30
9:22	116
9:24	25

10–11	160	5:17	120, 128, 143, 232	1:20–21	108
10:6–11	246	5:18	151	1:20	176, 212
10:11	200, 224, 232	5:19	40, 95, 149, 157	1:21	176
10:16	161, 164	5:20	182, 198	2:6	176, 213, 216
10:17	167	6:16	150	2:12–13	150
10:31	234	6:18	103	2:14–20	231
11:1	124	8–9	156	2:14–15	155
11:2	70, 189	8:3–4	156	2:14	7, 34–35, 150
11:18–19	161	8:6–7	156	2:15	151, 216
11:20	161	8:9	156	2:19	150, 158
11:21	161	8:14	156	2:21–22	216
11:25	101, 162	8:20	156	2:21	150, 210
11:26	162	9:8	157	3:1–14	216
11:27	161	9:12–13	156	3:9	59, 74, 78, 140
11:28–29	161	9:12	156	3:10	140, 204
11:29	163–65	10:4–5	135, 178	3:11	78
11:32	161	11:3	89	4:4–5	148
12:3	134	11:13	98	4:5	198
12:13	117	11:14	87	4:11	146
12:27	235	13:14	235	4:13	114, 204, 231
13:4–7	221			4:15–16	33
13:12	116, 203	**Galatians**		4:15	206, 216
15:3	1, 189	1:6–7	132	4:21	216
15:3–5	95	1:22	172	4:22	121
15:10	135	2:9–10	156	4:24	121
15:19	29	2:11–14	161	4:32	157
15:24	100	2:11	119, 161	5:1	123
15:26	156	2:12	119	5:8	64
15:27	156	2:13	119	5:15	205
15:28	79, 95, 178, 223	2:14	11, 119, 165	5:19	227
15:31	36, 125	2:16	122	5:23	149
15:49	86, 128	2:19–20	126	5:25–33	154
15:53–54	121	2:20	128	5:25	141
15:54	127	3:10	122	5:28	156
15:55	94	3:27	121, 136–37	5:31–32	233
16:1–4	156	3:28	117, 150	5:32	155
16:1	172	4:9	116	6:11	121, 135
16:3	156	5:23	182	6:14	121
				6:17–18	135
2 Corinthians		**Ephesians**		6:19	74
1:17	186	1	235	6:20	198
1:20	181	1:3	165, 176		
3:2	36	1:4	30, 77, 129, 194	**Philippians**	
3:6	127, 134	1:4–5	51	1:21	166
3:16	236	1:5	78	2:3	124
3:17	191	1:9–10	45, 74	2:5–8	94, 124
4:4	85, 129	1:10	59	2:5	221
4:6	64	1:12	52, 70, 236	2:6–7	43, 79, 95
4:10	129	1:14	236	2:6	190
4:13	229	1:17–21	209	2:7	79
4:16–17	224	1:18	134, 224	2:7–8	79
5:2	121	1:20–2:22	216	2:9–11	79, 214
5:17–19	112	1:20–22	79	2:10–11	95

Philippians (continued)

2:12–13	129
3:8	41
3:20	172, 177
3:21	127
4:4	224, 226
4:13	251

Colossians

1:13	126, 142, 172, 177
1:15	2, 129, 190
1:15–16	95
1:16–17	214
1:16	63, 70
1:18	149
1:25–27	9
2:12	142
2:15	7, 180, 209
2:19	149
3:1–4	129
3:1	138, 171, 178, 212
3:3	129
3:8	121
3:9	121
3:10	120–21
3:11	117
3:12–13	120
3:13	157
3:14	120
3:16	3, 227
3:17	119
4:2	230

1 Thessalonians

1:1	172
1:2–5a	130
1:5b	130
1:7–8	130
2:4	19
5:5	64
5:8	121
5:16	125
5:17	226

2 Thessalonians

1:8	40
2:9	88
2:9–10	88
2:10	111
2:15	70
3:7–9	123

1 Timothy

1:10	25
1:15	25
3:1	25
3:5	150
3:15	150
4:1	25, 88
4:9	25
6:20	5, 248

2 Timothy

1:13	25
1:14	5
2:11	25
3:15	204
3:16	246
4:2	248
4:3	25

Titus

1:9	25
2:1	25, 146
2:13	93
3:8	25

Philemon

6	17
14	195
16	159
17	159
20	196

Hebrews

1:1	4, 246
1:3	30, 38, 65, 190
1:5	190
1:13	212
2:7–9	86
3:3	108
3:6	150
3:12	98
4:15	86
5:10	108
5:14	191
6:19	211
6:20	108, 211
7:20–22	79
7:27	234
8:1–9:15	210
8:1	211
9:3	211
9:6–10	211
9:15	101
9:23–27	211
9:24	210–11
9:26	188
10:1	122
10:11	122
10:14	210
10:19–25	210
10:20	210–11
10:21	150
10:32–33	218
11:1–38	117
11:3	16
11:16	176
12:2	231
13:8	42
13:13	128
13:20	79
13:21	227

James

1:2	45, 193
1:4	220
1:13	105
1:22–24	19
1:25	19, 129
2:18	129
2:19	111
5:12	154
5:16	157

1 Peter

1:1	179
1:3	223
1:4	167, 223
1:5	224
1:6	223
1:12	140
1:16	129, 252
1:18–21	78
1:20	30, 194
1:22	40
2:5	150
2:9	7, 179
2:21	125, 218
2:22	86
3:14–15	224
3:15	47
3:22	212
4:13	218
4:17	40, 150

2 Peter

1:3	127
1:4	127
1:5–7	127–28
1:8–10	129
1:9	128

1:16	222	4:19	41	1:9	222
1:19	63–64	**2 John**		2:2–3	172
2:1	98	1	39	2:2	222
3:13	127, 178	2	44	2:4	172
		4	37, 39	2:5	172
1 John		7	41–42	3:10	222
1:1	70, 111	8	43	3:14	70, 217
1:2	207	9	44	5:5–6	109
1:3	151			6:10	110, 219
1:5	64, 249	**3 John**		12:9	87, 222
1:6	25, 40, 151	4	46	12:10	103
1:7	64	11	123	12:11	216
2:2	188			19	162
2:15	179	**Jude**		19:7	95
2:28	128	3	189	19:9	95
3:2	62			20:12	110
3:16	39	**Revelation**		21:1	99, 178
3:18	15	1:1	87	21:2–22:5	178
3:24	128	1:3	110	21:2	99
4:1	98	1:4	42	21:9	229
4:2–3	199	1:5–7	100	21:22	151
4:8	43, 67, 221, 249	1:5	109	22:7	110
		1:6	7		

Index of Subjects

Abbott, Rev. Roger, 196–97
act
    of play, 97
    of prayer, 229–30
action
    as essence of theater, 66–69
    as language of theater, 15, 66
    mimetic, 123
    propositional content of, 247
    as type of speaking, 15, 18
Ambrose, 144
Ames, William, xiii, 22, 33, 139, 141, 146, 234
analogia dramatis, 90
angels
    as supporting actors, 86
Anselm, xii, 15
antitheatrical prejudice, 239–40, 243
anxiety
    Augustinian, 122
    status, 186–87, 191–92
Apostles' Creed, 147–48, 151, 157, 212–13

Aquinas, Thomas. *See* Thomas Aquinas
Aristotle, 121, 133, 220
Athanasius
    as exemplar of faith speaking understanding, 190–91
attestation, 84
Augustine, xii 17, 57, 122, 133, 144, 155, 176, 182–83, 188, 207, 219, 241–43
authentic, authenticity
    age of, 61
    and being-in-Christ, 127
    crisis of, 10, 59–62, 69
    criteria for witness, 218
    defined, 60
    hypocrisy and, 117–19
    and identity, 115–18
    in theatrical performance, 69–70, 121

baptism, 10, 136, 177
    connection with teaching, 143–44

baptism (*continued*)
   as participation in Jesus' death and resurrection, 142–43
Barth, Karl, 83, 86–87, 133, 145, 213
Bartholomew, Craig, 97–98, 100
Bauckham, Richard, 36
Bavinck, Herman, 79
Beale, Greg, 99, 102
being
   as activity, 67
   authentic vs. inauthentic, 62, 69–70
   in Christ, 126–28, 176–78
   as communicative, 66–67
   creaturely, 67
   generic vs. personal, 38
   perfect, 38
   See also participation
being-toward-death, 62, 132, 223
being-toward-resurrection, 62, 71, 132, 219, 223
belief
   dispositional, 19, 66
Berry, Wendell, 41
Bible
   as divine address, 24
   relation to drama of redemption, 143, 244–46
   as stage lighting, 63–65
   See also Scripture
biblical authority, 2–3, 72, 200–1, 246, 248
biblical interpretation
   according to Augustine, 17, 183
   no alibi for, 36
   church life as, 24, 183–84
   and improvisation, 189
   inhabiting world of text, 246
   as participation in apostolic discourse, 35
biblical reasoning, 4
Biblical Theology Movement, 247
Bidermann, Jacob, 123
Bloom, Anthony, 225
Bonhoeffer, Dietrich, 19, 33, 46, 133, 137, 141, 151, 153, 157, 182
Borg, Marcus, 15–17
Bright, John, 100
Bristol Renaissance Faire, 184
Brook, Peter, 7, 46
Brueggemann, Walter, 106n76
Bunyan, John, 207

Calderon de la Barca, Pedro, 52
Calvin, John, xii, 17, 23, 28, 43–44, 63, 71, 127–28, 132–34, 139, 142–43, 145–46, 150, 152, 161, 163–65, 167, 204, 208, 242
canon
   as criterion of theodramatic correspondence, 202
   as rule of authenticity, 72
   sense, 205
catechesis, 134, 143–33, 146, 149–50, 205
catharsis, 220–21, 224
Chalcedon, Council of, 200–1, 203
   showcase for improvisatory wisdom, 201
character development
   discipleship as, 129–30, 147
   role of Holy Spirit in, 134–37
   preaching and, 131–34
   spiritual formation and, 135
Christ. *See* Jesus Christ
Christendom, 173, 176, 180, 182, 204
Christianity
   biblical, 20, 189
   creedal, 29
   intrinsically dramatic, 244
   early, 229
   essence of, 89
   nominal, 18
   theodramatic, 20, 189
Christology
   docetic, 199
   norm of theodramatic judgment, 199–202
   sets forth in speech *what is in Christ*, 90, 200
Chrysostom, John, 144, 159
church, 139–52, 154–67, 169–85
   "anonymous," 153
   as creature of the word, 166
   as body of Christ, 170, 175
   central ministry of, 181
   as company of the baptized, 184
   as company of grateful realists, 233
   current state of North American, 53–56
   defined, 141, 171, 175
   distinctness of, 153
   doctrine of, 150–51
   doing, 170, 178, 199, 216
   as domain of doctrine, 10, 46, 140
   on earth as in heaven, 216, 237
   as exhibit of the gospel, 140, 170, 234
   existence of as purpose of creation, 150
   and experience of Christ, 58
   fidelity as mark of, 154–55
   "fourth wall" in, 35
   generosity as mark of, 155–58
   God's encore performance, 236

hospitality as mark of, 158–59
as interactive theater, 9, 36, 169, 183
life of *ad extra* vs. *ad intra*, 140–41, 169
light of the world, 65
as living commentary, 2, 233
as living sacrifice, 235
local, xvi, 20, 169, 172–75, 215
mission of, 56, 169, 176, 178, 182–83, 185, 217
as parable of the kingdom, 7, 10, 173, 175, 178, 182, 185–86, 206, 215, 233
participates in Jesus' death and resurrection, 164
as "people of the book," 4
as place/people where Christ rules, 6–7, 182, 237
as place/people where God dwells, 150, 178, 236
as preview of coming attraction, 178
raison d'être of, 170, 232–33, 237
reciprocal relationship with doctrine, 5
role of catechism in, 144–45
as theater of gospel, xiv, 6, 20, 23, 37, 46, 58–59, 140, 149, 163, 171, 173, 175, 237
as theater of holy fools, 187
as theater of martyrdom, 220
as theater of reconciliation, 149–53, 216
as theater of wisdom of God, 204
as triune production, xiv, 140
vanguard of God's reign, 151
vocation of, 8, 17, 181–82, 232
witness to reality, 151, 197
and world, 35–36, 171, 173, 179–82, 184–85
church history
as history of biblical interpretation, 2
Cicero, 243
collection for Jerusalem saints, 155–56
communicative action
and covenantal relation, 84–85
communion
covenant blessing, 103
Father-Son, 75–76
of saints, 155–57, 164–65
and union with Christ, 132
community, 140
Christian, 153
godless, 152–53
See also church
confessing, 41–43
as inherently performative, 19

confessions. *See* creeds
contextualization
improvisation as, 198–99
covenant
aggravated assault on, 105
as content of divine communicative action, 84–85
defined, 101
lawsuit, 103–5
as material principle of drama of redemption, 74, 100–5
Cox, Harvey, 55–56, 61
creation
first act in theodrama, 96–97
new, 99, 214–16, 232
spoken into being, 68
stage of divine–human interaction, 68
as theater for communicative action, 66
as theater of God's righteousness, 74
creeds, 147–49
of godless congregations, 152–53
cries
as expression of human existence, 83
Crusaders, 182
culture
as location in the theater of the world, 203

Darwin, Charles, 230
Descartes, René, 115
Diderot, Denis
and concept of "fourth wall," 34
disciples
actors not spectators, 183
adverse effect of theater on, 240
and authenticity, 70, 157
acts out biblical scripts, 144
act out what is in Christ, 126–29, 136–38, 144, 157, 176, 188, 201, 215, 221, 230
church as company of, 139–43
definition, 20
endurance of, 222–23
hearts of, 224
identify with Christ, 142, 195
inhabit *eutopia*, 177–78
as improvisers of mind of Christ, 189–94, 201
imitate masters, 124
location in Christ of, 178–78
mandate of, 129, 132, 147, 188–89
paradigmatic reflex of, 154
as players in a subversive divine comedy, 95, 187–88, 216

disciples (*continued*)
   risk losing social status, 186–87
   sapiential imperative for, 205
   Stephen as model, 208, 214–15, 222, 225
   as story–dweller, 29
   vocation of, 114, 198, 219, 225
   walk in light, 64
   wardrobe of, 120–21
   wise, 205
   as witnesses, 109–10, 217
   word as bond of, 186
discipleship
   begins with baptism, 143
   as being biblical, 4
   challenge of, 3
   as character development, 130, 137, 147
   Christology and, xiv, 127
   confessing and, 42–43
   cost of, 19, 109, 181
   death and, 218
   distinctness of, 153
   and doctrine, 53
   drama of, 1, 153, 205
   everyday, 21
   formal criterion of, 72
   no geniuses in, 205
   goal of, 40, 148
   "Greats" curriculum as, xii–xiv
   hypocrisy and, 115–19
   as faithful improvisation, 191–99, 201
   martyrdom and, 71
   Pauline paradigm of, 124
   prayer as quintessential act of, 226
   as putting on Christ, 120–23, 136
   real work of, 129, 136
   as rehearsal, 140
   rejoicing and, 223–24
   secret to, 222
   as self-sacrificial offering, 235
   simul mimesis et authenticos, 138
   staying awake and, 230
   in theatrical model, 28–29, 177
   involves truth and love, 9–10, 33
Disney, Walt, 57
divine decree, 77–80
   dialogical, 78, 80
divine sovereignty
   and human freedom, 80
doctrine
   abiding in, 44–45
   of atonement, 199
   a bodily doing, 147, 231

   catharsis of, 221–22
   defined, 25, 230
   development of, 27, 202–3
   direction for greater understanding, 204
   direction for living to God, 216–17
   disappearance of, 54
   dose of reality, 231
   doxology and, 234, 236
   drama of, 19, 25–27, 183, 189, 231
   eclipse of, 53–56
   and ethics, 137
   false picture of, 5, 181
   fatigue, 59
   as grammar of faith, 17
   Great Curriculum of, 230, 232
   grows disciples, 5, 9, 110, 119
   inevitability of, 53, 71
   ingredient in improvisatory discipleship, 191–94, 197
   ministers understanding of theodrama, 235
   pastoral purpose of, 25, 170, 189, 249
   as performance pedagogy, 45
   performed daily, 235
   sacrificial offering of, 234
   serves church, 233
   sets forth what is "in Christ," 70–71, 114, 170, 181, 186, 224–25, 230–31
   "sound," 25–26, 146
   as "spectacles of understanding," 26
   as theatrical direction, 1, 8, 20–21, 26, 143, 146–47, 150, 160–61, 231
   transformative power of, 180
   uniqueness of Christian, 9
drama
   behind, of, and in front of doctrine, 27
   climax of, 209
   defined, 22–23, 27
   contrasted with narrative, 22, 251–52
   story made flesh, 252
   See also theater; drama of redemption
drama of redemption, 20, 27–29, 136
   as all–encompassing, 36–37
   baptism as initiation into, 142
   climax of, 207, 209–10, 213–14
   conflict in, 10–11, 37, 88, 98, 214–16
   cosmic scope of, 210–11, 222
   courtroom setting of, 103–8
   as divine comedy, 94–95
   ending of, 207
   as eucatastrophic, 95
   as improvisatory, 193
   and Lord's Supper, 160–66

material principle of, 74–82
missional, 82, 9–94
offers in, 193
plot of, 96–108
number of acts in, 95–98
small-scale summary scenes of, 235
summarized, 26, 102–8
as Trinitarian, 74–82, 89–94
See also theodrama
dramatic irony
in Fourth Gospel, 108
dramaturgy, 146–47

ecclesiology. *See* church
Eden Alternative, 60
Edwards, Jonathan, 69, 81
Ehrenhalt, Alan, 61
embodiment
as condition for communicative action, 170
empire
Roman, 186, 204
popular culture as, 186
endurance, 222
"Ephesian Moment," 204
Erasmus, 122–23
eschatology, 92–93, 214
and Lord's Supper, 164
and new creation, 99, 214
performing doctrine of, 108
essence
as communicative, 67
eternity
as form of divine life, 89
time and, 90
ethics, 137–38
eucatastrophe, 95, 221
eutopia, 177–78, 236
Evagrius, of Ponticus, 229
exodus
of Israel from Egypt, 92
of Jesus from the grave, 92
Experience Economy, 56–59
authenticity and, 60–62

face
as site of identity politics, 115
faith
created by God, 224
defined, 154, 247
as performance, 18–19, 189, 235
transmission of, 198–99
as virtue in improvisation, 193

fall of Adam
place in drama of redemption, 97–98
Feuerbach, Ludwig, 179
fidelity
marital, 154
as mark of godly congregation, 154–55
fittingness
missiological, 198
theological, 147
forgiveness
included in what is in Christ, 157
Forsyth, P. T., 163n66
"fourth wall"
between church and world, 35–36
defined, 34
between doctrine and life, 181
Francis of Assisi, 169, 180
Freytag, Gustav, 209

Gadamer, Hans-Georg, 4
generosity
as mark of godly congregation, 155–58
Geneva Catechism, 143, 212
Gentry, Peter, 102
Gilmore, James, 57–61, 183
God
audience of One, 34
Being itself, 67
calls into existence, 51
death of, 52
essence of, 66–68
faithfulness of, 154
foolishness of, 187–88
glorification of, 236
as improviser, 194, 219
as light, 63, 77
kingdom of, 99–101, 103, 126, 162, 173
knowledge of, 145
love of, 39, 43, 67, 77, 80, 82, 221
mighty acts of, 95, 248
name of, 67
perfect life of, 81
as playwright, 29, 136
reign of, 2, 6, 45–46, 178
revelation of, 30, 188, 247–48
right hand of, 176, 212
self-communicating, 20, 67, 76, 81
theater critic comparison, 19, 34
triumph of, 216
See also Trinity
Goffman, Erving, 28
Goheen, Michael, 97–98, 100

Goldsworthy, Graeme, 102
Gombis, Timothy, 216
Good Samaritan Experiment, 195, 198r
gospel
   actions that deny, 119
   climax of drama of redemption, 208
   defined, 5, 20, 75, 77, 93, 100, 120, 126, 166
   eternal foundation of, 78
   exodus from Egypt and, 92
   as historical outworking of divine decree, 80
   infinite translatability of, 189
   obeying, 40
   performative contradiction of, 43
   "politics" of, 8
   public dimension of, 7
   reality of, 9, 237
   theater of, 46, 164–65
   truncated, 7, 16
Great Commission, xii–xiii, 42, 142, 230
"Greats." *See* Oxford University
Gregory of Nyssa, 89

Haeckel, Ernst, 110
Hahn, Scott, 101–2
Harris, Sam, 52
Hays, Richard, 200
heaven
   citizens of, 177
   enacted on earth, 139–40, 150, 224
   Jesus' session in, 211–14
   as place of divine presence and activity, 91, 93, 176
   tearing of curtain that separates earth, 210–11
Heidegger, Martin, 51, 62, 69–70, 94, 132, 223
Heidelberg Catechism, 212
Herdt, Jennifer, 121–23
heresy, 148
   ad-libbing as, 192
Hilary of Poitiers, 236
Holy Spirit, 134–36, 251
   baptism with, 142
   conforms believers to Christ, 130
   enlarges church's understanding, 203–4
   equips church, 182
   firstfruits of, 190
   gift of, 233
   in theatrical model of theology, 250–51
   unites believers to Christ, 128, 134, 233
hope, 223–25
Hopkins, Gerard Manley, 38, 169, 171, 173
hospitality
   as expression of the gospel, 158
   as mark of godly congregation, 158–59
Houston Oasis, 152
Hugenberger, Gordon, 101
human being
   created forgiving praise, 235
   and dignity of communicative causality, 69
   eucharistic animals, 235
   face of, 115
   geography and, 174
   God's earthly representative, 84, 98, 127
   as holy icons, 129
   storytelling creatures, 252
   and what is in Christ, 120
Hunter, James Davison, 8, 180–81
Huxley, Aldous, 56
hypocrisy, 117–19, 130
   vs. "good pretending," 121

identity
   in Christ, 136–38, 219
   human, 115–20, 131, 235
   narrative, 251
imagination
   actor's, 118
   biblical, 4, 134
   eschatological, 126, 128–29
   social, 180
imago Dei, 83–84, 127, 129, 219
imitation
   of Paul, 124, 130, 189
   of Christ, 125–30, 189
improvisation
   characteristics of, 192–94
   defined, 191
   examples of Christian, 196–98
   as habitual church practice, 191–94
   parallel with discipleship, 193, 195, 205
incarnation, 42–43, 92, 111
indicative
   contrast with "as if," 126
   directive nature of, 249
   and justification, 128
   mood, 10–11
   Pauline, 136
   prime, 90
   relation to imperative, 53, 231
interpretation
   costumed, 184–85
Irenaeus, 71, 194

Jenson, Robert, 169

Jerome, 159
Jesus Christ
    abiding in, 44–45, 128, 178
    ascension of, 93, 209
    baptism of, 141
    being-in, 40–41, 176–78, 206, 214
    church as body of, 140, 149–52, 162–66
    coming in flesh, 42
    covenant faithfulness of, 221
    covenant mediator, 85
    cross of, 39, 76, 79, 92, 109, 125, 150, 187, 203, 209–10, 216
    deity of, 74
    divine Son, 75–76
    dramatic image of invisible God, 30, 33, 39, 85
    embodies heaven, 92, 213
    entry into heavenly sanctuary, 211
    as *eutopia*, 177–78
    exemplar of true humanity, 62, 86, 129, 138, 154
    faith of, 154
    heart of, 221
    heavenly session of, 211–14
    as high priest, 212–13
    historical enactment of God's being, 38
    identity of, 106–8
    incarnation of, 92
    as Inner Teacher (Augustine), 133
    keeping company with, 230–31
    light, 64–65
    Lord, 212
    martyr-in-chief, 217
    new creational reign of, 214
    paradigm for authentic existence, 70
    pedagogy of, 146
    place of, 176
    as preacher, 132
    resurrection of, 93, 223
    as temple, 99
    temptation of, 107–8
    transfiguration of, 64, 76, 222
    trial of, 106–8
    true witness, 70, 109
    victory over powers and principalities, 179, 216
    See also Holy Spirit; Son of God
judgment
    Christological, 201
    theodramatic, 199, 201

Kempis, Thomas à, 125

Kierkegaard, Søren, 18–19, 34, 109, 217, 223
King, Martin Luther, Jr., 151
kingdom of God. *See* God
Köstenberger, Andreas, 107
Kuyper, Abraham, 242

Lactantius, 159
Leighton, Robert, 76
Lewis, C. S., xi, 90, 113–14, 120–21, 126, 136, 138, 229
lies, lying, 87
life
    eternal, 77
    as fellowship with triune God, 6
light, 66
Lincoln, Andrew, 107–8
Loisy, Alfred, 150
Lord's Supper, 10, 175
    communicates Christ, 163
    corporately performs union with Christ, 165
    as précis of drama of redemption, 166
    rehearsing crucial scene of, 160–66
    as summa of the gospel, 160
love
    as essentially communicative, 67
Luther, Martin, 121–22, 128, 130, 133, 145, 188, 194, 224

Madson, Patricia Ryan, 192
marriage, 154–55
    as theater of reconciliation, 155
martyr, martyrdom
    early Christian, 70–71
    defined, 70, 217
    Stephen as, 208
    theater of, 217–20
    witness and, 109, 219
Marx, Karl, 179, 225
metaphysics, 231
Micah Network, 197
mimesis, 123–25, 230
mission, 182–85, 198
    and *dismissio*, 232
    integral, 197
    See also church; contextualization
missions
    Trinitarian, 81–82
Moralistic Therapeutic Deism, 54–55

Newbigin, Lesslie, 173
Newton, Isaac, 174, 200
Nicaea, Council of, 200, 203

Nicaea, Council of (*continued*)
    improvised creed, 190
Nietzsche, Friedrich, 223, 230
Nussbaum, Martha, 220, 223

offers
    accepting and blocking, 192–93
ontology
    defined, 66–67
Oxford University, xi

Packer, J. I., 80
pactum salutis, 78–80
paideia, 7
Pakaluk, Michael, 29–30
participation
    audience, 37–41
    in being, 37–38
    in Christ, 38–40, 126–28
    confessing as, 41–43
    in divine nature, 127–28
    eschatological, 126
    fitting, 147, 161
    in Lord's Supper, 162–3
pastors
    as doctors of the church, 146
    and dramaturgy, 146–47
Pelikan, Jaroslav, 1
performance
    authenticity in, 69–70
    Christian life as, 121–25
    defined, 22
personhood
    defined, 85, 116
    human, 83–85, 235
    and *persona*, 115–16
    in theatrical model of theology, 84
Peterson, Eugene, 246
Pine, Joseph B., II, 57–61, 183
place
    and being "in Christ," 176–78
    defined, 174
    local church as, 173–75, 183
    -making, 176
    new Jerusalem as, 178
    vs. space, 173–74
    storied, 175
    theatrical, 177
    vs. utopia, 172
Plato, 63, 186, 240–41
Pollard, C. William, 61
prayer, praying, 135–36, 226, 229–30

preaching
    Augustine on, 183
    as means of grace, 131–34
    presents Christ, 132–34
    supreme instance of faith speaking
        understanding, 131
processions
    Trinitarian, 81–82
providence, 192, 219

realism
    eucharistic, 236
    grateful, 232–33
    theodramatic, 247, 249
reality
    authenticity and, 60–61
    composed of beings in communicative
        act, 67
    defined by what is in Christ, 9, 129
    doctrine as dose of, 231
    prayer as tonic of, 136, 226
    preaching as ministry of, 133
reconciliation
    as aspect of what is in Christ, 150–51
    practices of, 154–59
reincorporation
    as improvisatory skill, 194
religion
    in modernity, 55–56
revelation
    corresponds in time to God's eternal life, 76
    as representational, 30
Ricoeur, Paul, 84, 251
Robinson, John, 64
rule of faith, 147, 201
Ryle, Gilbert, 124

sanctification, 128–30, 221
Sanders, Fred, 111n89
Sartre, Jean-Paul, 51–52
Satan
    "accuser," 103
    counterfeit communicative agent, 87–88
Sayers, Dorothy, 29, 59
Screwtape, 216
Scripture
    Christ's presence in, 132
    control story of Christians, 97, 198
    as divine discourse, 248
    following, 1, 72
    inspired transcript, 24, 63–64, 245, 251
    performing, 2–3

compared and contrasted with script, 23–24, 244–46
full of scenes of improvised wisdom, 232
"spectacles of faith" (Calvin), 23
See also Bible
Searle, John, 42
self
coherence of, 116
sermon
as ingredient in drama of redemption, 133
as ministry of God's word, 130–34
ServiceMaster, 61
Shakespeare, William, 187
Sheldon, Charles, 125
sin, 157, 193
Smith, Christian, 54–55
Son of God
and identity of Jesus Christ, 111, 190
and partner of *pactum salutis*, 78–80
speaking
as action, 15, 41–44, 66
Christian, 15–16
embodied, 66
as preeminent human communicative activity, 23
spiritual formation, 134–36
Stanislavski, Constantin, 118
Steiner, George, 17
story, 251–52
vs. discourse, 252
vs. drama, 252
suffering
speaks louder than action, 218
See also martyr, martyrdom
"superobjective"
Christian, 119

Taylor, Charles, 61–62
teaching, 44
false, 42
indirect, 45
temple
commemorates victory in battle, 213–14, 216
Eden as cosmic, 99, 213
tearing of curtain in, 209–11
Tertullian, 166, 184–85, 240–41
theater
action as essence of, 66–69, 248
audience participation in, 33–47
bridesmaid of theology, 242
business as, 57
defined, 22–23

distinguished from drama, 22–23
dramaturgy and, 146
embodied persons as medium of, 173, 233
formal principle of, 68
hypocrisy in, 115–19
interactive, 35–36, 182–85
of martyrdom, 218
means of character formation, 123
as metaphor or model, 28–32
people vs. place, 171, 173–74
Plato on, 240
ancient Roman, 240–41
and ancient Roman arena, 180
as sanctuary for display of the extraordinary, 185
See also church; drama
theodrama, 246
climax of, 216
conflict in, 215
divine entrances and exits in, 90–94
five acts of, 98, 235
purpose of, 194, 235
realism of, 249
substance of, 245
See also drama of redemption
theodramatics, 20–21
criteria for, 202
defined, 231
objections to, 29–32, 248–29
theology
Anselm's definition of, 15
as art and science of embodying the mind of Christ, 4–5
always dramatic, 203
as grateful realism, 232–33
as improvisation on a gospel theme, 192
makes wise for salvation, 204–5
as ministry of reality, 71
as ministry of understanding, 20
narrative turn in, 251
objections to theatrical model of, 239–52
public, 7–8
as science, 243, 247
study of what is in Christ, 231
systematic, 31–32
as teaching of living to God, xiii
theatrical model of, xiv, 21–23, 25–32, 46, 68, 117, 169, 189, 239, 244
theodramatic, 20
as training in Christian speaking, 16
as task of translating gospel into action, 17
theory/practice dichotomy, 21

theory/practice dichotomy (*continued*)
    and "fourth wall," 34
Thomas Aquinas, 67
time, 90
    See also eternity
Tolkien, J. R. R., 95
tradition
    guides church performance, 200–1
    as history of "great performances," 201
tragedy, 94
transcendentals
    Platonic, 37–38
    as theatricals, 39–40
translation
    of faith's understanding, 198–99, 204
    as transposing, 199
    world-for-world, 199, 200
Trinity
    drama of redemption and, 74–82, 214
    emergence of doctrine, 74, 111
    economic and immanent, 30, 75–82, 89, 110
    gospel and, 73, 80, 110–11
    missions and, 89–94
    mutual glorification and, 76
    processions in, 77, 81–82
truth, 40
    defined, 133
    doing the, 25, 151, 170
    Jesus as, 250
    as Platonic transcendental, 37
    representations of, 241
    speaking in love, 111
    suffer the, 206
    trial of in Fourth Gospel, 107–9
    walking in, 39
    as what is in Christ, 45, 159

understanding
    definition, 17, 20
    doctrine nurtures, 191
    ministering, 32, 113, 132
    theodramatic, 131–32, 202
    theoretical vs. theatrical, 27, 146, 170, 181
union with Christ, 137
    baptism and, 143
    and communion with others, 141, 151
    as condition for acting Christ out, 126–28, 154, 159
    and fellowship with God, 73
    and spiritual formation, 135

Verhey, Allen, 245

virtue, 121–23, 127
vocation
    human, 116
Volf, Miroslav, 183

Walls, Andrew, 198, 203–4, 218
Wells, David, 55–56
Wells, Sam, 96–97
Wellum, Stephen, 102
Whitman, Walt, 227
Wilken, Robert Louis, 229
wisdom
    improvisatory, 191, 201
    as lived knowledge, 21, 31, 205
    of Shakespearean fool, 187
    and theodramatic judgment, 199, 205
witness
    church activity as, 8, 217
    concept of in Fourth Gospel, 107–8
    in courtroom drama, 104–9
    disciple as, 109
    and doing Jesus' words, 18–19
    as faithful presence, 181
    Kierkegaard on, 217
    vs. onlooker, 217
    See also martyr
Wittgenstein, Ludwig, 44, 124
Wolfe, Alan, 53–54
word of God
    as criterion of ultimate reality, 8
    cultivates Christ in believers, 131
    exhibits Christ, 134
    as generative of drama, 24, 91, 104
    incardiated, 134
    as light, 63–65
    propositional vs. pragmatic, 247–28
    and relationship to Holy Spirit, 129–30
    as something to be done, 19
    See also sermon
world
    as stage for communicative action, 66–69, 170, 203
    as stage for human being, 51–53, 63
worldviews, 58–59
worship
    formal vs. informal, 234
    sets forth what is in Christ in symbolic action, 234–27
Wright, N. T., 96, 98, 100

Yoder, John, 173

www.ingramcontent.com/pod-product-compliance
Lightning Source LLC
Chambersburg PA
CBHW012251300426
44110CB00040B/2591